Congruence

The Playmaker's Guide
to High Value Companies

JOHN OOMMEN

First edition April 2022, published as *The Spiral Stairway: The System To Build A Holistic Company*.

Second edition January 2025, published as *Congruence: The Playmaker's Guide to High Value Companies*.

ISBN: 979-8-9860012-3-4 (Paperback)

979-8-9860012-4-1 (Hardcover)

979-8-9860012-2-7 (Ebook)

Library of Congress Cataloging-in-Publication Data has been applied for.

Inquiries: *info@acumes.com*

Congruence™

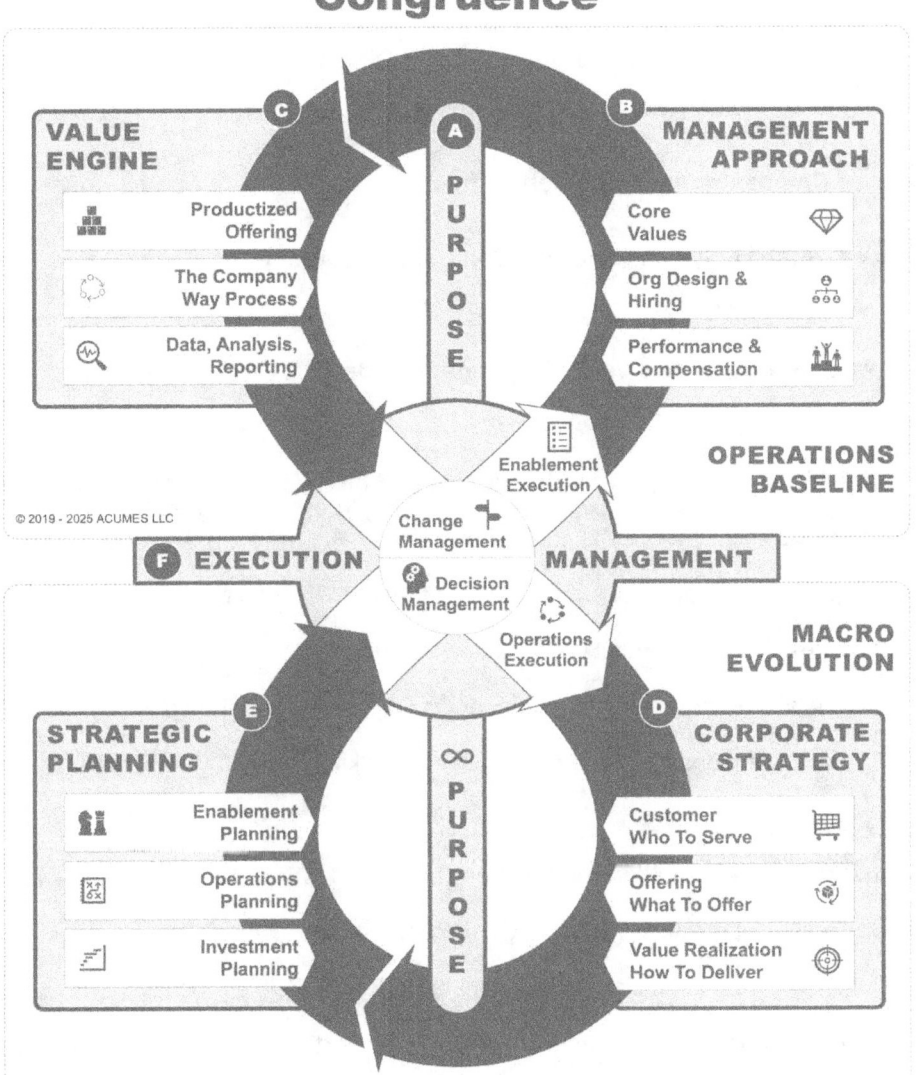

Table of Contents

Frameworks

The Choice Between Individualism And Congruence.

HUMANS once believed in the geocentric model, where Earth was the center of the universe. Religions flourished around it. Mathematics was simple and convenient. However, when we accepted that Earth is just another revolving body, starting with the heliocentric model in the sixteenth century, far more advancement became possible. This fundamental change in our view of the universe helped us ask increasingly profound scientific questions. These questions triggered an avalanche of physics and astronomical advancements in the centuries that followed.

The company lifecycles of today parallel the geocentric model in their entrenchment of individualism. This mindset does not capture the essence of capitalism, create successful companies, or even predict realistic personal success. *Congruence*™ reveals the underlying nature of companies and the vast possibilities that exist if we accept the reality that balance leads to optimal outcomes. *Congruence*™ is not about redefining nature, as nature remains constant. Rather, it is a comprehensive and cohesive guide to navigating the intrinsic nature of companies and embracing the truth that congruent value exchange is the lifeblood of sustainably successful companies.

We are all presented with a simple choice about our work and the companies we help build. We can choose a path where our motivations, decisions, and actions result in a sustainable and balanced value exchange among all parties involved, or we can hope that our individualistic gambles decoupled from value pay off before others notice the imbalance.

I fundamentally believe that most human beings find far more joy in earning their trophies than buying them. Even though the most predictable path to personal success is through value creation, *Congruence™* is not written to convince you to choose one path or the other.

It suits those with a fundamental instinct and desire to invest in what's required to build and manage healthy and profitable companies that make money and leave a positive legacy. The method, its underlying principles, and overarching philosophies are designed to help such persons and groups win.

Our first conundrum: Lack of a definition.

Imagine that we are in an urban area. Look around at everything you see. Every building, computer, book, streetlight, food item, sidewalk, tree, and article of clothing has been touched, moved, changed, or manufactured by companies. So, answer this:

What is a company?

What is a "good" company?

I searched for two decades, hoping someone else would have the answer. But I didn't find an unbiased, informative, and convincing answer that stood the test of time. Look for yourself.

We water down complex topics to 140 characters and thirty-second videos. We are inundated with clickbait headlines and search-optimized articles filled with trivial and tactical information designed to persuade us to buy something or follow the crowd. Large language models confidently answer questions with an assortment of important-sounding words they only understand in the context of sources chosen by their creators. Oversimplifying critical topics creates the illusion that we understand them, which is more dangerous than accepting that we must dig deeper.

Each business book and classroom covers only a fraction of a company's activities. Popular views on companies are often fueled by incentive biases, obscuring the fact that every company is a complex web of interdependent concepts. Thinking in a single dimension while ignoring the multitude of other dimensions is like trying to solve a Rubik's Cube while being colorblind.

Our alternative is to connect the dots ourselves across the vast array of complex and intertwined topics that make a company run. Just as a six-sided Rubik's Cube has over 43 quintillion combinations, the complexities within businesses can easily block our efforts to answer the question of how to build and manage a "good" company.

Our second conundrum: The comparison game.

There are over 1.3 million firms in the United States with ten or more employees. Yet, we subscribe to the fallacy that a handful of outsized success stories are the appropriate role models for all companies. All games focused on outsized wins follow the same model as a Powerball lottery: characterized by a low probability of success but with the allure of massive rewards. True outsized wins among companies are as uncommon as Powerball winners.

Losing a chase for an outsized win has a far bigger cost on the parties involved than a chase for realistic outcomes. Lost causes are apparent early on, and they lead to dysfunction among the parties involved. Dysfunction in a company is no different from dysfunction in a family. Regardless of who wins the disagreements, all family members are uncomfortable.

Dysfunction can be traumatic for employees. It can disappoint paying customers. It can fail to deliver returns to investors or lenders who are deploying retirement and pension funds, or whose investments are guaranteed by taxpayers. It can hurt partners who work with the company. A company can force the rest of society to pay for its mistakes. Whether we recognize it or not, we have all experienced such dysfunction, whether as consumers or active stakeholders.

Resorting to a take-what-I-can-get mindset is tempting. But what if there is a better way?

A single event early in my career triggered my search for deeper answers. A poorly run entity within a large company lured me away from my first job at General Electric, the largest company in the world at the time. After living through a comical series of blunders, the company laid me off in less than six months, along with many others. Armed with this new awareness of cause and effect, I dove into companies experiencing challenging circumstances to understand why bad things happen and how to avoid them.

I grew up tinkering with electronic and mechanical projects in my little home lab, enjoyed physics, chemistry, and mathematics in school, and eventually became an electrical engineer. Because of these formative experiences, I firmly believe in concepts that allow us to build on past lessons.

Regardless of what field we are involved in, we must not reinvent the wheel. Instead, we should find commonalities between situations to simplify problem solving. A firm grounding in foundational concepts and their relationships allows us to create robust formulae and move forward to address more significant problems.

Creating such formulae is complicated because companies are full of people, and people are complex with differing motivations. Companies are also a revolving door of people. So, the shifting collective incentives further convolute the implications of decisions and actions over time.

Companies include a wide range of personality types based on factors such as nationality, religion, culture, gender, prior work experience, and even personal upbringing. Such diversity leads to significant behavioral and interpretational differences within companies.

But let's think about the variations caused by individuals in companies as noise in the data and look for patterns. Then, we can develop an objective and structured method as our business formula. *Congruence*™ is my method for answering the question: *How do we build and manage a "good" company?* I have come to call such "good" entities **Holistic Companies**. I chose the word holistic because everything in the universe that isn't transient maintains a balance with its surroundings.

> **Things To Remember: *Congruence*™**
>
> ***Congruence*™ is a one-stop solution that connects every relevant aspect of a company and allows us to build and manage successful companies in a manner that fits the needs of its unique stakeholders. It focuses on intrinsic properties to build and manage holistic companies so as to maintain an equilibrium between the incentives of all its stakeholders – customers, investors, employees, partners, and society.**

Such methodical thinking creates a company that is truly unique and represents its stakeholders and their unique interests as opposed to an attempt to replicate a runaway success with vague and aspirational similarities. We do so by minimizing what I call **Incongruence**, which is our enemy. Incongruence is the unavoidable misalignment between a company's building blocks. We can never eliminate it, only minimize it.

I am not an investor, an academic, or someone who skipped the middle ranks in a company. Instead, I am an electrical engineer turned business engineer who spent a large part of my career rolling up my sleeves to fix almost every imaginable problem that arose in a company.

I have been a business operator and leader for twenty years, researching and gathering information through my hands-on work on how companies succeed or fail. I have worked in the bowels of over four dozen companies, solving strategic and operational problems. These experiences span a variety of sectors, including large public companies, early-stage startups, highly successful and profitable companies, and those that filed for bankruptcy.

I have helped young companies find early success and develop their offerings to become market leaders. I have assisted companies in pivoting from legacy business models to embrace market shifts and become competitive again. I have worked with companies to rebuild their operations and reignite growth.

I have seen miscalculated hiring frenzies and mass layoffs, rational business decisions that didn't stick, completed business acquisitions that failed to live up to promises, companies that caused their best employees to quit, and companies filing for bankruptcy. You get the idea. Attempting to turn around companies facing challenges has been a common thread throughout my career. These hands-on experiences led me to create *Congruence™*. It offers a cohesive path to balance the incentives of all stakeholders – customers, owners, employees, partners, and society at large.

This book isn't about creating another Tesla, Apple, Google, or Meta. There has always been a Carnegie, a Rockefeller, or a Jobs. They are successful freaks of nature aided by time and place. Our conversations here will not focus on a single outsized success story, since one or two data points don't make a trend. Instead, I've based it on my hands-on work performed at dozens of companies.

Congruence™ is written for **Playmakers**. It is an effective end-to-end method for building a holistic company focused on value. It is intentionally detailed. It's the kind of knowledge that is best absorbed with a notepad and a pencil.

Things To Remember: Playmaker

A playmaker is a critical thinker and problem-solver interested in connecting all the intrinsic parts of a company and creating and running better companies that uniquely and optimally represent all the stakeholders involved.

You may be a CEO creating or reassessing your approach to optimally manage your company. This method maximizes congruence across your institution. It offers a comprehensive set of frameworks and concepts to guide your company's playmaker through structuring organizational problem solving. You may want to be a playmaker and influence your company's future. *Congruence™* offers you comprehensive levers and principles in a how-to and what-not-to-do format.

We can all influence intrinsic value flow in our companies by asking critical and knowledgeable questions and focusing on optimally balancing the value realized by our unique stakeholders.

Holistic Companies Are Congruent.

As you will learn throughout this book, effective decision-making requires us to internalize our choices and their consequences. To illustrate this, our story needs a hero and a villain.

We are constantly presented with difficult, time-pressured choices and tempted with quick and easy short-term benefits that might not be in our best interest long-term and might even hurt others around us. Internalizing and practically applying "good" requires us to understand "bad."

Our team sport of making money in exchange for creating value – whatever name we give it – is crumbling under the weight of an increasing share of the global population who are treating it as a short game without rules of engagement or clarity on what even the most basic concepts mean. The speed of wealth creation among the lucky few is getting closer to lottery-winning timeframes through cryptocurrency spikes and opportunities to create or buy and sell companies quickly. This is compounded by unavoidable exposure to these lucky get-rich-quick stories. More and more people feel left out and motivated to follow suit by focusing on the self in the short term.

I am a capitalist and believe in its true essence. So, let's start by defining **Capitalism** so we can articulate our choices around companies. Turns out, a single global definition doesn't exist, but we can summarize its characteristics from various viewpoints as follows: Capitalism implies that the production of goods and services is based on supply and demand, is guided by private ownership, and income is distributed largely through the operation of markets. It also requires minimal government intervention.

In my experience, using specific words like "private" and "government" can give definitions a sense of authority yet distract from the fundamental essence. Capitalism is a beautiful and comprehensive competitive sport, and its incessant competitiveness and value-centered nature differentiate it from alternatives. Here is my simple definition of capitalism.

Things To Remember: Capitalism

Capitalism is a competitive, value-centered system in which individuals and groups access resources to solve problems experienced by other individuals and groups in exchange for corresponding compensation, where each shares and receives complete information transparently and makes rational choices based on the objective assessment of the information.

But like any sport, misbehaving players, teams, referees, or governing bodies can tarnish the essence of capitalism. Capitalism is misunderstood in twenty-first-century society, and knowledge gaps result from mistaking player and player group misbehaviors and irrational choices for the essence of the idea.

Whether you prefer my practical definition or the academic one, there is a very important takeaway hidden in capitalism's definition by omission. None of the definitions of capitalism include a keyword pervasively used in today's economy – **Growth!** Understanding why our economy and companies have developed a mutated reliance on growth will clarify the stark choice between holistic companies and the rest.

Unsustainable growth as the primary goal is a harmful interpretation of capitalism.

Last year, I started an incredibly beneficial habit of journaling daily. My early dedication to sit at my desk in the morning and truly introspect and consider the realities of my life was deeply beneficial. I had a daily checkbox for journaling, and I didn't miss a single day. But months later, I noticed I was writing down trivial matters while rushing from one thing to the next. I committed less time and mindshare even though I never missed a day. Measuring numerically, I had a perfect score. But intrinsically, the quality of my journaling efforts had been steadily declining. This decoupling of measurement from reality is referred to as the Hawthorne effect and exists everywhere in nature.

Gross Domestic Product (GDP) has been the core metric of quality of life and prosperity for decades. It is an important metric which is an estimate of complex underlying factors. However, using the same measurements for decades inevitably shifts focus to making the number look good while allowing the underlying behaviors to slide.

United States GDP has been rising like clockwork for decades. Like the adage of not trusting someone without flaws, the US GDP curve's perfection is artificial and deserves scrutiny. Many world governments follow the lead of the US and try to make their GDP figure rise smoothly . . . by any means necessary.

In 2022, the US GDP shrank by a small margin for two quarters in a row. This is the technical definition of an economic recession.

Elected and appointed US officials expended significant energy to convince everyone that the US was not in a recession. This reaction is far more telling than the numbers themselves. Why does it matter whether a number unrelated to practical realities decreases by a tiny margin? It doesn't. GDP numbers only have the importance that we give it, especially in wealthier nations where prosperity across all citizens is far beyond basic human needs.

Governments have three tools to prop up the GDP number. The **first** tool is the interest rates at which banks can borrow from central banks in their region. The US Federal Reserve in the US and the European Central Bank in the European Union are examples of central banks. Central banks lower interest rates to encourage more borrowing and spending in the economy.

When banks can borrow money cheaply from the central bank, they lower interest rates for companies and consumers. Low interest rates mean folks with excess cash and wealth must look for risky mechanisms to find a return on investment. Everyone without excess cash can borrow easily because individuals and companies can get cheaper loans, which triggers more spending. The intention is that increased consumer spending will show GDP growth.

The **second** path is for governments to spend money on big projects. We call this fiscal spending. The only money governments can spend comes from taxes collected from constituents. Alternatively, governments can borrow to spend hoping to collect more taxes later. The United States and most other rich countries' national and provincial debt has ballooned so far beyond their own country's GDP that their ability to pay off such debt has become questionable.

Governments can deploy a **third** and desperate tool by printing more money. The technical term for this is quantitative easing. It is another path to inject more spending into the economy, which makes existing money less valuable.

All three tools are blunt instruments and do not target specific problems in any country. Yet, governments have been taking bigger and bigger doses of these steroids to maintain GDP growth to the point that we have become addicted to them. The use of any performance-enhancing drug comes at the cost of harmful side effects.

Government officials have taken on the role of fiscally irresponsible parents to show GDP growth so that they can ask for votes in upcoming elections. What is this obsession with boosting GDP measurement doing to economies all over the world? What is the economic equivalent of the deteriorating journaling practice I mentioned above? Symptom-solving!

Symptom-solving implies addressing observable portions of a problem without tackling the underlying reasons why that problem occurs. In a simple sense, addressing symptoms has a place if we intend to move toward addressing the underlying reasons. But what if we live in a reality where we are disincentivized to address the underlying reasons for problems and perpetually address symptoms?

This is the distorted economic reality in which we live. I call it Duct Tape Economics. If our society focuses primarily on GDP and its derivations, the Hawthorne effect kicks in, shifting our focus toward activities that boost the GDP number, even if they fail to address the real needs of people in the economy.

Is it better for a patient to be given a symptom-solving pill that costs $1 each day for the rest of their life or a permanent cure that costs $100 today? The GDP number will rise more with the former. As a patient, we would prefer the latter.

Is it better to scrap a 5-year-old car today at the junkyard and get a brand-new car that lasts 5 years for $20,000, rather than give $10,000 to a mechanic who can make the car as good as new and run scot-free for 5 years? A rational thinker would choose the latter. GDP appears grander if we irrationally choose the former.

The same incentive challenge applies to every choice in our economy around food, clothing, shelter, and services we procure. This mutated economic environment is not the essence intended by capitalism.

> **Things to Remember: Duct Tape Economics**
>
> **An economic ecosystem that encourages trade that addresses symptoms of problems, as opposed to the root causes of problems, with the conscious or subconscious intention that symptom-solving will trigger higher and more frequent movement of money and create a perception of economic activity and prosperity through extrinsic measures like GDP.**

Like children who continue the cycle of poor habits demonstrated by their parents, companies may emulate their governments to create a perception of success by showing a high growth rate of new customers, new employees, new sales, and the endorsement of popular figures masking underlying risks and unsustainability.

Undue focus on unsustainable growth results in capital engineering.

A well-rounded athlete has great stamina, strength, flexibility, and mobility. As a byproduct, that athlete also likely has visually impressive biceps. But what if we start using only biceps to measure the athlete's overall quality? We will likely have weak athletes with otherworldly biceps.

Growth is a positive byproduct of running great companies, but it must not be the primary measure of a company. Growth has gained prominence because, over the past few decades, we have increasingly shifted focus from running companies that create value for all stakeholders to buying and selling them, just as one might flip a house. As the 2008 financial crisis proved, even too much buying and selling of real estate is problematic.

Our unhealthy focus on compounded metrics like GDP, where underlying fundamentals can be unsustainable while short-term measurements reflect progress, creates a noisy environment that incentivizes companies to follow suit. Capitalism is not intended to artificially inflate capital by constructing an illusion through the company's **Market Price**.

One of my finance professors used to say, "What is something worth? One cent less than whatever the next idiot is willing to pay for it!" That's the market price. Sheer focus on market price hides what something is intrinsically worth today or might be worth in the future.

Things To Remember: Market Price

Market price is the worth of a tangible or intangible item strictly based on what someone else might pay for it.

Capital Engineering explains every company scandal in history. It results in get-rich-quick schemes – however professional they appear. Make a list of the top ten company-level scandals or sector-wide disasters in history. Whether the actions were embraced by a single individual, executives in one or more companies, or all operators in an entire sector, we can trace the root cause of scandals to the tendency to inflate the monetary price of an asset significantly higher than the real-world value that the asset is creating. When we colloquially use the term Ponzi scheme, we refer to capital engineering.

Self-centered and opaque schemes built around growth are like a game of musical chairs with far more people than chairs. Only a handful of people in the game know and choose when the music stops. These schemes always result in a bust, with several disappointed stakeholders who didn't set up the game. It's inevitable.

> **Things To Remember: Capital Engineering**
>
> **The act of inflating the market price of a tangible or intangible item significantly beyond its intrinsic ability to create value with the conscious or subconscious intent of selling that item.**

Between the late 1990s and early 2000s, we experienced the dot-com bubble and bust. The internet was new at the time. Many internet companies popped up. Some improved the world. Many others made big yet empty promises that resulted in the dot-com bust.

During the height of the dot-com bubble, Yahoo!, one of the earliest internet companies, bought the unprofitable Broadcast.com for $5.7 billion. Yahoo! was a public company, and it was the largest acquisition Yahoo! ever made. Yet, Yahoo! gave up and shut down the Broadcast. com service within three years of buying the company. In other words, Yahoo!'s public shareholders got very little value from this acquisition. In this transaction, Yahoo! gave away most of the $5.7 billion purchase price to the handful of shareholders of Broadcast.com. Thirty percent went to the CEO and founder of Broadcast.com for creating an unsustainable company that Yahoo! shut down soon after. This CEO has since been considered a model investor and a startup advisor on Shark Tank, a popular TV show highlighting investors and wannabe entrepreneurs.

Soon after the dot-com crash, we experienced the housing bubble and bust of the 2000s. I actively worked on unwinding the mortgage-related mess that resulted from this financial crisis. How could something as simple and necessary as a home become a toxic asset that brought the global economy to its knees? Every stakeholder group in the home building, financing, trading, and owning ecosystem took part in causing the crisis because we preferred to show growth decoupled from the intrinsic value of the homes that people live in.

Loan originators worldwide indulged in their incentive to originate mortgages for fees from each new mortgage without considering whether the loans would be paid back. Underwriters failed to assess the value of homes under each mortgage.

Rating agencies became pay-to-play operators and gave mortgage concoctions the highest possible rating without digging deeper. Securitization firms took the money available to create paper asset classes with complex acronyms and sold those assets to the next buyer in the chain without considering their responsibilities to assess risk.

Real estate agents convinced many people to buy properties and artificially inflated the prices of homes without prudent negotiations. Home buyers got in over their skis and overpaid for homes or bought homes outside their affordability. We all played a part because we wanted money to grow by simply buying and selling and applying cosmetics between each stage.

The real estate crisis in 2008–2009 affected trade across all sectors and in most countries worldwide. Predictably, governments shot steroids into their economies to catapult themselves out of trouble. The post-financial crisis world involved excessive usage of all three government tools I mentioned earlier.

Large companies such as Google, Amazon, and Salesforce flourished shortly before we embarked on the post-financial crisis easy-money era of interest rates, excess government spending, and overzealous money printing. Those companies started and became behemoths quickly because they had once-in-a-decade successful and value-creating offerings.

Since the financial crisis, we have directly and systematically inflated the market price of companies with the primary intention of selling them. The methods and frequency with which entire companies are created, grown, and sold have changed.

We developed a tendency to create imitations of a few intrinsically successful companies and then hyperscale, the approach used to inflate a company's market price quickly. This approach infiltrated consumer-facing and business-facing companies across sectors, including software, hardware, packaged goods, services, you name it.

Figure 1 tracks the market price trajectory of a consumer apparel company. From its founding in 2016 through 2021, the company's shares were owned by the founders and a handful of private investors. During that period, only these individuals sat on the company's board. The extrinsic price ticked up like clockwork because these few owners who put money into the company internally decide the overall price of the company. Such a market price is not based on profitability or sustainable customer value creation. Each price increase is celebrated publicly to boost the brand. Cherry-picked information publicized about the company paints a picture of guaranteed future growth and prosperity. Such good news is directed toward potential future owners of the company's shares.

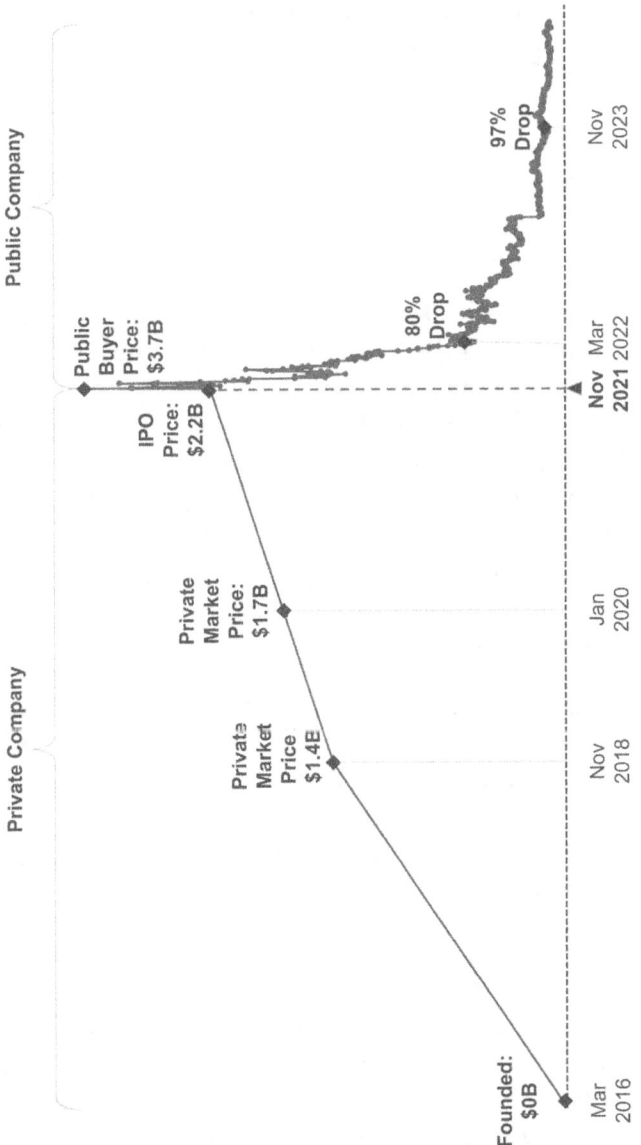

Figure 1. Capital engineering causes stakeholder disappointment.

The creators of a company can make money when they sell their shares to others. One exit path is an initial public offering (IPO), where a company's shares become available for the public to buy. The second option is to sell the company to a larger company, which is typically a publicly traded company. A third option is to sell the company to another private firm, which will eventually cycle back to the first or second path to make their money.

Under any of these circumstances, we would expect the company's market price to continue increasing or at least hold steady after transferring ownership, based on the prior market price increases and positive stories about the company's prospects. However, the reality is predictably not so.

As with this consumer apparel company, the market price of capitally engineered companies falls dramatically after the ownership transfer because new owners have access to the full story behind the company. Within four months of its public listing, this apparel company's market price decreased by 80 percent. Suppose the company's original owners sold $100 worth of shares to Average Joe who doesn't have all the information or the experience to inspect the information. This Average Joe, who bought $100 worth of shares at the time of public listing, had $20 worth of shares after four months. If Average Joe held on to the shares for two more years, hoping it would go up, Average Joe would have had $3 left.

I didn't select this one-off example for shock-and-awe. This was typical of the post-financial crisis wave. There were 1035 IPOs on the US stock market in 2021. A record. This figure was 120 percent higher than the 480 IPOs in 2020, which was also a record. These figures include Special Purpose Acquisition Companies (SPACs), a shortcut to list companies while skipping deeper scrutiny publicly.

Over 60 percent of companies that went public between 2019 and 2021 lost over half their first day's market price within a year, and many went bankrupt. SPAC listings have a far worse track record. These unsustainable companies lead to massive investor losses, negative net value for customers, poor experience and growth for employees, and risk for partners. Ultimately, this hypergrowth push is the underlying cause for the persistent inflation which mostly affects those with the least disposable income and wealth.

The meme stock craze during the pandemic was intentionally driven by retail investors who understood that the market price of any institution can be manipulated regardless of its intrinsic value. Through social media signals and coordinated buying, they inflated the price of a handful of small public companies. Their actions proved that capital engineering is real. They successfully raised the prices of companies such as GameStop, which traded at less than $1 before their intentional game to prove a point. This demonstrated that we can simply rush money towards any institution and temporarily increase its market price.

The cryptocurrency mania is another extreme example of the prevalence of buying and selling assets that don't have or create intrinsic value. Buying cryptocurrencies with the plan to sell to someone else when the price goes up is a textbook capital engineering investment mindset. It's like selling an empty box to another person, with a near certain guarantee the price will decrease significantly within a reasonable period.

Whether it's the dot-com cycle, the mortgage-centered financial crisis, the easy-money era market price bubble, or any other economic cycle in history, a simple pattern repeats. Intrinsic value creation for all stakeholders, effective capital deployment, and transparency about business model sustainability are traded away to show significant growth in the short term to claim a high market price for the asset. The promise is always the same – the asset is a low-risk and high-return investment option, and it will come to dominate the world. It's a nice story to handoff the asset to new owners.

The undercurrent for such short-sightedness stems from disconnecting incentives and behaviors from the creation of intrinsic **Value**.

What is value?

The standard business school definition of value is "everything that the customer is willing to pay for." It's catchy and easy to repeat in an interview but is equally impractical and, in many ways, harmful. It's another way to say quid pro quo. I don't like this definition for two reasons.

First, it is a circular reference. Willingness to pay is essentially the price. So, the definition means "the value of a thing is its price," which must be set based on value. Which comes first? This definition implies we don't know either, and the best haggler decides what it is. This recursive logic is why individuals overpay for homes based on the sale price of other homes in the neighborhood, which has no direct connection to the individuals buying or selling.

Second, what does "willingness" really mean? In my experience, willingness often encompasses situations where a person is forced, misled, lacks choices, or is irrational. Would a person struggling to pay down a massive education loan say that their hopeful willingness to pay for a degree that didn't lead to a decent job reflects the true value of their degree? I doubt that.

Things To Remember: Value

Value is the benefit of solving a problem experienced by a person or group.

We all live in the real world, doing real things. In this natural flow, we experience problems across various dimensions – functional, emotional, social, relational, cultural, spiritual, intellectual, physical, ethical, aesthetic, and perceptual.

These problems are opportunities, like gold in a mine, waiting to be dug up. We create value, or value is created for us, when the benefit of solving a problem is realized.

Quantifying value must begin with simple, practical benefits – like resources, feelings, abilities, and opportunities – within or across the dimensions where we experience the problem, without jumping straight to a spurious association with money. Qualitative articulation and quantitative measurement of value must start with these attributes in the natural flow of our lives.

The value of a college degree lies in its ability to address specific intellectual, societal, or earning needs unique to an individual, not in what the teaching institution believes students would pay based on spurious promises. Individuals, groups, markets, or even countries can behave irrationally when value associations are decoupled from real-world problems and benefits.

Disassociation from value and overreliance on short-term measurement of money is the root cause of capital engineering. Capital engineering at a sector level leads to bubbles that get noticed after the bubble bursts. The same patterns show up at a company level as well, which is where each of us operates. To truly internalize the intrinsic nature of companies, we need to start with a cohesive and comprehensive definition of a **Company**.

What is a company?

Early associations with the term company are the French word *compagnie*, which implies "large group of people," and the Latin word *companio*, which means "bread fellow." By the fourteenth century, we started using the word company for its present intention, "a number of persons united to perform or carry out anything jointly."

> **Things To Remember: Company**
>
> **A company is a relationship between people who have agreed on a mutually beneficial contract to conduct trade together. The people involved partake in this complex relationship to bring value to the collective and extract value that satisfies their incentives. To summarize, a company is a value exchange relationship between people with incentives.**

This sounds simple. But simple is not easy. This definition implies that we must consider all the people involved in an endeavor and their incentives and meet the promised exchange of value.

We often misinterpret the term company in two ways.

The **first** is excess individualism. In our increasingly individualistic world, discussing ourselves and our incentives and fighting for personal benefits creates a fractious perception of a company.

An investor- and owner-first mindset implies that companies are managed solely for the benefit of current investors and none of the other stakeholders or future investors. In such a mindset, employees, customers, partners, and even society – in the form of public shareholders – may disproportionately pay for owners' gains.

Workers under the employee banner advocate for personal outcomes and the advancement of others who fit a specific profile. But what is truly the difference between an employee and a supplier who could perform a task or build an object in lieu of an employee? Very little.

Customers are always in the frame. But who knows the customer's mind or speaks for the customer? Yet, there is no business without customers.

Society is easy to ignore. But current and future regulations and fiscal and monetary policy changes represent society, and companies that navigate them are far more successful than ones that don't.

It's easy to think that owning shares or wearing a badge with the company's name makes us a more integral part of a company. This is not true.

As shown in Figure 2, every company has five equally important stakeholders: customers, investors, employees, partners, and society. Conversations that don't include all these stakeholders don't solve problems for the whole company.

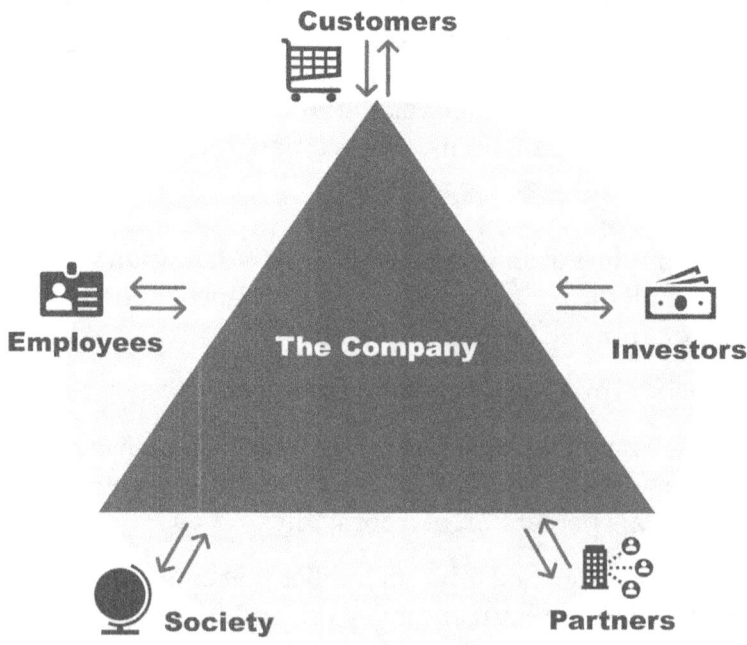

Figure 2. A company is a five-stakeholder relationship.

A company is not one or more stakeholder groups, the things created, or activities performed. A company is a relationship between five stakeholder groups akin to a marriage between two people. Focusing on balancing the value exchanged between stakeholders through the relationship creates optimal outcomes.

The **second** misinterpretation is conglomeration. A company is not a legal document created by a lawyer. A company is not a government registration. A company is not an acronym listed on a public market where people buy and sell. A company is not a brand that we love or hate.

Let's use an analogy to internalize how to think about companies. Imagine a house. Our customer is the future resident who rents or buys the house. A builder must consider that customer when creating housing options. Investors must consider the resident's desired lifestyle and affordability and the builder's skills when investing money. All of them must consider the lives of others in the neighborhood. A company involves these types of considerations regarding a single house.

A house might sit in a larger compound of adjacent houses that are constructed and owned by the same builder and investors because they can make more money this way. The residents might get a marginal benefit from a shared swimming pool or gymnasium.

Adopting this house-company metaphor can help us internalize the importance of intrinsic value flow. The formal name I use for this concept is **Single Market Problem Entity (SMPE)**, which, using our housing analogy, describes a focus on companies that are equivalent to individual houses rather than on an entire housing complex.

Things To Remember: Single Market Problem Entity (SMPE)

An SMPE has five stakeholder groups – customers, investors, employees, partners, and society – and solves a specific market problem for customers who benefit from the solution to that same problem.

We often legally attach businesses to each other like Lego blocks and place them under a single brand while each block intrinsically serves disjointed markets. This tendency is called conglomeration, and it distracts us from the most practical aspects of value creation.

I started my career at General Electric, the largest company in the world at the time. I worked in the company's electronic motors division. As an employee, every aspect of my work revolved around designing and manufacturing motors. The customers I worked with only purchased motors and were not customers of General Electric's aircraft engines, plastics, or medical divisions. The partners that supplied parts for my motor's offering were also smaller businesses that had no relationship with other parts of General Electric.

Then why do I love to talk about General Electric? It makes me feel good. In reality, I worked for a motors company that happened to be owned by General Electric. The motors business I worked for is an SMPE, and General Electric is a brand association I brag about.

Talking about the equivalent of a housing complex with many houses under the same brand is convenient for newspaper articles and business school case studies due to name recognition. But intrinsic value creation and problem solving happen at the SMPE level. So, throughout the rest of this book, when we use the word company, we refer to an SMPE.

Understanding that a company is a complex agreement of value exchange between five stakeholder groups – customers, investors and owners, employees, partners, and society – focused on addressing a single market problem helps us choose the type of companies we want to build and be part of.

Capital engineering results in incongruent companies.

We often see waitstaff putting a few of their own dollars into the tip jar at the start of their shift to create a perception that customers have been tipping generously. In this scenario, we empathize with the person because it's a hard job, even though, technically, the waitstaff is creating an illusion to mislead the customer.

What if we replace the tip jar with an investible or purchasable asset, and the pre-stuffed money runs into hundreds of millions or billions of dollars? Where do we draw the line between acceptable and unacceptable illusions?

The term "lemon" describes a car that runs well enough for a test ride and appears clean and shiny but has an underlying flaw the buyer only discovers after the purchase. Lemons are bad assets. Any asset, including companies, can be a lemon. Capital engineering encourages us to create, sell, or work with lemons.

It is against the law to sell a lemon car or lemon company shares. However, a lack of awareness of underlying causes, lengthy and long-winded contractual terms, and the inability to definitively prove intent allow such activity to go unaddressed. So, our individual choices about the ecosystems we create, invest in, and contribute our energy and skills to are far more critical.

From a customer perspective, capitally engineered companies may cause unsustainable customer behaviors in order to show short-term growth. They may create a perception of value for customers that cannot be maintained. Ask yourself: *How much power do you typically feel you have as a customer?* Most of us would agree we feel very little.

Such powerlessness can apply to investors and owners who buy shares in companies as well.

Over the past decade, social outlets, conferences, and teaching forums have given significant airtime to extrinsic growth in company size through investment dollars and market price figures decoupled from business model sustainability and intrinsic value creation.

Growing a company quickly implies investing significant amounts into a business model very early on. What if the business model is not as optimal as initially assumed? We don't shut down the business. Typically, even more money is poured in.

Even if a business model is sound, too much investment creates problems. Throwing too much wood onto a fire relative to its size has the counter-intuitive effect of dampening the fire because not enough oxygen flows in. Growing companies too quickly implies decreasing organizational productivity with scale. We measure productivity as the amount of output created using a specific input, which in this case is investment dollars.

If a company continues to invest in unproductive areas, each additional dollar invested creates less value. The larger such a company gets, the further productivity decreases until it hits a stall point. Once low productivity sets in, it's nearly impossible to reverse.

So, why would anyone throw even more money into a questionable business model or an increasingly unproductive entity? To show short-term growth! As we mentioned earlier in this chapter, we are increasingly inundated with the fallacy that what goes up will continue to go up.

Nowhere in nature is this true. It's not true in economics, either. This happens because present owners of shares are hoping to create an illusion for future shareholders about the return on their investment.

In all these scenarios, the stakeholders in our company definition are competing with each other. This is what capital engineering does to a company. The company destroys itself because the incentives of stakeholders are not effectively balanced. The ramifications are the same as a marriage characterized by infighting.

> **Things To Remember: Capital-Engineered Companies**
>
> **Capital-engineered companies are entities in which stakeholders are consciously or subconsciously at odds with each other. In other words, they are incongruent.**

The We Company, a shared workspace provider that owned the WeWork brand, offers us a play-by-play example of a capitally-engineered company.

The company was founded in 2010, and it spent investor money to open shared workspaces worldwide. On my first visit to a location, it was clear that the business model was unsustainable from a customer perspective because it cost too much for the value it delivered. Meanwhile, each location had many employees, while the value I received as a paying customer from their employment was unclear. This indicates low capital productivity.

Softbank, the world's largest investor in entrepreneurial companies, funneled over $10 billion into WeWork over several years to spike its market price to $46 billion in 2019. This meteoric increase was decided by insiders, which included the founders of Softbank and WeWork. However, when the company tried to list publicly in 2019 at such a high market price, prospective investors asked hard questions, and the company's price dropped by over 80 percent in the subsequent months.

Over 8,000 employees were laid off, and many commercial real estate owners who leased space to WeWork were holding on to unfulfilled contracts. Softbank's investment was significantly underwater. However, the founder was paid $1.7 billion to vacate the CEO role.

We might think the story ends there. But it doesn't. WeWork was listed publicly through a shortcut method in 2021 at an 80 percent lower extrinsic market price than the $46 billion peak in 2019. In other words, Softbank and other private owners sold shares to outside public shareholders to recoup some of their investment. After that, WeWork stock declined steadily, and the company filed for bankruptcy in 2023 when the public shareholders were wiped out.

Capital-engineered companies intentionally or unintentionally leave some stakeholders holding the bag. They benefit a subset of stakeholders for a certain period at the expense of the rest until time and information transparency result in a breakup of the collective.

Capitalism is intended to funnel capital to intrinsic value creators who can uphold their end of the bargain. Return on capital must come from an agreed-upon fair exchange of intrinsic value. Holistic companies uphold this balance.

Holistic companies are congruent.

We consider Adam Smith the father of modern economics. His political economics theory suggests that if every person, entity, and nation acts in its own best interest, the overall outcomes will be the best.

Under the Adam Smith model, present investors focus on their returns and don't care at whose expense. Employees ardently maximize their compensation and titles, regardless of customer value creation or balancing value exchange with partners. Even adopting societal incentive schemes such as easy money or affirmative action can lead to an unfair value exchange that penalizes the most capable value creators.

Operating strictly by the Adam Smith model encourages a capital-engineering mindset in which stakeholders within a company fight each other, and value extraction and creation across stakeholders is imbalanced.

John Nash revised Adam Smith. He proposed that the best outcomes happen when each player in the ecosystem considers the downside and upside of all the other players and then makes choices that will likely benefit both themselves and others.

The most significant difference between the two mindsets is the importance of time and information. Adam Smith's everyone-for-themselves mindset assumes that no one knows anyone else's hidden motivations and actions, nor will they change their mind over time when they learn more information. But that is not reality.

Every relationship has a state of sustainability based on how value is created and consumed by each party involved. On the positive end, this state can be a happy and balanced relationship where every party is content. On the opposing end, the state is a relationship dissolution because the parties cannot agree on a mutually beneficial set of criteria. This state of sustainability in any multi-party relationship illustrates a concept called Nash Equilibrium.

This concept applies to any situation involving multiple people or groups, each with unique incentives. Unless an ecosystem balances the incentives of every person or group of similar people involved, the ecosystem breaks down, and the collective no longer exists. Imagine a marriage where two people have different interpretations of fidelity. When this difference becomes apparent, the marriage breaks down.

In the context of a company, any stakeholder group or specific individual can only unfairly benefit from others in the ecosystem for a short period before others recognize the imbalance. Once the imbalance is identified, prior agreements to collaborate as a company fail.

However, it is critical to note that balance does not imply equality. In a competitive, capitalistic system, balance implies a fair exchange based on the value created. Confusing fair exchange of value with equal outcomes only creates further incongruence in a company.

For two decades, I have searched for a model to build and manage holistic companies. I learned that such companies create ecosystems that aim for a Nash Equilibrium where all stakeholders' incentives are considered, communicated, and fulfilled. I started calling such institutions that balance the incentives of all stakeholders "holistic companies."

Things To Remember: Holistic Companies

Holistic companies maintain an equilibrium between the incentives of all stakeholders – customers, investors, employees, partners, and society. They transparently balance the value exchange between all stakeholders over time.

Beyond a handful of people doing business together, building holistic companies is not easy because it requires solving a five-dimensional problem that understands, evaluates, and balances the incentives of customers, investors, employees, partners, and society. This cumulative responsibility is precisely why the temptation to create self-serving outfits that create a perception of short-term growth is easy to fall into.

Examples of holistic companies are plentiful. Most sustainably profitable businesses where the owners are happy to continue ownership maintain a congruent exchange of value across all stakeholders. Even a dry-cleaning store owned by a middle-aged couple who operates the shop for thirty years as a source of income and shuts it down in time for retirement satisfies all the conditions of a holistic company.

Multi-generational family businesses tend to lean towards the holistic company model because the current owners and investors care about the future owners and shareholders who may be their loved ones. Such owners are incentivized to leave a company with balanced customer, employee, and partner relationships, along with effective regulatory and legal compliance.

We will build on the holistic company model of maintaining congruent value exchange between stakeholders in Part A of our method: *Company Purpose Sets Value Exchange Boundary*. For now, chalk away this important takeaway.

Things To Remember: Holistic Company vs. Capital-Engineered Company

Holistic companies transparently maintain congruent value exchange between stakeholders. Capital-engineered companies are incongruent.

I present this stark choice to inform you about our two options and their implications. The choice is yours to make. If you are inclined towards building and contributing to holistic companies that are highly congruent, the rest of the book will give you a comprehensive and cohesive method for achieving sustainable and profitable outcomes for all stakeholders.

Fundamentals, A System, And One Company Underpin Congruence.

THE competitive ecosystem for most companies is closer to a golf tournament than a boxing match. Very rarely do companies truly compete head-to-head, and perceived competitive threat does not prohibit most companies from being successful. An oligopoly is a market condition where the solution to a specific problem is dominated by a small number of companies. However, this applies only to a few behemoths involved in highly lucrative market needs like energy or smartphones.

Outside of oligopolies, the success or failure of a company is determined by its ability to perform at its best. External factors like economic conditions and competition are often discussed and analyzed by outsiders because they are conspicuous and juicy tabloid fodder. They are also tempting topics for insiders to get distracted by because introspection and self-improvement are harder than hoping for externalities to change.

As we dive deeper, we will learn to choose market problems that are more optimal for companies to address and develop solutions that are more likely to be successful, while also considering our competitors. Our efforts to build a holistic company will focus on releasing the best version of our company. That's all we can control and all we are legally allowed to do. If a competitor dominates our chosen market problem to the point where we cannot be successful despite our best efforts, we have either poorly chosen the market problem or built a suboptimal solution. That's what capitalism is: fair competition.

In this chapter, we will introduce our cohesive and comprehensive method for balancing the incentives of all our unique stakeholders by creating the best version of our company. Our method is *Congruence*™. It has six parts, and each part will embrace three philosophies.

Philosophy 1: Focus on fundamental levers.

In the 1980s classic, *The Karate Kid*, the kid wants his sensei to teach him fancy kicks and attack moves from the get-go. Instead, the sensei asks him to polish his car in a specific circular wax-on, wax-off motion for multiple days. What the kid didn't know was that the waxing rhythms were the exact motions needed to learn both defense and attack, giving him the chance to master them and build strength without worrying about outcomes.

Although this lesson feels obvious, in a company setting, incredibly high mindshare and investment go into attempting to directly influence outcomes such as revenue, profit, number of users, or stock price with far less focus on the optimal inputs and the way we process those inputs. Creating intrinsic value in our company is like learning the principles behind a complex math problem. We could copy the answer from an online source to get points on our exam. However, we would have gained zero intrinsic knowledge because we still don't know how to do the math problem.

Successful athletes never talk about trophies they haven't won or their recent winning streak. Athletes are in a profession where outcomes are clearly defined. They internalize that the only things they can truly influence are their training, game plan, and similar fundamentals. A company has fundamentals, too.

Our method for building the best version of our company uses specific fundamental levers that we can influence directly. If we use these levers effectively, we will have optimally designed our company's makeup, and our desired outputs will manifest. Each lever, independently or in conjunction with others, creates, cuts, shapes, smooths, and improves the various building blocks and system that collectively form the design of our company. The fundamental levers needed to create these congruent building blocks and system are the foundation of our method and will be explored extensively throughout this book.

> **Things To Remember: Fundamental Levers**
>
> **Fundamental levers are cohesive variables that directly influence the design and build of a company and empower decision-makers to predictively balance the incentives of all stakeholders.**

Our goal is to use these levers to optimally design incentive schemes, decisions, and actions across all the people involved and the tangible and intangible assets we invest in.

From a timing perspective, business challenges are like dangerous late-onset diseases that allow us to live with negligible symptoms for a significant period before the situation becomes acute. I've worked with multiple companies over the years that believed the challenges that cripple other companies would never happen to them . . . until they do!

Any executive team can fall prey to this bias. Predicting business challenges and achieving outcomes is more about influencing and observing the intrinsic behaviors of employees, customers, partners, and investors. They translate into outcomes weeks, months, or years down the line. Any observable challenges result from the immature deployment of fundamental levers. Conversely, positive outcomes hail from the effective use of these levers. The time to focus on fundamentals is now, not after the challenges and outcomes become apparent.

> **Things To Remember: Philosophy 1 – Focus On Fundamental Levers**
>
> **Proactively embrace fundamental levers as influential tools to design and build the best version of our company, while allocating minimal mindshare to controlling outcomes directly.**

The fundamental levers in our method apply to the making of any company, regardless of the market problem, business model, or customer profile. Meanwhile, the principles within our levers allow us to design, build, and manage a uniquely optimal company that fits the people involved.

Philosophy 2: Build with a One Company mindset.

No two people or companies are alike, nor are the problems they need to solve. Ideas we perceive as critical success factors at another company are unlikely to fit our company's needs unless they are harmonious with all the other building blocks of our company. Remember that all building blocks must fit seamlessly with each other and function symbiotically.

First, choosing our company's optimal design isn't about standalone tactics. It is about stringing together a set of cohesive answers that fit our unique company and executing them to perfection.

Would we ever buy one pearl or a random assortment of pearls? Unlikely! As beautiful as one pearl might be, it is practically useless on its own. It's also hard to do anything with several dissimilar pearls. Finding more pearls that match the one in our hand will also prove extremely difficult.

In this analogy, a single pearl is a specific company tactic. Applying the same thinking, we should never get too excited about one-off tactics, especially popular ones deployed by other companies. Standalone ideas are often mistaken for game-changing answers and result in significant distractions. Such ideas can be valuable inputs for brainstorming exercises, but they are not ready-made answers for employee challenges or customer problems.

Replicating bits and pieces of successful companies is tempting because it reduces our onus to solve the problem and makes it easier to convince other company stakeholders that it is a good idea. But it is unlikely to yield good results if it is incongruent with our company's entire design.

How much more valuable is it if we can string together a set of matching pearls into a beautiful necklace? We immediately know that the creator took the time to find and assemble pearls that match, ensuring that the whole is more than the sum of its parts.

This is a critical foundational philosophy in our digital age because we live in a time of information abundance and access. It's easy to observe what other companies do through social media posts and marketing campaigns. Employees routinely move between similar companies. Scenarios like these create the temptation to follow a comparable company's recent tactics or deploy an idea that a new hire brings from a prior employer.

For example, companies send employees to conferences to generate leads and market the company. However, the return on such an investment is only likely to be high if the chosen conference strongly aligns with the company's overall strategy and the employees have the operational prowess to generate conference leads and close deals. Investing in conferences primarily because the companies we consider peers are attending is rarely a good investment.

Attempting to solve our problems with popular, borrowed ideas can not only be ineffective but also expensive due to wasted investment. It also often results in a period of paralysis where more cohesive ideas could have driven the organization in a better direction.

Buying technology to banish challenging operational problems is another typical rinse-and-repeat tactic. Operations technologies are compelling and, when used well, can create significant efficiencies. However, value realization challenges from such investments are more common.

Years ago, I oversaw major parts of an operations technology implementation at a large distribution client. The project was budgeted to cost over $100 million a year. However, it didn't dovetail with the overarching company-level strategy and the rest of the operations components. Implementation didn't include employee training or upskilling, and many oversight and governance steps were skipped. Despite the enormous investment, the company saw a minimal positive impact on operational effectiveness, revenue, and profitability.

Second, designing and building a company in fiefdoms is another manifestation of the distraction from the One Company mindset. Human beings prefer to build walls because it makes us feel secure and in control. But walls also limit our ability to align the whole company.

Imagine visiting our friends in their homes and seeing how they use each room. Every home has a typical layout of living rooms, bedrooms, kitchens, dining rooms, etc. But not everyone uses the rooms the same way. A home office may be in a living room, bedroom, or standalone office. Some people eat in a dining room, and others eat in front of the television. So, why do we bother with such a stubborn classification of rooms? Habit, ease of communication, and groupthink are stronger reasons than practical relevance.

Similarly, we overly invest mindshare in constructs such as sales, marketing, finance, operations, and product development. But every company uses these classifications differently, and remembering this can help us create the best version of our unique company.

> **Things To Remember: Philosophy 2 – Build A One Company Mindset**
>
> **Effectively use fundamental levers to design and evolve building blocks that fit together symbiotically and align our entire company without relying on borrowed popular tactics or falling prey to silo thinking.**

Philosophy 3: Embrace system thinking.

When multiple people are involved, there are differing opinions, perspectives, and human biases at play. In the same way a country requires a constitution, laws, regulations, and law enforcement, a company needs well-articulated and well-understood rules of engagement to help its people operate. This construct, which is akin to our central nervous system, is a company's **System**.

Let's consider a top sports team. There is a massive difference between consistently winning for multiple seasons and collecting trophies, and winning a handful of sporadic matches celebrated by passionate fans. Winning consistently and predictably requires more than talent and heroism. Certain aspects are common among consistently top-performing teams.

- *They often win even when their top players are injured or sitting out games.*

- *Many players excel and contribute to winning games instead of only the top few players.*

- *The scoreboard does not heavily influence their style of play because they believe in their approach.*

- *They don't elaborately celebrate regular season wins or look for excuses for losses.*

- *Everyone is aware of and embraces their accountabilities, which allows the team to win together or lose together.*

If a company were a sports team, great individual employees and their stand-alone performances could win a few customer deals or build one exceptional portion of an offering. However, individuals do not win seasons. Sustained success requires teams with robust systems. So, root causes for organizational challenges should always be attributed to the system, not the individuals.

For example, Mercedes AMG Petronas is a Formula 1 racing team with the most consecutive championship wins ever. Their team principal frames their approach as, "We blame the problem rather than the person."

Manchester City is an English football club made famous for its near-impervious nature over multiple seasons. The club has fantastic individual players, but none of them are the world's best in their position. The club fields different sets of players for different games, but collectively, they have been unbeatable over multiple years. That's the power of a system.

This translates into a cohesive approach to running an entire company that senior executives, employees, the board, analysts, regulators, partners, and even customers understand and believe. Objectivity and transparency are the determining factors of an effective system. Each lever of our method adds decision-making and governance factors that collectively form a system that works for our company.

> **Things To Remember: System**
>
> **The system is a company's transparent framework that maximizes the probability of objective decisions and actions and minimizes the impact of individualism and human biases across all stakeholder groups. It is a predefined construct that everyone internalizes and commits to executing.**

Why is this philosophy critical? An effective system defends well-designed building blocks and people from poor decisions, while protecting the company from getting derailed by misaligned building blocks and suboptimal personnel choices.

As we discussed in the previous chapter, a company is a relationship between people and their unique agendas. Most of us are not heroes who can single-handedly save the day. We will all make mistakes. However, we cannot allow our personal justifications for these mistakes to overshadow real performance gaps and root causes. Individuals must become high-performing commodities in an organized team for it to succeed over time.

Conversely, many organizations fall into the trap of blaming individuals for systemic problems. Sometimes they blame a lack of talent, experience, or motivation within their ranks for poor results. Other times, individuals may be considered misfits in the organization. However, these gaps may not be caused by those specific individuals.

They could be caused by a flawed system that allows ineffective managers to hold senior positions or the wrong senior executives to make hiring decisions. Possibly, their hiring practices are underdeveloped, or they have people management practices that don't align individual skills with a role's requirements. Sometimes it's training and coaching that are overlooked. Focusing on individuals perpetuates the same mistakes without addressing the underlying causes.

It's easy to indiscriminately hire individuals only to replace them when a company faces challenges. It provides a quick fix that kicks the proverbial can down the road. Not long ago, I led turnaround efforts at a mid-sized company that had challenges with customer retention and new sales. The root cause was an ineffective system that the CEO didn't address. Unfortunately, instead of addressing the root cause, the company replaced three successive sales executives, as well as the sales reps and supervisors those executives had hired over the course of three years, with no change in prospects.

A strong system brings together people in every stakeholder group with the right skills, experience, and motivations to perform at their best. The reverse is rarely true. Focusing on finding heroes that can save the day will not serve the best interest of all the company's stakeholders or the company's long-term future.

Creating an effective system takes patience and discipline, which is why it often gets displaced by short-term tactics focused on individuals. The lack of an effective system results in human biases and individualism taking precedence. This results in subjective decisions and actions that cause the deterioration of the fundamental building blocks and their alignment, and even the loss of strong performers.

However, we must not confuse focusing on developing a strong system with staffing the company with inexperienced or unmotivated individuals. A strong system is intended to attract and retain people with optimal skills and maximize their contribution.

Throughout our method, we will frame recommendations that enable objective, transparent, and decisive choices and protect our company's building blocks, avoiding the distractions caused by individual personalities and agendas. A strong system moderates these influences to achieve collective success.

> **Things To Remember: Philosophy 3 – Embrace System Thinking**
>
> **Using our fundamental levers, build a transparent company system analogous to the human central nervous system. This will enable the effective deployment of symbiotic building blocks with a One Company mindset while minimizing the impact of individual incentives and biases.**

Focusing on the fundamentals to design cohesive building blocks unified by a strong system will allow revenue growth, profitability, customer satisfaction, investor confidence, and employee morale to follow. The alternative is to invest heavily in rinse-and-repeat ideas, symptom solving, and reactivity, resulting in poor intrinsic outcomes.

To that end, what is the essence of the problem each company is facing? Let's examine the problem that prevents our company from living up to its full potential: incongruence.

Incongruence is every company's biggest enemy.

In the last chapter, we introduced the idea that a holistic company is congruent. We framed the primary condition that such a holistic company effectively balances the incentives of all its unique stakeholders. But how?

A holistic company is an outcome, and we cannot directly control it. We can only control the inputs and how we process those inputs. We learned that building the best version of our company involves a relentless, proactive focus on fundamental levers to influence the optimal building blocks and to create a strong system.

Let's formalize the term congruence.

> **Things To Remember: Congruence**
>
> **Congruence is the harmony across a company's building blocks and its system. The greater harmony we achieve, the less waste is created by the capital invested in the company and the more value it creates.**

Incongruence always exists in the present state.

Congruence is akin to a vacuum. Just as sucking more and more air from a container gets us closer to achieving a vacuum, through our method, we will focus on minimizing what keeps us from finding harmony within our company.

Let's examine our company's inner workings, starting with the assumption that we can completely freeze time and the world around us while we continue to run our company. Imagine that we are cutting the company open like a watermelon to take a cross-sectional view.

Every company in the world will reveal incongruences, like watermelon seeds, that directly cause obvious and subtle issues the company experiences. Incongruences always exist. It's only a question of how much, not if. Everything we experience as a gap in a company stems from an underlying incongruence.

> **Things To Remember: Incongruence**
>
> **Incongruence is the lack of harmony between a company's building blocks and its system. Incongruences are the root cause of all obvious and subtle challenges a company experiences.**

Incongruence is also analogous to electrical resistance in a wire. Electrical resistance is the unavoidable counterpressure that the wire applies against the flow of current. Similarly, the more incongruence within a company, the more resistance we will experience in our efforts to create value and use investment efficiently.

What if customers feel that employees who work in the company do not adequately respond to their needs? What if the employees who build early connections with potential customers are ignored by the people who complete the sale, and they choose to find their own customers? What if the people who sell feel that the company's offering is inadequate? What if the employees who perform the day-to-day tasks feel that the executives' plans are unrealistic? What if the executives feel that the people who perform daily tasks aren't as productive as they could be? We could go on with examples of common symptoms of disharmony within companies.

When scale, time, and environmental inputs are held unchanged, it is the incongruence between the building blocks and weaknesses in its system that is the first enemy of any company.

Scale, time, and environment changes inject incongruences.

Let's say we worked hard to harmonize our company's building blocks and create an effective system to run an efficient and optimally value-creating entity. What happens as scale, time, and environment change? A shift in any of these delivers new complications and demands, which create new incongruences within a company's building blocks and impacts the effectiveness of its system.

Our decisions and actions around what "good" looks like for each building block and how we dovetail them also need to evolve over time, with scale, and with changes in our ecosystem. Incongruence is like untidiness in our homes. To maintain a tidy home, we must clean up periodically and maintain good living habits. It's not a one-and-done effort.

Like any living thing, a company is born, lives, and eventually dies. The company's lifecycle, from the early stages, when founders work to acquire the first few customers and validate the company's offering, to reaching a steady state and eventually ending its value-exchange cycle, is a non-linear path, as illustrated in Figure 3.

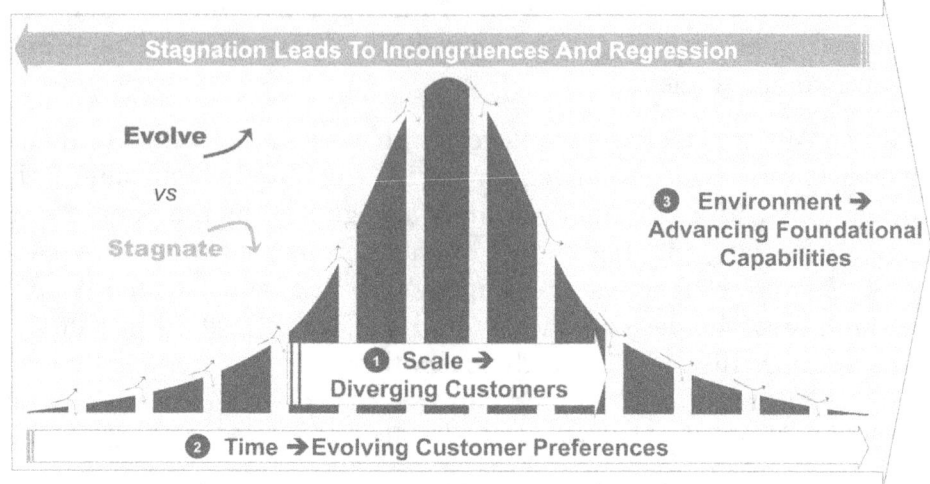

Figure 3. Congruence throughout a company's lifecycle demands evolution.

It is a multi-phased journey that requires the company to evolve its composition to accommodate the demands of scale, time, and environment.

First, a larger scale presents its own challenges. Typically, the company's entire market opportunity, often described as an **Addressable Market**, has a normal distribution, as shown in the figure. Unfortunately, capturing a larger share of the addressable market becomes increasingly challenging.

> **Things To Remember: Addressable Market**
>
> **The addressable market is the universe of customers that the company can realistically serve, given its current offerings and abilities.**

Companies are always launched to solve niche problems. Early success brings a company a small group of customers who greatly appreciate its offerings. Those early customers feel the pain of the problem significantly or have a high-risk tolerance for trying new solutions. Favorable pricing is another incentive for some early customers. Early customers are characterized by low expectations.

As a company grows, there are fewer and fewer easy customers. Beyond the early few, customers will become increasingly demanding. This means the company must evolve its offerings and increase the value created to acquire more significant portions of the addressable market.

The cost to acquire and serve customers further to the right of the addressable market is intrinsically higher because they are more demanding and more reluctant to buy. As a result, a company will have to evolve its efforts to be incrementally more effective to move further to the right of the addressable market curve.

Serving an increasing portion of the addressable market implies the company is getting bigger. Running a larger company requires a greater level of sophistication, without which the company will crumble under its own weight.

Suppose a company continues to operate at its early-stage maturity level and resorts to spending more money to scale. In that case, the company is resorting to capital engineering. Growth will stall, and even the early customers will eventually be disappointed.

The **second** reality that every company must live with is time. Every customer demands more or different value over time. Imagine that normal distribution in Figure 3 is placed on a treadmill moving forward. Our company is always experiencing a myriad of shifting preferences.

Preferences can be superficial choices like fashion, where customers simply prefer something different and invigorating. Preferences can be predictable scenarios like favorable or unfavorable monetary policy or government spending policies. Preferences can be harsh realities that stem from geopolitical posturing or war. Preference can change due to black swan events such as COVID-19. Regardless of the source, predictability, and gravity, we can be sure that our company will experience changes in expectations over time.

Third, regardless of the market problem we address, our company is built on a foundation laid by people who came before us.

A common foundational shift is technological. The internet completely changed how companies buy and sell. The smartphone invention changed when and where investors, employees, customers, and partners could contribute to the activities of companies. Artificial intelligence will likely bring another tectonic shift in the foundation of how companies do business and the way value can be created and consumed.

However, foundational shifts are not restricted to technology. New ideas can be equally powerful change triggers. The advent of behavioral economics, the idea that psychological triggers and reactions among humans are predictable, and its mainstream application has revolutionized how companies sell, develop solutions, and keep customers engaged.

In the late twentieth century, companies like Toyota and General Electric made developments that proved that operational exceptionalism can be packaged, taught, and replicated. Companies universally tried to emulate these groundbreaking ideas to transform their own businesses.

These three realities – scale, time, and environment – provide a constant stream of new demands, forming the second enemy every company must address as it tries to build and maintain its best version.

To wrap up our problem statement, any company's greatest enemy is itself, not competitors or the economy. Externalities are typically easier to focus on because we can see them. Incongruences between building blocks and a weak system hurt most companies far more than any competitor or external conditions can. Recognizing incongruence as the root cause of our problem, let's outline the method we will discuss throughout this book: Congruence.

The *Congruence*™ method.

Did you know that the overall winner of the Tour de France, the world's most prestigious cycling championship, only wins an average of two out of the twenty-one stages each year? Some years, the overall winner doesn't even win one of the twenty-one stages. The Tour attributes significantly more value to being extremely competitive across all twenty-one stages than to winning a few and performing poorly among the rest.

Developing the best version of our company is similar. I didn't create the *Congruence*™ method because I am the foremost expert across all levers in its six parts. However, through many positive and negative experiences, I realized that creating a holistic company requires maximizing congruence using all fundamental levers. It is crucial for us to operate with high **maturity** across all these components while dovetailing them effectively. Ignoring one component allows the rot to start and spread to the rest of our system.

A lathe is considered the mother of all machine tools. Every lever and principle in our method has similar power. However, we can use a lathe effectively or poorly, which reflects the usefulness of the object we create. Similarly, we can deploy our fundamental levers with a high or low level of maturity, which dictates the ability of building blocks and our system to create value and use investment efficiently.

Things To Remember: Maturity

Maturity is the efficacy with which we deploy each fundamental lever, which directly influences congruence across building blocks and the company system. Mature use of levers optimizes congruence in our company's design across lifecycle stages, the effects of time, and environmental factors.

The *Congruence*™ method starts with three assumptions.

First, we will assume that our company has already performed early-stage market validation of its offerings with a few customers besides friends and family. So, if you are an aspirational entrepreneur who is starting a company, *Congruence*™ can give you foundational principles to consider. Although you may not yet have people filling the roles of customers, employees, partners, and owners, which the method's effective application requires, it can still guide you to the realities you will encounter as a business executive.

Second, we won't address topics around money management. Finance is a discipline that focuses on money, which is crucial for a company. However, there is a reason we emphasized the stark choice between holistic companies and capital-engineered companies and chose the former. In a holistic company model, we are determined to win by maximizing intrinsic value, optimizing our fundamental building blocks, and building a strong system. Money is simply a token intended to represent intrinsic value.

> **Things To Remember: Money**
>
> **Money is a token of reward that flows in the opposite direction and as a direct result of value creation and delivery.**

A banker can help you with borrowing money for your company. But remember, playing with money decoupled from value is capital engineering.

Third, mergers and acquisitions (M&A), which involve efforts to buy and sell companies, have a role in the business world. However, balancing our unique stakeholders' incentives happens organically within the boundaries of a Single Market Problem Entity (SMPE).

The difference between formally buying another company to increase our customer volume and paying an external partner to find us new customers quickly is merely optics. Similarly, there is little practical difference between buying another company because we want to own their offering and paying a third party to create that same offering for us.

This is the uniqueness of the *Congruence™* method. We are constructively challenging the myths around the effectiveness of popular practices, returning to the basics, and focusing on value, which is why humans started creating companies in the first place.

With these clarifications in mind, Figure 4 introduces *Congruence™*, which is our six-part method. I suggest displaying this figure in your office so that each time you assess a company, you focus on its intrinsic, practical aspects rather than being distracted by extrinsic themes and silos. The six parts are:

A. *Company Purpose.*

B. *Management Approach.*

C. *Value Engine.*

D. *Corporate Strategy.*

E. *Strategic Planning.*

F. *Execution Management.*

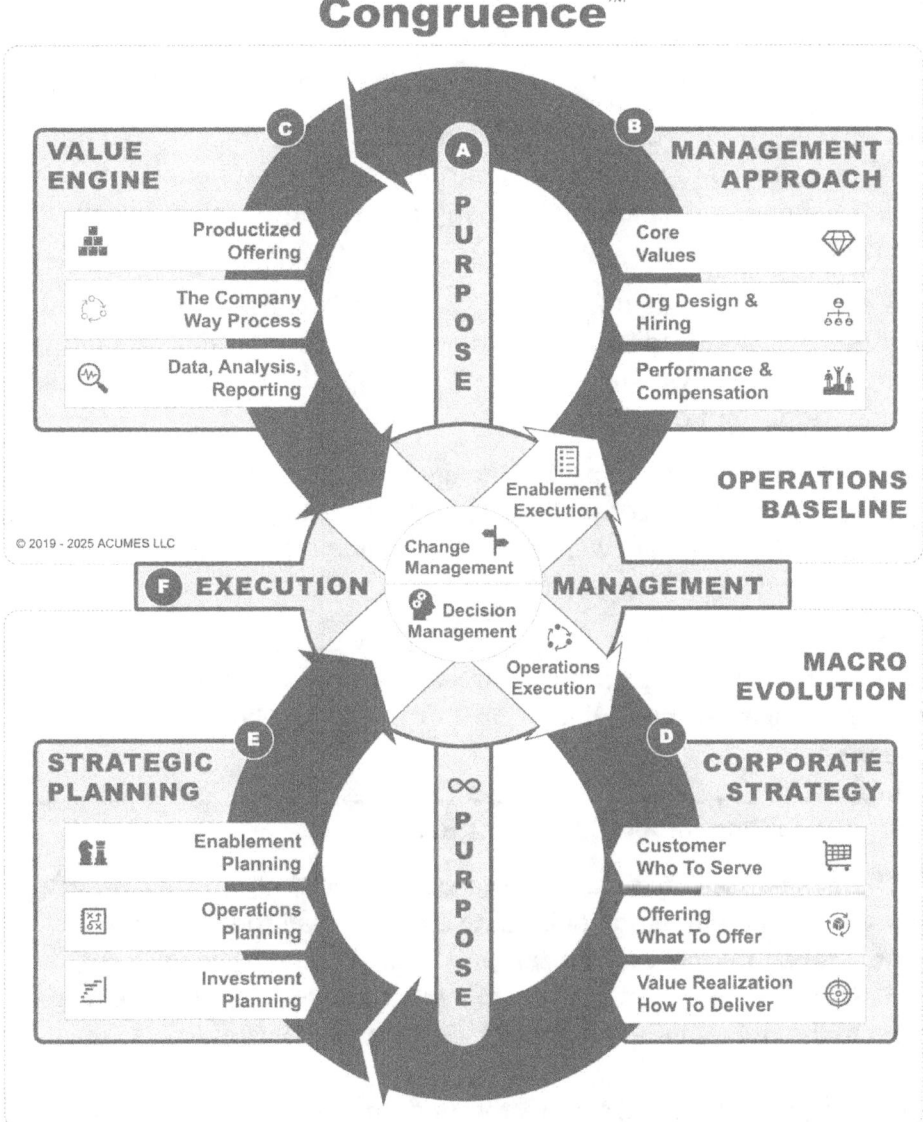

Figure 4. The Congruence™ method builds holistic companies.

As we go through each part of the method, we will explore fundamental levers we can control and principles for each that help us design our company's unique building blocks and system. We achieve greater congruence through the increasing maturity with which we deploy fundamental levers.

A five-level maturity model will be provided for each part. Our effectiveness in wielding each lever impacts the congruence between our company's building blocks and its system, and, thus, the balance in value exchanged.

We will also discuss common but avoidable pitfalls that often derail the best intentions and result in incongruence. I suggest you work through each of the six parts and underlying levers sequentially because the concepts build on each other.

The first part of the method, **Part A: Company Purpose**, is the cornerstone that helped me decode all my unanswered questions about a company. The first question we must ask about any topic is "why," and we will ask that all-important question in Part A.

The following two parts, **Part B: Management Approach** and **Part C: Value Engine**, describe our company's present-day reality. They encompass all the fundamental levers we directly influence regarding the company's people agenda, our offering to the market, and how we deliver it.

These parts also measure the maturity with which we have deployed these levers in the past, indicating the effectiveness of our building blocks and system in the present. Collectively, they form what I call our **Operations Baseline**.

Things To Remember: Operations Baseline

The operations baseline is the company's day-to-day reality. It articulates the balance of incentives among all the people involved, how those people are chosen and interact, and how we create and deliver value. It reflects all past efforts to build the company leading up to the present and characterizes its intrinsic value.

Even if we have designed a perfectly congruent operations baseline, where people are involved, we make mistakes. A strong company system includes defensive measures, just like white blood cells in our body, to maintain the efficacy of our operations baseline.

Through our fundamental levers, we can develop systemic defenses that prevent mistakes. But we also must set mechanisms in place to quickly identify and remedy mistakes that slip through. These defensive measures are called **Microevolutions.** Our operations baseline can and must make ongoing tactical adjustments to improve performance while maintaining the level of congruence through microevolutions.

Things To Remember: Microevolutions

Microevolutions are continuous defensive measures that identify and remedy breakdowns in our operations baseline to improve performance without injecting incremental misalignments between building blocks and systemic aspects.

As we covered earlier in this chapter, the present state of our company will have incongruences. Does the makeup of the company's offerings and people lead to outcomes that balance all stakeholders' incentives? Does the value realized by customers balance their expectations? Do the employees and executives who create the most value also extract the most value in return? Will the company make enough profits to meet the expectations set by investors? Microevolutions will not address such incongruences.

Incrementally, we must address the three complicating factors of scale, time, and environment and maintain a high degree of congruence across our company.

The following parts, **Part D: Corporate Strategy** and **Part E: Strategic Planning,** launch the offensive **Macroevolution** cycle. The bottom portion of Figure 4 reflects how a company must operate as an evolving machine. The macroevolution cycle enables the company to make major forward-looking decisions, act on those decisions, learn from those actions, and improve on past decisions to address present incongruences or accommodate curveballs from scale, time, and environment.

Things To Remember: Macroevolutions

Macroevolution cycles identify and inject comprehensively higher congruence into the operations baseline to create greater value for all stakeholders and optimize the use of capital.

What worked last year may not work the next because the complications created by scale, time, and environment are accelerating. A well-run company gets larger every year and requires a changing set of skills to help it effectively serve a larger customer base.

Typically, one year is a reasonable timeframe to macro-evolve our company, during which we also execute our operations baseline to create value. The start and end of a company's execution cycle are also effective start and end points to inject macroevolution improvements into the operations baseline. We will cover the company's operations baseline evolution and execution in **Part F: Execution Management**.

Each part of the method will require people in different executive roles to take ownership and execute. Figure 5 breaks down the roles that senior executive positions must play. Every lever requires appropriate ownership, the ability and willingness to execute, and a support structure to empower accountable and responsible parties. I also recommend that you use the finer details throughout the book to frame the responsibilities of important roles, as opposed to succumbing to popular siloed approaches that we touched on in our second philosophy.

Roles and Responsibilities Matrix

	Accountability	Responsibility	Enablement	Impacted
Part A: Company Purpose	The Board of Directors	Chief Executive Officer	Congruence Architect	All Stakeholders
Part B: Management Approach	Chief Executive Officer	Human Resources Executive	Congruence Architect	All Stakeholders
Part C: Value Engine	Chief Executive Officer	Functional Executives	Congruence Architect	All Stakeholders
Part D: Corporate Strategy	Chief Executive Officer	Congruence Architect	Functional Executives	All Stakeholders
Part E: Strategic Planning	Chief Executive Officer	Congruence Architect	Functional Executives	All Stakeholders
Part F: Execution Management	Chief Executive Officer	Functional Executives	Congruence Architect	All Stakeholders

Figure 5. Executives have precise accountabilities to maximize congruence.

Responsibility is paramount for effective outcomes. The board and Chief Executive Officer (CEO) are accountable for balancing all stakeholder incentives. But who will own and manage the levers of *Congruence*^{TM}? A CEO cannot simultaneously be the coach, captain, and evangelist while crafting and running plays on the field.

Every company needs a true playmaker who takes on the responsibility of a visionary athlete who can connect the past, present, and future and every building block of the company. I have found that practical applications of traditionally used role titles have become highly fungible, and a silo mindset is more prevalent than ever. So, I propose that building the best version of our company requires a new role: **Congruence Architect**.

> **Things To Remember: Congruence Architect**
>
> **A Congruence Architect is an experienced, objective, analytical, and transparent on-field playmaker who operates as the CEO's right hand. The role governs the effective use of fundamental levers to enable a One Company mindset and an objective system and leads all microevolution and macroevolution efforts to minimize incongruence across the company.**

The company's purpose is owned and managed by the board and no one else.

The management approach levers are ideally owned by the CEO and executed by human resources, with the guidance of the Congruence Architect. They align the company's purpose with definitions of roles and responsibilities, performance management, incentives and rewards, and day-to-day behaviors.

The third part, the value engine, enables our company to build an optimal offering and a predictable, transparent, and data-driven environment that uses capital efficiently. It covers the constructs that form a compelling offering for customers and the foundational processes and tools to take that offering to customers. The CEO must empower the hands-on Congruence Architect to collaborate with executives across functions, such as sales, marketing, and production, and deploy the value engine levers to design and evolve the company's building blocks and system.

In the fourth part, we will start the macroevolution cycle to build a cohesive and comprehensive strategy based on a deep understanding of the market and the company's strengths. We will cover how such a formulation will dictate all company-wide efforts. Much of this effort will be the responsibility of the Congruence Architect, while the CEO owns and oversees the outcomes.

In the fifth part, we will explore how the CEO and the Congruence Architect can use a company-level strategy to build a strategic plan that quantifies and qualifies all execution efforts. We will learn that creating a company-wide plan is only effective if we follow a structured method.

Lastly, senior executives, supervisors, and individual contributors must play their respective roles articulated in the strategic plan and execute it effectively. Our senior executives and supervisors must develop a path to plan, manage, and track day-to-day execution and course-correct where necessary. We will discuss this in the sixth and final part of our method.

My choice of the lemniscate form, symbolizing infinity, to represent the *Congruence*™ method is intentional. All six parts are symbiotic and interlocked. They support one another, and the whole is exponentially more valuable than the sum of its parts. They are not standalone topics, and without congruence across the building blocks, outcomes will suffer. As you go through each fundamental lever, notice how incremental maturity minimizes incongruence and nudges us toward the conditions of a holistic company.

Company Purpose Sets Value Exchange Boundary.

IF Bobby owns a chicken farm and a chicken sandwich shop in town, are they the same company or two different companies both owned by Bobby? If Bobby runs an amazing chicken sandwich shop in town but allows his friend to franchise the name to run another similar shop in the neighboring state for a fee, are they the same company or different entities?

A company is a closed-loop relationship, and we can draw the boundary anywhere we want. The effectiveness of the boundary determines the effectiveness of our company. Whether we draw a boundary to help us build our company or not, a natural boundary of effectiveness exists. Think about it as the optimal size of a village around a lake. At a certain distance, the fact that the lake exists doesn't help a villager's life.

A company's purpose is its boundary. Entities that run into trouble often extend themselves too far beyond reasonable boundaries.

To build the best version of our company, we will need to arrive at congruent answers to the following questions and live by them: 1) Who is involved in the company? 2) What does the company do? 3) How will the company do it? Choosing the appropriate answers forms the company's strategy, and translating that decision into real life is its operations.

But to answer these questions and live them, we need boundaries. Unlimited openness is the same thing as the emptiness of space. Without boundaries, we are lost. As we will see throughout this method, problem-solving is iterative, as well as time and resource intensive. If all possibilities are on the table at all times, we will end up chasing our tails or following other people's lead when we can't arrive at good answers. So, we must embrace limitations, which are useful because they help us focus on our options and make coherent choices.

Principle 1: Purpose articulates "why" the company exists.

Milton Friedman is an American economist who most modern capitalists look to for guidance. In his 1962 book *Capitalism and Freedom*, Friedman says, "There is one and only one social responsibility of business – to use its resources and engage in activities designed to increase its profits so long as it stays within the rules of the game, which is to say, engages in open and free competition without deception or fraud." As I explain later in this chapter, I agree with Friedman on the importance of profits.

However, the caveat of "so long as it stays within the rules of the game" is a gaping hole. In my twenty-year search for answers, I realized that there is no consensus on what the words "rules," "open and free competition," "deception," or "fraud" mean in practice.

Additionally, Friedman looks at a company as though time is constant. It never is. Ownership of companies changes hands. In the sixty years since his book, the speed of handoff is exponentially higher. Public company shares are traded in microseconds. Private companies are rarely owned to operate them but to be flipped like fixer-upper houses. So, we must ask, "Profit for how long?" and "Profit for which owners – the ones from this microsecond or the next one?"

Recall that our company is a relationship. In that vein, imagine two people dating and consider all the possible conditions that these two strangers will have to parse through to assess whether a relationship will be fruitful. Considerations may include family values, number of children, intellectual curiosity, growth mindset, health habits, spending habits, vacation choices, emotional connection, and thousands of others. A good relationship balances answers to the question, "Why do I want to be in a relationship?" for each person.

Some relationships work well because one person is a good breadwinner, and the other is a good caretaker. Others work because both parties challenge each other to do more.

Each person's "why" is different. So, for any relationship to be satisfying and sustainable, the why must align across people. As you will see through this chapter, alignment doesn't imply that the reasons are the same. Relationships are a value exchange equation, and it balances in good relationships.

Some highly talented individuals who could choose significantly higher-paying career paths, choose to become teachers, musicians, or social workers, knowing their career path will never bring them wealth. Why do people make such divergent choices?

We are all moved by our foundational motivations. We make decisions based on the incentives that we believe align with who we are as individuals. Actions that benefit us tend to flow from decisions that align with our incentives. Our mistakes flow from the motivations we don't understand or accept and the decisions that are based on them.

We must begin our journey to build the best version of our company by answering why we are in business in the first place. The "why" for our company is an objective, transparent, and practically discernible answer that I call the **Company Purpose**. It articulates the balance of incentives between stakeholders. Poorly understood, articulated, or balanced incentives lead to poor decisions and actions from a value creation perspective.

We translate these motivations and their balance into decisions about what our company looks like. This is our company's strategy, which is its overarching decision structure. We will learn about strategy in Part D of our method.

That overarching decision structure must rule the design of our daily operations, which is covered by our management approach and value engine. As Figure A1 illustrates, every company is a three-level Purpose-Strategy-Operations Pyramid that balances the incentives of our five stakeholders. We must also embrace key planning and execution concepts, covered in the final two parts of the method, to convert our intention to dovetail purpose, strategy, and operations into reality.

Figure A1. Every company is a three-level Purpose-Strategy-Operations Pyramid.

We are building a company with multiple people involved, so motivations will naturally differ. To build and manage the best version of our company that balances value exchange, we must have a "why" beyond moving money around.

As I worked with an energy data management company facing low employee morale, customer loss, and cash flow challenges, I asked the senior executives in a problem-solving discussion, "Do you want to be a high-growth company or a lifestyle company?" The CEO understood the relevance of my question; the remaining executives were perplexed. That confusion is key. They marketed and fundraised in a manner that aligned with a company that was going places quickly. But the hiring, performance management, compensation, offering's effectiveness, and processes reflected a company that was happy to be a lifestyle-focused, cash flow business. This incongruence caused chaos.

> **Things To Remember: Company Purpose**
>
> **Purpose articulates a company's objective boundary to all the people we want to be part of it - including customers, employees, investors, partners, and society's representatives, such as government regulators - by transparently answering the question:** *Why does the company exist?*

I have worked with several sales teams to help them operate more effectively. An absurdly significant share of sales representatives feel that sales quotas – the amount they are expected to sell each period – make very little sense. Sadly, sales quotas are too often set as a simple fraction of a company-level revenue goal based on the number of sales reps in the company. The revenue goal itself is often a simple markup from the prior year's revenue based on how much other companies increase revenue. I agree with those sales reps that their targets often don't make sense. They are not set based on why their company exists and imitate others in a vacuum of purpose.

Principle 2: The board of directors exists to own and manage the company purpose.

To buy and operate a car, the government requires it to be registered with a specific individual. Why? If the use of that car causes trouble to other people or property, the registered person is accountable.

A company also requires such registration. Regardless of size, every region mandates that we register specific members or directors when registering a company. That set of registrants is called the **Board of Directors**, and they are accountable for the company. Bobby's one-owner chicken sandwich shop may have only Bobby as the director on the board. But once we move past a small mom-and-pop business, companies become a complex web of interdependencies.

A board's mandate is also to be the de facto decision-maker on all aspects of the company. So, the board is responsible and accountable for ensuring that the interests of investors, customers, employees, partners, and society are considered and satisfied.

Suppose a company's operations spread harmful chemicals into rivers, its offerings hurt customers, or its management mistreats employees or misleads investors. In any of these cases, it's the board's fault.

Isn't it the CEO's fault? No! The CEO is an employee appointed by the board. The confusion around the CEO's accountability comes from the standard practice of having the CEO on the board and often also being the head of the board.

As outside observers, we often see the CEOs facing the brunt of significant issues associated with the company. However, it is better to think about this as the head of the board being held accountable and that person also happening to be the CEO.

> **Things To Remember: Board of Directors**
>
> **The board of directors is responsible and accountable to balance the interests of all company stakeholders - investors, employees, customers, partners, and society.**

The board of directors has accountabilities.

A good board is populated with individuals who understand and act in the best interest of all company stakeholders – customers, investors, employees, partners, and society. The converse is that a board is populated with individuals who do not represent the interests of one or more of these stakeholder groups or are primarily self-serving. All boards are legally accountable for three very loosely defined duties.

The **first** is the **Duty of Business Judgment**. The board is granted the power and duty to make business decisions, including establishing and overseeing long-term business plans and hiring and firing executives. This requires skills and experience to examine every aspect of the company's decisions and actions while considering the incentives of all stakeholders, including the customers across its market and the innocent bystanders who might face second-hand impacts.

The **second** is the **Duty of Loyalty**. This duty requires directors to act in good faith to advance the best interests of the company and refrain from conduct that injures it. Most importantly, the Duty of Loyalty prohibits directors from using their positions to advance their own personal interests. This duty articulates the importance of avoiding a conflict of interest for each director.

The **third** is the **Duty of Care**. It requires directors to make informed business decisions when evaluating information provided to them by management. Directors are expected to review the information critically and not accept it blindly. Every director must apply time, mindshare, and analytical muscles to seek and review objective data and explore business realities without depending on obvious or carefully curated information.

Despite the honor offered by a board position, the practical effectiveness of boards tends to be lacking. In a recent Price Waterhouse Coopers survey, only 29 percent of executives described the board's overall performance as excellent or good. 89 percent of executives agreed that "one or more directors on their board should be replaced."

Consider any company-level drama that leads to losses for investors, employment losses for workers, and value destruction for customers. A weak board is at the core. The board's ineffectiveness played a massive role in the Theranos, Nikola, and Wirecard scandals that led to senior management, consisting of people who were also board members, facing criminal charges. So, a board seat is not just a social status symbol.

Ineffective boards exist because competence in fulfilling these formal duties is often not the criteria used to select board directors.

The most prevalent path to a board seat is investing money. So, this board seat comes with strings attached to get the money back with a return within that director's time horizon. A director in that circumstance isn't really pulling for everyone else. An investment to buy a board seat is a conflict of interest that doesn't satisfy the Duty of Loyalty. Even nonprofit boards often set sizable minimum annual donations, pushing affordability as the top criteria for director selection.

The second most common reason to get a board seat is being on other boards as associative proof. However, how many board seats are too many for a director to handle in addition to a full-time job? Attending quarterly meetings to watch a picture-heavy PowerPoint presentation with scant details and voting "yay" or "nay" with the majority is not the call to action intended via the Duty of Care. Unfortunately, boards typically operate with a "don't have time for details" mindset.

Another common path to a board seat is personal relationships, which does little to filter for skill or experience and often results in directors who don't meet the Duty of Business Judgment.

Treat board selection as an executive search.

First, find an experienced board. Diversity statistics don't make up for lack of effectiveness. Retired or near-retirement folks have decades of experience with the highs and lows of business operations at their companies and macroeconomic waves. Late-career individuals also often have the breadth and depth of experience of many business functions and seniority levels and have a mature view of all stakeholders. Lastly, conflicting incentives like personal financial gain and career advancement are likely more muted, reducing conflict of interest.

Second, formalize board selection as a process because a board director seat has far more accountability than even a senior executive role. Stacking the board with investors who put money into the company or relying on personal references to source candidates results in groupthink and a board that exists to serve a subset of stakeholders. Choosing personal connections or references implies more loyalty to other directors than to all the company stakeholders.

The duties of business judgment, loyalty, and care focus on what each director brings to the company, not what the company brings to one or more directors. So, it is critical to rely on a formal selection process to source a broad range of candidates and create a funnel of mature candidates who put the company's stakeholders above personal motives.

Include a skill assessment because many board roles are paid positions, and each director has a job to do on the board. All of us get paid to bring a specific value. So, we must staff a board role as we'd staff any other role – based on the depth of topical expertise and experience.

Third, demand commitment and ensure board directors do not hold more than two or three board seats. Many boards operate as a check-the-box operation with several passive directors. In these situations, one or two strong-willed individuals swing all the decisions and actions in a manner that suits their incentives. For a board to be effective, all directors must bring their best skills and commit time and mindshare to think critically about the organization's purpose, strategy, and operations without being swayed by personal overtures or carefully packaged information.

Consider these design questions to ensure that the company has an effective board:

Are board directors selected based on a competitive search to limit dependence on personal relationships and loose brand associations?

Is the board's composition broad enough in terms of experience, industry, business function, and stakeholder representation?

Does the board represent the interests of all the company's present and future stakeholders without primary representation from one stakeholder group?

Does every board director have the time, interest, and mindshare to work on one or two topic-specific committees to create hands-on value and solve problems for the company?

An effective board is paramount because these individuals hold sway over every major choice about the company.

Principle 3: Purpose sets incentives for all stakeholders.

The board of directors is accountable for framing a company's purpose in a way that balances stakeholders' **incentives.** The first of two arcs of our company's boundary, framed by the company purpose, is the incentives that bring each stakeholder group to the company. Incentives are not absolute dollar amounts or formulaic metrics. We can frame stakeholder incentives using three elements: 1) benefit statements for each stakeholder, 2) sustainability of the proposed benefits, and 3) acceptable risks to achieve those benefits.

Things To Remember: Incentives

Incentives are sustainable risk-adjusted benefits that attract each stakeholder group to the company.

Incentives are benefits.

Incentives that benefit stakeholders must be practical and selfish, while also being true to self. We fear embracing the complete truth when we feel that our true intentions are too selfish or not socially acceptable. Alternatively, we may be afraid that our strengths aren't good enough for customers to realize value, investors to find lucrative, employees to find security, or partners to trust us. This results in a tendency to embellish.

Don't! Failing to fully embrace the truth can lead to incongruence in the value exchange between stakeholders or hurt our ability to convert our company's purpose into its decisions and actions. Let's use an illustrative example involving a fair-trade consumer company to explain benefits that must balance across stakeholders.

Owners and investors play the same role and are always represented on the board. Every owner has different motivations. Some want to make a lot of money quickly. Some want to replace their salary through a steady business. Some want to solve a problem they personally experienced. Some want to do something exciting with their life. Others want to build a legacy for their children. One individual owner may even own different companies and have different motivations for each. An owner-centric benefit isn't an altruistic mission or vision statement. It is brass tacks: *Why do the owners want to keep the company running?*

Let's say our fair-trade company owner spent a year in Colombia and, upon returning to their hometown, felt that running a small business was more in tune with their lifestyle than taking an office job with a salary. This is a good benefit statement for our new business owner.

To start this small business, our owner could ask their parents to invest some money and get the remaining startup money through a small business loan. This company's board includes our owner, who is also the CEO, the parent, who is the primary investor, and possibly an experienced third party who could bring independent thinking.

Our owner met local organic farmers in Colombia and is excited about partnering with them. Selling their items, such as organic coffee and handicrafts, at fair prices without being squeezed by large distributors is a strong benefit for those farmers.

Customers have a host of benefits when buying, some immediately gratifying, some longer-term, and some subconscious. Our owner feels that some price-insensitive customers would benefit from an opportunity to buy fairly-sourced goods even if it costs more than main street buying options.

Employees consider factors like career growth, stability, flexibility, personal passion, and societal status beyond salaries and bonuses. Our owner feels that retired neighbors could be thrilled to stay active and serve as employees to support the fair-trade outfit as a low-wage hobby.

Societal considerations can feel unimportant. That is never the case. Even a single retail store can begin to transform a mundane town center into an exciting and internationally flavored one, benefiting even the town's residents who don't shop there.

Such a practical and achievable set of benefits ensures congruent value exchange between stakeholders, but genuinely committing to these ideas is often the hardest part for us as human beings.

Incentives are benefits in the equilibrium state.

Let's contrast the fair-trade scenario with an overly aspirational board that hasn't grasped the importance of objectivity and self-awareness. The same owner with the same ingredients could watch too much Shark Tank and frame an incentive structure as follows.

The owner could claim deep relationships with organic farmers across Colombia and other South American countries and want the benefit of running a large company that reaches customers nationally. The farmers can be incentivized to produce more to bring higher volumes to market and make significantly more profits. Customers can be promised fair trade goods at the same price as regular items at other retail chains. The company can promise investors a high return for writing a large investment check to quickly expand nationally.

This is a different and outlandish purpose with the same starting ingredients. This shows that framing benefit statements can become inauthentic storytelling if we're not honest about our motivations. This story may be selfish, as we'd like incentives to be, but not true to ourselves. Our goal with framing incentives is to set realistic and sustainable ones.

We must examine benefit statements for practicality and sustainability to ensure we are setting a realistic boundary for our company that won't disappoint stakeholders. Whether in physics, chemistry, or economics, *equilibrium* is the most likely state of existence, given the ingredients at hand. If everyone in the ecosystem knew all the information as they interacted over time, the resulting reality would be the equilibrium. The benefits framed must be realistic and transparent so that the equilibrium state, which ensues after stakeholders learn all relevant information, is the same as our proposed one.

Recall the consumer apparel company in Figure 1 that saw its market price drop immediately after its public listing, once the reality behind the scenes became transparent. The disappointing share price reflects the equilibrium state, as the benefits promised to multiple stakeholder groups were unsustainable.

> **Things To Remember: Equilibrium**
>
> **Equilibrium is the sustainable and realistic outcome if we play the same game for a few iterations, where we learn others' real incentives, decisions, and actions, not just what they say.**

A thirteen-year veteran founder CEO's reaction to his company's selling price was: ". . . Not a positive outcome. . . . Many lessons learned I may write about." Employees who had exercised their stock options and spent years at the company received 30 percent below the price they bought those options. This means employees lost money on their time investment in the company and the real money they invested in buying those options. The company was sold for $100 million. How can a company that was sold for $100 million disappoint all these stakeholders? The company didn't have a transparent purpose, and the intended stakeholder benefits were always imbalanced. This imbalance remained until the company was sold, when reality became apparent. This equilibrium state was a disappointment for many.

Failing to balance the upside leads to incongruence between stakeholders and all the important decisions and actions. But our upside is only meaningful in the context of the downside in trying to achieve the upside.

Incentives are risk-adjusted benefits in the equilibrium state.

Smoking is injurious to health. Everyone knows it, yet people still smoke. As long as secondary smoke isn't hitting other people, it's a valid choice for a person to smoke. However, it is not valid for a tobacco company to frame smoking as having health benefits as they once did.

Driving down the road above the speed limit comes with risks. A speeding ticket is the smallest of risks; accidents we cause have far greater consequences. So, what is the point of taking this speeding risk? How much risk is reasonable? The answer is personal. But framing incentives has to be risk-adjusted.

Risks manifest in various shapes and forms. Three considerations collectively frame a risk: The likelihood of the harmful event, the severity of the impact if the event manifests, and any backstops or controls in place to mitigate adverse effects.

Risks are ever-present. But we choose our exposure to them. Risks must be intentionally uncovered, not hidden away. If we can't share the risks with our stakeholders, balancing all stakeholders' incentives is a short-term illusion, and our equilibrium will involve imbalance and disappointment.

Ownership structures and investment vehicles are increasingly complex. Companies are bought and sold far more often than a decade ago. Risks manifest in many ways, and there are many ways to hide risk through funky arrangements that can fall apart with a single trigger event. But there are a few common manifestations.

First, operating in perpetual unprofitability is a slow-burn risk that highlights an imbalanced value exchange where some stakeholders are extracting too much value compared to others. A company must be designed to pay its bills without perpetually taking on new investments or loans. Companies must be profitable or at least break even.

Second, taking on too much debt leaves the collective at risk when the company faces headwinds. Debt collectors can call in what they are owed and disrupt the balance of a company's ecosystem overnight. Managing acceptable debt levels and related covenants is part of balancing the risk profiles of all stakeholders.

Third, doing significant amounts of business with structurally unsound customers or partners and offering them imbalanced incentives puts other stakeholders at risk. This risk likely exists because we couldn't devise benefits that balance in the first place.

Fourth, if our incentives are set with unrealistic operational performance in mind, they can predictably lead to unethical behaviors over time that harm other stakeholders. No one starts with evil intentions, yet we end up with an opioid crisis, harmful fertilizer or talcum powder lawsuits, or predatory lending sanctions. Such events were caused by setting and chasing unrealistic sales targets or cutting too much cost, led by over-optimistic benefit statements for investors.

A "house of cards" is how an introspective CEO I worked with described his company's 25 percent revenue loss in a single year. I interviewed many customers and worked closely with employees. The theme that came through loud and clear was that the company had a perpetual habit of overpromising during sales and hoping to make it all work afterward. This operational behavior stems from framing investor benefits that require high growth rates that were incongruent with employee abilities or customer needs.

Consider this design question to frame incentives:

Have we uncovered the relevant risks to adjust the tangible and realistic benefit statements for each stakeholder group to ensure that they balance and represent the likely equilibrium state?

It is important to internalize that our benefit statements or stakeholders are not specific and tactical. At this stage, we aren't making any decisions about what our company looks like. The answers for "what" our company is will be framed later through strategy development. Notions about ideal customers and optimal offerings should be set aside, and the purpose must focus on simply the why. It will be tempting to muddle the why with tactical actions because framing and balancing incentives is challenging.

The incentive balancing act becomes more complex as the size and range of stakeholders increase. Companies are increasingly sophisticated arrangements, and each stakeholder's incentives have deeper layers and multiple dimensions. But if we want to create such complex entities, our board of directors is also accountable for balancing the incentive equation associated with them.

Principle 4: A company's purpose accounts for its lifecycle stage for present and future stakeholders.

Stars fizzle out. Humans are mortal. This is a normal part of life. So, why do we treat companies as though they will last forever and feel shocked when one fizzles? One answer is that the company's purpose didn't satisfactorily balance incentives, as discussed in Principle 3. The other is that its purpose didn't keep up with time.

Our **first** time-related consideration is a company's lifecycle stage. Just like everything else in the universe, companies are born, they mature and excel, they grow weak, and they end. Longitudinal thinking, which entails monitoring the same situation over time, is paramount for companies. The life of a company does not flow linearly. Time is a dimension we must live in, and so must our company incentives.

One of two owners of a twenty-year-old, mid-sized bootstrapped company asked for my advice. "I don't know what happens to our customers and dozens of employees if I get hit by a car." This is an extreme scenario. But having a "living will mindset" allows us to frame our incentives in a time box and revisit it periodically.

As we covered earlier, scale, time, and environmental shifts change our needs and our ecosystem. Our benefit statements and risk considerations must evolve with our company's lifecycle stage. A two- or three-year cadence is optimal for considering incentive shifts at a Single Market Problem Entity. Continuously questioning and reassessing our purpose is not helpful because it limits our ability to live in the present.

Imagine an athlete's career from their early days of pursuing recognition through their fame-filled stages and into their waning years and retirement.

Each stage requires a different purpose that dictates the clubs they play for, their salaries, training, style of play, and leadership skills. The same evolution in purpose through lifecycle stages applies to companies.

A holistic company frames its purpose so that the people involved have a realistic expectation of its current lifecycle stage, whether early, mature, or late stage. Would we buy an item at a going-out-of-business sale? If we find the right item at the right price, yes! This helps us understand the idea that, under the right conditions, customers are fine with buying something, knowing that no returns are possible. That sales event also has employees who are willing to work in a short-term arrangement without hope for pensions or promotions. So, it's all about setting appropriate incentives aligned with the company's lifecycle stage.

In the early lifecycle stages of our company, we are likely more dependent on our partners to provide the necessary inputs to create value for customers. However, as a more mature company, that dynamic may shift radically. Our partners may become more dependent on us. How does this change how we frame incentives?

Our **second** time-related consideration is balancing present and future stakeholders. For new companies, all stakeholders belong in the future. But companies that have been in business for a while have both present and future stakeholders. Our company is a relationship between the people involved, but people float in and out of it. Customers buy and stop buying. Investors come and go. Employees and partners are not perpetual value creators. New ones replace old ones.

At each lifecycle stage, we have people currently involved and others who will replace or be added to them. The board of directors has the duty to balance incentives across present and future stakeholders who may have different expectations.

For example, when a company is being sold, the board of directors is accountable not just to current investors to maximize the sale price of the company but also to ensure that the company's ability to balance incentives across stakeholders is transparently communicated to future investors. Current employees could resign en masse, hampering the company's ability to create value in the future. Change in investors doesn't necessarily mean the employees, customers, and partners change. Future investors impact current employees, customers, and partners. Even if the current board is disbanded at the sale because the buyer creates a new board, the current board is accountable for serving the incentives of soon-to-be past employees, customers, and partners until disbanded.

Operating our company led by a purpose is like running a relay race. We are constantly thinking about our current stage, the next stage, and the people running in each stage. A holistic company that maintains congruence is a strong relay team.

These time considerations do not imply that we write more benefit statements. Our company's boundary is still singular. It simply shifts.

I often ask CEOs who are also primary owners this question: What would you do differently in your company if you planned to run it for ten years, compared to the option of retiring this year and selling to a new owner? Interestingly, many don't have an answer to this question, which implies a lack of a well-framed purpose. Would you do the same home improvement projects if you planned to live in your house for ten more years instead of renting it or selling it this year? No! This simple question contains the essence of both time considerations.

Purpose influences what we do with our company and how we do it. Risk-adjusted incentives that account for the company's lifecycle and accommodate both present and future stakeholders are best seen through the lens of value creation and capital efficiency.

Principle 5: Frame purpose as value exchange between stakeholders at an agreed-upon capital efficiency.

Money is confusing. It is not benefits, time, or risk. It was always intended to be a token representing the essence of each. Our inclination to think that putting dollar signs next to things makes them official or effective could not be further from the truth.

Recall Hawthorne effect. If our purpose involves a bunch of dollars and percentages, our actions and decisions will likely devolve into forcing those numbers.

We also agreed that capital engineering involves turning money into more money with little intrinsic value creation in between. To well-trained eyes, dollars and percentages without evidence can prove insincere, so let's focus our purpose on the evidence.

Throughout this chapter, we have discussed stakeholders. Let's clarify that each stakeholder is a role, not a person. System thinking in the context of stakeholders requires us to view each role's responsibility and accountability without person-centric biases.

One person may be both an owner and an employee, like a CEO or senior executive. Many other employees may be part owners. Customers sometimes invest in companies they buy from and become part owners. Governments representing society invest in companies. So, our purpose goes beyond drawing lines of dollars and percentages between neat stakeholder boxes. It's never that clean.

Customers primarily benefit from the value created through the company, and society is a secondary beneficiary. Employees and partners create that value through their wit, skills, hard work, and other intangibles.

> **Things To Remember: Value Creation**
>
> **Value creation comprises real-world efforts by employees and partners to generate benefits primarily for customers and peripherally for society.**

Value creation efforts require investment. Capital may be injected from investors who own part of the company or through loans from banks. The price customers pay for the company's offerings should result in a profit, which we could use as an investment to further the company's ambitions. Employees might contribute to the investment pile. Regardless of the source, we need a rule of thumb for using investment effectively.

> **Things To Remember: Capital Efficiency**
>
> **Capital efficiency articulates the expected efficacy with which the board oversees the use of capital injected by investors, profits earned from serving customers, and support provided by governments on behalf of society, all to feed employees' and partners' value creation efforts.**

Investors' return was always intended to come from a share of the profits generated from the value created using capital efficiently. In fact, without continuous profitability, our company is not sustainable, and no rational investor should be interested in our capital-wasting scheme.

> **Things To Remember: Sustainable Profitability**
>
> **Profitability is a result of effective value creation combined with efficient use of capital, which is the only rational and intrinsic path for an investor to benefit from their risk.**

Recall the record number of companies that went public in 2020 and 2021, only for their share prices to drop dramatically. Guess what the single common factor was? Almost none of them made a profit. The purpose of a company is to exchange value between stakeholders by using capital efficiently. The proof is in its ability to generate profits consistently – not just once or twice through accounting gimmicks. I agree with Friedman on his focus on profitability: consistently generating profits is necessary for a company to be a sustainable entity.

These three success factors combine to form our powerful model for framing the purpose of a congruent holistic company.

> **Things To Remember: Holistic Company Model**
>
> **Balanced Value + Optimized Capital = Sustainable Profits.**

Now, is it okay for an entity's sustainable profits to be zero? Absolutely – as long as that's the equilibrium state outlined in the company's purpose and balances the incentives of all parties involved. We call such companies non-profits! They have the same five stakeholder groups we have been discussing.

Illustratively, a congruent purpose helps the board operate with tangible answers to questions such as the following.

What is the real-world situation that encourages us to create or keep running the company?

What is the uniqueness of our value creators that would enable our company to influence that situation?

What is our desired company scale, ranging from small to world-beating?

What is our desired reach between local and global?

Do we prefer to give profits to investors and employees or treat it as a new investment into the company?

Where does our comfort with new capital in exchange for ownership shares or loans fall on the spectrum between no interest and high interest?

Do the current owners want to continue running the company for at least five years, close it, or sell it in that window?

Note that writing quick answers to these questions does not constitute a purpose. These are illustrative, and the questions relevant to each company and lifecycle stage are different.

Setting a strong boundary using a clear purpose allows us flexibility in our company's decisions and execution regarding who, what, and how, without making our path too open-ended.

Things To Remember: Company Purpose [Refined]

Purpose is a well-written document, created and embraced by the board, that articulates a risk-adjusted balance of incentives between all stakeholders in equilibrium. It accounts for a company's lifecycle stage and is framed in terms of value creation and capital efficiency, with corresponding profitability expectations.

Figure A2 shows my Company Purpose Maturity Model that offers a self-assessment opportunity for a company you care about. Building the best version of a company requires all stakeholders to consider the balance of value exchange, effectiveness of capital utilization, and alignment on profitability expectations. Embracing these principles helps us reach *Level 5: Balanced* maturity. Not doing so leaves us close to the *Level 1: Individualistic* end of the spectrum, which results in a company that disappoints one or more stakeholder groups.

Figure A2. Company Purpose Maturity Model.

In a recent trend, a wave of young people in America are acquiring stable and profitable businesses owned by baby boomers for decades. Typically, those baby boomers have a purpose that focuses on long-term ownership and running a family-owned business that keeps the same employees and operates within their intimate customer relationships.

The younger owners, backed by high-risk investors, are likely going in with a different conscious or subconscious purpose. Their benefit statement involves faster customer acquisition through greater new investment, acquiring other similar companies, and an intent to sell the company to someone else in a few years. This changes the value exchange equation for all stakeholders. All decisions and execution around these companies will change with this ownership change.

Just as many humans prefer to avoid conversations about mortality, considering a company's purpose can be emotionally taxing. So, this first part of our method deserves to stand alone.

Purpose always guides what our company is and how we operate each day. It is better to consciously embrace purpose as a lever to set boundaries around all the remaining building blocks, rather than follow an unguided path of imitating others or creating an individualistic company.

PART B

Management Approach Sets The System In Which Value Creators Work.

IMAGINE throwing a perfect dart towards the bullseye, but it hits the board and falls on the floor. What if the board wasn't made of cork or any penetrable material and was just cloth covering a brick wall? An effective **Management Approach** is akin to a corkboard. It is a foundational people agenda.

Without such a foundation, developing an optimal offering will be impossible. We cannot design scalable operations, a winning corporate strategy, a related strategic plan, and an effective execution approach. For the first twelve years of my career, my transformational work with companies focused on such requirements, but I always felt that the real-world sustainable impact of my work was unsatisfactory. The reason is that I had limited influence on the fundamental levers under management approach.

The management approach levers are our CEO's most significant contribution. Almost every other responsibility in the company could be handled by another executive with deeper topical experience. However, the management approach cannot be delegated. It doesn't matter what the CEO's knowledge is about the market problem, sales skills to close big deals, or relationships to find investors; the CEO's primary contribution is building the management approach.

History has a handful of unusually visionary CEOs like Steve Jobs or company marketers like Elon Musk who conjure near-impossible outcomes through their personalities. But such personalities are outliers. If a CEO is a mere mortal like any of us, how is one person supposed to magically get everyone to behave optimally? The path is not what we have come to call company culture.

"Culture eats strategy for breakfast" has been an often-quoted phrase, commonly attributed to management guru Peter Drucker. Whenever problems arise in a company, pundits retrospectively criticize its culture and find correlations between the CEO and behavioral issues at the company. But what is culture?

> **Things To Remember: Culture**
>
> **Culture is a nebulous aggregation of behaviors and feelings – which we cannot directly control or measure – exhibited and experienced by stakeholders around a company.**

Each person experiences and expresses a combination of five core feelings – happiness, anger, shame, fear, and sadness. A company, as a collective, isn't responsible for each individual's feelings. We must all learn to choose circumstances that align with our feelings, which are heavily influenced by experiences outside of the company.

Similarly, we all have natural preferences in behaviors and stylistic differences. However, an effective system requires us to adjust those inclinations to attributes that suit the whole group.

That said, a company must offer transparency and objectivity about the expectations of each person so the collective can succeed. This allows individuals to choose whether they want to be part of one or more stakeholder groups within the company. Making that choice is each person's responsibility. Management approach is the set of levers that creates the result we call culture.

The management approach ensures that the company's building blocks and system to balance the agendas of all stakeholders are robust. A mature management approach correlates with our ability to maximize and balance value exchange between stakeholders while using our capital investment efficiently. An immature management approach creates work cultures that fuel individualism and infighting, resulting in what we typically call toxic cultures.

> **Things To Remember: Management Approach**
>
> **The management approach is a tangible path to developing an objective and transparent system within which optimal value creators work. Company culture is a lagging reflection of how effectively management approach levers are deployed.**

Management approach maturity dictates alignment of incentives, decisions, and actions across value creators.

A CEO has the toughest job in the world. With the help of the company's board of directors, this role is responsible for balancing value exchange between all stakeholders. We can broadly classify our company's stakeholder groups into value creators and value extractors.

Value extractors typically bring capital to the table. Customers bring money, and they expect the company to address their problems. Investors bring cash that greases the wheels of the enterprise and expect to share in the profits. In our holistic company model, we embraced the Single Market Problem Entity concept to focus on profits instead of short-term indicators of future profits that may or may not come.

Value creators take capital off the table to solve the problem the company focuses on. Employees of our company, which includes the CEO, senior executives, supervisors, individual contributors, and board members, are the primary value creators. They wear the company branded shirt, have emails with the company's domain, and are the day-to-day managers of the company. It is tempting to think that employees are the predominant value creators.

However, we are all building on others' work. Every company sits within a flowing chain of value. Partners create significant value that employees purchase with capital provided by investors or customers and add their own contribution to form the solution for customers. Partners might be suppliers of goods, services, or intellectual property. Other partners might help us sell to their customers in a mutually beneficial arrangement. Partners are just as important value creators in our company as employees are.

The management approach allows the CEO to create a system that attracts the best value creators and gets the most value out of them. A 2012 McKinsey Global Survey, War for Talent, shows that in complex job roles such as management and software development, the job productivity of high performers is 800 percent higher than that of average performers.

Our CEO's effort to maximize value creation starts with two priorities. **First**, the CEO must develop a system that attracts and retains top value creators, improves the performance of mid-tier players, and allows bottom players to improve or move on to other things. **Second**, the CEO must create a cohesive system that continuously improves the productivity of the value creators. This system should result in the best possible offering for customers while generating the expected returns for investors and owners.

Throughout the book, we may refer to value creators as employees for simplicity. It is critical to note that the boundary between a partner and an employee is semantics. The only practical difference is a badge. Every rule of thumb, measurement, assessment, and question we consider for employees applies to partners, both of whom are paid to create value.

Management Approach Maturity Model.

The model in Figure B1 gives you a reference guide to self-assess the effectiveness of the management approach levers in a company. We must strive towards the right side of the model. As we move from the left side to the right, the CEO has increasingly deployed mature building blocks bound by a cohesive system to allow value creators to collaborate effectively.

On the left side of the model, we operate in an individualistic mindset. The whims of the most opinionated and biased overshadow the rest.

At *Level 1: Egocentric*, the company's board and the CEO have not used management approach levers as intended. The company's purpose is focused on a few individuals. Aspects such as likability and homogeneity will likely rise to the top as factors that keep value creators around. Top performers who push for the company's maturity and cohesion will likely not feel equitably rewarded for their contributions.

These top performers who prefer to work at a meritocratic company will likely leave quickly. Lower performers who are satisfied with the status quo and are personally close to other tenured value creators will probably feel at home. Loyalty and groupthink are highly valued. Hiring, terminations, performance, and compensation decisions are likely to feel personal and subjective. A stagnant company at Level 1 of the management approach will find it impossible to evolve and mature on the other parts of the *Congruence*™ method.

At *Level 2: Subjective* and *Level 3: Democratic*, the company struggles to string together the essential levers of the management approach. Attracting, hiring, and retaining optimally talented employees or choosing the appropriate partners will prove difficult. The maturity of the organization design is unlikely to improve. As a result, it will struggle to retain top value creators.

As we move further to the right of the maturity model, the board, CEO, Congruence Architect, and human resources executive demonstrate knowledge and confidence in systems to manage people, behaviors, and related decisions.

To sustain a balanced value exchange, we must operate at *Level 4: Objective* or above. This maturity level allows us to attract and retain highly skilled employees and top-quality partners and align their incentives as framed in the company's purpose. This implies a system that evolves core values, organization design, and value creators' skills to efficiently deliver greater value for customers and investors.

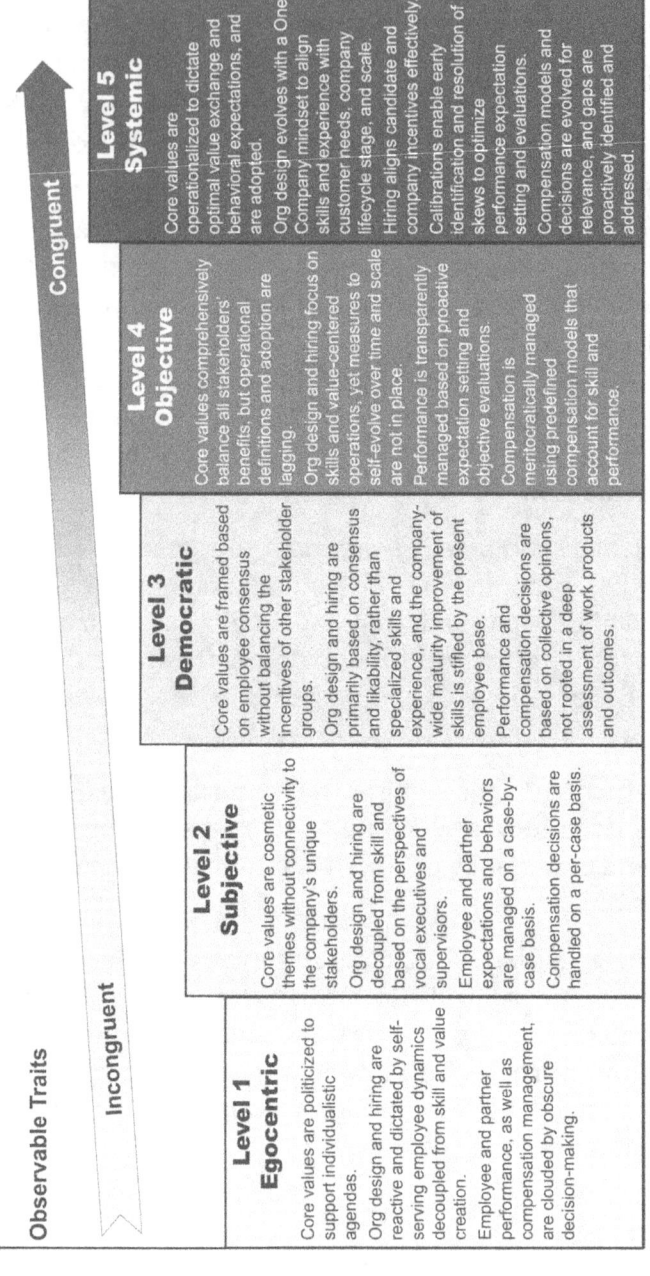

Figure B1. Management Approach Maturity Model.

Our optimal state is *Level 5: Systemic,* where we operate in an objective and transparent environment where all value creators know what is expected and what it takes to succeed. A mature management approach systemically ensures that value creators' incentives fully align with company values and are designed to meet the needs of customers and investors. Personnel decisions will not cause surprises. The highest performers will stay while the rest strive to catch up. Customers will look at the company as a cohesive unit and a trusted partner where most value creators can consistently deliver on their actual needs.

Taking each step to the right implies minimizing incongruences on how value creators are chosen and managed. Greater management approach maturity is no easy feat because it has to tackle the natural human tendency to prefer individualism and hold on to our biases.

I worked with an early-stage technology company with six employees that blossomed into a dominant leader in its space. The CEO focused on the components of this management approach before the company scaled beyond ten employees.

Conversely, I worked with a 200-employee technology company that prioritized the management approach levers after it experienced persistent challenges. Unfortunately, this delayed effort to improve the company's talent pool, work ethic, and productivity had limited success. Correcting subpar building blocks that are ineffective is exponentially harder than applying these foundational management approach levers proactively.

B.1
SET CORE VALUES AS BEHAVIORAL GUARDRAILS.

IF our effort to build the management approach is analogous to creating an organized religion, then core values are the actionable commandments that the priests and congregation must live by.

Most companies have an altruistic set of core values on their websites and office walls. Companies often talk about core values as their path to future success. However, there are core values that sound good, and then there are core values that have the desired impact. One company includes, "We don't have core values; we have core behaviors!" in all their job postings for future employees. This is the right mindset.

A holistic company effectively balances value exchange between value creators and value extractors. Core values are the fundamental lever that guides the day-to-day actions and decisions of the predominant operational value creators – employees. The CEO and senior executives are also employees; an owner or investor could also be an employee.

Core values dictate the day-to-day behaviors of all employees in creating and delivering value. They also guide employees in choosing the right partners, such as vendors or service providers, to help create value.

Each employee has their personal value system. Expecting individuals to override theirs with a company's value system requires them to understand and accept the core values and how they can best implement them.

Mature core values result in optimal value creation for customers without harming non-customer third parties, whether they are people who draw water from the river next to our manufacturing plant or loved ones of customers who use our medical solutions. However, core values are not meant to market a company's intent to customers. Customers only care about the behaviors demonstrated by the employees and the value created; they don't read the core values before they decide to do business.

Things To Remember: Core Values

Core values articulate the operational DNA necessary for value creators - employees and partners - to make good decisions and perform optimal activities to meet the needs of value extractors, who are our customers. Core values allow companies to attract and retain the right people to serve as value creators.

First, core values articulate the company's expected operational behaviors. The CEO and the human resources team must develop and operationalize them and consistently ensure adoption. Core values are a vaccine formulated, tested, iterated, and prescribed by the CEO based on market knowledge. Human resources must inoculate them as prescribed.

Second, the approach to defining core values should not be democratic. The CEO's decision and articulation are based on an adequate set of market and internal assessments. Unfortunately, the most common trap companies fall into is to start by asking the democratic question: *What do you think our core values should be?*

Core values are not meant to be an average of employee opinions or desires, including those of senior executives. If we create a perception that core values are a matter of opinion, we open the door to adoption challenges.

Understandably, taking the pulse of all employees is a much easier path to defining core values. However, this path rarely leads to the right behaviors that will help create value. Core values must lead employees, not follow them.

Mature core values achieve two things.

First, companies must focus on identifying the right behaviors, not fabricating perceptions. Although it is tempting to worry about the optics of core values, the only relevant optic is the ultimate impact.

Second, core values are effective when they become the operational DNA of the company. Every employee must adopt and live by the intent of the core values when they are within the boundaries of our company.

Core values must score well on adoption and impact. If our core values feel ineffective, we must be bold and change them. Forget all the rules about how often we are supposed to change them and what everyone else thinks. We will learn in Part D that corporate strategy development is an optimal pathway for the macroevolution of core values.

Figure B2 illustrates my Values Funnel Framework. The funnel has three levels that result in effective core values that can dictate the company's operations. I recommend leveraging it to determine and operationalize the correct core values.

Figure B2. Values Funnel Framework optimizes core values.

Principle 1: Core values reflect the needs of value extractors.

It is tempting to think that the management approach primarily addresses the needs of employees. Ultimately, a business exists to trade with customers. It is the only path to revenue or profitability. Even if a company has highly productive, top talent firing on all cylinders, the direction in which energy is expended is important. Such a group can spend its efforts in a direction that doesn't create enough value for its customers on the tepid end to one that misdirects stakeholders on the unethical end.

To identify the needs of value extractors, we must address two essential aspects. **First**, we must clearly articulate who our customers and impacted non-customers truly are. This answer entirely depends on our company's business model and the market problem we are solving. But a loose or inaccurate definition has dire consequences.

Second, framing mature core values starts with understanding our customers' real needs instead of perceived needs. Think about real needs as the root causes of problems customers are experiencing and perceived needs as symptoms. We must design employee and partner behaviors that meet customers' real needs. We will discuss both factors further in Part D: Corporate Strategy.

For example, I worked with a software-as-a-service (SaaS) company that took great pride in "responsiveness" as a value. Their responsiveness scores approached ten out of ten for years. But they found customer loyalty elusive. The truth was that customers wanted to take the results provided by the offering without investing time in the software and even less in troubleshooting.

The company mistakenly used a narrow measure of answering customer phone calls politely and chasing down problems quickly as success criteria. The customers' actual need was to get information quickly. My work with them revealed that the correct measure for customers' real needs was minimizing the number of hours customers spent getting the information in question.

The correct solution focus was to take the onus of using the offering away from the customer entirely. A core value of "turnkey" was more appropriate to lead the employees to a solution that met customer needs.

In this first layer of the funnel, value extractors' real needs help us frame our superset of employee and partner behavioral considerations. No employee can be good at everything. These behavioral traits provide prioritized guardrails for designing operational activities and decisions and managing and executing major initiatives. This alignment between behavioral expectations and customers' real needs is the only path to a congruent ecosystem.

Consider these design questions:

Does the company have a robust articulation of our optimal customers and impacted non-customers?

Does the superset of operational behaviors that dictate our core values start with the real needs of these value-extracting and impacted stakeholders?

For example, do our customers prefer to interact with a fun vendor or a serious, buttoned-up vendor?

If our company serves creative entertainment industry customers, they might prefer to interact with a vendor that makes their experience informal. On the other hand, suppose we are selling to banks or hospitals. In that case, they will likely expect our employees to demonstrate preparedness and discipline due to the high-risk environments in which these customers operate.

Southwest Airlines deftly translates their optimal customers' expectations into employee behaviors. A *Warrior Spirit, Servant's Heart*, and *Fun-LUVing Attitude* summarize the airline's values. It is evident that the employees strive to make flying fun and leisurely for their core market of middle-class occasional travelers and vacationers. It is a stark contrast to other US airlines that primarily profit from frequent business travelers who are used to a more formal flying experience.

All value creators' day-to-day behaviors must align with operational expectations that satisfy customer needs. Core value definition starts with articulating these expectations, and we must be able to execute them.

Principle 2: Core values align with value creators' strengths.

With the help of human resources and the Congruence Architect, the CEO has to continue to take stock of what our employees and partners are actually good at. Choosing expected behaviors that are not the core strengths of these value-creating stakeholders likely leads to disappointing outcomes.

Customers do business with the whole company. They do not interact with only one employee. Organizational behaviors demonstrated by employees must be consistent. Therefore, each employee must be able to repeat the desired behaviors consistently. Employees must reproduce the same behaviors as everyone else so that customers see the company as one united front. For instance, a company would not want the resignation of a top performer to risk the entire relationship with a customer.

The same applies to our choice of partners. The value our company creates will be disjointed if our partners do not consistently match the behaviors expected of employees.

Taking behavioral descriptions from large, successful companies or being biased by social conversations is not a good approach to defining our optimal behaviors. For example, a popular core value is "do the right thing." I have worked with multiple companies that used this as a core value. However, employees come from many geographical and professional backgrounds, and the "right thing" is subjective.

Consider three hypothetical employees. The first has a trading background, the second has nonprofit experience, and the third has an engineering background. They will all think about the "right thing" differently when interacting with various stakeholders. None of them are more correct, but their experiences vastly differ and shape what they consider the "right thing." Core values must align with practical strengths and be tangible and unambiguous.

This principle also gives the CEO the opportunity to demonstrate leadership and consider: *What type of people and behaviors do we want in our company?* Although we tend to stereotype the quality of people based on associations with other companies or educational institutions and past job titles, building our congruent company implies we are better off finding people who match the behaviors we seek. If one person can lift 200 lbs for $2 and two others can lift 100 lbs each for $1, which option do we choose?

Reconsider the question I posed in the earlier chapter to the senior executives to drive towards a company-wide purpose: "Are we a high-growth, fast-paced company or a cash flow-focused, lifestyle company?" That was not a good vs. bad choice. Instead, it intended to frame the strengths that the company's core values should incorporate. The company had to resolve the disconnect between its perceived strengths and the reality on the ground.

This second layer of the Values Funnel Framework impacts our organization design and the number of employees each role will need. It influences the depth of skills we can plan to hire. It impacts the expectations we set for our employees to measure their performance and how much we compensate them. It affects the quality, speed, flexibility, and cost of value creation for customers. Finally, it impacts the growth and profitability we can realistically achieve.

Consider these design questions:

Do we objectively understand our value creators' operational strengths and weaknesses?

Have we boldly framed the behavioral strengths expected from current and future employees and partners?

Principle 3: Core values are seamlessly demonstrable by senior executives.

At the bottom of the funnel, the final but equally important filter is the alignment between senior executives' behaviors and operational behaviors expected of all employees and partners.

Core values are an effective filter to consider while filling senior executive roles. Conversely, it offers an assessment of whether the right senior executives are in place.

A set of words and explanations is not enough to engrain the spirit of core values into the company's operational DNA. Core values require role models to demonstrate the true essence of expected behaviors. Senior executives are these role models. Every aspect of desired behaviors should be the natural state where senior executives operate consistently.

If core values do not reflect the natural day-to-day behaviors of senior executives, they just become words on a plaque. Employees will not have leaders to look up to and learn what "good" looks like. Furthermore, the misalignment between senior executives' natural instincts and documented core values will likely result in hiring and promoting employees who do not truly represent the essence of the core values, further devaluing their effectiveness.

One of the core values used by Uber's founding CEO, Travis Kalanick, was: "Meritocracy and toe-stepping – The best idea always wins. Don't sacrifice truth for social cohesion and don't hesitate to challenge the boss." Interestingly, this is a strong core value. Travis Kalanick successfully conveyed and demonstrated his idea of how Uber should behave. For years, Uber operated in markets worldwide with an "ask for forgiveness, not permission" attitude, constantly butting heads with local governments for starting Uber services without going through the proper channels.

We may or may not agree with Mr. Kalanick. But it shows the power of a well-framed core value – demonstrability and actionability. Intending to change employee behaviors, Uber's next CEO, Dara Khosrowshahi, changed this value to moderate the behavioral elements: "We value ideas over hierarchy. We believe that the best ideas can come from anywhere, both inside and outside our company. Our job is to seek out those ideas, to shape and improve them through candid debate, and to take them from concept to action."

The change in Uber's CEO and shift in core values were also associated with turnover among other senior executives who were better aligned with the company's more evolved global brand.

When we meet these three criteria, core values are aligned with the customer's value expectations and can be reliable guardrails that employees and partners can live up to.

Consider this design question:

Do the day-to-day behaviors of senior executives reflect the core values that employees and partners are expected to demonstrate?

What if the day-to-day behaviors that senior executives demonstrate do not adequately cover the values necessary to serve customers or, even worse, cause social damage? This is where a company's board comes in. The board must be aware of gaps between the senior executives' abilities and behaviors and how well that aligns with the company's agreed-upon core values.

Core values touch every aspect of managing the organization. The CEO can measure the leadership effectiveness of senior executives and the implementation prowess of the human resources department based on the adoption and impact of the company's core values across all components of our method. So, how do we drive adoption?

Principle 4: Operationalize core values for practical impact.

Once the CEO has developed the core values, taking it from paper to practice is not trivial. Every employee in the company must read, understand, and live by the core values without ambiguity or interpretive differences. In addition, every core value must have a detailed articulation that conveys what to do and what not to do. But getting the core values right and in operation is challenging.

I worked closely with a company that prided itself on the following core values: "accountability," "respect," and "agility," with a short sentence to support each. Unfortunately, after a decade into the business, the company lost 25 percent of its revenue in a single year and struggled with personnel conflicts. Negative customer feedback spiked due to persistent delivery quality challenges. So, what happened here?

First, these three core values were not derived from customers' needs or associated behavioral requirements. These behaviors could apply to any company in any market. Even more importantly, these three positively intentioned behaviors were not operationalized. The result was that the words on paper morphed into unintended behaviors on the ground.

- *Can one be too respectful when we aren't holding people accountable?*

- *Could one mix up agility with a lack of discipline and lack of planning?*

- *Could too much respect cause executives to fail to evolve the company's building blocks?*

- *Could respect lead to telling customers what they want to hear and being unable to deliver to expectations?*

- *Can accountability be tactical and miss the big picture?*

In this scenario, the ineffectiveness and poor operationalization of core values became one of the gaps that needed to be closed before other fundamental levers could have any reasonable impact.

Applying the first three principles during strategy development will generate the appropriate themes and actionable details for powerful core values. These values don't need to be ingenious; they just need to be effective and satisfy the first three principles we discussed. But their impact will elude us if we don't incorporate them into every aspect of our operations. Ineffectively operationalized core values are toothless.

As we review the remaining components of the management approach, core values will reappear as a constant backdrop. Our hiring and employee performance assessments must have the core values built in to ensure that they are a guardrail for all our people-related decisions. When new employees join us, we must conduct new-hire training to align on how to live our core values.

All employee meetings are valuable forums for communicating impactful ideas across the organization. We must use such opportunities to influence forward-looking behaviors through core values and spend less time on privately consumable information such as financial updates.

We must also incorporate core values into how we create and deliver the company's offerings and how employees work with each other, customers, and other partners. Larger gatherings to introduce new offerings and annual sales kick-offs are opportunities to demonstrate a throughline from behavioral expectations to customer value and desired company outcomes such as revenue and profitability. Continuously evolving employee understanding of the practical power of core values is critical.

It is also essential to monitor mutations in the interpretation and practical application of expected behaviors. Although company etiquette is increasingly focused on doubling down on good news and skipping tough news, effective leaders boldly highlight value creation challenges and operational disharmony caused by gaps in core value adoption to ensure that behavioral incongruence is addressed quickly.

Consider these design questions:

Is every employee and value-creating partner periodically trained on practical ways to inject behavioral expectations into creating and delivering customer value and working together?

When pop-quizzed, what percentage of employees get at least 80 percent of core values and the essence of its meaning correct?

Effectively designed core values are only a shadow of what effectively operationalized core values can be. Effectively operationalized core values will play an important part in the maturity and cohesiveness of every other component, including how we design our organization and hire.

B.2
ALIGN ORGANIZATION DESIGN AND SKILLS TO VALUE CREATION NEEDS.

To continuously mature and maintain the best version of our company, we need more than just people. We need the right value creators to do the right things. For example, if our company is a sports team, we first have to know our style of play and positions on the team; then, we can find the players to fill those positions. Organization design is the path to creating the most optimal configuration for our team, and hiring is the exercise of finding the players.

Let's start with an important concept that aids effective organization design and hiring.

Just because a child counts stars on a clear night does not mean they will have a reasonable estimate of the number of stars in the universe. So, why don't we tell the child to leave the estimation exercise to scientists who have spent their entire careers studying the universe? It's because we don't have the heart to tell the child about the universe's complexities, such as distances, gravity, light speed, time, rotation and revolution of objects, etc.

My point is not that we should disappoint children. But we often find it difficult to be objective if the truth causes discomfort.

Our inherent challenge with objectivity and transparency bleeds into professional decision-making and communication, which can hurt an organization's access to expertise and experience. The only way to balance value flow between stakeholders is to improve skills that directly or indirectly influence value creation.

Principle 1: Build a Comparative Advantage Ecosystem.

Our goal is to create a system that brings together the right value-creating talent and gets the best out of them. The first imperative is to overcome biases and groupthink, which are counterproductive and work against building the best version of our company. I call a state of balance between objectivity and expertise around skills a **Comparative Advantage Ecosystem (CAE)**.

First, corporate settings can allow decision-making based on committee and consensus rather than objective analyses and topical expertise. It feels easier to vote on difficult decisions because the vote count can be misconstrued as reliable data. It is more uncomfortable for an executive to disagree with a large group, even if objective analyses and insights indicate that an unpopular path is the right one.

If senior executives give in to this tendency, expertise, experience, and critical thinking will be overshadowed by consensus building and con-formity. The latter is important, but not at the expense of the former. As a result, analytical and critical-thinking employees will feel sidelined and perform below par or leave. Gradually, the company may only have employees who generally agree with each other but also align on a course that was not the right one in the first place.

A CAE delegates decision-making authority to individuals based on objec-tive criteria such as relevant experience and expertise, time dedicated to working on the specific problem at hand, and objective quality of work product.

A CAE does not delegate decision-making authority based on organizational seniority or job titles or reduce decision-making into popularity contests. It also ensures that each person knows the specific skills they bring and focuses on those skills while internalizing others' skills and allowing them to focus on theirs.

Second, every business sector demonstrates biases based on age, gender, sector-specific experience, and many other factors. Biases are human; however, they also create significant gaps in the company's strengths. For example, one type of bias that startups, especially in the technology sector, fall prey to is age, due to the misconception that youth implies innovation.

Several surveys, including State of Startups, consistently report that nearly 90 percent of respondents answered, "yes" to the question, "In tech, do older people face age discrimination?"

A market research firm, Statista, recently studied the median age of the largest fifteen technology companies. Ten out of the fifteen had a median employee age at or below thirty-three years. That means over half the employees in these companies are younger than thirty-three.

If we compare this to data from the US Bureau of Labor Statistics, Current Population Survey assessing workforce age breakdown across 283 industries, only shoe stores, clothing stores, restaurants and bars, car washes, and hobby and toy stores, which are all retail task-based jobs, had a lower median age.

A company could display other biases, such as gender and sector-specific hires only. Through all these biases, the company essentially excludes top talent with relevant expertise from hiring considerations.

Things To Remember: Comparative Advantage Ecosystem (CAE)

A CAE is an environment where every individual is optimally placed to focus on the activity where they are the best at creating the most value. CAE enables an organization to overcome biases such as age, gender, shared educational or professional institutions, sector-specific myopia, and similar factors. It creates an ecosystem where hiring, people management, decision-making, and execution focus on skills instead of spurious associations with expertise.

An effective organization design that fosters a Comparative Advantage Ecosystem is a bedrock to maximize value creation from the money invested. It is necessary to acquire and retain increasingly demanding customers and address the complexities of a large company. Placing individuals in positions where they cannot display their highest value-creating ability is suboptimal and limits capital efficiency.

Gallup's survey report *What Job-Hopping Employees Are Looking For,* conducted before the confounding impact of COVID-19, showed that 51 percent of all employees are considering a new job. The same survey asked for the motivation behind this, and 60 percent of respondents said their reasons to consider a new job included, "It allows me to do what I do best." Compare that to the 41 percent of respondents who said, "It significantly increases my income" as the motivation.

Unproductive environments make highly skilled and motivated employees feel the company is not utilizing their strengths. They become bored and will feel that a job search is a more challenging and fulfilling project than doing the work they are paid to do.

In addition to embracing a CAE, we must sidestep a few common mistakes.

Principle 2: Avoid organization design pitfalls.

No one in the world will disagree that a mature and cohesive organization design that aligns with all other building blocks enables cost-effective operations and maximizes value creation. So, how do companies end up with overstaffed and productivity-challenged staffing models? A few common pitfalls result in ineffective organization designs.

Pitfall 1: Confusing roles and job titles leads to poor hiring.

Have you ever started a new job with the same job title you held at a different company, only to realize that almost everything you do is entirely different? This is almost always the case because of the difference between roles and job titles. Organization design challenges arise when we mistake job titles for roles.

If a role is the candy, the job title is the candy wrapper. If we choose any job title and search for it on a job board, we will see little relevant differentiation between different postings. But the reality on the ground will be very different between those jobs. For starters, each supervisor will have a different experience. Every company's offering and process are different. Most job posts lack a clear, in-depth description of what a person would do, particularly beyond the first few months. Why?

Most hiring is reactive and bypasses organization design. Imagine a CEO addressing an unanticipated issue with a senior executive and saying, "I want it solved quickly, even if we have to hire a new person." The senior executive considers the hiring option as a directive and prefers to avoid another tough talk with the CEO.

The senior executive puts a supervisor in charge of hiring the new person with much less context than the CEO's original thinking. The supervisor, in turn, shares his interpretation of the hiring requirements with the recruiting team. The recruiter will ask, "What is the job title?" The supervisor will offer one without a clear view of how this hire might solve the original problem. The recruiting team then posts the job using details from a similar job title found online or an old job posting. Before you know it, there is a new person hired.

One of three things will happen to this new hire. One is that the original problem that the CEO faced resolved itself or was handled some other way by existing employees, even before the new hire joined. The second is that this hire's core strengths do not fit the problem due to a misalignment between the generic job title, the hire's experience, and the company's problem. The least likely outcome is that this rushed and job title-based search resulted in a new employee with the strengths to solve the company's short-term problem. However, this new hire does not have a clear long-term path, even in this unlikely scenario.

This tendency to use job titles to shortcut hiring leads to misalignment between longer-term needs and value creators' strengths and experience. Without a clear long-term path, non-employee partners are the ideal value creators.

Pitfall 2: Empire building is capitally inefficient and value destructive.

It is human to desire advancement, more compensation, and social status. All of this can come from visible seniority in an organization and the size of the team one manages. So, we are likely to have a natural bias towards hiring more people underneath us or asking for more significant job titles. But it should not come at the expense of capital efficiency.

In other words, the CEO and human resources must drive the company to focus on roles rather than candy-wrapper job titles. A Single Market Problem Entity should have no more than two supervisory layers between employees who perform most of the actual work daily and senior executives who report to the CEO.

The **first** reason is cost. Every dollar spent on underutilized organizational layers could be better dedicated to efforts that add value to customers or directly improve the company's congruence. Organizational fat triggers exponential productivity declines.

The **second** reason is the Chinese Whispers problem. Chinese Whispers is a game where each person whispers a word into the next person's ear and asks to pass the word on. Inevitably, we increasingly misconstrue words that have to pass through more people. In a company setting with complex concepts and individual incentives, unnecessary layers confuse accountability and communication, resulting in inefficiency on the simple end and vicious politics on the extreme end.

Pitfall 3: Lack of prioritization leads to diminishing returns.

As a company grows, more revenue comes in, and more investment is often easier to access. Under these circumstances, taking on many initiatives to create more structure and implement new solutions to address value or efficiency problems can be tempting. These might be the right things to do.

However, companies often underestimate the complexity of making necessary maturity improvements and overcommit. No matter how much money is available, a company can only work on a certain number of major initiatives at a given time. The reason is that many organizational problems can only be solved in a somewhat linear or triangulating manner. Too many people working in silos to solve highly dependent initiatives usually results in misaligned solutions.

Companies often overinvest in people, technology, and other assets and are forced to cut back. Laying off employees is terrible for a company's morale. Alternatively, executives try to reallocate these employees into roles that may not be their best fit. Both are suboptimal for investment efficiency and value creation.

Building an efficient organization requires prioritizing major initiatives and taking a tiered approach to investing. The company must see a return on present investment before investing further. If done well, the company can simply reallocate the same resources, improving investment efficiency further.

Pitfall 4: Failure to reallocate employees leads to inefficient investment.

To optimize every dollar we invest, it is essential to periodically consider whether value creator roles have become less time-consuming or unnecessary. This applies equally to employees and partners.

Imagine that our marketing team has employees focused on content generation to market the offerings. It is worth considering whether this is a perpetual need. After all, how much content do we need before it becomes too much content? Can the core skill of content management be reallocated to or shared with another need in the company after a certain period? Such prudence can even help us avoid hiring another employee in a different function.

Consider these design questions:

Do the CEO, senior executives, supervisors, and human resources rely heavily on standard job titles to describe complex organizational needs?

Does the company have growing fiefdoms managed by individuals that appear self-sufficient, which indicates a tendency to build empires?

Does the company have too many major initiatives managed by several owners simultaneously?

Do employees stagnate in their roles without effective reallocation?

Such incongruences stifle our company's three success factors: value creation, capital efficiency, and sustainable profitability. So, what does "good" organization design look like? To move to the right side of our Management Approach Maturity Model, we must embrace the following principles to optimize an organization's design and allow it to perpetually evolve.

Every company starts with a few employees, each with many overlapping responsibilities. This is not scalable. We must incorporate three principles while developing an effective organization design.

Principle 3: Delineate enablement and operations skill groups.

We can delineate every investment, whether people, technology, or other assets, into two groups. We invest in people, technology, or assets for time-bound efforts or to perpetually create value. This delineation is our first organization design concept – **Skill Groups**. I call it skill groups because I first arrived at this insight in the context of investment in people. However, the same principle applies to all investments. Although we will focus on people in the context of our management approach, we will see that the identical delineation applies across all our investment choices during strategic planning.

People fall into two general groups based on their interests, aptitudes, and experiences. The **first** group is most effective with time-bound efforts with specific goals, and once that effort is complete, they move on to a different effort that solves another problem. Thus, we can consider this skill group's focus as project work.

The **second** skill group is most effective in performing an activity many times over to achieve the same results, even if there are nuances each time. We can think about this as operations execution. The key delineations here are whether the work is time-bound or perpetual and how similar each iteration is.

In a CAE, individuals align with either of these skill groups, and roles should fall into one skill group or the other. Most of my experiences have been time-bound and project-based, and I am good at that. However, whenever I have been responsible for efforts in an operations execution skill group, I devise ways to make it project-like work. For example, I am atrocious at day-to-day sales activities in my advisory practice.

The reverse applies to anyone with an operations execution strength who is asked to do project work. They are likely to trivialize project work into tasks, which is far less likely to achieve the intended change. This has proven to be an invaluable practical insight in staffing teams and identifying and solving organizational risks around people and other investments.

Things To Remember: Skill Groups

All investments – people or other assets – fall into one of two skill groups based on their core ability to create value through either the time-bound execution of unique efforts or the perpetual execution of many iterations of predefined activities.

A company must mature towards knowing the core skill group for every investment item and categorizing them into one of these two groups. Let's name the first skill group **Enablement Resources** and the second skill group **Operations Resources**. They are equally crucial. Mixing these two skill groups into the same employee or role is similar to mixing milk and oil. It just doesn't work. Employees or assets not categorized into either of these groups should raise questions on how to leverage them. Let's define them formally as we will refer to these two skill groups throughout the rest of our method.

Skill group A: Operations resources.

Irrespective of the type of business, many tasks need to be performed on a regular basis. These might include selling efforts performed by sales representatives, marketers who create leads through manual or digital actions, service personnel who address ongoing customer needs, finance professionals who handle invoices to pay vendors and process payments from customers, and the list goes on.

The commonality between these roles is that the core tasks need to be performed perpetually. Such positions form a significant portion of a company's employees. The amount of work completed by these roles can be scaled up or down somewhat linearly by increasing or decreasing volume.

> **Things To Remember: Operations Resources**
>
> **Operations resources include all people (as well as supporting technology and other assets) that perpetually execute all day-to-day activities, directly leading to measurable outcomes.**

Simultaneously, a company needs to continue improving the maturity of its operations baseline, which includes the productivity of operations resources. This responsibility falls on the second group of resources – enablement resources.

Skill group B: Enablement resources.

Improving operations resources' productivity and effectiveness, designing our offerings, and similar efforts are necessary for us to improve maturity and cohesion between our building blocks. The critical difference is that all these efforts are time-bound and focus on achieving an end state.

These resources conduct research, develop forward-looking insights, create documentation, and socialize outcomes for others in the company to learn. Such efforts are identified and prioritized as part of strategic planning. Motivated self-starters and individuals who are change agents should fill roles that fall under the enablement resource category.

Things To Remember: Enablement Resources

Enablement resources include all people (as well as supporting technology and other assets) involved in time-bound efforts aimed at increasing the maturity of operations, including the productivity of operations resources.

We should take a prudent approach to adding enablement resources, as their efforts are always time-bound. In addition, we should consistently vet every existing enablement resource to ensure that we fully utilize them and that their strengths remain relevant.

One typical example of misallocation between operations and enablement skill groups is around sales teams.

The onus of revenue falls on sales representatives and supervisors, whose expertise is to execute sales transactions. Conversely, their expertise is not in defining the company's optimal customers, developing sales and marketing collateral, or conducting analysis. However, it is common for sales reps and supervisors to spend a large share of time on enablement efforts such as company strategy and process design, taking time away from their core selling responsibilities. This results in poor revenue outcomes. Meanwhile, enablement resources in roles intended to improve the design of sales activities are underutilized, and the operations remain immature, which further hurts revenue generation.

A CAE empowers both sets of value creators to focus on their strengths. Sales representatives and supervisors would focus on identifying and executing sales opportunities. Analytical experts would focus on data analysis and process design, which are typically part of time-bound efforts.

A similar paradigm plays out in the design and development of offerings, where skills for identifying customer needs can be confused with those for helping customers use the offering day-to-day.

We must begin organization design by delineating operations and enablement resources needs and aligning employees and other value-creating assets into these two divergent skill groups.

Principle 4: Increasingly specialize to focus on expertise.

In addition to delineating between enablement and operations skill groups, organization design must incorporate topical expertise. Even early in a company's lifecycle, we must define organizational roles carefully and narrowly to focus on the expertise of new value creators and the exact nature of their day-to-day work.

To move from the left side of the addressable market to the right side, where a company's market share continues to grow, the organization design and staffing will have to shift from a generalist mindset to a specialist mindset. Specialization implies that each role in the organization design has narrower and narrower responsibilities as the company grows. In addition, the ability to execute those responsibilities will have to improve as the company acquires and serves more customers. So, let's formalize **Expertise.**

> **Things To Remember: Expertise**
>
> **Every value creator – employee or partner – must have specialized experiences and natural inclinations for specific topic areas that form their expertise. Expertise is the most vital attribute that an individual can possess on their own.**

When we continuously evolve our organization design, it is important to articulate the necessary expertise for each role aligned with the company's lifecycle stage so that our hiring efforts can match candidates effectively to roles.

For example, I have built sales operations teams at multiple companies. Sales operations is a critical analytical function that provides sales and marketing resources with appropriate insights and process enablement, which requires two areas of expertise.

One is technical expertise to manage the software platform used for sales and marketing activities. The other is analytical expertise to design sales and marketing processes and optimally use data to improve future activities. These are very different and rarely found in a single individual.

If an organization can only afford to hire one employee, one optimal option is to hire an analytical problem-solving expert while finding a part-time partner to support the technical software needed. Alternatively, if the technical software is more onerous in a specific situation, we could assign an employee to the technical software expert role while an existing analytical expert doubles up as the sales operations analytical problem-solver. Combining the two areas of expertise into a single role often fails the entire function.

Even in the same role, the expertise necessary shifts with the company's lifecycle. The sales processes required for the first $1 million in revenue, where a minimal sales close rate is enough to meet the financial goals, are not the same as when the organization captures an increasing share of its market.

A similar shift in sophistication applies to the design, development, and commercialization of offerings. A common error is conflating "product management," which is an expertise in analytical problem-solving focused on customers to create offerings, with "project management," where a generalist tactically oversees the activities of others who create individual parts of customer offerings. Unfortunately, companies often place generalists based on poorly defined past job titles into customer-centric "product management" roles, resulting in a downward spiral in the quality of offerings.

It is suboptimal to have the illusion of complete coverage of expertise because the company continues to hire generalists and ask them to do things they aren't experts at. If we acknowledge that we have an expertise gap, we can prioritize and cover those gaps when we can afford to. On the other hand, if we live under the illusion that we have coverage, we will never understand the root causes behind areas of ineffectiveness and address them.

I worked closely with an executive who used to say, "We will just hire some smart people, and they will need to figure it out." It didn't work. The company was caught in a generalist loop where every employee was involved in everything, and decisions were either democratic or autocratic. As a result, the value created by the company slid further and further behind customer expectations while operations stayed immature. This company was in regression in its attempt to scale. We want to avoid this.

Even established companies can struggle if we underestimate expertise. For example, a senior executive at an investment bank that took significant losses after investing in a poor scheme framed the people agenda of the bank's CEO as ". . . came in with a mindset that you can appoint anyone clever into a job, and they will be a success even if they had no experience. . . . But that was inappropriate for risk and compliance."

It's inappropriate for any role. So, specialization via expertise is the second fundamental necessity for a congruent organization design.

Let's connect these two principles to formalize the term "**Skill**" for the rest of our conversation. Skill is the intersection of skill group and expertise.

Things To Remember: Skill

Skill is the set of ingredients that have the potential to create value. It is the intersection of a value creator's Skill Group and Expertise, combining the abilities related to time-bound projects or perpetual operations work and topic-specific experience, knowledge, and motivation to execute.

A sales rep role in a specific lifecycle stage will need an employee with expertise to sell within the constraints associated with that stage. This role falls squarely in the operations skill group, and the expertise needed to find prospects and close deals is likely different from that necessary in earlier or later lifecycle stages.

A sales operations role requires an expert in process design, data structures, and technology operationalization. This role falls squarely in the enablement skill group and requires different skills from a sales software administrator.

Roles need to have skill requirements formalized using the skill groups and expertise vectors to mature our organization design continuously over time and as our company scales.

Principle 5: Build an efficient structure.

Based on the two principles above, every individual contributor should have tangible, measurable, and fulfilling work that aligns with their strengths for which they alone are responsible. We should also choose to operate in a skill-based management approach to avoid too many chiefs and coordinators. Beyond the CEO and first layer of senior executives, an organization design with too many roles overseeing others' tasks alone is not capital-efficient. However, oversight and guidance for employees are also necessary. So, what does that look like?

Every company is different and must have an organization structure based on its lifecycle stage and its offerings to the market. So, drawing an actual organization chart isn't meaningful. But an efficient organization is simple and we can apply important parameters.

For a Single Market Problem Entity, the CEO, Congruence Architect, and the first layer of senior executives of functions such as finance, revenue generation, customer experience, offerings, and human resources will be general managers. They will own and manage the fundamental levers and resulting building blocks covered in various parts of our method. Their efforts primarily focus on the company purpose, management approach, value engine, strategy development, strategic planning, and execution oversight. The CEO is likely spread too thin if too many senior executives report to the CEO.

As a company grows, one supervisory layer for each group of similar operations employees can also be considered an operations resource. Most of that supervisor's work would be a predictable set of activities to coach, support, and manage a sizable group of operations employees. This supervisory layer helps operations meet the quantifiable measures for the group.

For example, one sales supervisor who coordinates and supports the selling efforts of several sales reps on a day-to-day basis and shares accountability for the measurable outcomes of that group can be considered a valuable operations resource. In a productive organization with top talent, the ratio can be around seven or eight employees to one supervisor.

Additional oversight layers between direct operations supervisors and senior executives can start causing organizational inefficiency. Although such additional operations oversight layers might become necessary as a company expands the same successful offering across the addressable market, these layers are also a sustainability risk if the skill group and expertise necessary for such roles are not clearly framed.

Like operations resources, enablement resources also require work design, coaching, work allocation, and quality checks. Typically, the work performed by enablement employees is not just time-bound; it is also constantly different. Given this evolving nature of work, supervising enablement resources is more time-consuming.

So, the ratio of supervisors to enablement resources is optimally four or five employees to a supervisor. If more than that, the supervisor will likely find it hard to utilize the enablement resources to their highest potential.

The specific share of operations resources and enablement resources is heavily dependent on the type of business and customers. If a company's offering is commoditized – think outsourced tax or accounting services – the share of operations resources as a ratio of total employees is likely high. Conversely, if the offering is unique and innovative, the company may have a much larger share of enablement resources.

In summary, an effective organization design that retains top talent to operate productively and creates increasing customer value achieves it by creating a high degree of alignment between the skill of each employee and the work expected of them and limiting unnecessary supervisory layers.

Consider these design questions:

How can we further delineate between enablement and operations roles?

How can we further specialize roles based on expertise to meet increasing customer needs and sophistication to address scale?

How do we further eliminate inefficiency created by unnecessary supervisory layers and poorly defined roles?

An effective organization design and mapping of skills to roles are necessary to enable the latter portions of our people agenda – hiring value creators and managing their performance and compensation.

The biggest staffing barrier that any organization can face is not in finding people to fill roles. Rather, it will be to define specialized skills for a greater number of positions while overcoming the generalist mindset that every company starts with in the early lifecycle stages.

Consider these reflection questions:

Does our company internalize the difficulty of acquiring enhanced skills from a base of generalists?

What are the checks and balances in place to acquire increasingly experienced and specialized talent with firmer skill group aptitude over time and scale?

It won't be easy, but possible in a CAE.

Our company must embrace a Comparative Advantage Ecosystem mindset as it goes through different lifecycle stages. If the CEO can ingrain this mindset with the help of the Congruence Architect, the company will evolve to stay congruent with the increasing expectations of time, scale, and environmental changes.

The alignment of skills to increasingly specialized roles will be part of ongoing microevolutions of our operations baseline and macroevolution cycle through strategic planning and execution. We will discuss these in later parts of the method. However, without a CAE mindset, the company will struggle to evolve its organization design, and it is unlikely that we will possess the necessary skills to create and deliver customer value within the company ranks.

B.3
HIRE FOR SKILLS TO FULFILL ORGANIZATION DESIGN.

THE next hire could be responsible for hiring several future value creators. That single thought makes this a critical lever.

Regardless of employment rates in the economy, hiring someone is not onerous if we have sufficient capital. Unfortunately, hiring the right people for the right roles is extremely hard, even with resources. But hiring with maturity is also the only path through which a value creator can come in and help the company evolve further.

Companies often say, "Our people are the best." How could anyone know that? There is no way to assess it accurately. Who even knows what "the best" means? There is no guarantee that we'd find the so-called best when we have a hiring need, even if we knew.

Hiring is a privilege that we must treat respectfully. It is a duty to do right by all potential value creators out there – whether they are prospective employees or partners who could create value that an employee may not be able to. Employment is where we all spend most of our time, and our lives and families are dependent on it. I was discussing how to handle an executive-level mis-hire with a CEO when he said, "We have to treat people with respect . . . he has to go home and tell the family about what happened and why it happened." I share that anecdote often. Such a frame of mind allows us to act objectively and responsibly. Hiring decisions have far-reaching implications on people's lives.

So, what exactly is hiring?

Principle 1: Hiring is an investment-efficient, incentive negotiation.

It is easy to fall into the trap of treating hiring as a simple transaction of a supervisor having extra work that needs to be done and choosing to find a body to do that work, especially if our company has the budget to add a new person. I worked with an executive who persistently urged that "we need butts in seats" to accelerate hiring. This tactical mindset leads to excess hiring as we witnessed during the post-COVID years. It eventually results in a 180-degree reversal that hurts the company's capital efficiency, operational effectiveness, and morale, and damages employee mental health and career prospects, not to mention the associated customer value creation impact.

In a mature management approach, we hire to fulfill our optimal and evolving organization design, which was discussed in the last chapter. We aren't just looking for interesting people; we are looking for people in the right skill groups and with appropriate expertise to fill the specialized roles framed by our organization design.

First, hiring is the operational end of converting the capital that we have decided to invest into choosing the right people who can create the necessary value. Note that I didn't say "right employees."

Our intention is to maximize capital efficiency and value creation, which requires a balance. To internalize this balance, we must understand the only true difference between an employee and a partner. This difference is the nature of the contract.

Things To Remember: Employees vs. Partners

Employees are value creators holding open-ended contracts with the collective company that one or both parties can opt out of, without which the relationship is perpetual. Partners, who can create the exact same value as an employee through skills, hold a timeboxed contract with an expiry date and require an opt-in for the relationship to continue.

Even though this sounds obvious when I say it, the practical application is not so. Those with open-ended contracts – employees – tend to see themselves as insiders, and those with time-boxed contracts – partners – are often treated as outsiders. Such a viewpoint is infighting amongst a company's stakeholders and constitutes incongruence that hurts value creation.

Companies also tend to lean far more toward perpetual relationships to avoid feeling any value creator volume constraints. Often, a time-boxed contract is the correct answer. Over-investment in value creators is capitally inefficient.

My violinist friend aspires to be a permanent member of a well-known symphony orchestra, which implies far more benefits and consistency. She is not . . . yet. But she substitutes for almost every gig throughout a season when a permanent member is unavailable. As an audience member, I see no difference between a permanent employee and my substituting friend, who is a partner. As a business engineer, I would stretch to say that my friend commits far more to each gig than a permanent employee because she wants to be invited back and is equally or more skilled. She is not paid any more than a permanent employee; in fact, permanent members cost the orchestra more on a per-concert basis. Could it be better for the orchestra to have several more floating seats and fewer permanent members?

A company's value extractors don't care about the combination of value creators. In our congruent ecosystem, the CEO, Congruence Architect, and senior executives must choose during strategic planning whether employees or partners are hired to fulfill the organization design.

Our organization design and strategic planning will inform whether we should hire skills from a partner temporarily or hire an employee perpetually. Would we buy a car whenever we need one in a foreign city? No, we rent one!

Second, hiring is also an incentive-based negotiation between a prospective value creator and the collective company. Hiring goes wrong when incentives are not aligned, and information gaps exist between candidates and our company. Our goal is to avoid both.

We can associate many hiring mistakes with putting blinders on and thinking that hiring is just about recruiting, which is a short-term act of signing a contract. But hiring triggers a long-standing relationship with a complete lifecycle. Relationships with value creators continue long after they leave the company.

Candidates are looking at opportunities to maximize their self-worth. However, each candidate independently defines self-worth, which could be monetary, the chance to do something they love, or fall into a range of other personal choices. Candidates want to optimally utilize their skills, feel valuable in their new environment, and continue to grow. The last thing candidates want is to land a relationship and be dissatisfied or disappoint their counterparty.

A company's goal is to find an optimal skill fit for our role where the incoming hire will feel that there is an excellent balance between their skills and the company's monetary offer or opportunity to learn and grow. There is absolutely no reason that these incentives cannot be aligned.

> **Things To Remember: Hiring Negotiation Mindset**
>
> **Hiring is a negotiation between present employees and prospective value creators – employees or partners – in a manner that optimizes across three factors: incentives of the prospect, value creation for the company, and efficient use of capital.**

In our hiring negotiation mindset, six actionable principles allow us to align incentives between the prospects and the company. Figure B3 shows the key incentives on both sides and the six principles that will enable us to hire well and maximize congruence.

Figure B3. Six hiring principles balance incentives.

Principle 2: Purpose and core values create an objective filter.

The foundational filter for all hiring is the alignment of purpose and core values. **First**, the company's overarching incentives are articulated in its purpose. Publicizing the purpose to prospects is easy in a congruent value exchange ecosystem. However, publishing something akin to a purpose doesn't imply the details are congruent. This is precisely why company-level mission and vision are often unhelpful because they focus on storytelling and not on congruence.

Throughout every stage of hiring employees or contracting partners, it is critical to convey elements of our company's purpose. If we are on a hard charge to expand into new geography instead of nurturing areas we presently serve, our demands of future value creators are different. If we intend to stop serving a specific portion of our offering in one year, hiring to support that portion for a year demands transparency about time.

Second, core values are intended to be the behavioral guardrails for all value creators. The CEO, Congruence Architect, human resources, and the hiring team must ensure that no new hires feel that they must change themselves fundamentally to fit the company and will be able to operate within the spirit of the core values. Although prospects can perform their own research and ask questions, it is hard to look over the walls of a company and really understand what is going on. So, it is the hiring team's responsibility to give prospects the clarity they need on core values.

Conversely, we need to operationalize core values effectively to hire candidates who can match skills with behavioral aspects. Poorly defined core values or poor operationalization could lead to a biased hiring team using core values as an excuse to filter out skilled candidates with a high degree of alignment between their skills and the role. In an immature management approach, core values can become propaganda to maintain the status quo of skills and groupthink even if it lags customer or investor demands.

Principle 3: Effective planning and year-round hiring enable a bench mindset.

When it comes to hiring, notions like "don't let 'great' get in the way of 'good'" lead to hiring bodies to fill seats. If we can use all the principles here, we will hire someone with the necessary skills to perform in the role. There are no great hires; hiring someone overqualified is another poor hire.

It takes a lot more time to make a quick hire, realize that they are a poor hire, and then spend more time moving that resource out of the organization. Then, we are back at square one and have to go through the exercise again. Even worse, some companies allow poor hires to stay in the ranks for a significant period for spurious reasons like likability or the hiring manager's unwillingness to admit a mistake. As a result, the hire's skills are underutilized and consume precious investment.

A slightly delayed hire where we must postpone onboarding a new customer or delay a design effort by two weeks or a month is a significantly more mature decision.

The **first** scenario that could cause hiring pressure is growth. A revenue executive at a European startup commented to me, "What's the biggest bottleneck in a hyper-growth tech startup? Hiring!" This can be mitigated through effective planning.

A **second** scenario where time pressure creeps into hiring is when a company has seasonal staffing needs. Again, for most companies, an effective corporate strategy and a strategic plan will alleviate seasonal pressure through preparedness regardless of offering and market.

A **third** scenario is employee turnover. Turnover is predictable. Involuntary turnover, which is a choice by the senior executives and supervisors to terminate employees, implies that the intentional path not to repeat past mistakes is not to hire fast but to hire well. Conversely, if a company has significant voluntary turnover, where employees choose to leave, why would it hire too quickly without addressing the root cause of the problems causing people to leave?

All these reasons can be mitigated with effective planning and taking the time to hire until all relevant incentives are aligned. I call this a bench mindset, where we are in a hiring mode all year round and meeting candidates. Effective strategic planning, which we will discuss later in our method, will give us a robust view into hiring needs and limit perceived time constraints due to poor planning and execution.

Hiring with a short-term mindset is a self-perpetuating revolving door ecosystem. It is a negative experience for everyone. An additional two weeks or a month spent upfront to find the right value creator is infinitely better. So, always take the time to hire by embracing a bench mindset.

Principle 4: Effective role descriptions enable optimal candidate leads.

On the same night that I was drafting this chapter, I caught up with a friend and colleague who has been turning around an ex-unicorn company for several years. Coincidentally, among the many challenges he described, one was hiring the right people.

When early success started plateauing, the CEO hired a president from a large company to right the ship. The new president then brought a large team of self-described "rock stars" from his past employer. After a few months of disjointed efforts, the group was let go. What went wrong here? My friend described the CEO as a visionary. Unfortunately, so was the new president. The company needed a true hands-on playmaker as a counterbalance to the CEO.

We often get referrals about a great person someone had worked with elsewhere. Other times, a team feels that a specific expertise is missing and tries to close that gap by poaching someone from a similar organization. These rarely work well.

Employee referral programs are very common, and almost every company has one. These are very popular with current employees because they can influence the company's trajectory and get generous referral bonuses. They are also popular with senior executives and human resources because they make hiring easier and create employee cohesion.

But is ease and cohesion all we are looking for? No.

Employee referral programs, investor introductions, and other tactics like posting job descriptions or using recruiting firms achieve the same outcome. They create candidate leads, which can be hard and time-consuming. However, it is still the responsibility of senior executives, human resources, supervisors, and the hiring team to convert these leads into hires objectively, just like we treat sales leads.

How do we generate optimal candidate leads?

The simple answer is an optimal role description, which articulates what the role would do within the unique environment of our company. A well-defined role description is tailored to the company-specific organization design and relevant building blocks of the company's offering and processes, which will be covered in Part C. It describes the role in a way that makes sense to an external audience.

Skilled candidates require such a robust articulation to self-assess their qualifications. Using generic descriptions based on job titles results in misfit applicants and often a deluge of applications, which has the same effect as zero applicants because the hiring team will give little to no attention to most of those thousands of prospects.

So, hiring should start with a well-framed, detailed role description covering our organization design principles.

Principle 5: Do not oversell or be oversold.

Buyer's remorse is real. It can make decisions feel sour. It is a feeling of regret after choosing, especially if one feels they got a poor deal. A senior executive can secretly look for a new hire with little cost to the company. But for an employee, taking a job is a life-altering decision. A candidate is likely taking the risk of passing on a more fulfilling career path elsewhere or sacrificing a promotion at their previous employer. In addition, a candidate might have made personal sacrifices like relocating.

So, an individual hire has many more reasons to feel buyer's remorse than the collective it joins. If the hiring party overstates the opportunity, it will likely result in an unhappy hire. The oversell can pertain to the environment the candidate would work in, the work the candidate would do, or the candidate's growth prospects. This often happens because the complete relationship lifecycle is ignored.

I worked closely with a company that struggled with employee satisfaction in the junior ranks staffed with several analysts. "Analyst" is often misused as an early career job title for any entry-level position. But to a particular candidate pool, the analyst title implies that they will be using qualitative and quantitative data to solve problems. In this company's history, hiring routinely allowed several candidates who went through data-focused education programs to believe that this analyst role would use data in powerful ways. In reality, the position mostly involved performing a large amount of manual work to take reams of data from one location and make it available in another without much opportunity for problem-solving.

A hire who wants to use the data to solve problems would be highly disheartened if that employee had to spend their entire time doing manual grunt work. A good organization design, role description, and honest hiring approach would have saved the company years of high employee turnover, which also rippled into customer dissatisfaction because these hires would probably have never taken the position if they knew what they would really be doing.

Suppose a company has a sub-par offering that is hard to sell. In that case, it is best to attract sales reps who find that risk exciting in exchange for potentially high compensation until our offering improves. If a company has revenue or cash flow challenges, being honest with candidates about bonus or commission criteria attracts the right type of risk-takers. Honesty always trumps short-term thinking in terms of hiring the right candidates.

Conversely, the hiring team must also remain objective and detail-oriented, not to be oversold by candidates who might know the right words to say or approach to demonstrate through the relatively short hiring interactions.

My recommended interview approach is to put all the cards on the table, including strengths and weaknesses. It is best for both parties when candidates feel that their expectations of the role and company are unchanged between the day they accept the offer and three months later. Many dissatisfied employees I have spoken with attribute their disappointment to the poor expectations set before hiring.

Principle 6: Focus on identifying the depth of skills to improve specialization.

There are many quotes about the importance of hiring A-players. Common anecdotes are attributed to Steve Jobs, the founder of Apple, who emphasized the significance of hiring A-players to ensure that the company doesn't end up with a lot of poor talent through a spiral down of hiring quality. I agree with this general sentiment, but the practicality is different.

Do you really think all one hundred fifty thousand Apple employees are A-players?

First, the grading of employees is a performance assessment, not a hiring metric. Talking about A-players during hiring is silly. We don't really know prospects. A person becomes an A-player only after they have performed the role for which they are hired, not simply based on their past work experience. How did the A-players at my friend's ex-unicorn fare?

Second, no one can be an A-player at everything. We must evolve past trying to find the best general employee to evolve toward an increasingly specialized outfit. Instead, we want to find the best specialists to fill specific roles.

Consider the World's Strongest Man competition. Several different events with individual scores are accumulated to identify the World's Strongest Man. The winner of the whole contest isn't the best at most individual events, such as the Hercules Hold or Atlas Stone Series. Hiring with the strongest person mindset perpetuates a generalist culture where niche skills are missing over time.

Third, A-players are rare, by definition. Therefore, attempting to hire A-players will inevitably lead to hiring lower-performing generalists and cause a downward spiral in both skills and performance levels.

The hiring process should reveal the core skills of candidates and how well their skill level aligns with the role we define. This principle is tough to execute without effective role descriptions and organization design. A good hiring team discovers skills that even candidates don't know they have. Often, candidates have skills that are unrecognized by past employers and lie dormant for us to unearth.

Objectively searching for specialist skills with deeper expertise may create discomfort among current employees looking for advancement. As the company's affordability and brand increase with size, the candidate pool will likely be more experienced and skilled than the existing employees and potentially even the hiring team. We have all let our insecurities win at some point.

Imagine a math Ph.D. holder interviewing with a bachelor's degree holder for a math teaching position, where the two will work closely at a school that suddenly rose in popularity and now attracts higher-skilled candidates. The interviewer's lesser math expertise will likely negatively influence their decision, especially if they see the candidate as a competitor. So, we must purposefully choose interviewers who are not incentivized to keep higher skills out of the company.

The CEO must ensure the company gives hiring responsibilities to individuals who understand the broad range of skills available in the wider world and are secure enough in their own skin to bring on new value creators with higher specialized skills than they possess. This is easier said than done, which brings us to our hiring process.

Principle 7: Trust a robust hiring process to avoid biases.

Regardless of any CEO's best intentions, every company will have biased individuals. Sometimes, we know who they are; sometimes, we don't; some are better than others at disguising biases. Our hiring goal is not to eradicate prejudices because we will not succeed. But we have to significantly reduce their influence on the hiring process to improve skill-to-role alignment with every new hire.

Conversely, candidates invest a lot of themselves into applying for roles, and they deserve a fair shake without allowing interviewer biases or poor processes to heavily influence outcomes.

Symphony orchestras use blind auditions where candidates play music from behind a curtain, and their identities are unknown to judges to limit biases. Such an assessment step is far more effective in reducing biases than affirmative action programs, which create different undesirable distortions.

I worked with a growth phase company to improve its skill alignment to roles. The CEO was onboard that a wholesale change in talent was necessary to improve the company's flagging trajectory. One simple change was to objectively document candidate interviews to ensure that hiring choices were less biased and subjective. If you journal, you know that we tend to be more honest when we write things down.

For our first turnaround hire, I shared a simple spreadsheet with a set of criteria to objectively document interview notes with the three other executives I had asked to join the search. Within minutes, I got a direct message: "I typically advise that we talk live about candidates. Our attorneys advise against documenting . . . very risky and discoverable." I know that this CEO had good intentions, but this revealed their subconscious recognition of what was happening beneath the surface.

We want to prevent the most opinionated and influential interviewers from hiring their preferred candidates. We want to avoid a "we will know when we meet the right candidate" mentality because that is entirely subjective and perpetuates groupthink. We want to evolve and improve skills, without which we will not evolve, and incongruences will creep in.

Therefore, define a robust hiring process that includes at least the following considerations.

First, an effective process includes a firm set of steps that every candidate goes through regardless of the lead source. Human resources must ensure that no one circumvents these steps.

Second, define a set of criteria that qualifies a candidate to move from one step to the next, how those criteria will be measured, and inform all candidates about the criteria. The more objective and measurable these criteria, the more effective the process is at limiting subjective decisions along the way.

For example, when I hire an enablement resource with problem-solving expertise, one key criterion is the person's understanding of the essence of data. For such a hiring sequence, I draft two or three discerning but straightforward questions for the recruiting team so they can explore every candidate's expertise with data with a reasonable degree of precision.

Third, invest in steps that allow candidates to show their skills rather than just talk about them. A very young startup that I used to work with invested in a practical skills interview phase for all candidates regardless of role. For roles that worked closely with customers to extract value from the company's offering, the company expected candidates to learn their offering and demonstrate an ability to create customer value during the hiring process. Interviewers ensured that candidates underwent a coding exercise to demonstrate skills for software development roles. Regardless of the environment, I include a problem-solving case for all positions I hire to allow candidates' tangible skills to rise to the top instead of their sales pitch.

Fourth, set definite interview and decision timelines uniformly used for all candidates. Intentional or not, delays can cause an excellent candidate to interpret that the company is not interested, or they may take a different offer and take themselves out of contention. Artificial urgency can allow interviewees or internal champions to influence the outcome of a hiring process even if a candidate may not have met the necessary skills criteria. Allow realistic and preset timelines to be a guardrail to prevent biases from influencing outcomes.

Fifth, for each role, leverage an objective hiring panel with interviewers who internalize our Comparative Advantage Ecosystem mindset. An interview panel that does not have the experience to discern the skills for the specific role leaves the company vulnerable to hiring for likability, other spurious criteria, or candidates who are good at selling themselves while masking skill gaps.

Lastly, document everything. There is absolutely no reason that any thought or action during a hiring process cannot be documented. If there are, the company's purpose is likely not congruent and transparently communicated. Secrets have no place around hiring.

Embracing a comprehensive but straightforward hiring process will allow the company to eliminate biases and mistakes that can creep into hiring. These seven principles will allow us to manage a skill-focused, objective, and unbiased hiring approach.

Consider these design questions to build a robust hiring approach:

How effectively are the company purpose and core values baked into candidate assessments?

Do we have a year-round and patient bench mindset for hiring based on an effective strategic plan?

Do we have a company- and role-specific articulation, which includes necessary tangible skills, for each role to generate candidate leads?

How do we effectively set honest expectations with candidates about the role and our company?

Does our hiring approach prioritize acquiring increasingly specialized skills for roles as our company grows?

Do we have a standard and objective hiring process that every candidate will undergo, including assessors, timelines, and objective skill-focused assessment criteria?

In our age, where there is an app for everything, using software tools to codify the hiring process offers efficiency. However, overreliance on tools without understanding their true limitations will backfire on the entire company. The perception that tools are objective is a fallacy. Tools are merely ruthless conduits for the quality of information fed into them. What if our company's organization design, processes, and role description are not optimal? Will a tool still choose optimal candidates that fit our company? No.

For the foreseeable future, we are unlikely to have tools that can truly discern and compare real-world past accomplishments, depth of knowledge, practical experience, upbringing, truthfulness, ability to handle pressure, and many other permutations of competencies relevant to hiring. Automatically filtering candidates by scanning words on a couple of pages that may or may not be the truth is treating hiring as a chore rather than the privilege and honor it is.

In an efficient organizational structure, a supervisor has only a few direct reports and is likely recruiting for no more than one or two roles at a time. So, what's the excuse for not manually reviewing candidate applications? In our increasingly sophisticated workplaces, where each role requires deep skills and experience, mindful reviews by one or more experienced humans are more likely to identify and prioritize genuine candidates with thoughtfully written applications.

When too many candidates lead to automated screening, it indicates an undifferentiated role description, ineffective hiring criteria, and too light an application that attracts too many leads. Let the depth of the application be the screen rather than relying on the outcomes of a tool with very little real-life information. Our company deserves that. Our prospects deserve that.

We covered three key levers of our management approach to shape the building blocks around value creators. We focused on the importance of core values and the necessity of an organization design and hiring approach to acquire the optimal value creators. Now, how do we use them optimally?

B.4
ANCHOR PERFORMANCE MANAGEMENT ON OBJECTIVITY AND TRANSPARENCY.

Now that we've acquired the optimally skilled value creators to staff our organization design, we have to figure out who our best performers are and keep them around. Start by asking yourself these questions:

Have you ever been an employee who felt that your supervisors or senior executives could not understand your true abilities and give you a fair shake? Whether an employee or their supervisor is naturally more competent is often a coin flip.

Have you been a supervisor or a senior executive who has been part of employee assessments where you felt the conversations were not data-driven, documented, or objective?

Have you worked with employees who may not realize their true potential themselves and work in roles that are well below their abilities?

Have you ever had toxic employees who lingered around because the company failed to remove them quickly and decisively?

Have you ever had to let an employee go when you knew that other lower performers would stay?

Such suboptimal scenarios are too common. Both a revolving door of top performers and a stagnant pool of poor performers impede sustainable value creation. A comprehensive performance management approach is a fundamental requirement to ensure that the right value creators stay motivated, and others are nudged to move up the value creation curve.

The term performance management evokes a focus on employees.

However, every principle to manage employees equally applies to partners, whether the partner is an individual contractor providing services or another company that we source goods from.

Principle 1: Accept that biases significantly impact performance measurements.

There are corporate environments that give too much feedback. There are ones that provide no feedback. Neither is optimal. The key to effectively evaluating ourselves and others is objectivity. As easy as we think it is, it is extremely hard in practice. Biases exist everywhere, including professional assessments.

Imagine working for someone who is primarily interested in their own career and popularity instead of developing and growing the people who work for them. What if you are a highly skilled value creator, and the person you report to feels threatened by you?

Another professional evaluation challenge is story-building. Think of a celebrity. It's unlikely we know this celebrity personally. But we often have firm opinions about their personality, relationships, and profes-sionalism. How is that possible? It's the art of branding or story-building triggered by spurious websites and social media portrayals.

People we work with every day also have opinions about others at work. Some of these opinions may have loose foundations, but most are sub-jective and imaginative. A friend's favorite line is, "We judge ourselves by our intentions, and we judge others based on their actions and words." Words and actions are contextual and interpretive.

Subjective stories become water cooler conversations, and they grow arms and legs. A colleague who switched from a company with a poor management approach to one with more mature foundations described the difference as "there is a lot less talking behind people's backs here." Subjective storytelling can propel or damage an employee's career.

We live among other humans, and they affect how we think about ourselves. In an ideal world, we are all keenly self-aware and can rate our strengths and weaknesses accurately. But the positive and negative experiences that hit us each day over the years inevitably influence how we think about ourselves.

An overly confident value creator can be harmful to the organization. Conversely, one who struggles to see their abilities positively and is not elevated to their optimal potential implies a missed opportunity for the company and a loss for the employee or partner.

This fourth lever of the management approach – effective performance management – is critical because an objective approach to evaluating professional worth is essential to creating a productive workforce with optimal skills. Two behavioral tendencies drive companies' need for an objective self-assessment and interpersonal assessment approach.

Dunning-Kruger Effect.

Professors David Dunning and Justin Kruger postulated and proved a cognitive bias through their 1999 study *Unskilled and Unaware of It: How Difficulties in Recognizing One's Own Incompetence Lead to Inflated Self-Assessments*. The simple idea behind this bias is that some individuals know very little yet believe and show very high confidence in their knowledge and abilities. The authors call this false confidence "mount stupid."

As an individual's enlightenment increases slightly, that individual realizes how little they truly know and hits a "valley of despair." However, if they can continue their enlightenment journey, their confidence eventually increases slowly over a significantly more extended span of self-growth to reach a "plateau of sustainability." Note that this journey of enlightenment has a focus on gaining competence and is not simply a passage of time. In other words, it is very possible to remain in a high confidence and low competence state for decades.

In practical scenarios, we observe this as confidence overshadowing competence. We ignore this concept in professional settings, but it is observable every day.

Consider this reflection question:

How does our company ensure that confidence demonstrated in decisions and actions is matched by underlying competence?

This is a cognitive bias, and individuals are often unaware of their own biases. We also don't know whether others' behaviors are based on confidence or competence. This lack of clarity on how we stand amongst others might encourage us to question our competence, professional skills, and quality of work. This leads us to be mindful of a second bias.

Imposter Phenomenon.

A second key cognitive bias around skills and self-worth that impacts an individual's ability to self-assess professionally is the Impostor Phenomenon. This bias is essentially the converse of the "mount stupid" phase of the Dunning-Kruger effect. Individuals may underestimate their own knowledge and abilities, particularly compared to their imagination of others' knowledge or skills. The operative word is imagination, which means it is perceived and not necessarily real. Irrespective of our line of work or past accomplishments, most people are likely to succumb to this bias. In their 2011 publication of *The Impostor Phenomenon* in the International Journal of Behavioral Science, Jaruwan Sakulku and James Alexander show that 70 percent of individuals will experience this phenomenon in their lives.

This phenomenon undermines confidence in ourselves and leads to underperformance or not claiming our deserved rewards. A study of high performers led to the original finding behind this phenomenon. If a company wants to keep and reward its best value creators, how will it do so if even the highest performers face such a cognitive bias?

Given that the "mount stupid" phase of the Dunning-Kruger effect and the Imposter Syndrome are opposites, this means most people in a workplace do not have an objective awareness and measure of their strengths and weaknesses.

So, if each value creator lacks perfect self-awareness, how will the company achieve it collectively? Effective performance management enables value creators to do their best work in a foundationally objective measurement system.

Over the past decade, many prematurely pronounced the death of the traditional annual performance review approach. Many companies use tools such as Objectives and Key Results (OKRs) or 360 Degree Evaluations. Foundations across all these tools are the same.

After working with dozens of companies, I believe the effectiveness of a performance management approach has absolutely nothing to do with the choice of tools. Instead, effectiveness comes down to our company's willingness to stand firm and execute the principles we are covering. Setting expectations and holding people accountable requires courage and experience.

Regardless of nomenclatures, an effective performance management approach must entail a few key principles. I have used the principles illustrated in Figure B4 to rebuild the performance management approach from the ground up at multiple companies.

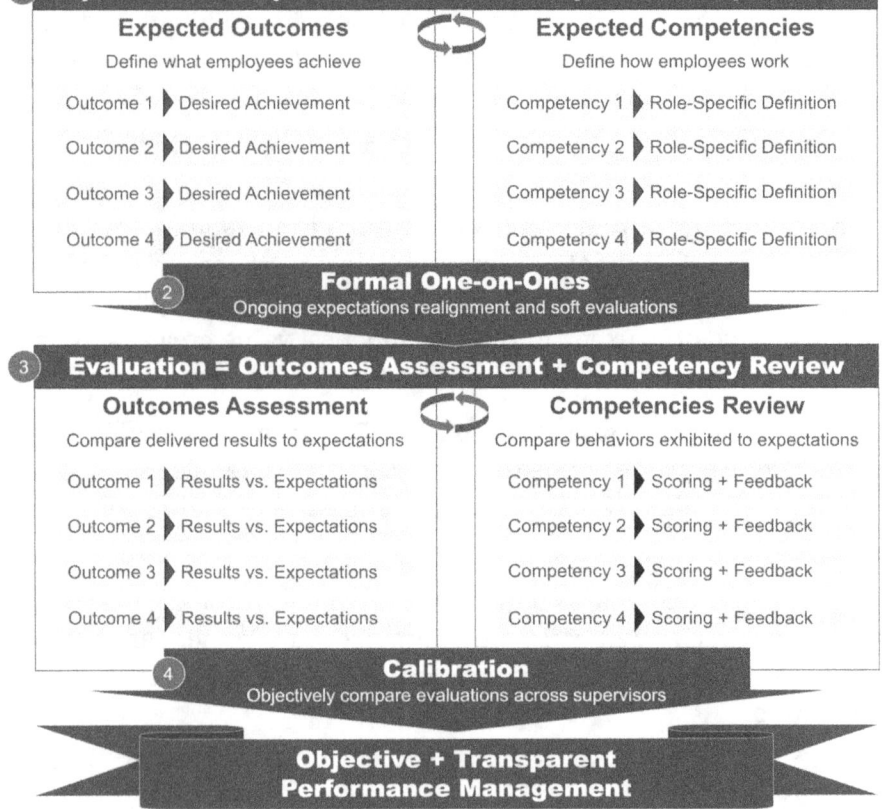

Figure B4. Effective performance management dovetails expectations and evaluations.

Principle 2: The goals of performance management are objectivity and transparency.

It is always best to start with understanding the company's current maturity. Almost every company invests in human resources staff and can point to spreadsheets, performance-related meetings, and annual compensation changes as evidence for performance management. At the same time, executives and employees consistently admit that their performance management process is a train wreck and creates highly politicized work environments with very little focus on productivity and value creation.

For example, I asked the chief strategy officer of a public company about the effectiveness of their performance management approach. He responded, "It's complicated. Yes, we have a process on paper, but it's always an argument. It's essentially a subjective evaluation."

No single external benchmark can measure the effectiveness of our performance management approach. This lever is not intended to drive employee happiness or win "Great Place to Work" awards based on employee surveys. Such measures do not reflect a company's ability to create value, use capital well, or create a profit.

Our holistic company balances value exchange across all stakeholders. To do so, we need a workplace that identifies and rewards the best value creators and helps everyone continue to upskill and evolve to meet the increasing demands of time, scale, and environmental shifts.

Things To Remember: Performance Management

Performance management is the objective evaluation, categorization, and transparent communication of value creator achievements and behaviors, compared against transparent expectations, to enable skill and performance elevation across all value creators.

The **first** crucial measure to assess the effectiveness of the performance management approach is how objectively our organization measures individuals. The first measure is spread. People fall into a wide range of effectiveness for any given skill. If the performance assessments of individuals in the same role are clustered together, it likely shows that the organization has a poor measurement mechanism. Irrespective of the position or company's lifecycle stage, the company must clearly distinguish between high and low performers. Even among high performers, there is a gradient.

Another measure of objectivity is skew. For example, if the overall performance for a specific skill in our company is low, but individuals are collectively assessed as highly skilled in that area of expertise, it reflects a reluctance to be objective or shows a lack of awareness about what "good" looks like for that expertise.

Transparency is the **second** necessary goal of performance management. I used to work with an executive who handed me the reigns of an underperforming division. The executive had very strong perspectives on who I should terminate on the team and relayed this to me almost daily. Yet, the company lacked any semblance of a performance management approach.

Even harder was the executive's two-faced approach. The executive would publicly and personally praise these perceived underperformers while I received private messages about how I needed to get rid of them. My efforts were focused on providing feedback to grow these employees or respectfully move them out of their roles.

However, employees weren't unaware. They became paranoid about trusting my feedback and growth path because they could sense the executive's praise and "twist the knife in private approach," as one specific supervisor who reported to me said. Sure, this supervisor had some growth needs, but other deficiencies pinned on this supervisor were systemic challenges. The conflicting information swirl eliminated the supervisor's trust, and the supervisor influenced employees who reported to them and others. This example illustrates a transparency gap.

Consider these reflection questions to assess the level of objectivity and transparency in current performance management approach:

Would most value creators agree or disagree with the statement, "I know where I stand with the company"?

Do most value creators operate as though they are a top 10 percent performer?

Would most value creators answer "yes" or "no" to, "I have clarity and confidence in the process that leads to promotions and internal changes"?

Would most value creators answer "yes" or "no" to, "I feel anxious about my position when another person is involuntarily terminated"?

If a large percentage of employees answer the **first** question in the affirmative, it implies that the performance management process effectively provides transparency for employees.

The **second** question addresses how well the organization objectively assesses employees' strengths and weaknesses, how transparently that assessment is communicated, and the alignment of that communication with employees' self-assessment. A large share of employees answering this question affirmatively implies that our organization isn't delineating performance effectively or the employee's perspective of their strengths is misaligned with the organization's assessment. This can be a strong predictor of turnover among true top performers.

A high percentage of affirmative answers to the **third** question implies confidence in the company's performance management process. You could analyze this third question further to see whether there is a significant disparity in responses between different organizational levels. For example, if individual contributors display considerable confidence while supervisors reveal lower confidence, it implies that the company is masking the ineffectiveness of the performance management process, which will eventually surface.

The **fourth** question reveals how employees think about the performance management approach in an adverse scenario. Involuntary terminations can shake employee morale, and it is important to understand how much confidence employees have in the company's objectivity in such a scenario. For the same group of employees, the percentage of employees who feel anxious should be higher than those who disagree with the first question, where we asked whether each employee knows where they stand with the company. The key insight here is the difference. A significant difference between the two implies that the general confidence in the performance management approach is shallow.

Once we are clear on our level of objectivity and transparency, we can use the following principles to develop an effective performance management approach.

Principle 3: Effective expectation setting kicks off performance management.

Professionally, I started in established and measurement-focused companies like General Electric and Accenture in their heydays, and the word "outcomes" meant a lot. Outcomes weren't contentious because these companies were stable. However, as I gained more experience and worked in environments that missed overarching outcomes, I realized it was time to fine-tune my definition of "objective" performance measurement.

If we decide to yell out loud, "Incoming!" and throw a ball towards a friend who instinctively catches or drops the ball, is the result of the attempted catch their doing or ours?

Rewarding a person for catching a well-thrown ball because it's the right place and right time or punishing someone for dropping a poorly thrown ball is suboptimal. Instead, we want to reward individuals for outcomes they earn and avoid punishing individuals for systemic challenges.

Objectivity in performance management implies that we must go beyond measuring outcomes. No person operates on an island. Many factors contribute to each person's work outcomes, and no one can control all these factors.

Objective performance management primarily focuses on assessing factors that each value creator can control and their contribution to outcomes affected by those factors they control. But before we measure value creators, we have to clarify what we expect of them. It takes significant forethought and planning to guide value creators to follow a set of behaviors and activities to achieve outcomes.

> **Things To Remember: Performance Management Expectations**
>
> **An effective performance management approach starts by setting clear expectations – encompassing both achievements and behaviors that each value creator can independently control – which also serve as the evaluation criteria for value creators.**

To achieve our transparency goal, we must communicate effectively. Our messages have to be consistent over time – before value creators set off to do their work, while they do their work, and after they finish their work. Transparent performance management implies that we measure employees only on those expectations we have communicated effectively.

Some might argue that "people want freedom in how they work." That's spin – anyone who believes that likely never had an actual job and was held accountable by another person. No one wants accountability for another person's unshared standards, whether it's a professional or personal relationship.

Others might say, "We have to be agile because we are a growing company." That's code for "I don't know how this will play out" or "Details aren't my forte; you figure it out."

Setting expectations for the entire company, a large team, or one person is challenging, requires hard work, and implies personal risk, which strong leaders must assume. Hiring and managing involves the responsibility to predict the future and take ownership of the prediction.

Expectations for partners are laid out through their contractual scope and desired expectations. The depth of specificity and guidance depends on the type of value created, which might even include niche expertise that our company's hiring team cannot provide guidance on. This is perfectly acceptable if the expectations of value and measurement are effectively set and aligned. A mindset of looking at partner contracts and employee expectations concurrently allows us to embrace objectivity as partners and employees are both people who create value.

To set expectations for all our employees, we need a detailed company plan articulating our strategy and operations. We will cover the development of this plan later in our method. For now, let's assume that such an effective plan exists in our company. Setting expectations for each performance cycle involves two parts: **Outcomes** and **Competencies**.

Competencies help employees achieve outcomes. Therefore, our company must define and communicate outcomes and competencies that each value creator can execute, and we can measure.

Principle 4: Outcomes are the first half of performance management expectations.

We touched on the concept of an annual macroevolution cycle that iteratively helps our company maintain and improve congruence. Value creators work within the same cycle, which is their performance cycle. We set company-level strategic and operations goals during each cycle. Those goals need to be broken down into outcomes that each employee or partner can influence individually or as a small group in the same role during each cycle.

One year, I was in charge of transforming customer relationships at a mid-sized company. One specific ask by the CEO was to create an automated customer satisfaction measurement mechanism. However, I pushed back because automation was far beyond the company's maturity at that stage, and it never came up again. Automating anything means we have stabilized its manual execution.

One of my meaningful contributions during that cycle was to understand our customers manually through conversations to improve the effectiveness of our offering and how we sell. Once we understood the customer, we could automate getting customer input during the following cycle with effective questions to give us meaningful data. I stuck to the plan I believed in and executed.

I could have easily created an automated survey with a few simple questions and achieved the CEO's expected outcome in an hour. But it also would mean that the company would rely on misleading information and make suboptimal decisions. So, this was not a win-win outcome for me as a value creator and the company.

However, at the end of the execution cycle, the automation survey was included as my only missed outcome. The root cause was that the company didn't have a cohesive strategic plan, and the CEO had included this automated survey as an important outcome for his team even though it didn't dovetail with other related work. The options were to admit that the misaligned item should never have been listed or penalize someone for it. Unfortunately, such perceived misalignment of expectations is very common, even when practical achievements surpass expectations.

The outcomes portion of setting expectations must feed directly from our company's strategic plan. For example, operations resources may have quantifiable outcomes such as sales pipeline conversion rate or the number of software bugs fixed. Enablement resources who handle time-bound initiatives may have outcomes such as meeting critical project milestones for their initiatives at the desired quality.

Senior executives and supervisors of operations and enablement resources are responsible for translating the company's strategic plan into bite-sized and reasonable efforts assigned to individual contributors as outcomes. Therefore, we must measure the effectiveness of supervisors on their ability to convert company-level goals into employee-level outcomes. If an employee is not clear on the quality or quantity of the desired outcome, it is a supervisory failure.

Things To Remember: Performance Management Outcomes

Outcomes are the first half of performance management expectations for each employee or partner. These tangible and unambiguous qualitative or quantitative measurements must directly roll up to the company's strategic plan.

Objectives and Key Results, commonly known as OKRs, is a very popular performance and execution management approach popularized at Intel Corporation. Google adopted it wholeheartedly. There is now an entire cottage industry around OKRs. There is no shortage of reading material or consulting services around a relatively simple idea. But I have also seen several organizations that have adopted OKRs and committed significant investment but never saw the value. Why? Companies often struggle with defining effective outcomes to set expectations.

If we poorly describe what "good" looks like for each outcome, the desired outcomes are highly interpretive; this creates a transparency gap and invalidates the entire purpose of defining the outcome. So, outcomes must be tangible and impactful and ladder up to the company's strategic plan.

However, measuring outcomes by itself is meaningless. If our company only measures outcomes, it offers a Get-Out-Of-Jail-Free card to supervisors and senior executives whose primary responsibility is to enable employees or partners they have hired to achieve outcomes. This brings us to the second part of setting expectations – competencies.

Principle 5: Competencies are the second half of performance management expectations.

Think about competencies as desired behaviors that correlate with outcomes.

> **Things To Remember: Performance Management Competencies**
>
> **Competencies are tangible, controllable, and learnable behaviors chosen carefully to enable employees and partners to execute their responsibilities and achieve performance management outcomes.**

A football coach shouldn't blame an individual player for not scoring goals or losing a game if factors are outside that individual's control. What if the team has very little ball possession to create scoring opportunities? What if the defensive line doesn't provide the necessary coverage?

There are observable and measurable traits that an individual can possess and work to improve regardless of anything else that happens around them. Therefore, a coach can hold an athlete accountable only to individual competencies and the outcomes correlated with those traits.

Besides translating company-level plans to outcomes for each value creator, senior executives and supervisors need to define a set of competencies and operational definitions for each competency to enable hires to achieve outcomes.

The first layer of accountability is competencies, as these are traits a value creator has complete control over learning and executing. Therefore, achieving outcomes set for them should be possible if they live by the spirit of the expected competencies. Conversely, if value creators cannot meet their outcomes after executing the competencies at the expected level, it is a supervisory failure to develop the right competencies or a senior executive-level failure to harmonize building blocks across the company to empower value creators to succeed.

Competencies are also only effective if operationalized and tailored for each role. Broad, commonly used traits are ineffective as competencies.

For example, a common behavioral trait relevant to all companies, functions, and seniority levels is "communication." However, telling employees that communication is a competency we will measure is not enough.

The type of communication that is important to master is different in a senior operational sales role compared to a centralized enablement analyst role. For example, senior sales reps need to communicate the value of offerings in the context of the price that customers will pay. We might call this competency "negotiation." On the other hand, an analyst will need to be good at sharing complex, data-driven concepts with a diverse audience. We might call this competency "structured communication."

Taking it further and comparing different sales roles, a junior sales rep responsible for talking to early-stage prospects will take notes and understand customer asks without trying to close a deal. We might call this communication competency "active listening."

The punchline is that we have to define specific competencies for each role, and these will closely align with the skills we define in the organization design. Next, the company has to determine the particular expectations for each position to ensure that they align with the outcomes set for that role. Expectation setting for performance is complete once outcomes dovetail with the strategic plan and role-specific competencies enable those outcomes. Once we do this, we can assess performance with confidence.

Principle 6: Use formal one-on-ones for interim alignment on expectations and soft evaluations.

Were you ever surprised by an end-of-year performance review? Have you canceled a partner's contract and they seemed surprised? Were you ever backed into a corner to fire an employee and seen a bewildered look on their face? No element of a performance management cycle should create a surprise.

Formal expectation setting happens at the start of a performance cycle, and formal evaluations happen at the end. But there is a lot of time in between, and much will happen in the interim.

Even with an effective strategic plan and expectations setting, we will learn new things as value creators execute. Senior executives and supervisors will need to adapt to changes objectively and intentionally. But changing the goal post without logical rationale or too often is a path to losing confidence in supervisors and executives and their ability to plan and manage.

No employee or partner wants to feel like a kite in a hurricane.

Formal One-on-Ones are a necessary people management tool throughout the performance cycle. This tool serves two purposes, and we will discuss the second purpose under Part F: Execution Management. Its first application offers a cadence-based, structured communication forum that smooths the jump from formal expectation setting to a formal evaluation on two ends of the performance cycle.

The choice of the word formal is not accidental. In my experience, every organization that refrained from well-prepared, documented, and consequential one-on-ones failed to mature in its management approach. Subjectivity and lack of transparency prevailed, and these companies saw performance stagnation or significant turnover, particularly among top performers.

I recommend formalizing a cadence-based, preferably monthly, one-on-one process. The process should include simple and effective documentation, preferably standardized to limit adoption challenges, that both the value creator and supervisor contribute to and are accessible to the human resources team.

> **Things To Remember: Formal One-on-One**
>
> **Formal one-on-one is a powerful performance management tool that enables both supervisors and value creators to continuously align and document their perspectives on actual ongoing performance compared to expectations set. It also creates a formal opportunity for supervisors to coach and support value creators to bridge gaps between actual performance levels and outcomes and competencies set as expectations.**

One-on-ones are only effective if we operate in a value exchange mindset. If we don't empower supervisors to coach and grow employees, then one-on-ones become a gripe session where most of the conversation focuses on someone else in the company, challenges with the offerings, the sales team selling poor deals, or talking negatively about customers. On the other hand, a formal one-on-one is intended to be a tangible and objective discussion about what the two people in the room are doing.

I have experienced situations where giving feedback was impossible due to a poor performance management mindset. A few years ago, a manager on my team twice missed a deadline that we had agreed to and had communicated to the whole company. My feedback was simple: "Let's agree on a reasonable date, but we cannot miss it a third time." The discussion was very contentious because he didn't want to set a deadline and be accountable. He said he wanted to think about it.

The next day, I got a message from human resources that this manager complained, "John is stressing me out." I spent thirty minutes in a "culture" conversation with the human resources executive, who also had not built a performance management approach after five years in the role. I listened, shared my perspective on the importance of deadlines, and left feeling that I cannot hold my team accountable unless the company embraces an effective performance management approach.

A few days later, the manager volunteered, "I know you are right about asking me for a date. But I wanted to see what would happen if I just went around you and complained. I know how this place works, and I was right that they would just make your life difficult."

After a few months of turnaround efforts, I handed over responsibilities to the long-term owner, the finance executive. Within a week, the finance executive fired this manager by "eliminating his position," which surprised the employee. This completed a cycle in which this manager and others felt the company was not objective and transparent because we couldn't set proper expectations, hold them accountable along the way, and share objective performance evaluations before making decisions.

Our performance management principles, including formal one-on-ones, are only practical if our company has effective and operationalized core values as a prerequisite.

The CEO, senior executives, and human resources must embrace formal one-on-ones to force a necessary, all-cards-on-the-table, and documented communication between supervisors and value creators at least on a monthly cadence. It allows both sides to improve alignment on the essence of outcomes and competencies throughout the performance cycle and transparently measure ongoing performance to avoid surprises at the end.

Principle 7: Evaluate only against expectations at the end of the performance cycle.

In a mature performance management approach, the evaluation portion at the end of the performance cycle will be easy because the difficult parts are already done. If they aren't, something likely went wrong between Principles 2 and 6.

The most disheartening evaluation phase I had to manage occurred with a company with a performance process on paper, but all the principles above were missing. The company never set outcomes or competency expectations. The concept of competencies was foreign to the team. Perceived top performers were the most liked and most social individuals. Everyone operated in a generalist mindset, where individual expertise was not identified and measured.

I distinctly remember that the only point of feedback that the perceived top-performing team's best performer received during the previous evaluation cycle was "[employee] should take care of self and work less."

Yes, self-care is important. But this person had four years of total work experience, all at small companies with far greater growth opportunities. My company let this high performer's skill growth stall and nudged the person to look for growth outside the company.

Performance management approaches that give value creators comfortable evaluations without providing objective and transparent feedback are not doing anyone any favors.

Both employees and partners require evaluations. Partner evaluations may follow the same timeline as employee performance cycles for long-term contracts or align with shorter partner contract timeframes. Either way, executives, supervisors, or individual contributors who hire partners as value creators must evaluate them objectively against expectations set in the contract. It is critical for us to objectively assess the value created by partners and provide them with an opportunity to elevate their performance.

Regarding employees, evolving their skills and managing their execution to achieve targets set through strategic planning and conveyed as performance expectations is a supervisor's primary responsibility. It is not to get high likability scores from their team. Instead, we should measure our supervisors' ability to set expectations, coach value creators through formal one-on-ones, and objectively evaluate them to grow in future performance cycles.

First, supervisors must objectively evaluate each value creator on specific outcomes set and provide detailed documented feedback on what worked well and what didn't. The key to an objective performance management approach is to be rigorous and ensure that we measure employees against the spirit of the predetermined desired outcomes. Value creators should never feel that we changed their goalposts in the middle of the game.

Second, an effective performance evaluation will focus less on outcomes and more on competencies. Many aspects of success and failure are outside the control of an individual employee.

We must evaluate based on each competency set as an expectation. Competency assessments should be independent of outcomes and not rationalized to fit the outcomes. Preferably, these competency measurements are quantified, which allows an easy and reliable way to compare value creators against each other. In addition, these quantifiable competencies also enable value creators to internalize their own relative strengths and weaknesses.

Use competencies to guard against organizational failures affecting a value creator's ability to achieve outcomes. For example, suppose we set a sales target for a sales representative for a specific offering. In that case, a delay in the launch or quality of that offering adversely affects their ability to hit the target. So, it is imperative that evaluating competencies isn't a retroactive exercise based solely on outcomes.

A company that wants to hold on to high performers will focus on what each person can achieve. Competencies are much more reflective of each person's ability than outcomes. Outcomes often depend on several value creators and the effectiveness of building blocks across the company. So, it is essential to commit a significant portion of the evaluation stage to objectively develop competency scores, articulate practical observations of each person's ability to demonstrate desired behaviors, and highlight detailed, actionable recommendations to improve those behaviors.

Formal one-on-ones throughout the performance cycle inject clarity on how value creators are tracking against expectations. At this stage, a supervisor following a well-laid out and adopted performance approach can use the formal one-on-one documentation created through the cycle to draft the evaluation.

No one remembers all the relevant details that happened over an entire performance cycle. Therefore, it is crucial to ensure that recency bias does not influence evaluations. Employees or partners can consciously change behaviors in the short term to get an excellent review, or a negative recent experience can cause a supervisor to hold ill will. Documented formal one-on-ones protect against such recency bias.

The formal evaluation combines the objective assessment of outcomes and competencies, which the value creator will feel accurately reflects their performance if we incorporate all our principles.

Principle 8: Calibrate value creators to ensure objectivity across supervisors.

Performance management in a vacuum where value creators cannot be compared is practically meaningless. Some supervisors are more demanding graders. Others are much more lax in their assessment. So, our last performance management principle is to put all value creators on a curve to compare them.

Professional environments are competitive. Attempting to hide performance levels or cluster value creators into equally performing groups is equivalent to under-rewarding high performers and over-rewarding low performers. Eventually, we will demotivate or lose high performers and encourage mediocre and low performers to maintain the status quo.

A mature performance management environment can successfully execute **Performance Calibrations** to effectively compare value creators in similar roles to ensure that we are genuinely objective across supervisors. We don't want to reward employees because they work for a strong-willed supervisor or punish employees because they work for a more conciliatory supervisor.

My recommended performance management cycle culminates with a simple and effective calibration step because supervisory biases can massively impact value creators. This is especially true in small companies, where every cycle is different as the company grows. We cannot expect supervisors to get aligned miraculously on what "good" performance means.

We can consider employees and partners as comparable alternatives through all the management approach levers and principles. We must analyze and compare outcomes achieved, competencies demonstrated, and the investment required for employees and partners in similar value creation arenas. As the difference between employees and partners in their abilities to create value becomes negligible – thanks to seamless collaboration opportunities across geographies and time – we must evolve our organization design and hiring choices to refine whether a value creator should be an employee or a partner.

However, due to differing incentives, contract lengths, and expectations, we don't want to compare individual employees directly against partners.

Calibration must compare employees against employees and partners against partners. The employee-partner stakeholder-level assessment described above must be owned and performed across our company by our Congruence Architect. This playmaker may also lead the calibration of partners. The CEO and the human resources executive can best own and manage employee calibration at the end of the performance cycle.

We can calibrate employees in similar roles in a critical thinking and debate-filled exercise in a matter of hours. Senior executives must support the exercise through active participation and work to maintain objectivity and engagement. If employee evaluations remain unchanged from the beginning to the end of a calibration session, it likely indicates a weak discussion where participants are simply agreeing with each other.

Things To Remember: Performance Calibration

Calibration is the objective comparison and ranking of value creators in similar roles and seniority levels based on their performance evaluations while eliminating supervisor-specific differences and systemic factors that may have influenced their performance.

A critical-thinking calibration step allows us to align on employee evaluations, learn more about all our employees, and further align on skill gaps and challenges across groups of employees. It will enable us to close our performance cycle with our overarching goals of objectivity and transparency.

As we wrap our discussion on performance management with this final principle, we should not underestimate the level of expertise and hard work it takes to build and manage an effective performance management approach with these core principles. Finding an off-the-shelf performance or feedback management technology tool and rolling it out is confusing a technology purchase for a performance management approach.

Alternatively, copying an approach used at successful companies without internally building out the foundational principles is a lazy effort. Therefore, I recommend putting in the groundwork to create a system that allows all value creators to perform optimally. Once we build a robust performance management approach, we are in an excellent position to align rewards with performance.

B.5

BASE COMPENSATION ON PERFORMANCE AND SKILL TO FOSTER MERITOCRACY.

WE tend to expect a reward from everything we do. Spending time with friends and family has emotional rewards. Watching sports or a movie, or reading a novel offers us entertainment. Meditation or prayer may give us peace and security. Charity work helps us feel more righteous or offers a sense of community. We always make conscious and subconscious choices based on each choice's reward.

So, our discussion about creating a management approach and a system that brings in the right people, keeps the best, and motivates the rest is only complete once we get the rewarding approach right.

Recently, discussions about pay gaps due to gender and race in the public sphere have encouraged companies to look at compensation more closely. But we can't solve biases with counter-biases. Instead, we must address the systemic gaps that allow biases.

Imagine an effective performance management approach that clarifies who the top performers are and who needs to improve performance. What if our company's overall results fall below expectations, and we give the top performers a meager salary raise or only a small portion of their bonus? What if the bottom performers keep their jobs with only slightly lower monetary rewards?

The most likely outcome is those bottom performers would feel happy to hold on to their jobs, yet we will have disgruntled high performers after putting forward a strong year. High performers will probably feel slighted when they only receive a small reward for performing very well, hurting our chances of holding on to them. Now we have a company that didn't do well, and high performers are heading for the exit.

A technology company founder described his company's experience this way: "By the time we reached 120 employees, we had to bring in a compensation consultant to address issues. Top performers did not get a good raise while we spent a lot more money on external recruiters, and then we were surprised when the best people left."

Holding on to high-performing value creators is as important for an organization as intellectual property. Top performers' skills are the asset that drives forward momentum; most other assets reflect the organization's past.

The timeframe and type of payment are slightly different for employees and partners. However, in a congruent ecosystem, we must truly embrace the essence of equal pay for equal value created. We can apply the same principles to set the pricing and conditional payments in a partner contract as we would for an employee's compensation. For simplicity, we will use employees as the proxy for both value creators throughout this chapter.

Before we discuss the principles to develop an effective compensation management approach, let's explore common pitfalls we must avoid.

Principle 1: Eliminate the common rewarding mistakes.

We have to remove the weeds before the plants can grow. Before building an effective compensation management approach, we must avoid some common, costly mistakes. Compensation mistakes are easily observable to employees and can quickly cause harm and trigger infighting among our various stakeholder groups.

Every management approach lever is about confidence in company-level transparency and objectivity and the senior executives' ability to build and maintain it. Even a few mistakes undermine confidence in our management approach and, thus, senior executives.

Losing confidence in companies' ability to manage compensation effectively can trigger a wage spike. We are witnessing a post-COVID era market-wide spike in the Employment Cost Index (ECI), which "measures the change in the hourly labor cost to employers over time" because several employee-centered influencers triggered a mass no-confidence movement, which encouraged workers to demand higher and higher wages.

Compensation is a significant grey area in most companies and creates major consternation among employees about their self-worth and career possibilities elsewhere. This opens the door for competitors to poach our employees through simple tactics like offering a pay raise because employees feel that the devil they know is bad enough to risk another one.

So, let's talk about the common rewarding mistakes.

Eliminate the "squeaky wheel" fallacy.

"The squeaky wheel gets the grease" might be the number one negative behavior reinforcement mindset of all time. Objectively, none of us would ever agree that the people who ask the most should get the most compensation.

But companies often entertain power plays directly from employees or their supervisors to secure promotions or raises. This exacerbates the situation when we lack a performance management approach. Encouraging one-off negotiations to determine compensation is suboptimal as it is not meritocratic.

Back-channel decisions often deprive top performers of rewards. These performers tend to stay focused on delivering the expectations set for them. An organization should never want top value creators to be distracted by the possibility that they might have to negotiate their way to their deserved rewards.

This mistake creeps in when we ignore our system thinking philosophy. Remember, no employee or hire is indispensable, including the CEO. If we feel that pressure, it is likely due to poor work planning or not adopting our bench mindset for hiring proactively. Here is an example of this mistake, where I didn't think through the details and acted too quickly because I felt my team was short-staffed.

Shortly after I took over a department, a supervisor informed me she wanted to raise an employee's salary because he had been demanding it. So, I signed off on it to appease my new team because, until then, the company had allowed direct supervisors to make independent decisions. That was the first mistake.

Within days, someone else on that team was gravely disappointed to find out that her base salary was now 35 percent lower than the peer who had just negotiated a higher salary and threatened to quit. The same supervisor came to me. The size of the discrepancy appalled me because it seemed unfair, and we were in the busiest period of the year to lose another person. I allowed a sizeable correction to be made to this employee's salary as well. That was the second mistake.

Did one or both of these employees deserve higher compensation? Maybe. Maybe not. But the timing and the process were all wrong. As I started analyzing my new team more deeply, I saw significant salary discrepancies between employees in similar roles across the board. Furthermore, none of the compensation figures were based on performance or skill.

The right choice was to absorb the pressure and advise the supervisor to wait until the end of the performance cycle to address these challenges comprehensively. The quick actions I allowed only made the discrepancies worse. The squeaky wheel scenarios indicated a weak management approach that I set off to fix soon after.

Unsubscribe from a welfare-state rewarding mindset.

Companies deploy "recognition programs" in which a few employees are highlighted as "Rockstars" or "Heroes" every month or quarter and given a small monetary gift in front of other employees. Each time, the recipients are different, and over time, these programs recognize most employees.

Although the intent of such programs is employee satisfaction, top performers will likely feel slighted. Senior executives' true intention through such programs is to create cohesion and win favor. However, such programs are often miscommunicated as performance-related while rewarding everyone equally. So, I think about them as welfare-state recognitions. Top value creators are more likely to find this frustrating.

If our goal is to celebrate and make employees feel appreciated, a better alternative is a monthly team dinner, collective attendance at a sporting event, or similar perks that cannot be mistaken for performance recognition. Framing morale boosters as performance-related is equivalent to poorly rewarding high performers.

Avoid history-based compensation.

We get what we pay for. I never want to know what a potential hire made in their previous job or other competing offers. I trust the employee to make the best choice for their own future.

Recruiters often ask, "What is your current and desired salary?" This is a poor way to assess an employee's worth. A company should have a value determination for every role, which we will cover in Principle 5. We should compensate our hires based on that value.

Compensating a value creator by weighing past remuneration heavily or giving them what they ask for leads to one of two possibilities. One is that an overpaid value creator is filling the role because of their past high compensation. Alternatively, the company fills the position with an underpaid person who will eventually realize the imbalance, which triggers underperformance or exit.

One key responsibility of the human resources executive is to translate the expected value created by each role into monetary compensation figures. This must go beyond outsourcing this task or depending heavily on compensation data purchased from third parties. Our company should focus on skill-based roles and not job titles. References to positions outside our company walls imply using job titles, which we called "candy wrappers" earlier. Compensation setting must focus on the value created by specific skills, strengths, and weaknesses. Benchmarking compensation levels from job titles provides basic guardrails, but this is not the path to determining monetary compensation based on value creation.

A US-based, mid-sized technology company always includes the bullet "Competitive pay based on the work you do here and not your previous salary" in their job postings. We need to embrace this mindset.

Do not reward employees based on tenure.

We must set aside government-like thinking and pay for skills and performance to build a congruent value exchange. Entitlements have never resulted in optimal performance or value creation.

Different people have different interests, and many of those interests could be outside the company boundaries. Employees have various career goals and levels of commitment to grow professionally. So, the company should never feel that salary increases should align with tenure. Yet, organizations resort to tenure-based rewards in the absence of a strong performance and compensation management approach. This is a shortcut to ensuring that mid and low-tier skill and performance remain at the company while disappointed top-tier performers depart, seeking rewards for performance elsewhere.

As a first principle, we must be wary of making these common rewarding mistakes. Once we embrace a meritocratic mindset, we are ready to build an effective approach.

Principle 2: Compensation management must be transparent and objective.

It is essential to internalize that the compensation management approach has the same goals as performance management – objectivity and transparency. We must cap our management approach with a reward system that mirrors our performance evaluations and calibration results.

First, employees should be able to correlate their performance management results to their compensation. Although performance results and compensation decisions are confidential, the organization must maintain transparency about this direct relationship to ensure that all employees are confident that they are not missing out on rewards.

Second, a compensation management approach that is congruent with other building blocks disproportionately rewards high performers, encourages mid-level performers to perform at a higher level, and nudges low performers to either improve radically or consider alternate employment options. Disproportionately rewarding top performers motivates mid-tier performers to improve. Excessively punishing a minority of poor performers may be convenient, but it's not enough. The key is to encourage mid-tier employees to push for the top. Compensation is not just a monetary reward instrument; it is also a quantitative mechanism to signal to every value creator their standing with the company.

Third, enable transparency by ensuring that all employees are clear on the details of their compensation packages. Whether it's understanding how sales quotas are used in commission calculations or knowing the exact details of bonus decision criteria, employees must be able to calculate their achievable compensation themselves and should never be surprised about their final compensation.

As simple as this sounds, the most common complaint I hear from employees across dozens of companies is, "I don't understand how my bonus and commission number is decided!" It is even more critical in smaller companies where compensation plans radically change often to accommodate new market lessons or changes in operations. Similarly, employees must be made aware of their role-specific pay bands and the performance levels that will allow them to earn more or less.

Compensation tends to be a sensitive topic. It rarely gets discussed unless it is in a negative light, such as pay gaps. It doesn't have to be. Certain American states, such as Colorado and California, already demand that employers share a salary range with all job postings. However, the intention here is not to check the box with a range that is so wide that it provides little specificity. Our motivations are intrinsic, and transparency comes with significant benefits.

Fourth, develop a proactive approach and set a cadence that matches the performance management cycle. We need employees to focus on their initiatives and processes throughout the year. It is much easier for employees to focus on their work when we have a specific cadence for compensation discussions and changes.

The lack of a formal cadence leaves employees constantly worrying about their compensation and motivates ad hoc back-channel discussions. We can mirror our partner relationships mindset for employee compensation cadence as well. It is uncommon for partners, whether they are service providers or sources of goods, to attempt renegotiations of their contracts mid-cycle, regardless of their satisfaction with the agreement they struck.

Contracts are reassessed when they are winding down. How are employees different?

Compensation typically invokes salaries, incentives like bonuses and commissions, and longer-term financial rewards like stock options. However, we must think more comprehensively to cover our company's entire lifecycle. I broadly classify rewards into three comprehensive groups: rewards that offer personal satisfaction, professional satisfaction, and monetary satisfaction. We must use each one differently to keep high performers and motivate others.

Principle 3: Rewards that offer personal satisfaction must be equitable for all employees.

For every hour we take away from a value creator's personal life, they expect compensation in some form for a fair, professional relationship. So, the first reward type is personal. It focuses on creating a playing field with fair value exchange.

A fair playing field is also not an overcompensating one. Companies experiment with various employee perks to attract candidates and keep employees happy. Topics that qualify for personal rewards have become even more important as more employees work from home or anywhere in the world. As more and more employees want remote or hybrid office jobs, other sectors like manufacturing, supply chain, and retail are finding it harder to find on-site labor.

However, it is not a company's place to make a value judgment between types of personal satisfaction rewards based on employees' unique needs. For example, one employee might value picking up children from school at 4 p.m. Another might want to go for a run before the sun sets at 4 p.m., while another might want to volunteer every week at 4 p.m.

Everyone gets happiness from different things. A company's role is not to determine which is more acceptable than another. For example, setting personal rewards can involve setting core work hours, where every employee officially works a day between 10 a.m. and 4 p.m. and completes the rest of the work at personally convenient hours. But our company must avoid the tendency to judge between the importance of family, health, public service, or entertainment.

Another example of a personal reward is vacation days. Historically, companies offered vacation days based on roles and tenure. However, younger companies have attempted to move to an "unlimited vacation" policy in recent years. This incentive eliminates the need to accrue vacation day pay as a financial liability should the company decide to terminate the employee. Of course, there are good intentions behind it as well. But it is worth considering whether the vacation policy skews personal rewards.

Do certain employees take a lot more time off than others? How do we ensure that employees have an equal playing field on vacation days across roles where some roles work longer days than others, especially when personal work ethic might be different?

> **Consider these design questions to test the effectiveness of personal rewards:**
>
> *Has the company designed all-employee rewards such that they are not more valuable for some employees than others?*
>
> *Regardless of intention, does the company have personal rewards programs that some employees draw on significantly more than others?*

Not long ago, I offered a candidate a position. The monetary compensation was based on the candidate's skills, the role I had designed, and the peer group we already have on staff.

A couple of days later, the candidate shared that the cost of the company's healthcare policy for her entire family would be significantly higher than the healthcare perks her current employer offered. The candidate asked for 20 percent more in base salary to compensate for the difference in healthcare coverage because of her family's specific needs. As much as I wanted to hire the candidate, I decided I could not make that accommodation because it was unfair to her peer group. I empathized with this candidate's healthcare coverage needs. Still, I would have created an unequal playing field if I had accommodated one individual's personal needs while the peer group would not receive comparable rewards.

A company's role is not to accommodate personal rewards based on our perception of its relevance. Instead, we must create a level playing field on personal rewards from which employees can leverage reasonably similar value.

Principle 4: Professional rewards offer a short-term incentive for high-performing employees.

If you remember the Gallup poll we referenced in Chapter B.2, only 41 percent of job-seeking respondents considered "it significantly increases my income" a motivation, compared to 60 percent who believed "it allows me to do what I do best."

Nonmonetary rewards motivate most high-performing employees for a reasonable period. So, we should never overlook the importance of such rewards to ensure that high-performing employees stay on the payroll. Top performers are often motivated by an opportunity to have an impact, the possibility of future income through new skills, and exposure to new challenges that help them grow with no association to other rewards.

There are several practical manifestations of nonmonetary professional rewards. For example, we might give top performers organizational visibility through greater responsibility and accountability that align with their skills instead of monetary or title elevations. These could include opportunities to work on important projects or invitations to critical meetings where they can observe and learn.

We could create an opportunity for a high performer to learn tangible and relevant new skills through lateral moves. If the employee has no prior experience, but the company grooms them with an apprenticeship mindset, such a move would increase their future success.

Another form of professional reward is to support high performers to graduate to the next stage of their careers. This could be higher education or roles at larger companies where the employee can take the next step. Paving such a path will attract skilled high performers who want a proving ground and will perform strongly for a relevant period. Top consulting firms, investment banks, and law firms embrace this mindset. Experience at these firms is a stepping stone for employees to take on challenges or rewards that these professional services firms eventually cannot provide for all their employees.

However, professional rewards have an expiry date. An employee's value from such a reward expires after climbing their learning curve. So, it is critical to think about professional rewards as interim and prepare for a longer-term path for the value creator, and this often means a new formal role. That new role elevates the high performer from the compensation in the current position to higher monetary compensation benefits of the new role. We will discuss this in Principle 5.

We must sidestep two common mistakes around such role changes.

First, new roles do not imply just moving high performers into supervisory positions because they are vastly different. Companies need employees with specialized skills to excel and deliver value in their roles. For example, companies often make the mistake of elevating excellent individual contributors into supervisory roles in sales teams. A top seller adds incredible value through revenue acquisition. However, putting that same employee in a supervisory position might be a double whammy. We might end up with a poor supervisor and lose our top seller.

Second, title inflation, which implies assigning flashier job titles without corresponding changes in underlying skills and responsibilities, does not qualify as a professional reward. On the contrary, it is a lazy, rewarding approach guaranteed to derail organization design, performance management, and compensation management maturity. Short-sightedness is the only rational explanation for title inflation.

In the dozens of companies I have worked with, I have never seen title inflation create anything but incongruences. Adding prefixes like "senior" while the employee continues to perform the same role only creates an illusion of career progression, especially if we did not formally define the new role with a new set of tangible skill requirements, responsibilities, and rewards.

Consider this design question to assess the effective use of professional rewards:

Does the company avoid artificial professional rewards through confounding promotions and title inflation and instead use effective nonmonetary professional incentives such as apprenticeship and skills acquisition to motivate top performers?

Professional rewards are not the answer for all employees and roles, especially beyond a few months. Often, the answer is to keep compensation simple and monetarily reward employees. So, let's talk about money.

Principle 5: Rewards that offer monetary satisfaction must be exponentially greater for high performers.

The third and most obvious type of reward is monetary. The equation for this third type of reward should be entirely quantifiable and based on the value attributed to a specific role and the performance and skills of the value creator in that role.

There is no reason for monetary compensation design to be creative. It's just math. We must have a formal compensation model that every employee should know and be kept within for their role. A compensation model accommodates both the coverage of skills and the performance demonstrated for each position.

The question, "How much should we pay for this role?" is incomplete. That question only considers the moment we extend the offer. What happens in a year? What happens when we have a few people in the same role? What happens when an employee has been in the position for a few years? Figure B5 illustrates my framework for designing compensation for each role. There are four elements to a simple and effective monetary compensation model.

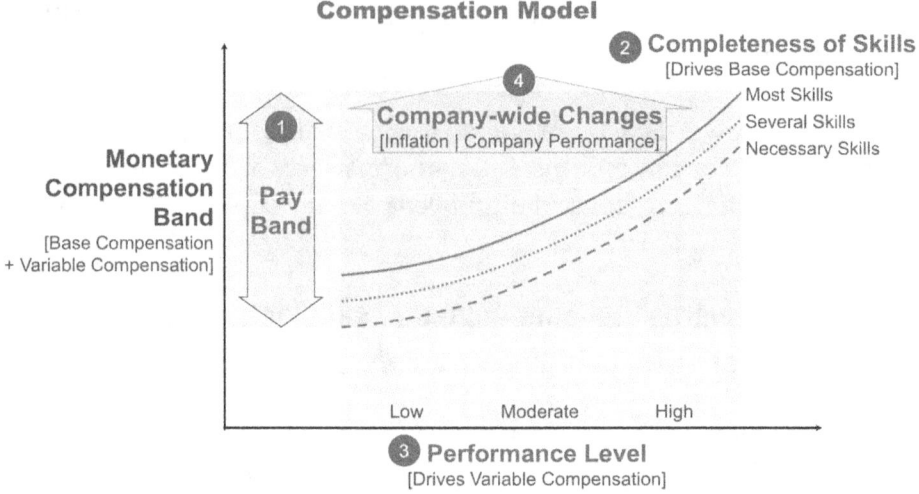

Figure B5. Every role must have a compensation model.

The **first** element of a monetary compensation model is to set lower and upper limits for total compensation for each role. It is the pay band for the role. Besides skill definitions in our organization design, the compensation curve offers a guardrail for the role definition. By defining the pay band, we can quantify each role. We must set intentional compensation boundaries for employees in each role to avoid the "squeaky wheel" mistake or personal biases creeping into compensation decisions.

To start the design process, consider at least two or three performance cycles for every employee in the role. Will we have room below the upper limit to reward a highly skilled, top performer for multiple cycles? On the other hand, is the lower limit too low, where it might create an opportunity for inherent biases?

If you remember the mistake I contributed to in the "squeaky wheel" story, the root cause was the lack of a pay band. When I got around to creating it, the company was already paying both employees, who escalated their pay demands, within the upper and lower limits of the pay band. A reactionary base salary change should have never happened. We should have based their compensation adjustments on an objective performance evaluation.

The **second** element of a compensation model is skills coverage. Skills coverage must dictate the fixed base salary.

When we talked about organization design, hiring, and performance management, we covered the importance of hiring for specialized skills. The reality of hiring and performance management is that we are unlikely to find and hold on to value creators with expertise in every area that we would like the role to have. Employees in the same role will have varying skill levels. A layman's proxy for this vector is the number of years of experience. However, this association is spurious and leads to the common mistake of rewarding based on tenure. I always look for tangible skills.

For example, if our organization has several product managers, it is unlikely that they all have full coverage in all areas of the necessary expertise. There are likely many candidates who can satisfy some of the skills and very few who might meet most of them. Suppose we intentionally hire an employee with expertise in tactical management of the building of the offering but not the customer-facing and design aspects. In that case, our performance evaluation for this employee should not punish them for their skill gaps. Their fixed salary must then reflect this lower skills coverage. This offers the employee the opportunity to vie for a high performer rating among the lower skills coverage group.

In practice, we may augment the employee's role with a partner with the necessary skills to help with the customer-facing aspects. We could think about the partner expense as a hidden compensation cost. If another employee in the same role can cover the full breadth of skills, we wouldn't need this partner and would place that employee in the higher skills and pay group.

So, a good compensation model would bucket areas of expertise together and create two or three skills coverage curves to ensure we offer higher base compensation to the value creators who offer higher skills coverage. Figure B5 visualizes how this might look.

The **third** element is performance-based, non-linear variable compensation. Higher performance levels are increasingly harder to achieve, and an effective compensation model disproportionately rewards improvements at higher levels.

Let's say our current running speed is fifteen minutes per mile, and we improve it by 20 percent to twelve minutes per mile. We deserve a reward for this. However, it is significantly harder to improve it by another 20 percent, and that requires an exponentially greater reward. Improving at higher performance levels is how trophies are won.

Imagine a scenario where our sales reps sell our company's wares in a highly competitive setting. A mediocre sales rep improving by 20 percent is not likely to change the outcome that the customer still buys from a competitor. But if a high performer elevates their performance by 20 percent, we might win that deal.

During a recent discussion with sales reps at a mid-sized company that struggled with employee motivation, their top sales rep rightfully took issue with their linear model. The company placed sales reps into five performance tiers, Tier 5 being the lowest performers and Tier 1 being the best performers. The company put the bottom 5 percent of reps into Tier 5, the next 20 percent into Tier 4, the middle 50 percent into Tier 3, the next 20 percent into Tier 2, and the top 5 percent into Tier 1. So far in the conversation, I supported the design. But the company limited the impact of all that excellent work by setting up a linear variable compensation model. They offered Tier 5 reps 80 percent of their expected variable compensation; Tier 4 90 percent; Tier 3 100 percent; Tier 2 110 percent, and Tier 1 120 percent.

It takes much more work for an employee to move from Tier 2 to Tier 1 than from Tier 5 to Tier 4. In this case, an employee's reward for improving any level would be the same. Essentially, the company is motivating lower performance.

Suppose the extra compensation of moving from Tier 2 to Tier 1 was important to an employee. It is likely easier for the employee to stay at Tier 2 and take on a part-time job that pays them a guaranteed additional wage than put in exponentially more work towards the small, uncertain extra incentive.

So, always develop a non-linear monetary compensation model that rewards high performers significantly more. We want to motivate lower performers to strive to move up the compensation curve, not the other way around. Although compensation models are easiest to explain using operations roles such as sales reps, the same principle applies across all positions.

Mathematically, combining the second and third elements of the compensation model – the distinct skill-focused base compensation curves and the performance-focused non-linear variable compensation potential – must result in the guardrails we set through the first element of the model, which is our pay band.

The **fourth** element of the model is easy. Simplify compensation changes because of externalities like inflation or the opportunity to increase salaries across the role or company by shifting the entire pay band upwards. Do not address these changes at an employee level because it creates another opportunity to allow personal biases to creep in. Always accommodate externalities by shifting the pay band and delineating this fourth element from compensation adjustments centered around performance and skill levels.

You might think – isn't it easier to negotiate employee by employee? No. If we spend one or two thoughtful days building and aligning on a compensation curve once for key roles, we won't have to waste hours going through stressful negotiations for each employee we hire or spend our days dealing with employee compensation issues months down the line.

Even for a role with one employee, which is valid for senior executive roles or cross-functional roles, the compensation cost and the expected impact are usually very high. Therefore, it is worth taking a few hours to develop a rewarding approach before spending several weeks hiring that impactful employee.

Consider these design questions as you build monetary compensation models:

Does every role have a compensation model that dictates total compensation for that role?

Does each compensation model have an upper and lower limit that sets the role's pay band?

Does each compensation model offer tiered curves to delineate varying levels of skills for each role?

Does each compensation curve reward top performers exponentially more than moderate and lower performers?

Are company-wide compensation adjustments applied to the entire role-specific compensation model instead of individual employees?

I promise you that if we don't start with a compensation model and have the discipline to stick to it, we will create distrust among employees that will be hard to overcome.

Principle 6: Implement a formal compensation management process.

As we design and manage compensation models, it is important to remember that every model can get distorted and needs a formal review cadence. Once we get past the first few employees, we can set an annual compensation review cadence that aligns with the performance management cycle.

Compensation structures are often tinkered with or radically changed reactively, especially when a company faces challenges. These reactive modifications are usually triggered by ad hoc inputs like highly vocal employees or board-level cost inquiries. Therefore, it is best to review the compensation models for roles and personal benefits across all employees proactively leading up to the end of each performance cycle so that all inquiries can be handled confidently.

It is also important to be mindful of how we handle evolutionary changes. For example, we may evolve our organization design or processes through major initiatives during the year. As these changes occur, we will be tempted to adjust compensation on the fly outside the scope of such an intentional change. Don't! It's a slippery slope that will lead us to misalignment between compensation, organization design, and performance across the company.

Apart from well-scoped major initiatives, all compensation activity throughout our performance cycle must focus on administration, not redesign. Of course, having a design is critical, but it is also crucial to adhere to its intent.

First, we must identify a **Compensation Czar** whose responsibilities go beyond payroll execution. One individual must be accountable to ensure that our compensation design principles are practically implemented and used. Our compensation czar may belong to a human resource or finance function and have other responsibilities or report to our Congruence Architect. Regardless of functional alignment, a critical thinker must be in the role.

Second, the compensation czar must manage a simple and effective set of controls that ensures that every new hire fits the compensation model for the designated role. A similar set of controls must ensure that compensation adjustments align with performance evaluations. Aberrations must be addressed in short order.

Third, the compensation czar must work closely with our Congruence Architect, senior executives, and owners of major initiatives whose evolutionary work impacts the organization design and associated compensation models. As we approach each new performance cycle, this role must understand and aggregate changes necessary to our compensation approach across all three rewarding types.

Lastly, the compensation czar and Congruence Architect must periodically analyze the cost of using partners as value creators compared to investments in permanent employee compensation. The best version of our company will maximize value creation and capital efficiency regardless of historical precedent. Skills and high-level performance are available at affordable prices worldwide.

In summary, rewarding starts with avoiding the common compensation mistakes. Then, develop compensation plans ensuring personal rewards create a level playing field. Professional rewards are an interim path for high performers. All monetary rewards must be formally designed using a compensation model that disproportionately rewards high-skilled, top performers. Lastly, limit compensation design and changes to align with the performance cycle while focusing on compensation administration throughout the cycle.

Effective compensation management is a powerful and necessary tool for creating an objective and transparent environment that encourages top value creators to stay with the company and motivates the rest to push the envelope on their performance and earn more.

We have now covered the management approach levers. We need to evolve these components continuously to maintain congruence, acquire the right value creators, and enable them to do their best work. As we leave this part of our method, remember the dart analogy that we started with. The management approach is the foundational dartboard that can absorb a perfect throw with a perfect dart. Everything else is predicated on a mature management approach that brings together the best value creators and allows them to operate optimally.

PART C

Value Engine Generates Customer Benefits.

IN Part A: Company Purpose, we outlined the levers that address the question: *Why does our company exist?* Then, in Part B: Management Approach, we explored the company's people agenda. Essentially, we answered the question: *How do we manage our people?* The maturity level of those fundamental levers helps the CEO and senior executives bring together the most skilled value creators into well-defined roles, retain the best, and ensure that the rest strive to improve while operating in a purpose-led system. We have the team.

Now, what does the team actually do?

Value creators operate in a company to meet the needs of value extractors in our ecosystem.

We are now transitioning from our approach of systemically managing our people to the reasons we are in business in the first place. So, the second half of our operations baseline, which comprises the intrinsically valuable parts of our business, is what I call the **Value Engine**.

Simplistically, a congruent company balances the value received by customers and investors. Value creators have to build and improve an offering that solves tangible problems for our customers. Then, we must devise ways to deliver that value to an increasing volume of customers profitably.

The more intrinsically valuable our offering and value delivery are, the more customers we will attract and the more they will be willing to pay. This generates profits that can be returned to the investors who put capital in. The capital could be cash from wealthy individuals, mass retail investors, or banks. It could also be "sweat equity" from owners who risked a lot and started the company without taking money for their efforts.

Boom! Easy! Done!

But then, why do incongruences keep a large share of companies from achieving these obvious outcomes?

First, the sequence of value extraction is paramount. Customers are the primary value extractors. Investors are served well if customer value is optimized. Serving investors first is a capital engineering mindset that quickly results in shortcuts that create significant imbalances across purpose, strategy, and operations.

With that foundation, let's do a thought experiment. Put five of your favorite ultra-successful executives in five separate rooms and give them five portions of a significant business problem to solve. What is the probability that they will propose five solutions that will fit together to solve the overarching problem?

In my experience, near zero!

We could take this further and replace them with relatively normal executives you have met in day-to-day settings.

Do you think it will be hard for them to agree on the best course of action? Indeed. What if the set of five were individual contributors in different roles with different incentives and far less experience?

Diversity in problem-solving, choice of solutions, and risk propensity will apply to any group of value creators operating independently, irrespective of their performance level or skill. We won't have a company if every person chooses what they feel is the right course. Recall that operating a congruent company is like running a system-led team.

So, we must choreograph the efforts of all value creators to act as One Company, where everyone sings from the same hymn book. This is the essence of the value engine. Our value engine injects a system mindset into how we serve our customers. As a growing company, it formalizes a cohesive offering that creates significant customer value. It articulates how we work with each other to deliver that value.

Things To Remember: Value Engine

The value engine comprises the levers that create benefits for our customers by solving a relevant problem. It includes our offerings to address customer problems and all day-to-day decisions and activities to deliver that value.

We can only create value by having something the customer doesn't have, doing something they can't or won't do, or knowing something they don't. The only way to achieve this is through scale. Whether our offering is an object, an action, knowledge, or a promise, we can only offer it because we are very good at it. To be better, we must do it many times. So, we must codify how we create value for our customers. This is called **Productization**, which is the first component of our value engine. Think about this lever of our value engine as the answer to the question: *How do we solve our customers' problems to create value?*

Once we choose, design, and build our offering, we still have to deliver it to the customer on an ongoing basis. Every offering in the world will have portions that require constant human or technological actions to create customer value. Above that, our sellers focused on acquiring new customers must take the same day-to-day steps that work for the company's chosen customers. All value creators who serve customers must solve customer problems consistently based on the expectations set. Marketers who attend conferences must establish the same expectations for prospects. Engineers or designers who build the company's offerings will follow the agreed-upon ways to work together.

The internalization that all such operations follow a collective way and not each person's way is critical to developing a system that enables sustainable customer value creation. I call this operational cohesion **The Company**

Way Processes, the second component of our value engine. It answers the question: *How do we execute day-to-day to deliver value to customers?*

The value engine also includes our defenses and problem-solving approach to protect against individualism, human mistakes, and unexpected events and enable microevolutions based on such experiences. Our path to identification of challenges and evolution must be based on the objective use of information and sound analytical principles.

If problem-solving discussions are analogous to looking outside a window and using present weather conditions as evidence for or against climate change, we don't have a sound system to create and deliver customer value. It is only a matter of time before enough arbitrary choices add up to a catastrophic mistake.

Our ability to gather objective information and use optimal problem-solving and issue-resolution frameworks forms the third component of the value engine: **Data Usage**. This lever answers the question: *How do we improve?*

These three levers intertwine to form the value engine, which allows us to deliver optimal customer value, drive all value creators to execute effectively, and continue to improve execution over time. Additionally, these three levers rest on the foundations laid via our management approach because none of this works if the right value creators are not in the right roles. Figure C1 shows the dovetailed relationship between the management approach and value engine components to form our operations baseline.

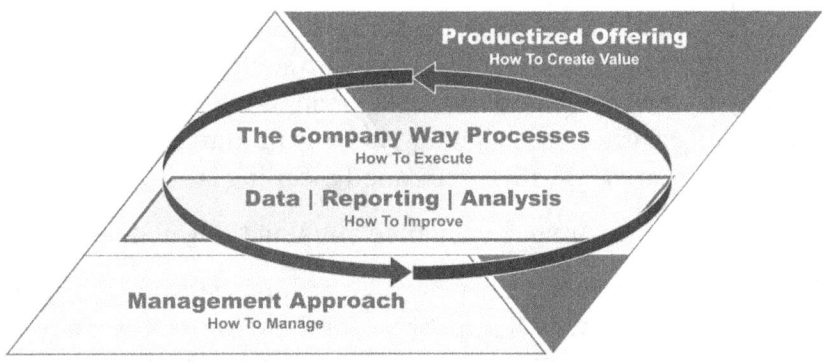

**Figure C1. Value engine dovetails with management
approach to complete operations baseline.**

Regardless of market, our offering will involve ongoing actions by operations resources to deliver value, which is part of The Company Way Processes. Similarly, management approach levers – hiring, performance management, and compensation management – have activities and decisions that are part of the company processes. Our data-gathering effectiveness and problem-solving have to envelop all the other levers of the operations baseline, including the management approach. They influence each other, and we will see the interplay throughout the rest of our method.

Why is a systemic value engine important?

The concepts under value engine have become layman's language. From a business perspective, this is a complication and not a benefit. We all tend to use specific words in general contexts, and over time, we lose the real intent behind important words.

When we want to search for something on the internet, we might say, "Google it." Or when we take a taxi, we might say, "Take an Uber." In both these instances, we might not even use Google's search engine or Uber, but instead opt for an alternative that provides the same service. Both concepts are only a little over a decade old.

How much more misused are the words I used in the three value engine components we introduced above, given that they have been part of business terminology for a long time?

We live in a world where software platforms take any question and provide answers by statistically connecting words into sentences. Their knowledge of meaning is solely based on statistics gleaned from information fed to them previously without ever having met any human beings. Saying that important words are losing their intended meaning is an understatement.

Data suggests that we are getting worse at using the value engine levers.

The U.S. Bureau of Labor Statistics (BLS) publishes productivity figures quarterly and annually. BLS publishes Total Factor Productivity, which "compares the growth in output to the growth in a combination of inputs that include labor, capital, energy, materials, and services." BLS also publishes labor productivity, which "compares the growth in output to the growth in hours worked."

Total factor productivity and labor productivity have to increase to produce more output with a given set of inputs, which is the essence of improving intrinsic value creation.

Both the 2007 to 2019 post-financial crisis economic cycle and the 2019 to 2024 post-pandemic cycle have the lowest productivity growth figures since 1948, except for the odd double-dip recession in 1980–81.

The annual average labor productivity increase since 2007 has only been 1.5 percent compared to 2.7 percent between 2000 and 2007. Total factor productivity growth has only been 0.5 percent since 2007 compared to 1.3 percent between 2000 and 2007.

So, with all our technology and automation, social connectivity, knowledge sources, and fifty times more data availability compared to a decade ago, how is it possible that productivity growth figures are at an all-time low?

We have overlooked the importance of foundational levers that create intrinsic value and enable productivity advancements. Over the last decade, we have subscribed to inaccurate themes like "efficiency and discipline are the enemy of creativity and agility."

This means hiring more people or spending more on assets to achieve slightly better outcomes rather than improving existing investments in people, technology, or other assets. As a result, it creates a lack of profitability among many companies.

As we established in our introduction, we have increasingly focused on dealmaking, which means buying and selling companies, to inflate market price instead of running companies to create more value and profit. But happy hour deals don't last forever. Sooner than later, we will have to start paying the regular menu price collectively and as individual companies by focusing on intrinsic value creation.

Figure C2 shows the two productivity paths a company can take. The value engine encompasses our path to revenue and our cost of achieving that revenue. The bottom left of the chart shows our company's budding phase, with little revenue and cost and almost no paying customers. Moving to the top right, we are growing and capturing more of the addressable market. The Y-axis represents our increasing revenue, which correlates with the value we create for customers. The X-axis represents the cost of serving those customers.

The first path is the lower, unsustainable path, where we are trying to grow at any cost. Our cost of delivering value to each customer increases as we acquire more customers. It's not a sustainable growth path because our growth will stall eventually, and we will likely get there without a profit. So, going down this path is ill-advised. The only reason to attempt it is to boost market price and sell the unsustainable entity to someone else. The further down this unsustainable path we go, the harder it is to restore the fundamentals necessary to be profitable.

The preferable path is the top one, where we seek increasing productivity from our ongoing cost of doing business. That is, we continue to do more with what we have. A mature value engine and its core principles will help us stay on this path. However, staying on this path is not easy. There will always be a continuous downward pressure to lose discipline and take the lower suboptimal approach, which is easier in the short term but won't get us to the best version of our company.

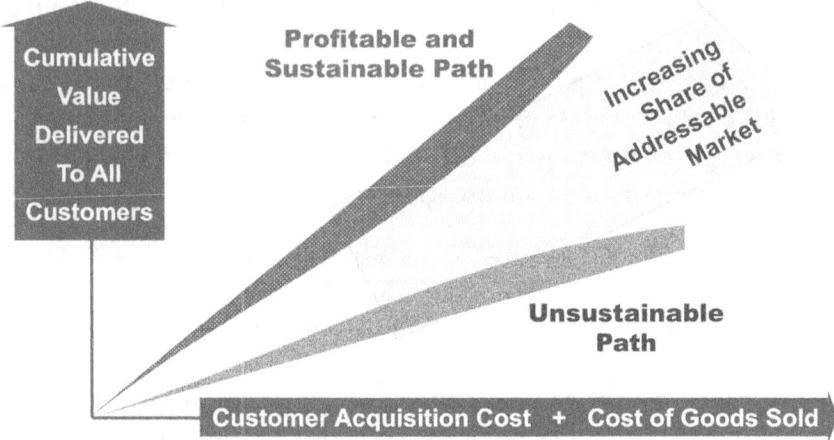

Figure C2. Optimizing value engine enables sustainable profitability through lifecycle stages.

Mistaking a weakness as a strength is a path to self-destruction. So, we must understand the present level of congruence of our value engine. A mature foundation can help us arrive at winning decisions and flawless execution. Conversely, a misaligned and misunderstood one can be analogous to trying to win a math challenge with a broken calculator. So, what does a good value engine look like?

Value Engine Maturity Model.

We are striving for two success factors across our value engine levers.

The **first** success factor is **Repeatability**. Repeatability means each entity takes the same execution path every iteration for a given action or behavior. So, whether it's an employee, a customer, a partner, or even a tool, repeatability implies that the entity executes in the same way every single time or at least close to it.

The **second** success factor is **Reproducibility**. Reproducibility means that all entities collectively adopt the same behavior for every iteration of a given action or behavior. In other words, everyone does the same activity the same way.

Reproducibility is a super-set that includes repeatability.

Repeatability and reproducibility span all components of our value engine. Building both into our value engine is the only path to sustainability.

The most important takeaway from our maturity model is that all levers are interdependent. They build on each other and are largely ineffective without dovetailing building blocks from other levers.

Think about our value engine as a missile. The payload is our offering to our customers. The rocket that carries the payload is our process. Finally, the guidance system that navigates our missile to its destination is our objective capture of data and its effective usage to micro-evolve our operations baseline. Without any one of these components, our missile is inert or will flame out.

Figure C3 shows our Value Engine Maturity Model. As you consider these five levels, think about who might be responsible for improving the current level of congruence. The responsibility of driving towards high levels of harmony and maturity must sit with a strong Congruence Architect role. Remember, the Congruence Architect is a role. Whatever job titles present senior executives have are inconsequential. The question is: *Who can the CEO entrust these responsibilities with to ensure that our company operates at a high level of value engine maturity?*

On the left end of the model, we operate at *Level 1: Chaos*. Here, the company's investors and value creators primarily focus on their own success without internalizing that customer value creation is the primary reason to exist. The company also depends on individual value creators' brilliance to win the day. Most companies operate here during infancy, but staying here without maturity improvements implies that scale is prohibitive without overspending, which is unsustainable.

Many organizations make minor attempts at building maturity around the value engine levers and operate at *Level 2: Ambiguous*. However, repeatability and reproducibility are not internalized as necessary success factors. So, there is limited incremental customer value creation or operations efficiency due to scale. Some misunderstand minor improvements to mean high maturity levels and remain at Level 2, which essentially stifles further evolution.

I worked with a mid-market technology company where a senior executive

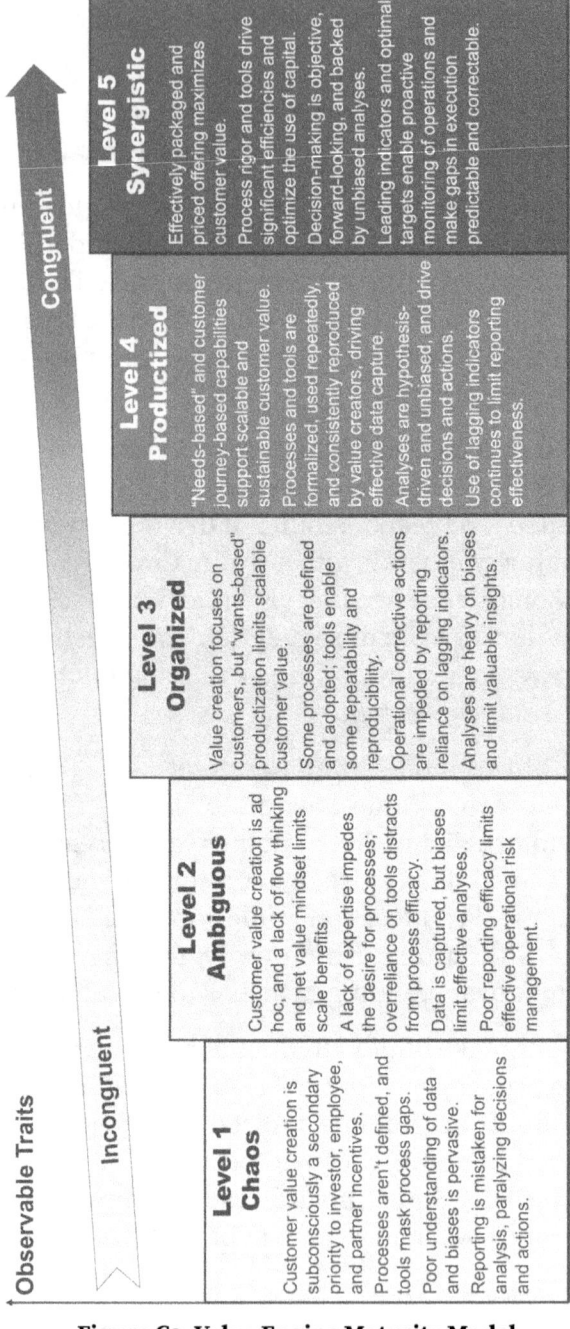

Figure C3. Value Engine Maturity Model.

and the supervisory layer wanted strong processes. However, their interpretation allowed each of the thirty operations employees to devise their own path to achieve the expected outcomes. This team thought that they were being "process centric." However, this is the antithesis of creating and executing The Company Way. Misunderstanding their maturity led this team to miss targets after repeated attempts to achieve expected outcomes without repeatability or reproducibility.

We must at least evolve to *Level 3: Organized* before the customers and value creators begin to see scale-related benefits. Level 3 implies that at least some value creators have adopted effective processes designed for them and consistently repeat the same desired behaviors. However, the company is submissive to all customers and places the onus of designing the offering on them, which is not scalable or sustainable. Effective capture of information enables access to usable data. But the power of objective analysis and reporting is not leveraged for decision-making and managing processes.

As we move further to the right to *Level 4: Productized,* the company has matured to develop value-focused offerings by understanding the root cause of customer needs. Groups of value creators in the same role adhere consistently to The Company Way. Additionally, analytical roles spearhead effective decision-making and microevolution of the offering and processes using objective data.

The desired value-creating state is *Level 5: Synergistic.* Our offering effectively solves the root cause of customer problems and is commercially sustainable through effective pricing and packaging. The company uses objective analysis to generate insights to improve well-adopted processes and tools continuously. The Company Way Processes and objective data enable effective reporting, which facilitates predictive execution risk management and issue resolution.

Over the following three chapters, we will explore each lever that enables a congruent value engine.

C.1
CREATE NET POSITIVE CUSTOMER VALUE WITH PRODUCTIZATION.

M Y first role was as a "Product Owner" of an electronic motor used in heating and cooling applications at General Electric. Over several years in consulting, I experienced many different definitions of "product" across industries and companies. In the past few years, I have worked with many technology companies with a narrower view that software is a "product." It is a nebulous word that anchors value creators too much to the historic practices of the worlds they spend their time in. Some tribal knowledge is helpful. This one is limiting.

Employees and senior executives move from one industry to another. Employees play musical chairs between companies. So, how do we work together effectively and create value using a nebulous seven-letter word that no one appears to have a firm articulation of?

Can you name Google's, Meta's, or Amazon's "products"? I bet a customer's list would differ from the list we would get from employees. So, rather than spin our wheels by restricting ourselves to this one overused word, let's focus on themes and principles around creating value.

We will not use "product" as a noun in our method because it is overused and misinterpreted. Instead, we will continue to use the plain English word "offering" as our catch-all box to describe our value-creating payload.

Our congruent company's value creation effectiveness rests on three overarching themes that run across seven design principles.

Theme A: Customer first is our Hippocratic Oath.

Some companies claim an investor-first mindset, which has been the traditional path for decades. Recently, there has been an employee-first wave, and many companies have jumped on this bandwagon. Of course, there are employee-owned companies, which is a logical overlap. However, not a single company in the world is sustainably successful because it operates as an investor-first or an employee-first company. These result in value exchange incongruences.

As the old wisdom from many, including Plato, goes, "The person who doesn't want to be king should rule." This brings us to the first of three themes about how our company creates value.

Holistic companies prioritize customers and societal impact because those stakeholders are never in the company's problem-solving and decision-making room haggling for themselves. The people in the room – employees, investors, and partners to some extent – tend to make sure they are well-represented.

So, who speaks for the customers? It's a conscious choice by investors, employees, and partners on the importance of creating value for customers. Without doing so, our value exchange is incongruent, and eventually, the company disbands.

Every methodology that focuses on value creation would tell you to start with customers. Now you also have the psychological reason. Rational investors will not put a cent in our company if they don't believe our customers are willing to pay for our offerings. Likewise, we won't have a cent to pay our employees if our customers aren't willing to pay for our offerings.

Recently, we have had many more companies funded by investors when customers aren't buying enough or paying enough. We have also increasingly given company shares to employees in exchange for lower cash compensation. But none of these changes the fact that we will only be sustainably successful if we can generate value for customers who are willing to pay for what we are offering. If customers don't pay for the party, the party ends sooner or later.

Why is this important?

If we serve our customers exceptionally well, we have all the revenue and profit necessary to make our investors and employees happy and prosperous, and partners will be easy to find. On the other hand, if we focus on making our investors and employees extremely happy and place a lower conscious or subconscious priority on our customer needs, our party will likely end after we drink the champagne that we paid for with borrowed money.

When I started working with a founder who had just replaced his co-founder as CEO, he told me, "I am going to change our company mindset from customer-first to employee-first because our employees are not happy."

As I worked to diagnose their challenges, it became apparent that the company lacked a consistent, core customer offering. Employees were unhappy when a new deal was sold because they had to fend for themselves and somehow provide what the sales team promised the customer. The company desired to be customer-first but hadn't matured its customer offering. Employee unhappiness was a symptom of a lack of maturity in serving customer needs.

The CEO, the board, and senior executives, who collectively represent both employees and investors, must look in the mirror and ask whether our company purpose from Part A is true to its essence and whether we have empathy for our "ruling" stakeholders – customers – who will almost never represent themselves. If we prioritize physically present stakeholders, it's only a matter of time before current or new competitors prioritize our customers and lure them away. As I said in our introduction, our competitors don't usually beat us; we usually beat ourselves.

Theme B: Flow thinking optimizes our understanding and measurement of value.

Creating and delivering value implies understanding how we make a difference in the recipient's life. Flow thinking allows us to internalize the lives of our value-extracting stakeholders effectively.

Would a series of pictures or a continuous video of a given situation have more information? Obviously, the latter! Flow thinking is the concept of visualizing everything as a continuous streaming video, which is what the real world truly is. Mistakes are made when we view a situation as a series of disconnected snapshots because we are operating with a loss of critical information.

Things To Remember: Flow Thinking

Flow thinking implies that we view the entire world as a connected series of physical or mental actions, including review, analysis, decision-making, communication, etc. A human or a machine may perform those actions.

Let's consider the market ecosystem for last-mile delivery of consumer packages. A critical block of value is the front-door package hand-off. It sounds self-explanatory, and everyone who has ever received a package at home has a perspective on what this means. But does this really clarify how much value is created? I argue not.

The front-door package hand-off is not a well-defined block by itself. The dovetailed flow of the entire last-mile delivery ecosystem determines the specific value created by the front-door package hand-off portion. How does the package recipient know when to be at the front door? How long will the deliverer wait? How many times will they return? All these ancillary actions to front-door package hand-off dictate the effectiveness of that specific value creation intent.

According to Newton's third law of motion, actions have an equal and opposite reaction. Although this isn't a physics class, the same mindset applies to how we create value. For any given situation, if we represent all the actions in our ecosystem or all the actions of our customers as a flow with no loss of information, then we are also capturing the complete flow of value accurately. Otherwise, we operate with spurious interpretations and expectations based on commonly misused words and might miss critical information.

Theme C: Customer value is multidirectional.

As much as we hope to deliver value to customers, we can also cause regret through our offering. How many times have we put our heads in our hands and said, "Why am I paying for this?"

The flow of value is not single-directional. Value can flow to a customer through our offering. But value can also flow out of a customer if the customer makes sacrifices to use our offering. Think about these value outflows as friction for the customer. The higher the friction caused by our offering, the lower the overall value gleaned by the customer.

We must consider this value outflow as we design and build our offering. We must ask ourselves, are we creating net positive value for our customers? Or is our offering costing the customer substantial undesirable adjustments that leave their net value close to zero or negative?

Imagine sending a loved one a gift we feel is meaningful. But the loved one has to reschedule their busy day to pick up the gift. Where is the balance between the value to the recipient and the adjustments that make this gift potentially value destructive for them?

Our customer value creation principles must create significant net positive value, which is all the customers must pay for. Let's keep this definition in mind throughout our discussion.

Things To Remember: Net Customer Value

Net Customer Value [EQUALS] Value inflow from our offering [MINUS] Value outflow due to our offering.

Now that we have aligned on the importance of a customer-first mindset, flow thinking, and the multidirectional nature of customer value, let's talk about seven non-negotiable principles of value creation.

Principle 1: Productization requires repeatability and reproducibility.

Wait a minute! Product what? We said we are not using the word as a noun, and we aren't. **Productization** is a verb and a concept.

Customers buy from us at a fair market price because we can create value that they can't or don't want to create on their own, regardless of the offering. We can only create increasing customer value for existing customers and deliver that value to an increasing number of new customers if we design our offerings with repeatability and reproducibility.

> **Things To Remember: Productization**
>
> **The act of creating a repeatable and reproducible offering is called productization.**

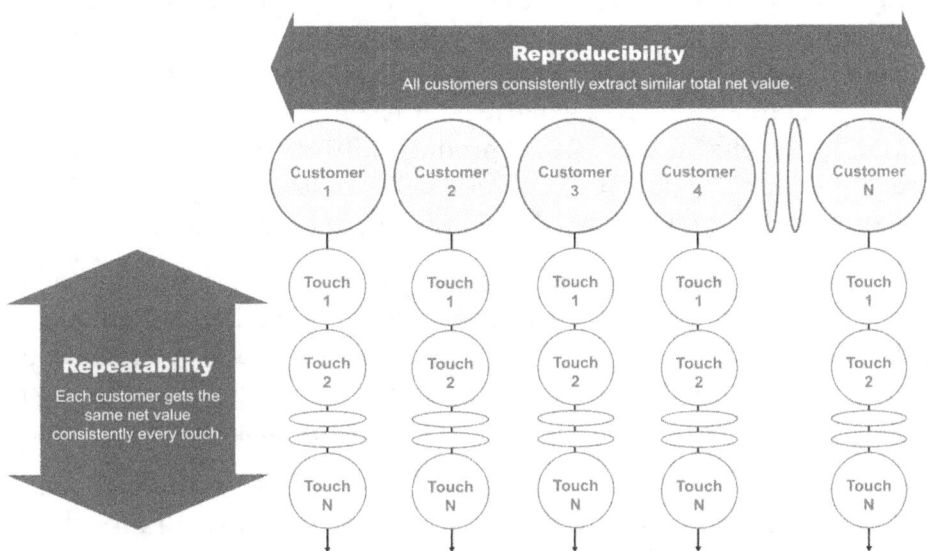

Figure C4. Repeatability and reproducibility enable productization.

In the context of creating value for customers, repeatability implies that we are able to deliver the same total net value to any given customer consistently. Thus, whether our offering is a widget, service, advice, or any other perceivable creation, the customer must predictably get the same value each time they buy or use it.

Additionally, we are only a sustainable and profitable company if we can consistently deploy our creation to many customers. This is reproducibility. Otherwise, we have no economies of scale, and we will take the unsustainable productivity path that we covered in the value engine introduction. As summarized in Figure C4, congruent value creation requires us to productize, which combines both repeatability and reproducibility, because it generates the most consistent value for customers and allows us to do so profitably.

Suppose we are offering our customers a simple widget. In that case, repeatability and reproducibility imply that we can source the ingredients and build the widget at a large enough volume consistently that it is a lot cheaper for customers to buy from us. It is also less time-consuming for our customers than creating it themselves.

Repeatability and reproducibility don't imply making the same simple widget for every customer. For example, we could be a custom mechanic who refurbishes vintage cars. Our productization here focuses on our experience, flexibility, and ingenuity. Our repeatability comes from our ability to demonstrate this expertise for each unique vehicle that a customer brings in over time. Our reproducibility comes from showing our breadth across a range of customers with similarly unique cars. In this situation, price is likely not a primary concern for a customer.

If we are offering our customers a service, the only reason they would choose us is if we can do it cheaper or at a better quality. This means we either have many people doing the same service so that we can gain economies of scale, or we have gained experience by doing it many times and can deliver higher quality or bring knowledge the customer doesn't have.

Even if we own a Michelin-star restaurant or a hole-in-the-wall family outlet, customers come to us due to scale. A Michelin restaurant's reputation comes from the chef's and team's expertise channeled into customer value. A family outlet might be valuable because of deep experience with a cultural cuisine or access to tried-and-true family recipes.

This mindset of embracing repeatability and reproducibility to design our offerings applies regardless of our market. The crudest way to frame the importance of productization is that we cannot use customers as perpetual test subjects. Beyond the first few customers, we must be good at what we're offering and continue to mature.

In my experience, most company-level challenges that lead to existential crises stem from the failure to effectively productize. Selling something to a few customers at a discount or a high delivery cost is acceptable at the start. But to run a sustainable company, repeatability and reproducibility are table stakes.

Each macroevolution cycle must include major initiatives, triggered by strategic planning, to improve the productization of our offerings. Enablement resources will execute such initiatives to create and enhance our productized offerings. We will dive into this macroevolution cycle further in the corporate strategy, strategic planning, and execution management parts.

Principle 2: Align company strengths with market problem.

I am 5 ft. 10 in. and slim. No amount of fitness training, food consumption, or mindset shift would ever help me be a heavy-weight boxing contender. We all have specific abilities and limitations. Introspection and humility will always serve us well. At the very least, it can save us from misallocating capital, especially if it comes from others.

From the get-go, we agreed that our goal here is to build a path to sustainable profitability, optimal value creation, and capital efficiency that normal people can strive for and have a reasonable probability of success. That implies that there must be tangible reasons for success in productizing an offering.

I have seen the inner workings of plenty of motivated businesses that began with the thought, "We want to be successful, and we will create a company!" This is an admirable entrepreneurial spirit. This isn't usually enough.

For instance, I have worked closely with companies that tried very hard to develop technology solutions, but the know-how that got them early revenue was through staff augmentation services. Without a fundamental rebuild of the entire company, including the management approach components, productizing what the value creators did for each customer's desire and then baking that into a single technology doesn't come naturally to a service-minded group.

Suppose our founding and operating spirit is, "We have experienced a market problem, and our experience is unique enough that we are likely to be best placed to create value for our customers!" In that case, we have a customer-focused path. Obviously, anyone can say this, but only some can say it with objectivity and honesty.

To learn this principle, let's define the term **Market Problem**. For now, let's simplify the formal definition below to think about the market problem as the collective essence of the challenges customers face. In the next part of our method, we will expound on this formal definition and dive into how to analyze our market.

Things To Remember: Market Problem

Market problem is a three-legged stool that frames the situation that customers could draw value from. The three legs are 1) Non-core Activities, which encompass all customer efforts that do not have to be 100 percent owned and performed by the customer, 2) Voiced Pain Points, which are value-diminishing challenges that the customer feels and is aware of, and 3) Unvoiced Imbalances, which articulate undiscovered gaps due to unfair systemic elements that the customer lives with. Thus, market problem and value are two sides of the same coin. Customers are willing to pay for the value they receive from solutions to their market problems.

Can we look at our company's value creators and objectively say that we have something that no one else in the market has? Where does this belief come from? What are our proof points?

Ask: *Why us?*

I empowered the early success of a three-person founding team that had worked in the consulting world. They witnessed a client problem in the risk management space in their previous jobs. They built a solution for that client in a consulting project. Then, they founded a company codifying this project that they had successfully delivered once before. That's enough. They understood their customers. In my experience, this is far more unique than most companies make it sound.

Investors call this Founder-Market Fit Story when they fund companies. But anytime there is a formal term for anything, we start overusing it. Every founder has a founder-market story, and it's tempting to focus more on the story than the fit. We want to focus on the fit portion.

Established companies can fall into the same trap of telling stories based on success from several years ago and assume that the world hasn't changed.

This **first** essence behind the "why us?" principle is the company's intimate understanding of its market. It can be learned.

Conversely, the "why us?" principle is not intended to highlight one person's decades of experience in a market. Such historical knowledge and anchoring to it could also backfire. We want to focus on our unique understanding of the market, which empowers us to solve the problem.

Regardless of our company's origin, gaining a deep understanding of the market must go beyond experience. History may help us land our first few customers. But sustainability requires that we genuinely dive into the depths of how the market functions and evolve our knowledge of it.

Second, we must have the strengths to solve the market problem. Just a desire or will isn't enough. Compared to other competitors, why would we win? We will dedicate two chapters to answer our "why us?" question under Part D: Corporate Strategy. To build and evolve our offering to solve the market problem, we must know the market better than others and hold the relevant strengths to solve the problem.

For instance, if we are a technology company trying to build operations improvement software, coding or technology infrastructure know-how is not the differentiating strength we need. That is table stakes for any technology sector company. Our market understanding and design strengths around processes and the ins and outs of how people work together must be exceptional. When building a data-centric technology solution, we need to have the internal horsepower on how data is gathered and leveraged. No amount of software expertise will cover gaps in our knowledge and skills around data-specific value creation.

Consider these design questions:

How deep is our ability to empathize and understand the root cause of our intended customers' market problems?

How differentiated are our core strengths so as to create a repeatable and reproducible solution to the market problems?

Weaknesses in these answers will reveal incongruences that hurt value creation.

Principle 3: Focus on customer needs, not wants.

When was the last time you sat a friend down and said, "You are not thinking about this correctly, and if you go the opposite direction, you will be more successful."? Society encourages us to mistake appeasement for empathy. This leaves most of us afraid or unwilling to invest the personal risk to take someone to a place they aren't considering. Pandering to maintain near-term comfort can feel like value creating. Yet it doesn't create sustainable value.

Asking customers what they want and giving them exactly what they asked for is easy but not the appropriate interpretation of customer-first.

Customers are focused on their pain and not on effectively resolving it. Instead, they think about getting back to core actions and decisions they consider in their control. I call such customer-expressed symptoms and sentiments "wants."

Addressing wants is easy. It doesn't require problem-solving skill to replicate specific asks by customers, at any cost. If it costs too much to replicate what a customer wants, it can even be an excuse to say that the customer is unreasonable. Does it make sense for a patient to ask a doctor for specific pills and dosage?

Productization does not address wants because it doesn't lead to repeatability or reproducibility. Customers are our children; not our parents. We don't know why a child cries and we often say, "No!" We are constantly problem-solving on the child's behalf. Our productization role is not to say, "Yes, sir!" as we might to a dominant parent.

Every single problem-solving methodology highlights the importance of root cause identification and resolution tied to that root cause. Five-Whys is a root cause identification tool that drives us to ask "why" five times to drill deeper into a symptom to address the essence of the problem. A Fishbone Diagram is a tool that drives us to comprehensively assess the entire landscape and underlying contributors that result in a symptom. All such tools hint at the same message – focus on the root cause.

I call the root causes of customer wants "needs." Most of our company's customer value creation ability through productization depends on our problem-solving skills and risk propensity to invest in identifying and creating a solution that addresses the underlying need.

Things To Remember: Needs vs. Wants

Customers know and share how they feel, which are their "wants." Wants are symptoms. Our problem-solving skills must translate those symptoms and constraints in the market to underlying root causes, which are customer "needs."

Current or potential customers are our source of information to address problems in our market. However, we must frame appropriate questions in the right circumstances to capture useful information, which can be transformed into tangible customer needs that we can solve. While gathering market intelligence, our questions and surveys must be framed to capture customer sentiments while understanding that such answers are not the root causes or solutions. If a customer says, "I wish the service were faster," their real need might have been that we set accurate expectations on delivery time so that the customer could use their time effectively.

Our conversations with customers must always allow them to share their visceral pain and feelings through open-ended questions. Once we have objective and unbiased information about feelings and symptoms in the market, we can translate those to underlying customer needs. Then, we must productize to meet those needs, which by extension also takes care of customer wants.

Principle 4: Operate within the customer journey.

Value creators could brainstorm in a vacuum, develop great ideas that might help customers in a market we understand, and try to convince customers to buy. But how would that be a customer-first mindset? It's a value creator-first mindset. Net positive customer value creation is only likely if it addresses a very specific and well-defined problem.

Recall that productization for customers is the act of developing a repeatable and reproducible solution to address a real-world problem.

Customers are either individuals or groups of individuals. Our offering might intend to impact their personal or professional lives. Nevertheless, every person follows a natural flow that is also their path of least resistance.

What did we do if we wanted to take a taxi at the turn of the twenty-first century? We walked to the street corner, looked around, and raised our hands when we saw a taxi with "for hire" lights on. What do ride-share platforms that disrupted the space do?

They replicated this human flow and solved some challenges we faced as consumers. For example, these platforms placed all nearby cars on our phone screens. We may not have wanted to wait outside and raise our hand to get one. They replaced a hand-raising with a button we could push without waiting outside. Even if we hailed a taxi, someone else might have jumped in front of us and snagged our cab. The platforms eliminated the possibility that someone else could commandeer our taxi. Rideshare platforms replicated our old human behaviors, systematized the steps we would take, and removed some of our hurdles.

This exemplifies our fourth principle, and it applies to developing solutions for any market problem.

We always serve customers who operate in their own natural flow. Therefore, productization is not about dreaming up a magical answer disconnected from that flow. Instead, designing our offering must internalize and optimize the natural path our customers are used to taking or create a more lucrative new path that improves the old one. Therefore, putting a customer-first hat on implies that we are drawing a process flow for customers' behavioral journey, which is called a **Customer Journey**.

> **Things To Remember: Customer Journey**
>
> **The customer journey is the natural path of least resistance that any customer would take if we were not in the frame. It is a process flow with steps and transitions between those steps.**

The concept of customer journey is commonly accepted. However, the challenge is its practical application. Our natural flow is obvious and consistent in a business-to-consumer problem-solving setting because we are all familiar with and follow basic societal norms.

However, most companies solve niche consumer challenges or challenges other companies face. We personalize our behaviors even for most consumer activities. For example, each individual's exercise habits are more unique than hailing a taxi.

Similarly, every company is unique because of its people, history, maturity, and the market problem it is solving. Therefore, serving customers that are businesses implies serving behaviors that are somewhat unique even for the same market problem.

This tendency to personalize our behaviors creates two challenges and complicates the practical application of the customer journey mindset. **First,** the tendency to personalize behaviors makes solving the problem for all customers in our market space challenging. **Second,** personalizing makes commonalities between customer behaviors difficult to observe. So, how do we productize our offering through repeatability and reproducibility to serve customers in our space if behaviors are not exactly the same?

Unless we are trying to solve a nonexistent market problem, some customers will behave more similarly than other customers. In other words, there are always clusters of customers with similar enough behaviors. Let's call these clusters **Customer Groups.** We will dive into customer groups in more detail when we discuss corporate strategy.

> **Things To Remember: Customer Groups**
>
> **A customer group is a cluster of current or potential customers who demonstrate very similar behaviors within the context of the market problem we are focused on.**

Clusters of customer behaviors also imply that we can paint a customer journey for each cluster. We will have to study the customer behaviors in-depth to connect the dots to paint the customer journey. We must analyze customer behaviors qualitatively to remove the noise of individualism and tease out these clusters and the common ground within each cluster.

Such deep analysis helps us address the practical application challenges of the customer journey. Productization implies that we cannot serve all customers and cannot practically allow every customer to follow their perfect natural flow. But it allows us to serve many customers exceptionally well by minimizing deviation from their natural flow.

If we can choose our optimal customer group, we can tease out a customer journey that reflects the common behaviors within that customer group. I call this specific and optimal journey, a **Use Case**. The effective choice of a single use case is our success factor of the customer journey principle.

Things To Remember: Use Case

A use case is an end-to-end flow that reflects the common behaviors of an optimal customer group that we want to serve. It is the customer journey that reflects the optimal customers we prioritize to create value for.

Peloton, an in-home exercise solution provider, originally built and marketed their offering for an affluent family member who doesn't have time to get to the gym and wants to exercise at home. The customer journey they focused on revolved around a person at home who was also a fitness enthusiast. It is an effective use case. The company addressed the market problem: How does one solve the needs of a motivated exerciser who lacks the time or flexibility to go to a gym? It worked.

Conversely, my exercise journey always revolved around a brick-and-mortar gym's social setting. I enjoyed getting to the gym first thing in the morning on my way to work and seeing other people. I didn't mind the extra time lost because it was a social experience for me. As such, I did not fit Peloton's primary use case.

However, the COVID-19 lockdowns changed almost everyone's exercise journey, including mine, and forced us all to try exercising at home. It took me three stubborn months of being stuck at home to consider what a long-term home-based exercise journey might look like. I started using Peloton when my journey had converged with their original use case. I became an avid fan of Peloton classes and did 100 percent of my workouts at home. I was part of a large customer group that embraced Peloton because our exercise journey changed.

However, as the world reopened, how likely was my customer group to break our new exercise journey again and revert to exercising in social settings? Peloton's productization decisions to try to serve a mass market imply a bet that the second customer group would continue to behave like the company's original loyal customer group. Sadly, they bet wrong. This single choice proved fateful for Peloton as most of the world was eager to return to social settings and back to past behaviors of visiting gyms in person. Peloton has been deeply unprofitable due to loans the company took on to serve the mass market that vaporized after the world opened back up.

The few who found significant incremental value in the time savings and convenience of exercising at home during COVID lockdowns maintained their customer journey. I am part of this small group and am still an avid Peloton user. This story underlines the power of understanding customer groups and their respective journeys and this principle's impact on company-level success and profitability.

Consider this design question:

Do our productization efforts firmly lean on the end-to-end customer journey of our top customer group or two, framed as our prioritized use case?

Principle 5: Create value via comprehensive capabilities.

I often kick off productization discussions by using a planned city analogy. Some cities in the world are planned, and others aren't. Planned cities have guidelines that dictate their evolution. Drone views of such cities make it obvious that there is a design and a longer-term vision behind them.

Then there are unplanned cities. An aerial view of such cities gives us little comfort that there was any method behind the madness. Such landscapes are often built for the short-term goal of creating a big mall, a skyscraper, or large highways. The outcome is a traffic-heavy, pedestrian-unfriendly, and public transportation lacking landscape. Essentially, the freedom to build has created an unwieldy patchwork. Unplanned cities are a microcosm of an incongruent ecosystem.

Offerings can be designed using either a planned or unplanned city mindset. The former results in an offering that solves the root cause of customer needs and can be organically evolved to support macroevolutions to keep up with time, scale, and environmental shifts. It also limits customer value outflow. The latter approach implies a patchwork of short-term symptom-solving efforts that eventually become unscalable and leave customers with higher value outflows.

We now know that we must strive to serve a specific customer journey, which is our use case. The shaded middle pathway in Figure C5 illustrates the use case for our top customer group. Regardless of the market and the use case we focus on, the customer journey can always be represented as a continuous flow. The steps and transitions in this illustrative journey represent the path that the customer flows through without our company's involvement. An effective customer journey flow will frame every step and transition such that each such activity has tangible benefits and challenges that the customer is experiencing. In aggregate, it adds up to the customer's entire experience.

Now, let's superimpose two rules of thumb to create optimal value.

The **first** rule of thumb is to avoid trying to address the entire span of the use case, however tempting that might be. Every use case in the world is broad, whether it is a simple consumer home-based exercise flow or a more complex customer journey in a business setting. The entire use case will require a broad set of strengths that even a conglomerate of several Single Market Problem Entities might not have. So, stretching our limits to address all steps and hand-offs in the use case will distract us from effectively productizing the parts of the use case that we are strong enough to address. Increasing our coverage may eventually be possible once we dominate a narrow area of focus. However, low net customer value with broad coverage is not the path to sustainability and definitely not domination.

The **second** rule of thumb is to focus intently on addressing the root causes that trigger symptoms throughout the use case. Don't solve symptoms. Root causes congregate in specific parts of the use case. So, our offering maximizes net positive customer value by comprehensively handling the specific portion of the use case that holds the root cause. Where do

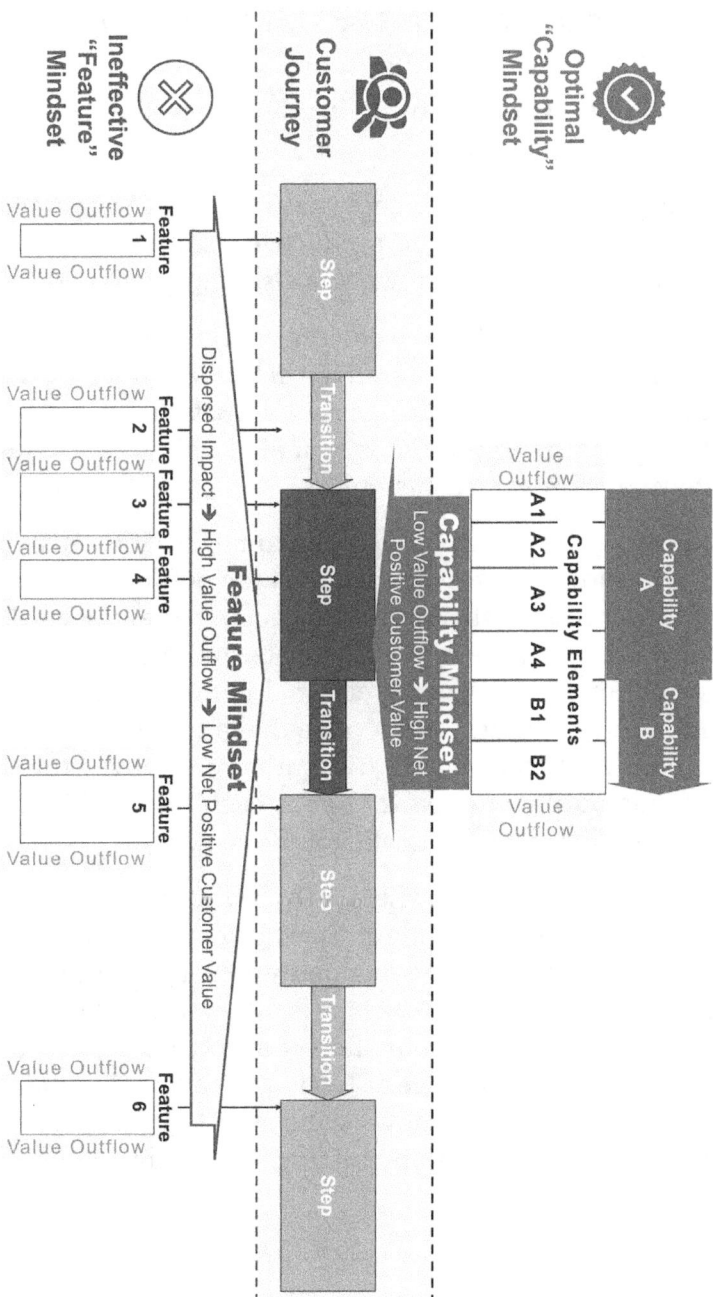

Figure C5. Capability mindset enables net positive customer value.

demolition experts put each explosive? They place it in load-bearing spots. The root causes are our load-bearing spots.

Capabilities and **Features** are two critical concepts that we need to learn to optimize value creation in a use case.

Capability is an important concept that we want to embrace and use throughout our method to help us productize effectively. We want to avoid using a feature mentality, and thus, it is also important to understand.

Creating a feature by itself is like putting up a residential condominium building without much thought to what will be around it. Yes, the building is fine. But what if there is nothing around the building we can walk to, and the traffic congestion in the area makes using a car a nightmare? Features have this impact on customers.

Disconnected features do not create much net positive customer value because each feature causes significant value outflows from customers as they try to incorporate that narrow widget into their journey. Outflows are the equivalent of friction or a tax for customers to use our offering as we covered under the multidirectional nature of value theme. This outflow often negates much of the value that a standalone feature could create. In Figure C5, the shaded friction points convey the incredible customer value outflow necessary to use each feature. Therefore, this is a counterproductive productization approach.

If we build many such narrow widgets, they become unmanageable over time because our cost to maintain these disconnected widgets would increase. i.e., if we create features, our delivery cost per customer will likely rise as we sell to more customers, which is the opposite of what we want. It also becomes harder to mature our offering on top of disconnected existing features. Imagine playing a game of Tetris and having a jumbled base that covers most of the playing window. Features leave us with a disorganized Tetris base that prevents us from building effectively on top.

> **Things To Remember: Feature**
>
> **A feature is a creation in our productization effort that focuses on customer wants and symptom-solving. A feature is a narrow widget that solves a symptom without effectively considering the whole market problem or its root cause.**

Have you ever felt an overall body ache, while the source is a single knot in your back muscle that connects to those other achy parts? Ironing out that knot releases the pain from the rest of your body.

A capability addresses the root causes in the market by analytically transforming customer wants into needs. Thus, a capability is a solution that intentionally addresses the specific portion of the use case that causes the customers' broader challenges.

> **Things To Remember: Capability**
>
> **A capability is a comprehensive solution to the root causes of the market problem associated with our use case. It is an intentional and organized productization approach that enables scalability, maximizes positive net customer value, and limits wasteful investments in symptom-solving.**

Think of a capability as a modular construct that can replace an entire portion of a use case that triggers most of the customers' symptoms. This is a far superior approach for two reasons.

First, a capability is a plug-and-play approach that creates far more positive net customer value by addressing one comprehensive part of the use case. Given its modular nature, integrating a capability into customers' natural flow requires fewer integration points between our solution and the customer's journey. Each intersection causes value outflow for customers. Fewer transitions for a capability imply far more net positive customer value.

Second, capabilities are the only path to scalability. Symptoms of the market problem are very personal and unique because they are interpretations and feelings that change from one customer to another. However, root causes across divergent symptoms shared by many customers are often the same because they are objective and non-interpretive. A capability addresses a root cause that spans our optimal customers, allowing reproducibility.

Choosing a specific capability as our value creation path implies laying out a long-term productization plan. This allows us to organize our design and build our offering with a long-term view. A capability's superior reproducibility means our cost to deliver value to an increasing number of customers would be far more amenable compared to symptom-solving features, which lead to unsustainability due to the escalating cost of serving new customers.

So, our productization effort must always focus on creating one or two comprehensive capabilities that drive positive net customer value. Conversely, avoid a slew of features that cause significant value outflow from customers and result in little positive net customer value.

For instance, a hypothetical metals manufacturer embracing the capability mindset may productize ten metal tools sold as a single set targeting urban homeowners. The same manufacturer operating with a features mindset may create ten metal widgets that go into different uses in a home and are sold individually.

I worked closely with a software company that focused on an end-to-end invoice data extraction and processing use case. The use case spanned identifying source invoice documents, gathering those documents, extracting the data, and storing the data in a software platform. The company then transposed the data to connect with other non-invoice customer data, delivered the transposed data to customers, and generated takeaways from that entire data set.

That is an enormous span to cover, even for conglomerates. Unfortunately, this company set expectations with customers that it would cover the entire end-to-end flow. These were good intentions, but they were impossible to accomplish.

The company deployed a narrow widget to address every part of this customer journey because the customer felt pain everywhere. One widget tried to gather documents but missed many. Another widget tried to highlight missing documents ineffectively. One widget was an extraction method that resulted in low data accuracy. Other widgets tried to interlink invoice data and non-invoice data with limited effectiveness.

Essentially, almost all widgets left alarm bells ringing for customers and the company's value creators working with customers. The reality was that customers could never remove themselves from any one of these steps in their workflow. Dealing with several transitions back and forth from the customer's natural flow to support each widget caused too much value outflow for customers. It cost the company too much to deliver all these widgets and deal with perpetual customer dissatisfaction. This epitomizes challenges with a feature mindset.

With a capability mindset, the company would have served this use case much more effectively. The biggest value creation opportunity was the document acquisition and data extraction step. This single step was the root cause of timing delays and data quality symptoms throughout the use case.

If the company had only taken responsibility for consistent document acquisition and high-quality data extraction while leaving all the other steps to the customer to continue in their existing journey, the odds of net positive customer value creation would have been much higher. Customers would have been able to completely offload this step from their journey and thus embrace the comprehensive impact with limited value outflow to use this capability.

But this didn't happen. Customers churned off when they realized that even a low price wasn't worth the net negative value they received. Customers found it frustrating that they still had fires to put out throughout the entire flow. Eventually, the company stopped serving this entire use case and terminated the employees involved in the manual processing steps.

It is necessary to distinguish between features and capabilities because sustainability and profitability are unlikely without a capability mindset. However, it is significantly easier and more tempting to create features rather than capabilities. It's alluring for three reasons.

First, the most common source of feature creation is customer complaints or customer wants. Customers share their feelings, not root causes and solutions. Companies often do not demonstrate thought leadership and create features to address symptoms. The best-case scenario here is that we have added something that makes a few customers happy in the short term. However, congruent value exchange requires us to solve the root causes of customer problems.

Second, value creators build solutions, and no individual will ever complete an entire capability design and commercialization alone. So, individualism can tempt each value creator or small team to talk about small widgets that they can quickly create and feel proud of.

Third, suppose the company hasn't embraced the power of a Comparative Advantage Ecosystem that we covered under our organization design lever. What if the productization responsibility sits with a value creator or team that is more experienced in detailed execution instead of wearing a customer-first hat to identify the optimal use case and focus on a capability mindset? We are more likely to end up with features.

Operating in a customer-first and capability-focused mindset requires a mature organization that can internalize the principles we are covering and ensure that all our productization efforts focus on net positive customer value. This mindset allows us to expand to a second comprehensive capability over time because customers are already committed to us.

If we are going to build a capability, we need to understand its innate nature.

Principle 6: All capabilities are multidimensional.

Imagine that our office hired a landscaping company to plant trees. What exactly is the capability they delivered? Is it the tree? Is it the act of planting it? Is it expertise to make sure the trees take root? Is it a promise that the trees won't fall over on people or cars the next day? Yes, yes, yes, and yes.

Figure C6 illustrates the multidimensional nature of a capability. Any solution that creates value comprises one or more of four dimensions – object, action, knowledge, and promise. In our complex world, we almost never consume in one of these dimensions anymore. Instead, everything we consume is a complex permutation of these four mutually exclusive and collectively exhaustive dimensions.

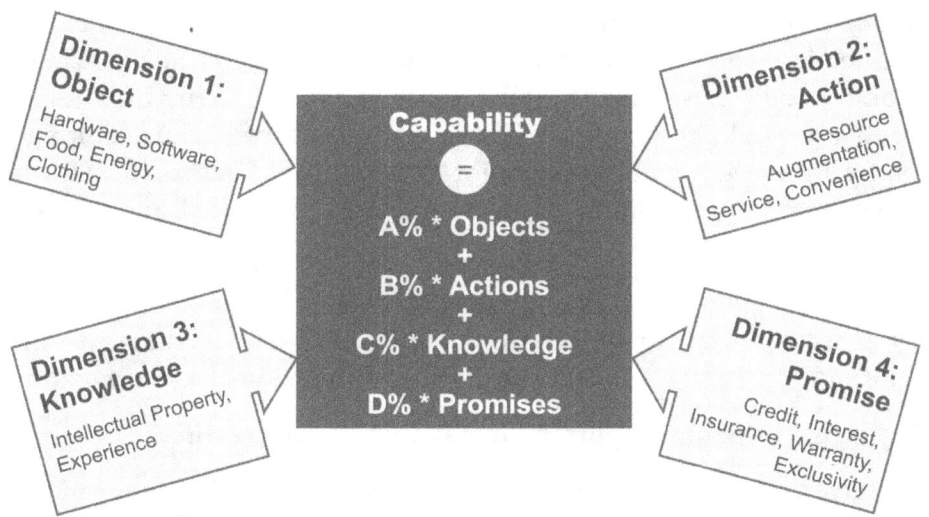

Figure C6. Capabilities are multidimensional.

The first dimension is **Object**. All goods in the world fall into this dimension, including the food we consume, the energy we use, the physical phone we have, and our phone's software operating system.

The second dimension is **Action**. We gain value from others performing actions on our behalf, whether it's due to convenience or our inability to perform it.

The third dimension is **Knowledge**. We don't know everything. We must depend on others to give us information, whether it is their licensable intellectual property or their know-how due to their experience.

The fourth dimension is **Promise**. This intangible category includes bidirectional promises. For example, an institution might give us money today in exchange for us paying interest or vice versa. Alternately, we sign insurance contracts and pay someone else to mitigate risk. A warranty is a promise of quality. Even restricted access to a thing or an action can be considered a promise of exclusivity.

It is nearly impossible to create positive net customer value in our complex world by focusing only on one of these dimensions. Therefore, every effective capability is a solution that spans multiple dimensions.

I hired editors to help me put the finishing touches on this book. I am gaining value from their intellectual property as writers and their experience helping others like me. What if my editors only offered advice? I might be able to edit myself if they tell me how. However, using their advice effectively would cause me significant value outflow because editing is not my strength. My net value might be negative if I get frustrated with the process. So, my editors also perform the action of editing the book through my grammatical mistakes.

There is a tinge of warranty in our relationship because we set up our payment terms to ensure we are making progress before I pay for the work. As a single customer, I seek three of these dimensions from my editors.

Why is this principle important to maximize value creation?

For a given root cause, there can be a range of solutions that could all have the same impact from a customer perspective. In our multidimensional approach, we could potentially create the same value for the customer by focusing heavily on any of the dimensions while augmenting with the others.

Think about a polynomial equation with four variables. We can change the constants for the variables to achieve the same specific solution. The solution here is our capability, and the variables are the four dimensions.

Amazon offers free shipping with a predefined guarantee on the delivery timeframe for customers paying for Prime shipping. Essentially, this seamless delivery is an Amazon capability that solves all sorts of divergent customer challenges. As customers, do we care whether this delivery happens through the United States Postal Service (USPS), Amazon's direct fulfillment staff, or flying robots? In fact, Amazon used to deliver Prime packages through the USPS. Then, they transitioned to using their own staff and vehicles. Regardless of how Amazon delivers its packages, its Prime capability is to deliver the package for free within a given timeframe.

Amazon shifted from operating in the promises dimension of signing contracts with USPS to the action dimension of delivering themselves to whichever dimension we want to put flying robots in. The multidimensional principle allows us to evolve the contributing dimensions of our capability to become more scalable and profitable. If done well, it could be seamless for our customers.

Conversely, embracing a capability's multidimensional nature is not optional. Creating a comprehensive capability in only one dimension is nearly impossible.

At the invoice data software company, my team owned and managed customers. The company thought of and sold its software as the "product." However, the software portion also had many of the challenges I described. My team tried to reactively add a vast array of action and knowledge dimension aspects to address persistent customer value outflows. Yet we struggled to keep customers happy because the company had a single-dimensional capability mindset focused on software.

So, we must think of productization as the act of creating a multidimensional solution to the root cause of customer problems that we can evolve and mature over time. This brings us to the last customer value creation principle: *How do we commercialize a capability?*

Principle 7: Customer value is always consumed as a commercialized package with a price.

We made a somewhat controversial decision earlier that we wouldn't use the word "product." So, here is the final nail in that coffin. A customer never buys our "product." In simple words, a customer gets what we sell.

Regardless of the market, use case, and specific root cause we are addressing, our customers always consume a commercialized version of our productized offering. The only question is whether we have commercialized well or whether our commercialization is ad hoc and reactive. Commercialization is the last step of our productization path, and it has two elements: **Packaging** and **Pricing**.

Staying with Peloton, the company introduced a corporate wellness angle to its offering in 2021 as employees working from home returned to the office. Did Peloton introduce a new capability here? No. Almost everything about their capabilities remained the same except for creating a new package and price to sell to companies to reach their employees, unlike previous packages sold directly to consumers.

Customers buy our packages at the price we set. Let's explore both these elements further.

Optimal packages balance customer value via complementary capabilities.

We covered the importance of a capability mindset to create tangible value and avoid feature creation. We also framed the importance of creating multidimensional capabilities that comprehensively address root causes in our chosen use case. There is a nuance we must incorporate.

There is only a very small chance of creating a capability that perfectly fits our chosen use case for our optimal customer group. Think about it this way – even the best capabilities have seasonality or customer-level variation in value.

First, we are productizing for our optimal customers. As we will discuss further under Part D: Corporate Strategy, even our optimal customers aren't exactly the same. There are likely at least a couple of similar groups that form our optimal customer. Further still, each customer will be different within each of those groups, even to a small extent. So, no two customers have precisely the same customer journey, which means we are asking both to make a small adjustment.

Second, no customer will ever value a given capability exactly the same at all times. Unless it's the air we breathe, we just don't use anything else 100 percent of the time, including water. So, how does this time-based variation in value delivery impact the net customer value?

How do we deploy our ever-maturing capabilities to create optimal net customer value while accounting for customer-level difference and seasonality? The answer is packaging.

Customers always buy packages. Packages allow us to normalize value delivery to each customer and across customers. Packages help us solve both the time-based and customer-level variation in value realization.

> **Things To Remember: Packaging**
>
> **Packaging is the act of creating a figurative customer-facing box with more than one complementary capability to normalize the net value created over time and across customers. Packaging allows us to sell the same box to our optimal customers while minimizing the variance in value extracted over time and between customers.**

Amazon Prime is an extraordinarily effective package that delivers at least two effective capabilities. I signed up for the Prime package almost fifteen years ago, thinking that free shipping would be valuable. It turns out I don't buy that much stuff. But I continue to be a Prime customer. Why? I attribute about half the value of the Prime package to Prime Video, which is Amazon's version of streaming services included in the Prime package. When I buy something where I get free shipping, I am willing to overlook the lack of quality shows on Prime Video. When I find a decent show to watch on Prime, I don't mind that I haven't shipped anything for free for a while. Prime is a package that accounts for my personal seasonality.

Similarly, a customer who buys a lot online but never watches Prime Video also gets a lot from the Prime package. What if a customer enjoys a lot of Prime shows but rarely shops on Amazon? The Prime package takes these customer-level differences into account.

Packaging is a necessary value-optimizing step to commercialize our capability because there will always be at least a small gap between our capability and the customer journey.

Sadly, most popular packaging efforts fail to focus on creating customer value. Common discounting activities such as "Buy 3, Get 1 Free" are psychological nudges to encourage customers to overbuy, likely creating waste and essentially causing negative customer value.

An example of value destruction through packaging is shrinkflation where retail offerings are sold in the exact same packet with the same price, but the volume of content is reduced. A packet sold with 16 oz. of walnuts last week could be sold for the same price next week with only 14 oz in the packet, and the customer may not notice because the packet has not changed except for the volume noted in small font.

Another non-value-focused packaging is to bundle together items that may not complement each other but create the same psychological nudge for customers as discounts where they buy more hoping it's a good deal. This is also a sales tactic and not necessarily geared towards the value extracted.

Non-value-focused packaging efforts will likely create more incongruence between value and price for customers. These efforts only work in highly commoditized environments or situations where customers lack choices due to oligopolies.

Our focus with effective packaging is to deliver consistent value across customers and over time, not sales tricks. There is a massive difference.

Consider this design question to develop effective packaging:

Based on 1) the cadence at which each customer will likely extract the intended value, and 2) the variance in value that different customers might extract at peak use, which complementary capabilities can be packaged to smooth net value delivered across customers and maintain value delivered over time?

A marketing software company that I worked with developed a capability to deliver executive-level awareness about the effectiveness of the customers' marketing expenses. But this capability had a value creation cadence of once in six months or longer for most customers. It meant most customers were only learning something new every six months or so. There was also a large variance in the value customers extracted because some customers managed their marketing expenses far more actively than others. So, many customers stopped using this capability after a couple of cycles because they weren't learning new information often enough.

The company had a second capability that offered daily actionable suggestions for responding to marketing leads. The actionable suggestions from the second capability allowed customers to extract frequent tactical value. However, the value created by this capability may not have been used by the operations teams if the overarching measurements were not delivered to executives through the first capability.

Both capabilities had limitations. We packaged both capabilities together, and they augmented each other. This package normalized the value delivery frequency and the net value delivered across customers.

Embracing the power of packaging to address time-based variation in value delivery and customer-level variation in value realization allows us to maximize, maintain, and sustain customer value.

Leverage value-based pricing.

Finally, to sell our package to our customers, we have to price it. In today's highly transparent world, where every entity has a website and third-party sources of price and value comparisons are ubiquitous, pricing is a more critical lever than ever.

Website messages and social media can create perceptions about value. Any company can purchase rating services and reviews. Misinformation has always existed, but each new tool introduced to help companies sell makes it even more prevalent. So, how do we price our package in our ridiculously competitive world?

Customers understand value because they are acutely aware of the market problem they live with. They are willing to pay for the value they can extract, and pricing is a monetary translation of that value. To build the best version of our company, we must stay focused on congruent value exchange.

This also means avoiding temptations to overstate the value of our offerings or misdirect customers about competitive offerings in our highly public selling ecosystem. I have never found these to be sustainable, and they are also ethically questionable.

Hooking a customer with undeliverable expectations is more likely to hurt us than help. It's the equivalent of stepping into quicksand. Every oversold customer is an increasingly heavier burden to create value for, which distracts us from improving our offerings or selling to more customers.

With that, let's price our package.

The only reference points in a market are us, our competitors, and the customer. Pricing based on the first two reference points results in unsustainable and unprofitable business models. Our only sustainable option is to focus on our customers and the net value we create and increase that net value. This allows us to increase our pricing, which, in turn, enables our company to increase revenue and profit.

Our first option is to set pricing for our offering based on our operations. This is generally called **Cost-Based Pricing**. In this mode, the company adds up the expenses incurred to build and deliver the offering to the customer and adds a margin on top to set the price.

The practical manifestation of cost-based pricing starts with a feature mindset. In this mode, we are likely selling disparate single-dimensional features, trivializing our value to customers as a collection of widgets. Here, we expect the customer to figure out how to draw value from our widgets. Customers will think about our widgets as commodities they can shop around for because they understand value more than we do.

There are two primary problems with cost-based pricing. **First**, if we price based on cost, we will inadvertently share our cost model with customers because we haven't enabled our sellers to discuss value. We are inviting unnecessary downward pressure on price because the customer knows exactly how we create our package.

I often advise companies that customers don't need to know the sausage-making process. Effective packaging and pricing let us talk about the quality and taste of the sausage rather than nickel and dime based on what it cost us to create it. Once the customer knows how the costs add up, they will find ways to question each cost component and shrink the offering's profit margin.

The **second** problem is that we will never be able to raise the price beyond periodic inflation adjustments if we anchor it to the cost. So, we can only improve our profit in this mode if we reduce our costs. But the cost can only go down so far. Thus, we have severely constrained our ability to use one of the two key levers to make money – price.

Our second option is to arrive at a pricing model based on our competitors. This is a war of attrition. **Competition-Based Pricing** is most common when our value creation is not unique among our competitors.

Alternatively, if we do not understand the customer journey and the effectiveness with which our offering addresses it, we might feel insecure and feel the need to defend ourselves against our competitors. This is especially true if we operate in a very story-focused environment instead of a value-focused one. Customers will always test us on our value proposition and our pricing by comparing us to others in the market.

Objective self-awareness determines our confidence in addressing customer probes about comparisons with competitors. Beyond playing in a market with trivial low-value offerings, a lack of confidence in the value created by our offering is usually the primary reason for operating in a competition-based pricing model.

Our third and preferred option is to focus on our customers and set pricing based on the value we create for them. This third option is known as **Value-Based Pricing**. Value-based pricing is a congruent mindset with our customers where we are taking a cut of the loot. If we create value for customers by addressing their market problem, it is only fair that we can extract a portion of the value attributed to the problem we solve.

> **Things To Remember: Value-Based Pricing**
>
> **Value-based pricing focuses on monetizing the upside we create for our customers by addressing the market problem. Therefore, customers are willing to pay for value upside that directly links to the market problem, regardless of the cost to create the solution.**

To embrace value based pricing, we must understand the incremental value that our customer group can create if we solve the market problem in the use case. The better our package addresses the root cause of the market problem, the higher the value we are creating.

Why could Peloton price its bikes and treadmills significantly higher than anyone else in the market in its early days? They primarily sought a customer group that values each saved hour of time. The customer group was willing to share a portion of that increased value with Peloton regardless of what it costs Peloton to make and ship a bike and create programming.

A counterexample can be found in book editing services. Every quote I received for my book editing request was a competition-based price with only a 15 percent difference between the highest and lowest quotes. Do I believe they all offer similar value? Absolutely not! In fact, I am willing to offer an incentive model where the editor can get a share of the earnings because it is a win-win to create the most optimal outcome.

Rational customers are happy to embrace a value-based model if we take the time to understand the value we are collectively creating and our contribution to that overall value. This requires our value creators and investors to see customers as part of our company, not as outsiders.

Use the questions below to gather information, analyze, and arrive at pricing figures that can be tested with customers. Quantifying the monetary value associated with each portion of a use case isn't easy. Our alternative is to sell our productized offering with an unsustainable cost-based or competition-based pricing model. So, it's worth taking the time to answer these questions.

Consider these design questions to determine a fair price based on the value we deliver:

Can we quantitatively map the value flow throughout our customer's journey, particularly parts of the use case we are addressing?

How much value outflow do our customers incur without our involvement?

How effective and differentiated is our package in addressing the root cause of the problem, and how much incremental value would we create?

How much value outflow would our customers incur when using our package and underlying capabilities?

How effectively does our package normalize value delivered over time and across customers?

Using the above, can we quantify the net positive value we create at any given point in time and from the perspective of our most demanding optimal customers?

What is a fair share of the quantifiable net positive value that our more demanding customers feel is reasonable to share with us as our price?

The high-level considerations above will help us quantify the positive value we create for customers. Our path is to quantify practical activities and decisions. Getting carried away by tagging dollar signs to nebulous perceptions or storylines will lead us to overestimate the value we create and overprice. This will hurt sales and customer satisfaction. As we are trying to serve many customers who derive slightly different value, it is important to price based on the value delivered to the more demanding ones.

One of the key impediments to value-based pricing is a lack of effective productization. If we cannot internalize the concept of repeatability and reproducibility, we will never arrive at a scalable offering. Without scalability, our cost of creating customer value will inflate with new customers. This increasing cost will distract us from focusing on the value we create for customers. Our price-setting approach will then quickly become operations-focused, and we fall into a defensive mode of ensuring that we meet our cost to survive. This leaves us with a cost-based pricing model.

I have worked with multiple companies that use the term "value-based pricing" but have a cost- or competition-based pricing in reality because they didn't follow the principles we discussed. Operating in either of these pricing models implies that our value is largely commoditized or our productization is ineffective. Once we enter this cycle of cost-based pricing or competition-based pricing, it is a downward spiral that is almost impossible to get out of unless we hope to be the last one standing in the marketplace, which isn't a sustainable mindset.

So, we must productize and become highly effective in understanding the value our packages create for customers so that we do not doubt that our value-based pricing is fair.

Most companies struggle to internalize the customer-first mindset as well as appreciate the importance of solving the root cause of the market problem. Our starting point is understanding the customer journey and focusing on an optimal use case. Then, we must productize a capability to drive positive net customer value. Finally, effective packaging to optimize net customer value and embracing value-based pricing are necessary to commercialize and deploy our offering.

These principles articulate the quality of the offering that spearheads our value engine. An offering that maximizes net positive value for customers increases congruence across all our stakeholders. We must constantly micro-evolve our offering's alignment with the use case we are serving and create increasingly higher customer value.

Now, let's talk about how to deliver our offerings.

C.2
ENABLE CAPITAL EFFICIENCY VIA
REPEATABLE, REPRODUCIBLE PROCESS.

WE have the right people and the right offering. We compared our offering to the value-creating payload of a missile targeting our customer.

Countries spend decades developing and reimagining their long-range missile capabilities, even if they have a powerful payload. Our offering can only create customer value for a large portion of our addressable market if we employ effective operational processes, technology to support those processes, and data to enable improvements and decision-making. Together, these components complete our value engine.

We categorized our people, technology, and other assets into operations and enablement resources and supervisors for each group under organization design. Operations resources perform all the ongoing activities. This spans all functions from marketing, sales, customer management, ongoing management of our offering, finance, human resources, and any other activities that we need to deliver customer value. The specific tactics for these ongoing activities are almost exclusively dependent on our offering and the market we serve. But several fundamental principles drive the maturity of processes and data across the company.

In this chapter, we will focus on **Process**. Like many other common words used in business environments, the meaning of "process" has undergone unhelpful distortions. So, let's formalize it.

> **Things To Remember: Process**
>
> **Process is the well-articulated set of guidelines, criteria, and conditions that we expect performers (employees, customers, or partners) to execute or we design technologies to replicate. Processes are intended to achieve behaviors that are repeatable (the same performer executes the same way every time) and reproducible (several performers execute the same way every time) and ensure our company uses investment in people, technology, and other assets optimally.**

Most companies talk about process rigor and support its criticality. However, some consider it a growth killer, creativity destroyer, or momentum staller.

These anti-process sentiments have been prevalent in environments that prioritize capital engineering. They incorrectly presume that creativity and structure cannot coexist. The truth is that creativity without discipline sends us down an unsustainable trajectory. So, let's start with a fresh outlook by framing common misconceptions around processes.

Principle 1: Overcome myths and awareness gaps around processes.

A strong process mindset makes everyone's life easier and creates more value for companies. No company grows slower because of process rigor; we don't value a company less because they are operationally excellent.

So, why does the concept of process get so much flak? Let's explore the common myths.

Myth 1: Process slows us down.

Many entrepreneurs try many ideas. Many of them fail, and some find a fit between their idea and a market need. An entrepreneur must be agile in the early stages to find a fit between their ideas and the market as they stumble around in the dark with one or two people. Running a company beyond the early stages requires a mindset change where discipline becomes just as important as agility.

Discipline in a company takes the form of processes. A clear understanding of processes enables operations to move extremely fast, not slower. Is a well-mapped and well-traveled path easier or harder to take than stumbling through an arbitrary, untraveled one? Obviously, the former.

Saying that processes slow operations down is like saying that it is faster to get in a car and start driving immediately without looking up directions or knowing the roads. Usually, it results in drivers taking wrong turns and stumbling their way to the destination, if at all. Operations resources in companies are analogous to individual drivers.

Well-defined processes remedy the need for individual discovery of optimal paths. They allow value creators performing similar tasks to follow predefined directions on the fastest route to reach the desired destination quickly and at similar times. The Company Way is essentially point-to-point directions created for operations resources through enablement initiatives, which we will discuss in the final two parts of our method.

Myth 2: Process design is resource intensive.

Cleaning up a mess is different from doing it correctly the first time.

Misconceptions around process development and adoption arise from confusing process design and process reengineering. Process design is a proactive effort to run an efficient organization that starts well before poor operational behaviors have taken root and outcomes have started failing. Process reengineering is a cure for past sins where an organization exists in operational chaos and outcomes have suffered.

Process reengineering efforts are far more demanding because they require change management to revert poor behaviors that may have taken root, which is onerous.

Imagine that your car stalled on the road. Do you think you can put your car in neutral and push the car? Most people can make some headway with effort. Now imagine that same car moving at even ten miles per hour. How about trying to slow down that car and move it in the opposite direction? It is much harder or somewhat impossible.

In physics, inertia is the force that helps objects continue on their current path. Human beings also demonstrate inertia by continuing to do things the way they have always done them. As a result, managing change is challenging. We have dedicated a chapter to it under Part F: Execution Management for this reason. Most myths around the difficulty of building a process mindset come from stories where companies were struggling to reengineer poor behaviors and dealing with the high cost of change management.

Myth 3: Process design is an option.

The choice isn't whether we define processes or not – the company always has processes. The only option is whether they are good or bad. Even if a company chooses not to mature the day-to-day activities of its critical teams, value creators are doing things. Unfortunately, the default state is *Level 1: Chaos,* where every employee chooses their own way and leaves the organization in operational chaos.

Every person develops good or bad habits, and we can change them as we wish. Unfortunately, process chaos leaves the company in a state where it cannot explain what value creators are actually doing or which activities are working well. So, our only choice is to improve upon the default state of operational chaos, where individuals and groups of individuals operate their own way and not The Company Way.

In addition to overcoming such myths, our process mindset will be most effective if we understand and communicate its overwhelming benefits.

Principle 2: Internalize the benefits of a process mindset.

The temptation to ride a company growth wave without developing consistent operational behaviors is understandable because it is easier, but it is not advisable. Lack of behavioral consistency is a considerable tax. Problem-solving and microevolutions of our operations are impossible without processes. So, let's dive deeper into the benefits of a process mindset.

No data without process.

Often, data and process are considered separate concepts. Nothing could be farther from the truth, and this misconception often undermines the amount of effort that goes into process design. Data is nothing more than an ongoing recording of measurements associated with behaviors demonstrated during specific steps in processes. These measurements are only meaningful if we design the process well and the performers have adopted the design and executed it as expected. Conversely, measurements are practically useless if the underlying behaviors are not well-defined or not adopted.

Let's imagine that a restaurant employee has the simple role of counting the number of people visiting the establishment. An establishment with an immature value engine will ask the employee to count. What is likely to happen when the employee counts? What if different employees are handling this role on different days?

There are several ambiguities that these employees face even in such a simple experiment where they are forced to do it their own way. An example of ambiguity is the exact definition of a visitor to the establishment. Should the employee count someone who enters the main door, peeks inside, and leaves without entering further? What if a visitor looks at the menu to understand the prices and then exits without making a purchase? Should the employee count neither of them, one of them, or both? Every employee who performs this role will have a personal perspective of the correct definition of a visitor.

If you are an analyst at this establishment's head office, how dependable are these daily tallies if you are trying to understand how visitor volume changes from one day to the next?

If you are an analyst at heart, you know what I am talking about. Making sense of information and making decisions from it is fraught with risks. We could call the information from the above scenario a "bad" data set. But the truth is that data is just data. It is the underlying process that is bad.

One of the most important reasons to have well-defined processes is to capture coherent data, allowing us to understand the real state of affairs objectively.

Processes improve the efficiency of operations resources and supervisors.

A strong process mindset enables operations resources to focus on executing their core strengths that drive the most value. Leaving operations resources and their supervisors to stumble through and find a path to achieve expected outcomes leads to incongruence with how our offering is delivered and how we manage value creators, not to mention inefficiency in the use of investment. Operations resources and supervisors would lose significant time and mindshare away from their core strengths and likely trigger poor outcomes due to no fault of their own.

As a practical example, sales reps should focus on selling activities with prospects outside the company and closing deals. However, in a process vacuum, many sales reps spend too much time on internal design activities or mapping out their own selling steps. A company where sales reps spend a large share of their time not interacting with prospective customers is essentially throwing away a significant portion of revenue potential. In turn, the company will end up hiring several more sales reps to meet sales goals compared to an operationally efficient environment. This unnecessary spending on additional sales reps also takes investment away from improving our offerings or marketing efforts to find more prospects.

To add insult to injury, a supervisor to those sales reps can likely only manage fewer sales reps than at a company with a strong process mindset. Even an effective sales supervisor will have to spend much more time managing each rep in a company with a weak process mindset. Every rep operates differently, and there are no economies of scale for the supervisor's activities. Now, we have a company that also needs more sales supervisors on staff due to poor sales processes, compounding the company's woes around investment efficiency and quality of value creation.

Figure C7 illustrates the heavy toll of a weak process mindset, which requires more operations resources and supervisors. The weak process mindset environment on the right side of this visual illustrates why labor productivity is lower in such conditions. This is a practical manifestation of the unsustainable path where the cost of delivering value accelerates faster than the value created.

Strong Process Mindset
High Capital Efficiency

Weak Process Mindset
Low Capital Efficiency

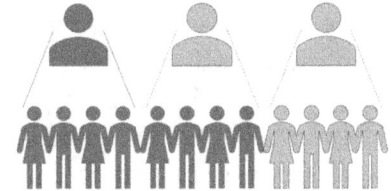

Figure C7. Capital efficiency demands a strong process mindset.

A strong process mindset allows operations employees to focus strictly on value-creating activities that are core to their role and align with their skills.

Operations resources must be empowered with The Company Way Processes, which articulates solutions to repetitive problems. This prevents each employee from wasting time solving similar problems independently. A process mindset doesn't just create efficiencies; it eliminates significant waste, allowing for increased focus on customer acquisition and value creation initiatives.

Process design is a necessary problem-solving frame of reference.

Imagine getting lost in a huge shopping mall while looking for a specific store. What do we do? We look for a map of the mall. The map orients us, tells us where we are in the enormous complex, and tells us how to get where we need to go. Well-documented processes serve the same purpose in operational problem-solving.

If a specific operational problem arises, key players get together and discuss the problem and how to solve it. But how do these individuals communicate their understanding of the current state? Too often, senior executives, supervisors, and individual contributors talk in circles about operational problems and have little success explaining their perspectives to each other. This happens because there is no frame of reference that everyone can look at and work from to understand each other and solve problems. That frame of reference is a well-articulated process design.

We must codify process designs to ensure they can be reviewed, understood, disagreed with, iterated, and improved. Once such a codified definition that articulates The Company Way exists, problem-solving can start by using this articulation as the frame of reference.

A process mindset is the first and foundational step to maturing as a congruent organization. After sidestepping common design pitfalls, we can deploy a streamlined set of principles to develop operational processes quickly and effectively. But before we explore the core principles of process design, let's avoid a few common design mistakes.

Principle 3: Avoid common process design mistakes.

A few common mistakes typically set back efforts to mature The Company Way Processes.

Avoid trivializing operational expertise.

We wouldn't try to diagnose and cure diseases with communal voting, would we?

We would go to a doctor with years of training in specific health conditions and parts of the human body. The only difference between a health issue and a business operation is that health issues impact us personally and could have serious and immediate ramifications on our lives. Business operations can feel less personal, and the impact can be slow-moving and may even only take hold after our association with the company. But that doesn't change the relevance of expertise in process design. Recall the Comparative Advantage Ecosystem principle. Process design requires designated experts with relevant experience.

Process design is more scientific and more studied than most other business areas. It has proven frameworks and formulae. People dedicate their careers to this space. So, do not hand off this critical responsibility to resources without relevant expertise.

The company must grant the ownership to develop a process mindset to an effective enablement resource with deep operations design skills. A Single Market Problem Entity only needs one primary process designer, who might also have other related analytical responsibilities. This resource ideally works under the guidance of our Congruence Architect. Spreading ownership will cost far more due to distracting and unnecessary involvement from too many individuals while causing incongruences across the company.

Do not succumb to a reactive top-down design.

As a company grows, senior executives naturally feel the need to understand what value creators are doing and what is working well. This implies looking at the company's quantitative information. However, senior executives often find that the required information doesn't exist because there is no process rigor to dictate data capture.

So, what happens next?

Senior executives often reactively urge the supervisors to collect the needed information. These supervisors, who are unlikely to be expert process designers, ask their operations resources to capture new information regularly; this ask essentially changes existing process.

The operations resources now have the additional responsibility of collecting new information during their existing day-to-day activities. Since this doesn't fit their usual activities, they tend to forget, ignore, or just do a poor job. Supervisors and senior executives are likely to scratch their heads trying to make sense of this poorly captured information or, worse, make decisions with it.

This is a common scenario that leads to more disruption and poor information in an ad hoc attempt to create process and data. This design mistake essentially ignores our flow thinking, which applies equally to value creator activities as it does to customers' worlds. Here, our process design customers are process performers.

Process design has three stakeholder groups. Process performers, which include internal operations employees, customers, and partners, are our primary stakeholders. Processes intend to give them more clarity and predictability and ease their path to achieve outcomes, not make it more complicated. An expert process designer will base the design on what works best for performers who execute day-to-day activities as long as it works in the company's interest.

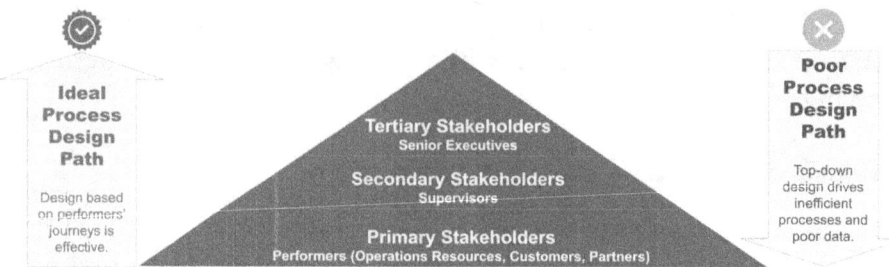

Figure C8. Effective process design focuses on performers' journey.

Supervisors and senior executives, who are secondary and tertiary stakeholders, respectively, will reap the benefit of proactively laid processes and learn from consistent and unbiased data captured seamlessly through the normal flow of process performers' execution. Figure C8 provides a visual reminder to prioritize process performers above supervisors' and senior executives' short-term needs when designing processes to achieve optimal results.

Do not forget that processes are alive.

We often misunderstand process design as a time-bound initiative. Although a process design effort will have milestones, it is never a one-and-done effort.

A mature operations baseline implies that we are continuously learning through our data and tactically improving the day-to-day process execution by value creators. These improvements are first reflected in the process design. Then, value creators adopt those improvements and execute them.

A common mistake is the temptation to make knee-jerk changes to execution without leading with appropriate objective assessments and codification of decisions through The Company Way. Reactive and hasty changes are typical of value engines that lean to the left side of our maturity model. When a problem arises, senior executives, supervisors, or operations resources might present off-the-cuff ideas to remedy the situation quickly.

These unproven ideas may feel like cohesive solutions in an undisciplined value engine. Suppose senior executives or supervisors ask operations resources to adopt such spontaneous ideas into their day-to-day execution while circumventing any analytical reasoning and without consulting the process design expert who originally designed the process. In that case, we are essentially breaking the process. Even a handful of such spontaneous changes, however small, can completely break down a simple and efficient process design and make it ineffective.

So, an effective process design will also include a governance approach owned and managed by the process design expert, where fast-paced objective analytical assessments and codification always lead to tactical improvements in design before execution changes begin. Doing nothing is often more effective than doing incorrect things.

Now, let's frame up what constitutes a good process design.

Principle 4: Leverage six design elements to build processes.

I spent my early years developing processes at several large conglomerates, and I can guarantee that it takes years of practice to get good at it. At the same time, every value creator needs to have a sense of a good process design so that they can demand improvement when they see gaps.

My proven approach to process design has six elements, and I've highlighted each of them in Figure C9. These six elements can be used to develop the foundational processes required at a company of any size. For each element, I will lay out a set of questions that you can use to determine your current process maturity, and you may use answers to those questions to drive improvements.

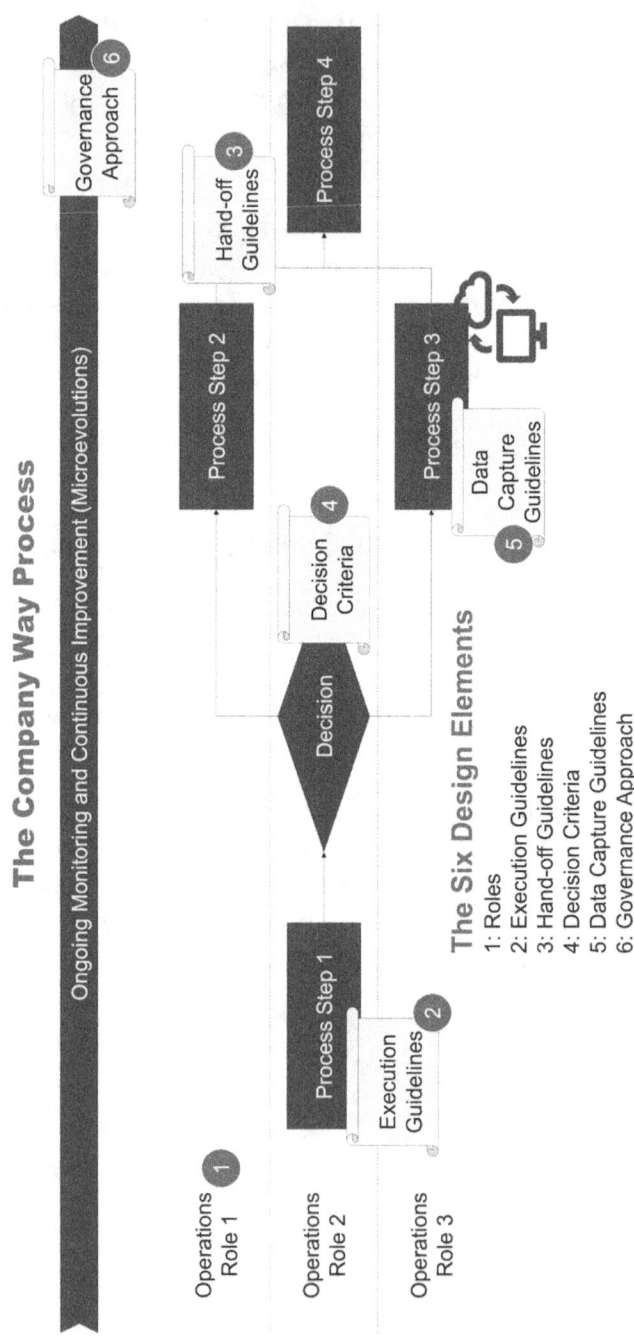

Figure C9. Effective process design has six elements.

Irrespective of your role, look around and assess whether process definitions account for at least these six elements. If not, have a conversation with your Congruence Architect or CEO. See what steps can be taken to achieve foundational process maturity that enables repeatability and reproducibility in operations execution and captures unbiased decision-making data.

Element 1: Cover all operations roles and their activities.

Operations employees, partners, and customers are our primary process design stakeholders. Therefore, the most important outcome of a process definition is that it communicates details of day-to-day execution to these stakeholders.

First, a process design must account for every performer role. If it doesn't cover all such day-to-day execution roles, many inefficiencies and incongruences will likely remain unaddressed. These roles will include individuals who are business customers or consumers buying from us, along with partners enabling value creation.

A common mistake is to focus only on high-volume roles such as sales reps or builders of our offerings, such as software developers or manufacturing line staff. This leaves significant holes in mapping our entire value creation flow.

Second, process design must clearly articulate the entire scope of every operations value creator role. Placing a microscope on some parts of each role is not enough. Process design intends to eliminate unnecessary work as much as it means to articulate the appropriate way to execute commonly discussed topics.

Consider these design questions to scope processes:

Do process designs cover all operations employee roles, customers, and partners to paint a complete value flow?

Does our process design include all execution efforts performed by operations employees, customers, and partners in the context of our offering as well as cover our management approach and data usage?

Asking these overarching questions gives a strong sense of the coverage of our process designs. At *Level 1: Chaos,* these are the first two questions we need to convert to "yes" to begin our process design effort.

Element 2: Execution guidelines dictate day-to-day actions.

Simplistically, we build a process by sequencing activities and decisions, which are steps. Each step should involve a set of instructions that can convert a given input to an output, whether a human or a machine performs it. A good process step with the appropriate execution guidelines delivers the same output every time, which indicates repeatability and reproducibility.

No human wants to feel that they are being micromanaged, and the intent of process design is not to do so. So, process design is also a prioritization exercise.

The designer must carefully choose which execution elements are most important to choreograph to achieve the outcomes without burdening process performers with too much direction. This awareness comes from the process designer's expertise in using operations technology as a process enabler and their understanding of manipulating unbiased data and performing analysis.

A process step must also have quantitative thresholds to monitor performance against. Without measurability, framing specific instructions is meaningless, as a process performer, supervisor, or analyst will not know whether execution meets expectations. We will discuss how to set such measurements in the next chapter.

Putting these two together, our second element of process design is that every process step must involve execution guidelines, which are specific instructions and measurements, to enable the same outcome every time the stakeholder in the role performs that step.

Consider these design questions to set execution guidelines:

What is the specific, measurable outcome expected from the execution of each step?

What is the prioritized set of key activities that qualifies the completeness of each step?

What does "good" look like for each activity?

If the process designer can articulate answers to these three questions for each process step, then the company's design effort is well on its way. Alternatively, take any process step and ask these three questions to see whether the answers are codified, communicated, and adopted to know whether your process design is effective.

Element 3: Prevent common vulnerabilities via hand-off guidelines.

If we watch team sports of any kind, when is a team most likely to make a mistake? Mistakes often happen when the ball passes from one player to the next. It is much more uncommon for a player to drop the ball or stumble over themselves. Company settings are not different. The probability of mistakes is relatively low if we look at one value creator's work in a vacuum, particularly with skilled, high performers.

Most operational breakdowns happen when one process performer hands off responsibility to another. This simple concept is common everywhere in nature. Where does a plumbing leak usually occur? The joints. So, it is critical to ask a few simple but highly effective questions to ensure that each hand-off in a process is pressure-tested.

Consider these design questions to assess hand-off effectiveness:

How will the preceding role logistically send the work to the succeeding role?

How will the role in the succeeding step know that work is being passed on?

Do specific actions need to be taken to confirm the hand-off?

Once the hand-off is complete, when should the succeeding role start working?

Is there a specific technology involved to record or simplify the hand-off?

These questions are not exhaustive. They get us started on asking hard questions about how interactions between two roles can fail and how we can articulate those remediations into process design.

Element 4: Decision criteria must be predetermined.

Knowing the future is difficult. So, articulating and making future decisions is also challenging. But that's the onus of effective process design. The enablement effort to design processes includes assessing available information, predicting the decisions that process performers might have to make, and proactively articulating that choice in the process design.

As a practical example, imagine an operations resource who handles inbound calls from prospective customers interested in buying the company's offerings. This role might have to decide to pass the call to the right sales team based on the type of customer. For example, if the company had two sales teams where one sold to large customers and the other sold to small customers, how would the call-handling process performer know what constitutes a potential large or small customer? The process design should articulate exactly what large and small mean for the process performer, how to find out whether the prospective customer is large or small, and what the performer should do if they cannot arrive at an answer.

Putting the onus of figuring out all the potential choices of answers and making the choice on the performer is not a good process design. Instead, to ensure reproducibility across several process performers with the same role, the process design must articulate the decisions that each step or hand-off entails.

Consider these design questions to optimize decision guidelines:

What decisions might a performer have to make to move forward to the next step in the process?

Does the performer have permission to complete the task, or will a review be required?

What are the possible choices that the performer might encounter?

How many different ways can each choice appear in a day-to-day environment?

What should the performer do if a decision is impossible to make with the criteria articulated in the process design?

By comprehensively examining every decision point in the execution flow, we can ensure that performers have clarity on the decisions we want them to make and specific guidelines to enable consistent and accurate choices.

Element 5: Data capture guidelines enable intentional information collection.

We have already touched on today's ubiquity of data. This part is true. There is more valuable data available today than ever before. However, it is important to think about where this reputation for data comes from. Most valuable data in the world are captured and mined by a handful of organizations, and they mostly focus on a handful of very common use cases.

Google has massive amounts of data enabled by search behaviors. Meta has vast amounts of social behavioral data. OpenAI has ingested publicly available written information. Amazon has troves of online shopping behavioral data. Netflix knows a lot about people's entertainment preferences. Major banks know a lot about people's debt worthiness. These companies dominate their space and use information from millions of users.

This is nothing like the reality most companies live in. With fifty, one hundred, or even a thousand employees – and a similar order of magnitude for customers – a Single Market Problem Entity cannot use the same data principles that big consumer-facing companies use for a few everyday market use cases.

Data capture must be very intentional and premeditated to understand internal operations or customer behaviors. Looking at spurious information when the sample size is small will not reveal valuable information with any level of confidence. SMPEs often struggle to make decisions using data because they do not follow an intentional path to capturing data.

So, what does this mean in terms of process design? We can tailor process design to extract just enough of the right information without burdening process performers.

First, do not capture information for the sake of it because it drains process performers. It is the responsibility of the Congruence Architect and process designer to predict the necessary and optimal information needs.

Second, avoid capturing complex and compounded information, as we often misconstrue them during data capture. Don't ask whether something is good or bad. Instead, ask for the underlying information that might help determine whether something is good or bad. The company's definition of good or bad may change over time. It also prevents process performers from trying to make another decision.

Third, avoid capturing information outside the flow of steps defined based on process design elements 1 through 4. If we try to do so, we will often incorrectly capture data. Again, it is human nature to take the path of least resistance.

Fourth, make every attempt to capture information systematically. Manually captured information is often spurious because human beings tend to make execution errors or imprint their biases onto information.

Consider these design questions to ingrain effective data capture:

What are the most important analytical answers that the company might need?

What is the rawest form of information we can capture to arrive at those answers?

Which process performers need to capture such underlying raw information?

Are data capture activities firmly within the flow of process performers' optimal journey designed based on the other process design elements?

Can an automated data capture mechanism be built in?

For the unavoidable manual information capture activities, what specific guidelines must the performer follow to ensure that the raw information is accurate every time?

By building answers to these questions into our process design, we can capture objective information without burdening process performers. This element is critical in our information age because we want to avoid operating with poor data, which stifles micro- and macroevolutions.

Element 6: Governance approach enables microevolution and process monitoring.

We talked about the common process design mistake of forgetting that processes are alive. Without an overarching governance approach, process design can quickly become outdated shelf decoration.

Process governance has two parts.

The **first** is to ensure that process design always comes before execution. Changing execution hastily and reactively is symptomatic of a value engine on the immature end.

The **second** is that we must micro-evolve process design on an ongoing basis to protect ourselves from becoming reactive. We must monitor processes using the key measurements we set through our execution guidelines, and actions must be taken when those measurements breach critical limits. We will discuss this further in later chapters.

Consider these design questions to guide process governance:

What quantifiable measurements imply process performers aren't executing as desired?

What is the quantifiable measurement that would trigger a reevaluation of the process itself?

What is the design and approval path to revising a small or large portion of the process?

Our microevolution path involves developing a simple governance approach and cadence for evaluating and improving processes through reporting and analysis. This keeps processes alive. A strong governance approach guards against undisciplined and ad hoc changes to execution that can rapidly cause a company to become chaotic.

These six elements are a simple and uncomplicated foundation for meeting any company's process needs. However, it takes discipline and an expert process designer to develop The Company Way Processes that are cohesive and comprehensive and adopted by all operations employees, customers, and partners.

As you might have noticed, we discussed process design and barely mentioned technology. That is intentional because technology always follows process.

We often misunderstand the purpose and approach to using technology to mature our company. A congruent value engine effectively uses technology to turbocharge process design without attempting shortcuts.

We must invest in technology to boost productivity, improve safety, keep records, analyze data, and make decisions. Even a small company has at least ten to fifteen relevant pieces of technology, and that number goes up as the company gets bigger.

But then why are so many technology implementations failing and their day-to-day usage frustrating value creators as well as not resulting in the expected efficiencies? Significant amounts of investment go into technologies at companies trying to circumvent poor processes, hoping that technology purchases can work miracles. They don't.

So, let's dive into how we can leverage technology to mature our value engine.

Principle 5: Process design comes before technology.

It is easy to buy something and turn it on. But buying technology as a silver bullet to solve process immaturity doesn't work. Technology is never intended to be a shortcut. Rather, it is an aid. Unfortunately, a shortcut mindset leads to ineffective use of technology and eventual dissatisfaction.

In 1987, Robert Solow, a Nobel Prize-winning economist, famously wrote, "You see the computer age everywhere but in the productivity statistics." That was true in the early computer age, and it is still true today in the digital technology age. The Solow Paradox, as this conundrum has come to be known, aligns with the low productivity increase since 2007 that we covered at the start of our value engine discussions.

For example, companies regularly replace their sales and marketing technology, and the most reported reason is that "the previous technology didn't have the right features." Would we give credence to someone blaming the number of buttons on the treadmill for subpar fitness results?

Having worked with many technology offerings over the years, I can say that they are usually not at fault. Typically, a lack of effective design, implementation, and adoption renders the technology ineffective.

On average, most technology platforms have become powerful enough. So, it is often not about what the technology is capable of; it is about what we are capable of doing with the technology.

The **first** step is always to articulate operational needs, ensuring those needs are evident in the process design. Always think of process design as the foundation for identifying the specific areas where technology can aid in executing the six process design elements.

As a **second** step, the company can explore technologies that meet those needs. As a warning, it is essential to avoid stubbornness about existing process designs and the tendency to force technology to fit them. Processes are malleable, like a Rubik's cube, and can be reconfigured in many combinations to achieve effectiveness. An effective process designer can triangulate between the capabilities of technologies and the process design combinations to use the best of both.

Once the technology is designed, simply throwing it in front of process performers never works.

A strong teaching and enablement mindset is the **third** and necessary step to ensure that process designs aided by technology are adopted and used to their full potential. This is not a one-and-done exercise. Every time the process changes, a teaching and enablement mindset must follow.

A mature value engine continuously evolves. How well do we execute processes? How well does our technology support processes? What are opportunities to improve? This **fourth** step is the governance approach, which is ongoing oversight of our day-to-day execution.

Over time, changes will be necessary as we learn new information through the effective use of our data. As our process performers execute operational activities, effective process governance will periodically uncover breakdowns and improvement opportunities that can trigger microevolutions. But under any such circumstance, where a change is appropriate, it is critical to circle back to Step 1 of this cycle, which is process design.

Figure C10 shows the nonnegotiable sequencing necessary to use technology effectively to empower processes.

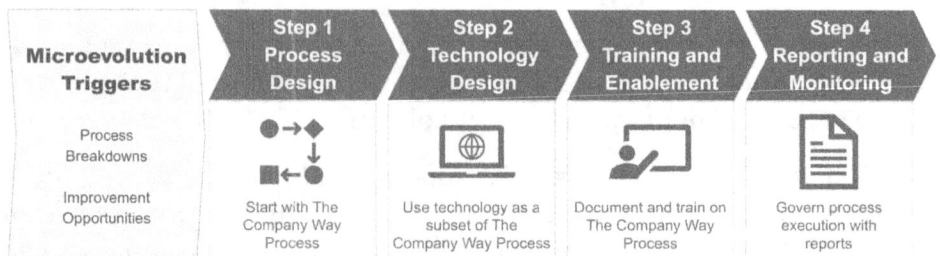

Figure C10. Operations technology always follows process design.

As obvious as this cycle sounds, most environments fail to follow this discipline. Once this cycle breaks, even companies with a mature value engine can find themselves in process chaos. Breaking the value engine is quick and easy. Fixing it is nearly impossible.

With this process-led mindset, let's examine how technologies can support processes in more detail.

Principle 6: Leverage operations technologies to augment process design.

If we take out buzzwords and complex categorizations, technologies fall into two groups.

The **first** group includes operations technologies that automate or simplify actions that humans perform regularly.

The **second** group includes infrastructure technologies that operate behind the scenes to help a company function. This includes computers, servers, and cloud storage solutions, but it also includes assets like the building we work in and security solutions for it. Although this group is extremely important, we will assume that our company's infrastructure supports the value-focused elements of our company.

So, let's talk about operations technologies in general and the value they can create. The value of operations technologies mirrors the six process design elements.

Manage roles and responsibilities.

Technologies allow us to separate the responsibilities of process performers in various roles from each other. Sometimes, these separations are for convenience to ensure that every performer knows where their responsibilities begin and end. These separations also create necessary walls to manage information security or critical authority. Such separations are necessary to empower day-to-day collaboration between value creators and customers.

Time and again, I see scenarios where value creators or customers can't perform tasks using the intended technology aids and resort to manual or email communication, which breaks down their natural flow. Other times, such frustrations lead to too much access to responsibilities for many individuals with few boundaries, risking information security.

In such scenarios, the company is working in process chaos, limiting the operational effectiveness of value creators and customers, leaving them to perform tasks that may not align with their skills. A company cannot leverage this technology element unless the process design firmly lays out all the critical roles and responsibilities. Implementing technology whose roles and responsibilities do not reflect an effective process design triggers process chaos.

Automate execution guidelines.

Technology solutions also help performers eliminate the need to memorize how to execute a task or the information necessary to execute a task.

Most roles require a specific sequence of activities that may not follow our natural instincts. Executing those activities may require access to troves of information about thousands of customers, multiple packages and underlying capabilities, and their prices.

Technology offers significant help for these otherwise herculean efforts. For example, technologies have workflow capabilities that can guide performers to the following predefined activity without having to remember anything at all. Technologies also have large databases where vast amounts of information can be stored and accessed at the click of a button.

But we could also cause execution challenges that appear to be the fault of technology. For instance, what if the process performer finds data stored in a software technology confusing or cannot find it at all?

The workflow paths in technologies are always flexible and configurable, and a company can choose what that path ought to be. Technology databases always come empty, and we fill them with the company's information based on historical execution. Using technology automation elements well starts with getting the process execution guidelines correct and driving the adoption of those guidelines. Everything included in the technology for execution comes from the process design and nowhere else.

Optimize hand-offs.

Imagine trying to complete an online application form of any kind, and when you hit the "submit" button, you get an error code. What exactly is happening here? The technology design ensures that the hand-off between you and the next person in that application process is effective. The form is likely telling you that you are not handing off enough of the correct information to go to the next step.

Technology can be a spectacular aid in ensuring that hand-offs are effective.

Most operations technologies can direct work to the correct next person in line. Most can do basic checks on whether the performer completed the appropriate amount and quality of work before passing to the next step. However, this also means what "good" looks like for each step is clearly articulated and coded into the technology ahead of time.

These are the same details articulated through the third element (hand-off guidelines) of process design. When the process design does not involve such clarity about hand-off criteria, any use of technology to aid hand-offs can easily trigger execution challenges. This might cause process performers to think that the technology is at fault. Far from it.

Automate or verify decisions.

Recall our fourth process design element – decision criteria. Every process performer makes several decisions as they execute their day-to-day responsibilities.

Let's revisit our inbound call handler. We can empower this role to discern between large and small prospective customers based on criteria coded into a technology solution. But that also implies that the decision criteria are first clearly defined via our process design.

In this same illustrative example, imagine a situation where a supervisor decided that the criteria determining between large and small prospective customers had to change. Suppose they directly coded that change into the technology. How would that affect the call handler? How would that affect the sales team who are working without appropriate changes in their execution guidelines or receiving training around it?

Such knee-jerk actions are more common than you think. Technology has the power to aid decisions during execution. However, it can cause chaos unless all microevolutions start with process design to ensure that our execution is congruent with intent.

Automate data capture and use.

When we send through an online application form, imagine a process performer manually writing down submission time so that the company can track how long it takes to process applications. That was the reality a few decades ago. Today, we don't even think about it. That timestamp can be automatically captured in a data table the moment our form is submitted.

Technologies bring so many powerful data-related capabilities that require careful design and codification. For example, extending our form submission scenario further, what if the form submission had to involve support documentation that was incomplete during the first submission, and the responsibility reverted back? Should the submission timestamp get overwritten when the form is resubmitted, or should the original timestamp be maintained? The company has to make many such unique choices as part of process design for effective data capture using technology.

You can see how quickly this can get complicated. Getting it right is nearly impossible if we make these choices in a vacuum. Process design is the only path to effectively decide what, when, how, and by who information should be captured using technology.

Enable process governance.

Information gathering and charting tools are commonplace and affordable these days. Data visualizing solutions allow us to slice and dice information easily and deliver visual reports to senior executives, supervisors, and employees almost without effort.

But how effective are these information packets if we have not chosen the right quantifiable measurements for various execution roles? How will all the recipients of these information packets know how to act if the measurements do not highlight breakdowns in execution?

The ease with which we can create pretty charts often distracts companies from focusing on whether a chart is practically useful. Instead, we must first design how we intend to govern execution, including responsibilities, cadence, and measurements. Building a mature design into a technology solution is easy.

If the process-first message throughout these six technology capabilities sounds repetitious, it is intentional. I cannot stress enough the importance of aligning the six process design elements and technology capabilities and the necessity of sequencing technology after process design.

Know this: operations technology investment has consistently increased by 9 percent each year for a long time. Yet our total factor productivity measurements are barely moving. Investing in technology only leads to impact if we design the "why" first – which is The Company Way Processes.

In addition to process alignment, each operations technology is only effective if its congruent with our broader technology ecosystem.

Principle 7: Ensure operations technologies are congruent with our ecosystem.

Whatever operations technology we procure, the vendor developed it to be sold at scale. Hopefully, we are buying from vendors who have effectively productized using the principles we laid out in Chapter C.1. Best-in-class vendors provide a range of configuration options to tailor various capabilities to fit our execution needs. These configuration options can add up to millions of combinations of how each technology could be leveraged.

These technologies must dovetail with other technologies, each serving a different purpose. Now, we have multiple technologies, each with millions of configuration options. Simply buying a technology off-the-shelf and plugging it into our process environment should sound like a suboptimal idea.

It is!

Think of a single technology purchase to improve our process maturity as looking for one piece of a large jigsaw puzzle. Technology choices and design must focus on how they fit our ecosystem as much as the technology's standalone capabilities.

From an operational perspective, a technology can serve only three general purposes.

The **first** is to serve as a core technology. A few technologies enable major, broad portions of our process across multiple functions. Examples include sales and marketing technologies and financial reporting technologies.

The **second** is to be a niche technology in our ecosystem. Most technologies fall in this second category, meeting very narrowly defined needs. Companies use dozens of such peripheral niche solutions. Examples may include third-party data sources, customer communication solutions, email marketing tools, and payment processing solutions. To be effective, they always have to link to a core technology and potentially other niche technologies.

The **third** is a data platform. Most companies use a central database that integrates information from all core and niche technologies and is considered a single data source. Such platforms offer strong options to manipulate and visualize data, and well-run companies choose one such platform.

Beyond process-first, the most critical aspect to remember during technology selection and design is that all these technologies must link together seamlessly. Like our process design hand-off principle, technologies also break down most often when they link with other technologies.

Consider these design questions:

What does the company's operational technology ecosystem look like?

Have we ensured limited overlapping capabilities between technologies that we have already chosen or are considering choosing?

Have we ensured seamless transitions between each technology and across our ecosystem?

Articulating answers to these questions provides our company with an operations technology landscape necessary to support our process design and improve our value engine maturity. If technology solutions aid effective processes in a well-designed ecosystem, we can significantly improve the repeatability and reproducibility of process execution.

In such a congruent system, employees, partners, and customers work together effectively to enable balanced value exchange through our productized offerings and the processes to deliver them. Mature use of technology opens the door to using information to continuously evolve our company.

C.3
ATTACK AND DEFEND USING DATA, ANALYSIS, REPORTING.

THE third lever of our value engine is a path to understanding how well we're doing as a company. How do we know what we could do better on an ongoing basis? The answer is objective data.

Data is supremely powerful, and its applications are everywhere. However, mistakes are often made due to a lack of awareness about the extent of that power. It is analogous to a chainsaw that can be as helpful as it can be harmful, depending on the user's ability to wield it. So, it is worth dedicating a chapter to this conversation on how we might look at data objectively as a path to improving the maturity of each building block and congruence across the company.

The Congruence Architect and the analytical resources guided by this role are accountable for identifying actionable opportunities to improve the company's productized offering, The Company Way Processes and their execution, and the effectiveness of the management approach using objective information. However, every value creator has a role to play.

All individual contributors must understand how the company creates and uses its information. Supervisors and senior executives are responsible for monitoring their teams' execution and making objective decisions based on opportunities presented by analytical resources.

In a world where words such as big data, analysis, data science, artificial intelligence, and machine learning are commonly used, we must dig deeper to ensure that we are benefiting from the power of data and not harming our prospects through poor usage.

Principle 1: Data is always a byproduct of Process-Data Symbiosis.

Many data companies and executives claim, "Data is the new oil!" I once had a summer internship at ExxonMobil. The consumable petroleum we use in our cars starts with exploration of where oil is located, drilling, and extraction. These early stages take years before oil companies get to process oil into usable forms.

Despite being inundated with data and our efforts to use it, most companies or users of data pay very little attention to the source and true essence of data. This lack of attention to the source is one of the key risks associated with data usage.

After working deeply with qualitative and quantitative data-related situations for almost two decades, a simple but incredible realization dawned on me. Data is always a byproduct.

> **Things To Remember: Process-Data Symbiosis**
>
> **Process-Data Symbiosis is an unbreakable relationship in which all recorded information reflects real-world activities or decisions. Whether captured manually or automatically, data is always the qualitative or quantitative byproduct of behaviors in a process.**

In other words, data is always a reflection of a process.

I asserted in the last chapter that there is no data without process. Now, let me explain.

We usually see data in tabular formats. It is stored, edited, and manipulated to create charts and make decisions. But how does a data table come to exist?

If we recall our inbound call handler who directs leads to the two sales teams, one of the tasks that the role is likely to execute is logging the information provided by the inbound caller. For example, maybe this role asks a few questions about the caller's company, role, and the reason for their call. Each piece of information collected becomes a cell in a database in our operations technology.

On one extreme, a process performer in the role could be highly talented, well-versed in our offerings, understand our customers well, and know exactly the right way to ask follow-up questions to understand the caller. That is, the performer executes the process admirably. On the other extreme, another performer in the same role could be undertrained or may not be a motivated value creator. This performer may only spend a few seconds on the call before passing the caller to the next stage in the process. Here, the performer is executing the process poorly.

How different will be the quality of information captured by the two performers across several calls?

The data logged by the high-performing value creator tells a story about the customers who call. The data logged by the low performer tells a story about the person's low performance and spurious information about the customer. If we just look at the data without understanding how it is being created and whether the process is being executed well, it is impossible to know which story the data is telling.

Should an analyst use all this data or only part of it? Regardless, we'd be working with spurious data due to poor process execution. This is our data conundrum.

Data is nonexistent without some action or decision that triggers its creation. That action or decision is always part of a process, and that process may involve any combination of employees, partners, and customers.

Consider all the information stored in our brain - this is our data. Where does it come from? Every bit of it is created over time through the activities of our body, using its five senses, and then transferred by our nervous system from the body to the brain. This is Process-Data Symbiosis.

Figure C11 illustrates how best to think about data and its creation, building up from our processes. We always collect data as a byproduct of the efforts within a process. In this illustration, two of the process steps trigger the creation of new data or the change of existing data. It is a symbiotic relationship where well-designed and executed processes capture useful data, and poor ones capture tarnished and misleading data.

It is easy to forget about the origin of data because big consumer conglomerates have zettabytes of data, and one could think it appears miraculously. No! Every such data byte is triggered when normal people like us move our mouse or click a button while executing a process in our consumer journey, whether we recognize our role or not.

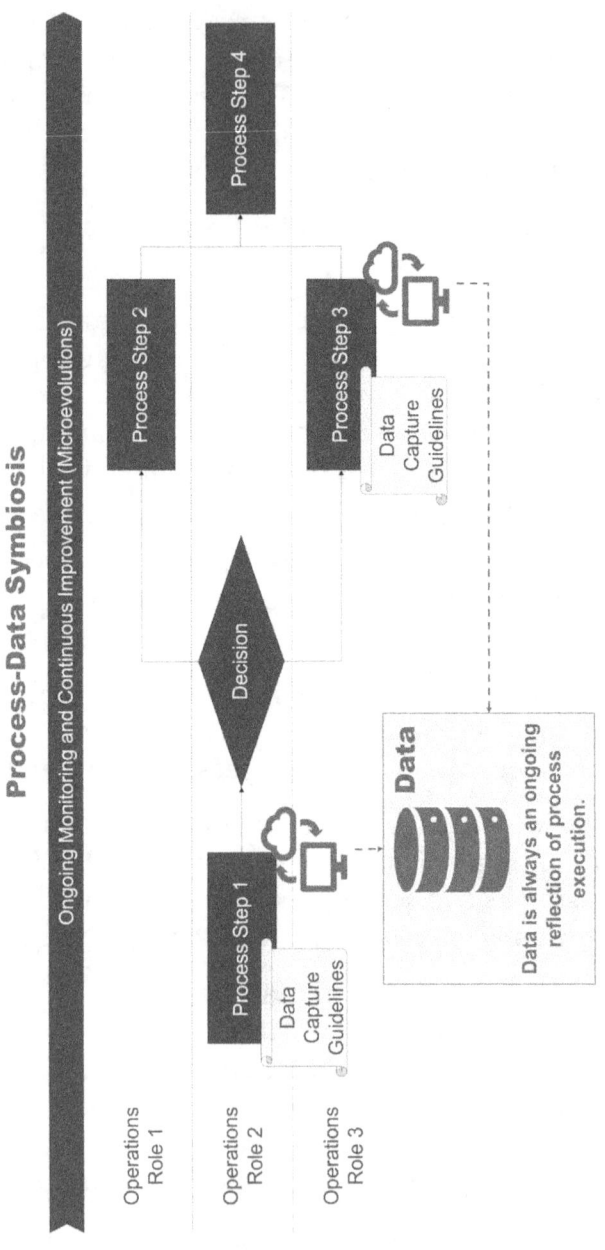

Figure C11. Process-Data Symbiosis prescribes company's information prowess.

Every exploration into understanding data begins with understanding the design and execution of the process that created it. Data is rarely perfect because the process of its creation is never perfect. The question we must ask is, how imperfect? Data always has flaws and biases. Anyone using data to generate conclusions or make decisions must understand the potential flaws and biases inherent in the data and how effectively they have been accounted for.

Principle 2: Data often has flaws due to process governance failures and process breakages.

There are two common types of data flaws. Both create the illusion that a meaningful message can be drawn from the data, but such patterns in the data are created by undesirable aberrations in the process itself. Therefore, every analyst should evaluate the data for various manifestations of these flaws before considering the information ready to be analyzed.

Process governance failures cause data flaws.

Imagine a perfect scenario where our company has well-articulated and adopted process designs and process performers executing their tasks repeatably and reproducibly. The data capture mechanisms gather all the correct information. The Congruence Architect and analytical enablement resources slice and dice the data to uncover underlying messages to make decisions about improving any number of activities. These enablement resources and process performers are in sync about how data needs to be captured, and these expectations are met. All is well, and the messages make sense.

Now, let's move into reality. The sixth process design element, the governance approach, which requires disciplined process improvement and subsequent use of technology, is the hardest to live by. Large and small companies regularly fail to maintain such discipline. Executing a governance approach is a risk management effort. It's not about all the situations effectively managed; it is about the situations when the governance approach didn't hold up.

Failures in the process governance approach may mean decisions about changes in how performers execute are made through quick in-person conversations or via email communications without formality. If these decisions and changes do not formally start with The Company Way Processes, no one trains all the performers consistently on the changes. Governance has failed.

If we ask process performers to make a change and execute without following the governance sequence, we are distorting the data captured through this process. Essentially, the data before the change cannot be compared to the data after the change.

Let's use a simple illustrative example.

Smartwatches allow users to track their exercise habits. Most can be used to track manually or automatically.

Imagine that a close friend who cares about our health outcomes gives us a smartwatch as a gift and offers to be our accountability coach. We agree with the friend that we will use the smartwatch, and the friend can see how well we are tracking via the data on the smartwatch's online data portal, which both parties can access without even speaking to each other.

At the start of the first month, we agree that we will manually trigger the functionality to track each exercise. This is our process. Throughout the month, our friend keeps tabs on the portal. We don't speak to each other because all the data is on the portal. This is our governance.

At the end of the first month, we realize that we tend to forget to trigger the watch on certain exercise days manually. We learn about the automated logging option and turn it on at the end of that first month. Another month goes by, and we receive a congratulatory note from the friend commending us on the improvement in exercise habits during month two. This is akin to receiving a reward in a work environment.

The question is – did we deserve this reward?

The truth is that the data is lying to the friend. The only difference between the first and second months is the toggle from manual logging to automated logging. The friend is the analyst in this example and does not know about the toggle and thinks we are exercising more. We broke the governance pact by changing the settings on the watch without telling the friend.

Such occurrences are very common due to a lack of value engine maturity. Every company's data will contain flaws created by process governance breakdowns that could be mistaken for meaningful knowledge. The only path to using such data is for an analyst to perform detective work and understand where governance failures might have happened. If the analyst identifies these failures, they could carefully use data within a window between governance failures where the data is at least comparable.

In reality, it's nearly impossible to know whether such patterns are aberrations or what the sources of such aberrations are. Incongruous data can mislead senior executives into making incorrect decisions or sharing incoherent stories about our offerings or customers. Maintaining process governance is the only mature path.

Process breakages cause data flaws.

Process breakages are essentially poorly designed processes that cause poor execution. When we capture data as part of poor execution, the data is poor. Process breakages pollute data with incorrect entries and offer few obvious clues as to which entries are wrong.

Let's revisit our smartwatch example. Assume that our friend also planned to track the number of steps we walked each day and set a target of 10,000 steps.

Let's say that we have two watches – a smartwatch and a luxury Swiss watch that we have owned before but never mentioned in conversation. In our minds, we agreed to wear the smartwatch every day, but subconsciously, we intend to wear the luxury watch on the days that we have an important meeting.

How much will the friend learn by tracking our steps in an information vacuum without knowing about the luxury Swiss watch?

In this scenario, the data does not reflect the designed process, which involves wearing the smartwatch every day to track steps consistently. We could think of this as a poor process design by our friend, who didn't ask all the right questions to create a process and predict the potential process breakage caused by the arbitrary addition of the luxury watch to the mix.

This is a prevalent data flaw, and an analyst would need a deep understanding of the process and its execution to know whether the data is sensible. Unfortunately, there are no easy fixes after the fact in such circumstances. Attempting to go back and "fix" the entries will most likely create other distortions in the data, causing a different set of problems. Furthermore, an assumption of only using available data can backfire. What if our walking habits on days when we wear the luxury Swiss watch are significantly poorer because those are busy meeting days?

Both types of data flaws are likely hiding in most data sets. Therefore, analysts and decision-makers must be aware of these pitfalls before capturing and using data.

The common practice of gauging the skills of analytical resources solely based on slicing and dicing data or using visualization solutions is suboptimal. An analyst who cannot transcend between numbers in a database and real-world behaviors that created those numbers is likely to arrive at suboptimal conclusions from data.

Recall our definition of skill from the management approach. At the very least, analytical resources must have experience and expertise around all the concepts we cover in Chapters C.2 and C.3. Value creators at all seniority levels who make data-driven decisions must have the wherewithal to pressure-test recommendations and ensure they aren't based on flawed data.

Principle 3: Data is always likely to have a capture bias or observer bias.

Unlike data flaws, which are potholes in the data caused by process immaturity, biases are natural human tendencies that affect the creation and use of data. Process execution has skews because all employees, partners, and customers exhibit individual cognitive skews, and those skews are imprinted into the data created from those processes.

Data users such as analysts and decision-makers also bring their own biases and look at the available data, however perfect, in a skewed manner. Human bias around the capture and use of data is akin to poorly calibrated measuring equipment.

Cognitive biases form an entire branch of economics. We can broadly classify sources of biases into two themes that impact how we create and use data: biases in data capture and biases in the observer mindset.

Data capture triggers biases.

We demonstrate natural biases that create a personal slant to everything we do. Then, we bring that same bias to our work. So, every performer is likely to execute the processes they are responsible for with that slant, and the resulting skew is captured in the data. Let us look at two examples of biases and how they might impact how process performers capture data.

One bias that could skew data is framing bias.

Framing bias is evident when a person uses an overtly positive or negative positioning statement to get a corresponding positive or negative response. Framing bias skews information received in a more positive or negative direction based on the way the question is phrased.

Imagine an employee developing a new capability being asked to get customer perspectives before senior executives decide whether to continue funding the project. First, the employee would ask customers for their perspectives. For example, the employee could ask potential customers, "Would you buy our upcoming capability with three benefits that the current offering doesn't have at the same price?"

They framed this question too positively to get a positive answer, particularly if the employee failed to mention that the new offering would no longer include two existing benefits, which was a necessary adjustment to keep the price unchanged. If the same question was asked of many customers, it results in a very skewed perspective about the prospect of the new capability.

A second bias that could skew data is anchoring bias.

Anchoring bias most often applies when a person is looking for an answer to a question and phrases the question in a manner that nudges the responder to choose a specific answer.

Let's say that a customer decides to leave our company and choose a competitor, and we want to understand why. An unbiased question could be,

"Could you tell us the top three reasons you decided to leave us?" This question would likely lead the customer to share their own perspective. But what if the question was phrased as, "Would you say that you decided to move to our competitor because they offered you a lower price?"

Irrespective of the real reasons, the customer is more likely to provide a cancellation reason involving pricing.

These skews don't technically make the data wrong. However, the messages that analysts and decision-makers can take away from such data can be very misleading, especially if they don't understand the impact of biases and how they might have skewed the data during capture.

Observers induce biases.

Even if we assume that the data captured has no biases, biases can creep in as the data is being analyzed or used for decision-making. These biases occur due to personal or professional incentives and life or career experiences that have molded our general perspective about the world.

Strong analysts must take a stand on what the data might say, also known as developing hypotheses, and then assess whether the data agrees or disagrees with the hypotheses. Senior executives have to advise the analytical team on the information they want to see before making decisions. Confirmation bias, self-serving bias, herd mentality, and narrative fallacy are all cognitive skews that can lead us astray unless all the decision-makers understand that these tendencies are always around us.

Consider these design questions to self-assess our objectivity when developing hypotheses:

Do I have a preconceived notion about what the decision or answer ought to be? This assesses confirmation bias.

Do I have a vested interest in proving a point and thus missing the real answer? This assesses self-serving bias.

Am I tempted to look for messages that align with the thinking of the whole group? This assesses herd mentality.

Am I tempted to create a positive storyline and search for that story in the data? This assesses a narrative fallacy.

These biases are not exhaustive. They are also not anyone's fault. We all fall for them. They are natural human tendencies. However, countering them is a practiced skill and requires self-awareness. The Congruence Architect, analytical resources, and decision-makers operating in critical roles without internalizing these concepts risk misleading our company. Understanding these concepts and using them in decision-making is paramount for a congruent value engine.

These three data principles of Process-Data Symbiosis, the existence of flaws in data, and biases in data are as prevalent as the common cold. But underestimating them causes existential threats to a business as bad as cancer.

Like an iceberg, the data capture principles are the significantly larger mass hidden underwater. But the groundwork is paramount. Leveraging value from the data is the smaller visible mount of the iceberg. But it has a massive impact.

Our ability to micro-evolve and macro-evolve the company's management approach and value engine depends on the effective usage of data. We always use data in one of two ways – analysis or reporting. Unfortunately, these are two very different and powerful parts that are often confused with each other and poorly leveraged. Both analysis and reporting involve graphs and numbers but serve very different purposes.

Many even use catchphrases such as "analysis paralysis," which is propaganda against the value that could be created by objective data use. It is not analysis that causes paralysis. It is skill gaps around what constitutes quality analysis or effective reporting that cause this misconception.

Both components are the sword and shield of value creators at all seniority levels on a day-to-day basis. Not internalizing the difference between analysis and reporting is a massive drain on customer value creation, senior executive and supervisor decision-making effectiveness, and value creator execution efficiency.

Principle 4: Analysis enables forward-looking problem-solving.

Analyses drive forward-looking improvements from our current state. It is our attacking sword. Let's start with a definition of analysis.

Things To Remember: Analysis

Analysis is a time-bound objective effort to improve a given situation using data. Analyses always start with a forward-looking objective to solve a problem, find a path to improve outcomes, or quantitatively answer questions that enable decision-making.

Once an analysis starts with the problem statement, the performer identifies unbiased hypotheses, assesses whether hypotheses hold true based on the available data, and recommends tangible actions to improve the current situation to achieve the objective. Such tangible and actionable recommendations are called insights.

The word insight is often incorrectly used to describe a collage of data or charts, which is a considerable loss. Visually capturing charts or complex data presentations do not constitute insights.

Things To Remember: Insights

An analysis must result in answers that articulate the path forward to achieving the objective that triggered the analysis. This answer is an insight. An insight is a cohesive and actionable answer and recommendation directly drawn from the data used in the analysis. Without insights, data jugglery is not analysis.

A good litmus test for quality analyses is to look for a sound problem statement, hypotheses to solve the problem statement comprehensively, an objective and systematic path to test those hypotheses, and finally, the arrival at one or more insights that chart the path forward. If any of these four elements are missing, it is likely not a quality analysis.

Imagine taking our car to a mechanic, who is the analyst in this metaphor. We expect the mechanic to listen to the symptoms we experience, run only the necessary tests based on their experience-based hypotheses to keep our costs low, and tell us the objective and precise fix we need without ambiguity. That is good analysis.

Principle 5: Reporting predicts breakage of the expected current state.

Let's start with framing what we are trying to avoid with reporting.

I worked closely with a conversation data technology company as a turn-around leader. The company believed poor lead generation was causing sales to plateau. The commercial team had a widely accepted marketing and sales dashboard built in a data visualization platform. Whenever I tried to get some quantitative answers, they referred me back to this dashboard because everyone had access to it, and they received it via email every day. It was clear that a lot of work had gone into building this dashboard, which was a colorful page full of numbers.

So, I asked around, "What do you usually do with this dashboard?"

Most would say, "We look at it."

I followed up with, "Then what happens?" I never got a good answer. They were basing their decisions on data they didn't understand or not making decisions at all. This team's misinterpretation of what good reporting looks like was symptomatic of costly incongruences across the value engine, including the incorrect interpretation that lead generation was their biggest challenge.

Things To Remember: Reporting

Reporting is an ongoing effort to use objective data to maintain the status quo of a given situation and prevent adverse outcomes. Reporting continuously monitors a big or small process using previously identified and articulated metrics and compares its current measurement against a predefined threshold to identify breakdowns in execution.

The key takeaway is that reporting does not improve the expected current state. Reporting is intended to protect against downside risk. It is truly a defensive shield, not an attacking sword.

A process monitored by reporting can span multiple teams to a narrow portion of a single value creator's responsibilities. To protect against downside risk, reporting must have three key elements. These elements are 1) a predefined and quantifiable metric, 2) a threshold that qualifies what "good" looks like for that metric, and 3) a remediation path for threshold breaches. Without any one of these elements, reporting is not effective.

Effective use of these elements grants us two benefits. **First**, the most beautiful part about effective reporting is that our company will dedicate little time or effort to monitoring execution once we set it up. **Second**, effective reporting provides us with predictability. What is the use of looking at information if it is too late to do something about it?

A practical example of a well-functioning report is a car's oil change light. The process is the car's entire systemic operation as it is designed to perform. As the owner and driver of the car, we are the senior executive or supervisor. The car's electronics are constantly "reporting" on the volume of oil, which is the metric. It does so in the background, comparing the oil levels to a predefined threshold set by the manufacturer. A driver never has to think about it until the oil change light comes on, which is the trigger that asks for intervention. The manufacturer has designed the car to report on oil performance.

Unfortunately, many practical applications do not achieve the two benefits above because of poor reporting development, which is far more common than effective reporting.

First, many companies do not dedicate enough time and discipline to identifying and using predictive measurements for their processes. These gaps go back to immature process design and ineffective execution guidelines, which are intended to include effective measurements.

Second, companies also often spend a significant amount of time and resources reviewing a poor collection of data without setting thresholds for metrics, even when predictive ones exist. We will discuss the reason for this gap soon.

If you are somewhat familiar with cars, you also know that cars have an oil dipstick. Imagine a world where your car didn't have that automated oil change light. You will have to open the car's hood often, pull out the oil dipstick, and see how much oil is on it. The dipsticks in a car have a marker that shows how much oil should be visible on the stick to validate that the car has enough oil. What if this marker didn't exist?

Unfortunately, many companies operate in the dipstick scenario, where the dipstick does not have a marker that signifies how much oil there should be.

Without a firm understanding and definition of what constitutes an execution breakdown, we are left to hope that we will know a breakdown when we see one. It leaves our company committing significant time and effort to look at trivial and repetitive information, and we are unlikely to know breakdowns when they occur.

Principle 6: Effective data ecosystem dovetails analysis and reporting.

Figure C12 shows a mature data ecosystem. It illustrates the core application difference between analysis and reporting. The center of this ecosystem must look familiar to you from our earlier discussion about Process-Data Symbiosis. It creates the necessary data we can leverage for either analysis or reporting.

The key to the data ecosystem is the diverging, non-overlapping, yet dovetailing relationship between analysis and reporting. To reiterate their purpose, analysis allows the company to assess problems, irrespective of their scale or situation, and develop forward-looking solutions. By contrast, reporting monitors execution risks by comparing ongoing performance measurements against preset thresholds. Breach of these thresholds triggers previously defined remediations.

> **Things To Remember: Analysis vs. Reporting**
>
> **Analysis is the forward-looking problem-solving sword. Reporting is the risk management shield to protect against breakdowns.**

Well-performed analyses allow companies to identify and solve strategic and operational problems related to any part of the management approach

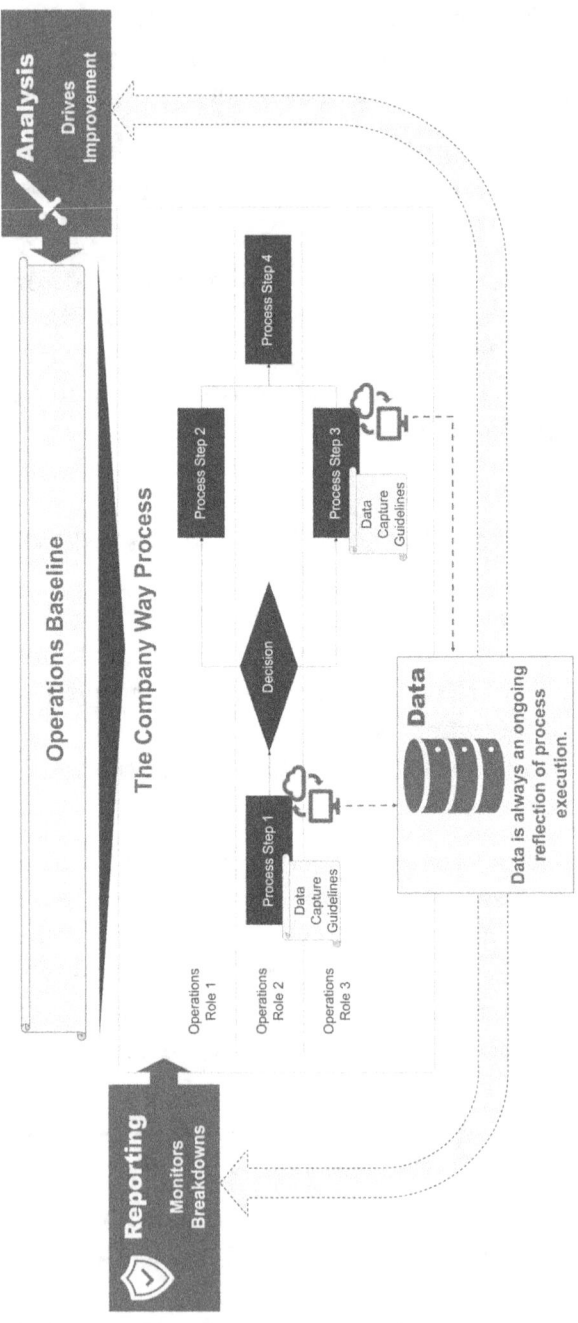

Figure C12. Analysis and reporting have divergent applications.

and value engine. Insights from analyses may drive microevolutions of building blocks in our operations baseline or support our macroevolutions that we will start discussing in the next chapter.

Analyses also identify predictive measurements to monitor processes and associated thresholds where processes are at risk. These are the metrics and thresholds that we would use to monitor processes using reporting. In other words, analysis leads to identifying two of the three elements of effective reporting we listed earlier. Let's give these predictive metrics a name – **Leading Indicators.**

Things To Remember: Leading Indicators

Leading indicators are performance measurements that offer predictability regarding a process' likely outcome. Monitoring leading indicators through reporting allows us to take preventative and corrective actions before undesirable outcomes manifest for the entire process.

Ongoing reporting triggers predefined corrective actions when thresholds are breached. Such breakdowns triggered by reporting can reveal unanticipated problems, which will trigger further analysis.

The Congruence Architect and analytical resources must internalize and leverage the unique purpose of analysis and reporting and their intertwined relationship. Failure to do so is akin to fighting with both arms tied behind the back in our fast-moving information age.

I worked closely with a highly talented and motivated data tools expert who was quite a magician at making data available for hypothesis-based analysis and predictive reporting. However, this gentleman was not an analyst. The company mistook all the available information and charting tools to think they had achieved data maturity.

Many senior executives and supervisors were not aware of the core concepts around analysis and reporting. They would spend hours in meetings looking at charts and data presented by our data magician and discussing endlessly what the data might mean. However, the group seldom recognized impending execution failures or made vital decisions based on forward-looking analysis. Actions and decisions were based on the executives' personal views. Eventually, the data magician quit because he felt that his hard work wasn't producing any actual results.

So, yes, paralysis can happen, but it is caused by mistaking data overload with high-quality analysis and predictive reporting and their intertwined relationship. Every company needs analytical skills that can guide the use of data and lead analysis and reporting efforts effectively.

Principle 7: Define effective reporting metrics, targets, and limits via analysis.

Reporting allows us to monitor our company processes once we identify the appropriate leading indicators. A hypothesis-driven analysis is the source of the optimal set of leading indicators. Analysis is an integral part of our process governance approach and is always a critical part of our strategy development and strategic planning effort. So, we will discuss leading indicators again later in the method.

To internalize what "good" looks like for leading indicators, we must first internalize what is not a leading indicator – a **Lagging Indicator**. The names are intended to be descriptive. Lagging indicators measure outcomes and are always significantly easier to identify and measure. But they offer no predictability of the outcomes. Lagging indicators are often permutations of revenue and expense outcomes, which are important but only as outcomes.

Imagine going to a big conference and meeting many new people. If we tally the number of people who seemed to have a terrible cold, that could be a leading indicator of our health prospects. Using a thermometer to measure our body temperature is a lagging indicator because it only reveals useful information after we have a cold.

Things To Remember: Lagging Indicators

Lagging indicators are non-predictive measurements of outcomes, and their future measurements can be estimated using carefully chosen and measured leading indicators.

We will further discuss the appropriate use of lagging indicators during our strategic planning discussion.

Figure C13 demonstrates the simple lessons I learned as a Six Sigma Black Belt in my early career. There is nothing complex or new about it. However, over the last two decades, I have been surprised that many companies and teams do not internalize or apply these simple concepts to use reporting effectively. So, let's frame how to leverage our objective data to track leading indicators via reporting.

Figure C13. Targets and limits dictate the effectiveness of reporting.

Regardless of the situation, perfectly designed and executed processes deliver outcomes randomly around a center point – this is a law of nature. Such an even distribution around a center point is called a normal distribution. Although no processes are perfect, and many have skews, this is an acceptable simplifying assumption. For all practical purposes, we can assume that processes deliver outcomes somewhat randomly around a center point, even if it's not a perfectly normal distribution.

If a well-designed process is also well-executed, the measurement of each iteration stays very close to the center and does so consistently. If they are poorly executed, the measurement of iterations spread far from the center. In Figure C13, this distribution of measurements of a leading indicator is centered around the dotted line in the middle. Most of the measurements are close to the center; fewer are spread farther away. The normal distribution illustrates this. This simple idea that outcomes are spread around a center point helps us effectively design reporting for our processes using leading indicators.

If we are trying to hit the bullseye on a dartboard, would we shoot straight for the bullseye? Anyone who has aimed at something knows that we all have a natural skew, while gravity and other conditions take a toll on our intended actions. So, we would never go for the bullseye. Instead, we would aim for something slightly above the bullseye with an adjustment for any natural skew that we may be aware of.

Unfortunately, companies with immature value engines make a fundamental mistake – they instruct value creators not to breach the extreme breaking points and put the onus on the performers to figure out how to stay within those limits. This results in poor outcomes.

Effective tracking of a leading indicator has three core elements. We must identify and set them through analysis.

The most important part of a distribution of outcomes is the center point. Think about this center point as the most likely outcome if we perform the process an infinite number of times. This should be the realistic expected goal we must set for the process as measured by the leading indicator. Let's formally call this the **Target**.

Things To Remember: Target

The target is the median measurement of the leading indicator over time. Critically, this is the quantifiable outcome of the process that should be expected over time across all performers executing the same process.

Recall setting performance expectations for value creators. The target must be practically achievable for most performers in an effective system, not just a handful of heroic overperformers. If the process involves customers, then this must be the expected median outcome across all customers, not just a handful of dedicated ones. During strategic planning, the targets for key leading indicators must be set to this median measurement. It is the realistic anticipated predictive measurement of processes.

Similarly, all operations value creators must be measured against the target for processes they are responsible for. We must set the 100 percent achievement of incentive compensation against this target. Top performers will likely achieve significantly higher output beyond the target and, thus, incentive compensation beyond the 100 percent mark.

The most important aspect of the target is that we always derive this figure from our analysis. The target is only known to us because of effective process design and measurement using objective historical data. The target is our expected outcome from the execution of the process in perpetuity, not each iteration of execution.

Why is this important? We want to avoid the temptation to use non-analytically sourced information as our target.

For example, if one of our processes is solving customer complaints, a leading indicator of customer satisfaction could be the number of hours to close complaints. However, let's also imagine that we captured customer sentiments and learned that customers are likely to be very unhappy if it takes more than twelve hours to close a complaint. What should we communicate as the desired complaint closing window with our customer service team?

Shockingly, I have seen many situations where such a customer service team would be told, "We have to close all complaints in less than twelve hours." Unfortunately, most complaints will likely be closed on either side of the twelve-hour mark, which means a significant number over twelve hours.

The correct answer is to design a process that closes customer complaints at a much lower expected timeline, say eight hours. If we created such a process where the measurements fall on something close to a normal distribution with the vast majority of complaint closures around the eight-hour mark, we could confidently set our target as eight hours. In this scenario, we will seldom breach the twelve-hour limit that irks customers.

The measurement that leads to dire consequences is not our target. Target is the expectation we set for our leading indicator, such that our process can meet both value creator and customer expectations almost every single time. In the scenario above, the twelve-hour mark implies that our process to close customer complaints has failed. Let's call this the **Breaking Limit**.

Things To Remember: Breaking Limit

A breaking limit is the absolute edge of performance for a process or part of a process that misses the minimum requirements of stakeholders. The stakeholders can be customers or value creators awaiting the completion of the process to perform other processes.

Breaching this limit implies that the process has broken down, particularly if it happens several times. Figure C13 illustrates our breaking limits with two bold lines on both extremes. Triggering this red flag for our leading indicator must result in a reaction. This reaction is part of our process governance and is a perfect opportunity to analyze the root causes of the breaches and micro-evolve our process design.

For an effectively designed and executed process, the breaking limit is the point at which the hand-off guidelines for the process or process step are broken. In other words, this process is giving lower than acceptable value to other stakeholders, which sets them back and triggers a domino effect. Triggering the breaking limit is grave and requires a comprehensive assessment of what went wrong.

But we cannot operate in a world with only two realities – good and bad. That epitomizes a firefighting ecosystem.

A process can be functional and effective, while execution lags. So, how do we manage a process beyond designing it and setting a target? We must base day-to-day oversight on a more acceptable limit where corrective actions can be taken before other stakeholders are left to suffer. This is the **Management Limit**.

Things To Remember: Management Limit

The management limit is the oversight trigger. Senior executives and supervisors proactively monitor this threshold to ensure that operations value creators are performing to expectations. Management limits offer a yellow flag that triggers corrective actions or coaching of employees or partners to deliver to the target.

Each iteration of process execution will naturally deviate from the target. Performance between value creators also varies. Senior executives and supervisors need an acceptable range around the target within which process performers must stay.

Focusing on setting and using management limits is the mature path to proactively overseeing our organization. Effective use of management limits has far-reaching implications.

First, most reporting activities revolve around these management limits of leading indicators, without which reports are ineffective. **Second**, ongoing individual training and coaching are triggered when performance breaches the management limits. **Third**, we can use management limits to set performance management expectations and evaluate performance.

How does a supervisor or a senior executive know that the process is working well in our customer service team or when to coach laggards? It's too late to coach someone when the breaking limits are breached because we will be doing so at the expense of another dependent stakeholder. In our customer service example, we will miss our desired eight-hour target. We expect this variation. A management limit is an effective threshold, say ten hours, that allows a supervisor to intervene and coach the process performer back to the target well before hitting the breaking limit.

We must anchor process oversight on management limits, which drive specific, predefined remedies when breached. This is the third important element of effective reporting. Mature process designs anticipate these breaches and codify these remedies, and effective governance ensures their use.

Often, companies don't design and train on the recourse necessary to address management limit breaches. Poor process governance definitions and supervisors' and executives' desire to maintain freedom of action are often to blame for operating without a predetermined definition of corrective actions. The escalation and actions associated with management limits cannot be unstructured demands and ad hoc efforts to improve performance. This leads to the gradual deterioration of the process to reach breaking limits.

We must develop and use management limits to monitor and govern processes and ensure corrective actions can be taken when performance breaches the management limit. A strong analytical team will use targets, management limits, and breaking limits as intended and embrace the importance of governance for all leading indicators across processes.

Principle 8: Prioritize insightful analysis triggered by reporting limits.

Time commitment and cadence are necessary to optimize the company's use of analysis and reporting to drive forward toward the mature end of the value engine. Time implies how much time various resources in the organization dedicate to analysis and reporting. Cadence implies the frequency at which these resources spend time on analysis and reporting.

In today's world, where data manipulation and automation technologies are prevalent and affordable, we must spend the vast majority of our data usage time (say, 80 percent) on analysis that solves problems to evolve and only a small share of time (say, 20 percent) on downside protection efforts via reporting.

There are two reasons for this.

The **first** reason is that almost every reporting aspect can be set and forgotten using automation technology if our company is mature enough to use analysis to identify the correct leading metrics and appropriate management limits. There is absolutely no reason for value creators at any seniority level to stare at reporting if they have suitable thresholds and flags to indicate breaches. Conversely, there is nothing to learn from reporting if the process execution measurements are within these guardrails set via process design and analysis. But if the process has breached these thresholds, then it's time to take remedial action or perform analysis.

The **second** reason is that sustainability as a company requires us to dedicate more effort to forward-looking assessments than downside protection. Every company has to continue solving problems to improve the value created for customers and optimize operations efficiency.

So, strong analytical enablement resources must lead senior executives, supervisors, and, where appropriate, individual contributors through forward-looking and problem-solving analyses often and at a cadence.

These reviews will require the deepest mindshare and preparation from decision-makers to understand the assessments and recommendations presented to them. They have to understand and embrace the power of data and its possible flaws and biases to ask hard questions and ensure they make the right decisions to improve the company's management approach and value engine.

A mature company ensures that such analysis development and decision reviews are part of ongoing efforts and not just reactions to bad news. We must set the timing of these events on a cadence to ensure that day-to-day distractions do not inhibit such forward-thinking.

The urgency of problem-solving will differ depending on the company's lifecycle stage and level of success with its offerings and customers. So, the specific cadence will vary from company to company. Regardless, a monthly commitment is generally appropriate.

We must formally define responsibilities for report creation, access, dissemination, and governance in the context of this analytical decision meeting cadence, which we will discuss further in Part F. A skilled Congruence Architect and associated analytical resources must ensure that operational performance reporting is seamless in terms of time commitment for all senior executives and supervisors.

Our ability to invest in analysis depends on our ability to limit distractions from reporting. A common data usage gap stems from a lack of clarity around reporting management limits, associated corrective actions, and predefined ownership of such tasks. This results in reactions that distract from forward-looking analysis.

Consider these design questions to mature the use of analysis and reporting:

Do we dedicate a significant majority of data usage time to hypothesis-led analysis (say, 80 percent) compared to reporting (say, 20 percent)?

Do senior executives, supervisors, and individual contributors commit mindshare to understand and objectively assess the effectiveness of analysis developed and socialized?

Do the Congruence Architect and analytical resources maintain at least a monthly cadence to review and discuss analysis and insights?

Have we effectively identified leading indicators, used management limits, and developed corrective actions to address aberrations in process execution?

These four considerations will highlight whether our company is adequately committed to discerning value from analysis and reporting.

Principle 9: Mature use of data requires effective organization design and strong skills.

Process design expertise, developing objective and comprehensive hypotheses, choosing the appropriate analyses, and assessing the available data to tease out the right insights – while being wary of Process-Data Symbiosis, data flaws, and data biases – are not easily learned skills. It takes years of practice in the proper teaching environments to hone these skills.

No classroom experience or quick-fire certification can replace learning from experienced mentors and mature work settings. As part of the organization's design and hiring approach, we must ensure that our most essential hires can use data objectively in today's information age.

We live in an age of many information-capturing tools, and the world's largest companies trade information. There is also a proliferation of ways we can create charts and tables with minimal effort. So, it is tempting for everyone to jump on the data bandwagon and loosely use the words "analysis" and "reporting" to describe any kaleidoscope of information.

Although data-related concepts aren't rocket science and can be mastered, they require discipline to learn. Even more importantly, experience is necessary to gain humility about the true power of data, where what we don't know often proves far more important than the little we know.

First, every company must have a Congruence Architect with deep expertise in hypothesis development, forward-looking problem-solving, and risk management using objective data. This role must be able to do the work independently, influence the rest of the company regarding operations baseline performance, and guide micro- and macroevolutions. As our company serves more customers, this role will require additional enablement resources with similar skills to focus exclusively on problem-solving.

Second, ownership of analysis and reporting optimally resides under the same role. These two components are highly intertwined, even though they serve different purposes. There is no value in splitting analysis and reporting responsibilities into separate roles because they require the same skills. Furthermore, creating separate roles can lead to turf wars about who is accountable for what instead of seamlessly and collaboratively slipping between analysis and reporting. A well-done analysis leads to reporting, and breakdowns triggered through reporting lead to analysis.

Third, analysis and reporting are company-level skills that must be placed under our single Congruence Architect without piecemealing responsibilities across teams. Spreading this responsibility across resources under different teams creates unnecessary confusion and collaboration gaps because they are likely to use misaligned approaches and frameworks.

Fourth, this single team led by the Congruence Architect must report to the CEO. The CEO is the only value creator in a company empowered with broad oversight to own and improve every aspect of the present and future state of the operations baseline and manage downside risks. This aligns with the independence and objectivity expected from the Congruence Architect. Aligning the Congruence Architect under specific functional specialties will create conflicts of interest and a lack of independence.

Consider these design questions to evolve organization design and hiring in order to achieve mature use of data:

Do we have a single leader with deep hypothesis-based analysis and data-driven risk management experience?

Does this leader own both analysis and reporting responsibilities?

Are all analysis and reporting responsibilities across all functions assigned to one independent owner?

Does this independent owner of analysis and reporting directly work for the CEO?

A mature value engine that embraces the core principles around analysis allows our company to use internally developed insights to micro-evolve its offerings, processes, and management approach.

As a company grows, the number of employees and partners, critical initiatives, and customers increase, which may come with increased expectations from investors. This also means risks increase. A proactive and predictive reporting approach will allow us to foresee and resolve execution breakages and limit downside risks preemptively.

We have now covered our value engine and management approach, which form our operations baseline. These building blocks and systemic elements cover our people, offerings, processes, and information and, thus, our company's present state. Maintaining congruence between all these building blocks optimizes value exchange across stakeholders, investment efficiency, and sustainable profitability.

But what does the future bring? We must macro-evolve to keep up with time, scale, and environmental changes.

PART D

Corporate Strategy Is The Macroevolution North Star.

W E are at a pivotal point in our method.

Our management approach has a maturity that reflects our past efforts to embrace our company purpose and dictates our core values, organization design, hiring practices, and performance and compensation management. Our value engine demonstrates the effectiveness of our past productization efforts to create value for our customers. It also reflects the maturity of our processes, technology, and data to take our productized offering to our customers. Collectively, this is our company's operations baseline.

If our past actions were absolutely perfect, our sustainable value exchange would satisfy the risk-adjusted benefits we set forth for each stakeholder group in our purpose. We would do so within the capital efficiency and profitability parameters we agreed to in our board-approved purpose.

In our purpose-led Single Market Problem Entity, we will want to continue to create incremental value for customers and profits for investors, which also allows employees and partners to capture value through compensation and deploy their best skills and capabilities. Such a best version of our company can capture more of our addressable market.

Even in such a perfect scenario, the world around us changes so fast our customer incentives and needs will change. Our company's scale will demand more sophistication, and our environment might trigger tectonic shifts with new technologies, ideas, or social themes. Any or all of these will inject incongruences into our operations baseline's ability to maintain value creation and do so efficiently.

In reality, no company operates in its best version and will have significant incongruences that are hurting value creation. We may not have perfected our choice of customers, our offerings, or how our processes deliver value to customers. Our management approach building blocks may not be operating to a guiding purpose and our value creator performance and skills may not be congruent with our value engine.

Corporate strategy starts our macroevolution cycle that connects our past to our future.

Companies commonly use the word "pivot." Often, it refers to shifting the direction of the company. But such pivots often ignore the past and rarely learn why mistakes were made in an urgency to jump to a better future with little clarity on what that looks like. This is not macroevolution. This is gambling because an arbitrary pivot is another attempt at trial-and-error. This tendency correlates with an incongruent company purpose and a board that is largely focused on self-serving outcomes, failing to represent all stakeholder groups.

Our effective transition from our past and present to our future starts with our corporate strategy while staying within the boundaries set by our purpose.

Moving from our present to the future also implies making investment decisions. We need to decide how to use our existing investment more efficiently and how to create even greater value with it. We may also generate a profit, some of which we can reinvest while the rest is paid to owners and investors. Or we may want to deploy new investment from existing or new investors.

As a prerequisite to investment decisions, we need to articulate the north star of our purpose-led company, its corporate strategy, based on deep analysis and objective decisions, without which we would be nomads walking around the desert in circles.

Corporate strategy is a value creation and capital efficiency prerogative.

A frequent philosophical debate that I have engaged in is the importance of structure and discipline, especially in this age when growth is a widely considered proxy for success. The true essence of a well-vetted strategy is lost among key decision makers such as investors and executives who are operating in an individualistic mindset. Individualistic decision-makers tend to see others as less important and rarely understand and appreciate their risk-adjusted incentives. Such a company's board often operates without a concrete and well-balanced purpose beyond creating near-term extrinsic perceptions to sell the entity.

Without a balanced purpose, decisions and actions tend to become self-serving and misaligned with the incentives of the collective enterprise. Storytelling and operating reactively without effective overarching decisions that articulate what the company really does becomes more typical. Tactical day-to-day busy work or lack of resources become excuses for a lack of clear direction. "We don't have time for it" or "We already know" followed by a rehearsed story is a telltale sign of such companies.

Embracing structure and discipline backed by a well-balanced purpose starts our strategy journey. A guiding corporate strategy is just as or more critical to an early life cycle company because resources and time are more constrained. Unfortunately, this is counter to how many companies think about their priorities in the haste to tactically firefight problems or spend newfound investment to demonstrate short-term progress without an in-depth assessment of investment effectiveness or sustainable value creation.

Imagine that we are trying to solve a company-level problem.

What if we had a time machine that allows us to return to the same moment an infinite number of times and try all possible paths to solve the problem? Think Groundhog Day.

Or . . .

What if we had infinite resources, both people and tools, to do what we ask them to, and between all of those resources, we get to try all possible options to solve that big problem?

If either of these were possible, we wouldn't need a corporate strategy because we could tactically try each option and eventually get lucky with the one that works best. But that's not the real world. Companies have finite resources and time. So, a tactical, trial-and-error approach is a capitally inefficient and often impossible path to find the best answer to company-level sophisticated problems.

Once our company has a valid offering that some customers want to buy, we must learn to operate with an effective strategy. This is the most efficient use of investment and exponentially improves the probability of sending our resources down the right path to maximize value creation.

As a transformation partner to a twelve-year-old managed services company, my mandate was to evolve the company's operations baseline, which had significant incongruences. I shared a six-point plan with the CEO based on my analysis to uncover why the operations baseline wasn't supporting new customer acquisition or profitability and causing dissatisfaction among existing customers. I agreed to focus on the bottom five points that would mature fundamental levers across the operations baseline. The top point in the plan was the need for a decisive corporate strategy, and the CEO insisted on owning it without my support.

Nine months later, initiatives around the bottom five points made significant inroads. But their adoption and disciplined execution were always a challenge because the company continued to operate in a strategic vacuum. Any strong-willed person could take the company in the direction they pleased. For example, choosing a specific customer group was impossible because selling followed the sales reps' instincts and personal preferences; use case-focused productization efforts were distracted by tactical ideas that weren't creating value. The company's investment to improve its operations baseline had limited impact because it didn't have a concrete strategy.

Our journey to mature our operations baseline must start with an effective corporate strategy. We can dance around this all we want, but the strategic planning that frames all our work for the next execution cycle and that plan's actual execution depends on this important but poorly understood concept. So, our company's macroevolution from our current operations baseline requires a deep dive into corporate strategy.

Corporate Strategy Maturity Model.

Study the Corporate Strategy Maturity Model in Figure D1 to assess your company's current strategic effectiveness and then chart a course to a higher level of congruence. Like our maturity models for management approach and value engine, the far left and least mature state implies a lack of corporate strategy in any sense. This leads to a reactive company without much of a forward-looking plan. This immature state is *Level 1: Reactive*.

In this state, the company operates like a kite in a storm, with the path forward unclear and decisions essentially gyrations from one big or small idea to the next in quick succession, based on very little formal structure or analysis. The company gives employees, customers, investors, and partners minimal comfort that there is an actual path forward other than getting to the next day or week. A company at *Level 1: Reactive* is unlikely to create considerable value for customers and investors or deploy capital efficiently.

I once led the efforts to expand a new business division of a mid-market company. The CEO pitched this new division to me as the company's future and how the current division that created most of its past revenue no longer demonstrated a sustainable opportunity. My first few weeks focused on shoring up operational challenges for the new business division and improving the value creation efforts. However, within ten weeks, the company decided that the new market was no longer the priority, and it would start focusing on its legacy business again, which implied writing off the investment and laying off several employees in the new business division.

What triggered this change? A board member asked some basic questions that the executive team didn't have good answers to.

The reality was that the company never found out whether the new market

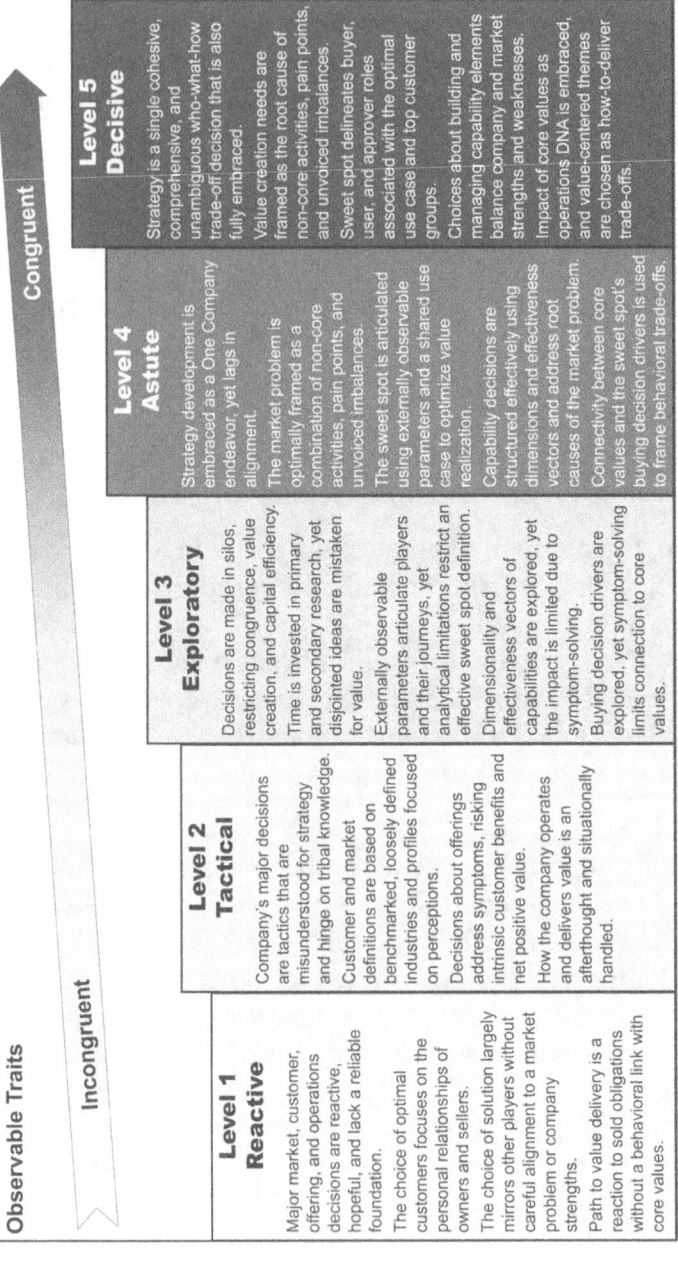

Figure D1. Corporate Strategy Maturity Model.

could have been a real opportunity or not because a few short-term uncomfortable events led to a complete change in priorities. This exemplifies *Level 1: Reactive.*

Moving to the right of the maturity model implies that the board and executives are inclined to make forward-looking decisions. But the commitment to objective analysis, comprehensive decisions, and decisive choices to chart a dependable path forward is weak. In a practical sense, the outcomes at *Level 2: Tactical* are unlikely to be better than Level 1 because the company relies heavily on tribal knowledge and isn't investing time and mindshare into objective information.

A good shot in the arm, like significant customer losses or a new CEO, is often a necessary trigger to move a company from *Level 2: Tactical* to the right of the model, where valuable strategic concepts are explored and leveraged in the company's go-forward path.

At *Level 3: Exploratory,* strategy development is less intuitive and reactive and more objective and analytical. The company uses relevant analytical principles to identify and embrace the sweet spot – a blueprint of customers that greatly value its offerings and offer a large enough market to focus on.

Becoming market-aware involves scientific exploration. Going after the wrong customers in a suboptimal manner is a poor investment of capital and contributes to an unsustainable path. Although a CEO's gut feeling may be enough to validate a company's market in the early stages, it will not be enough to operate profitably and sustainably beyond that.

Knowing who to sell our offerings to is a good start. But what should we offer, and how should we deliver it? The second and third pieces of the strategy puzzle are knowing exactly what to offer and how to deliver that offering. To do this well, the company must know its strengths and weaknesses. *Level 3: Exploratory* also begins a qualitative and quantitative introspective exercise to define these.

However, Level 3 is also plagued by silo thinking and limitations in analytical insight generation. A One Company mindset and a robust internalization of critical market-focused insights backed by objective analysis raise a company to *Level 4: Astute.*

Knowing the market and internal strengths and weaknesses takes a company to the doorstep of a good strategy, which implies translating our insights into a cohesive and comprehensive decision structure. To achieve *Level 5: Decisive,* we must develop a comprehensive set of choices and decisively choose a path forward that all stakeholders can embrace. Making hard choices comes with risk, but that's a leader's job. The company must have strong leadership to enable Level 5 maturity.

We will frame how we can create a tangible and impactful corporate strategy for our company through the following four chapters.

D.1
INTERNALIZE TRUE ESSENCE OF STRATEGY.

OUR modern company ecosystems are eerily similar to the biblical city of Babel, which collapsed due to conflicts triggered by citizens speaking many different languages and not understanding each other. Sadly, strategy has become business jargon just like the components that we discussed under Part B: Management Approach and Part C: Value Engine. But it does have real and necessary meaning. So, lets rediscover it.

I give a quick exercise on analytical interviews. I provide a plain piece of white paper and a pen and ask, "Draw a line."

What would you do?

Incredibly, a very large portion of my interview candidates draw a line right away without asking any questions and look at me with a proud smile that conveys, "Done!"

I hope your response is to ask for more information without any doubt in your mind. Geometry 101 – even the simplest straight line has a starting point and an end point. I ask this question to understand how a person thinks instinctively.

How will we know exactly where the starting point is on a piece of paper? First, you can ask for coordinates such as one inch from the bottom and two inches from the left. Then you must nail down where the endpoint is, which will require different coordinates. Do you see how the idea of drawing the simplest form of a line – a straight one – can become a worthwhile exercise?

What if your designated pen has a limited amount of very precious ink, and there is only so much of it? How does this change your perspective of the entire exercise?

Welcome to strategy!

Our draw-the-line exercise is akin to strategy development in a fundamental sense. Strategy development is a conceptually simple but practically difficult exercise of articulating how a company can move from its present state to a desired future state.

We can think of our operations baseline as the starting point of our line. I often ask people I meet about their level of clarity around the present state of the company. Whether they have a board, executive, supervisor, or employee role, I typically get a confident "Yes!" But this is also often followed by storytelling, and the same people are surprised by events around the company months down the line.

No company knows its current reality without an adequate analysis based on all the levers in this method. Therefore, it is essential to remain humble about our company's current coordinates.

The same applies to where we want our company to be one, two, or three years in the future. If it's not easy to determine where we are now, imagine how much more difficult it is to say where we want to be and mobilize many people in that direction!

The precious ink in our pen from the analogy is resources. We have limited investment, top talent with specific desired skills, and time in the real world. Strategy development is not an exercise of wishful thinking; it is an exercise of practicality. How far can we go from the starting point with the twists and turns we must take by being mindful of our constraints?

Using this draw-the-line exercise, can you see how overused and underestimated the word strategy has become? In colloquial English, we say "strategizing" to mean "think." We are dedicating an entire part of the method to corporate strategy because it is the lynchpin that dictates our company's path forward, including all investment choices, regardless of the current maturity of our operations baseline.

Principle 1: Strategy is not tactics.

We often think about great chess players as great strategists. Great coaches of successful sports teams also have this quality. Unfortunately, people often associate strategy with the importance of a person's position, which is where the word's overuse comes from. Who doesn't want to sound important?

What do chess players, renowned coaches, presidents, and CEOs have in common? They make big decisions in the context of their environment. Others often live with or follow those decisions. We all make decisions. But the simple truth is that not all decisions are equally important.

A person's life might involve five, ten, or fifteen strategic decisions that offer nerve-wracking and unknown paths that can change the course of our entire life. I am not referring to events of chance such as "if I had missed that bus by ten seconds, my life would have been better because of the accident it led to" or "if I had known that the company would become such a prosperous one, I would have continued to work there." Instead, strategic decisions imply purposeful choices after considering all options and outcomes.

What is the difference between such strategic choices and decisions and tactical ones? Three key aspects differentiate strategic choices.

Differentiator 1: Outcomes are probabilistic for each choice.

The choices preceding a strategic decision leads us down a path that we have never walked before. A well-defined choice in a strategic decision will give us a clear view of what "good" looks like for that choice, but we will not know with certainty whether it will result in the outcome we seek. We can assess our chances of achieving the outcome for each choice through the experience of others or objective assessment of information. But we will not be able to guarantee that it will lead us to the preferred outcome. This is exactly why strategic decisions are hard.

Differentiator 2: Decisions have an outsized cost.

We have to give up something to get something. A strategic decision always implies that we must sacrifice something we consider valuable.

If we cannot articulate the cost of a decision, then we are likely not making a strategic decision or aren't committing to a strategic decision, but just think we are.

Differentiator 3: Scale of impact is high.

Strategic choices are win-or-lose options. The outcomes are not passive. They are intended to create a significant positive upshot or avoid a major downside. Either way, the difference between a good and bad outcome for a strategic choice is considerable. This is precisely why it is important to frame what "good" looks like for a strategic choice. Without a clear articulation of what "good" looks like, we will be unable to compare each choice's upshot or downside limitation to the cost of making that choice.

Combining these three aspects that differentiate a strategic decision leads us to a simple fact: strategic decisions are not reversible. We cannot undo a strategic decision once we make our choice. We may make another strategic decision to try to go back to square one, but we cannot erase the cost and impact of the first decision. A strategic decision always has a significant cost, and there are no refunds in the real world.

Is going to Las Vegas and putting half our net worth on one roll of a roulette table a strategic decision? The outcome implies a significant cost, and the impact of win or lose is also high. So, if we are rational and clear-minded, "yes" because we have many options on what to do with half our net worth, and if we compare those options and choose this one, it is a strategic decision.

On the other hand, tactics cost us very little, and the predictable impact is also marginal. Thus, choices aren't often very relevant, and we can make many tactical decisions. Misunderstanding tactics as strategy blunts our opportunity for purposeful and impactful decisions when they matter.

Tactics and strategy are also dependent on a frame of reference. They are not absolutes. One person or entity's strategic choice can be another person's tactical choice and vice versa. A $1 million investment can be a strategic choice for a small company. At the same time, a $1 million purchasing approval might be a tactical decision that happens every week at a large established company because the outcome is likely guaranteed. The cost is low for their relative scale. Overlaying our three differentiating factors into the context of a given person or entity helps us focus on strategic decisions where necessary.

Things To Remember: Strategy vs. Tactics

Strategy is a decision that always satisfies three conditions – probabilistic outcomes, outsized cost, and significant scale of impact. Such a choice is irreversible and contextually colossal to the person or entity the decision pertains to. In comparison, tactics are choices with at least a relatively guaranteed desired outcome, relatively low cost, or only have a marginal impact.

When I shared this definition with an Executive MBA classroom full of experienced students, one stated, "I disagree; my start-up venture's strategy was to quickly hire the people we needed and not think too much." I quipped, "Thanks for confirming the importance of rediscovering strategy." If we don't understand our probabilistic choices and their cost and impact, we aren't thinking strategically. Such mistaken associations of tactical actions as strategy are pervasive.

Our three differentiators highlight why true strategy development is uncommon yet universally associated with positions of power. Know that a strategic decision has nothing to do with who is making it. Conversely, people with power often make tactical decisions when strategic ones are necessary.

A few simple day-to-day observations will reveal whether our company has a strategic inclination or whether we are consciously or subconsciously hoping to win with tactics. Our corporate strategy guides our entire operations baseline, including building and selling our offerings, which is where strategy-related incongruences are easiest to observe.

Consider these reflection questions to self-assess the company's strategy development and execution history:

Do the company's marketing collateral and channels reflect the actual value customers can receive without exaggerating to the point of unrecognition?

Do sellers set honest customer expectations about the breadth and depth of the value the company can deliver without setting unrealistic expectations?

Are value creators comfortably able to create promised value after selling without struggling to meet customer expectations set during sales?

Are we disciplined and productizing based on objective and practical market studies and avoiding poorly executed existing priorities?

Does our offering follow a comprehensive capability mindset that focuses on a specific use case and the root cause of the market problem without reactively building a slew of disconnected customer "wants"?

Are we methodically seeing our productization initiatives through to completion without leaving investment-consuming and non-value-creating loose ends?

Companies end up in the latter scenarios of these assessment questions because there is no cohesive corporate strategy or strategic plan, and execution did not follow the strategy. Not prioritizing a strategy-led approach leaves our company with little confidence in its self-worth, which is essentially the maturity of its operations baseline, leading to reactivity and setting expectations the company cannot deliver.

If we aren't performing well based on these questions, our company is likely gyrating between various tactics without much forward momentum. The most rational and hard-working employees and customers with options will consciously or otherwise sense the lack of direction and look for alternatives.

So, let's codify what "good" corporate strategy entails.

Principle 2: Corporate strategy triangulates answers for who-how-what questions.

The most important strategy development concept that enables macro-evolution of our operations baseline is "we can't have our cake and eat it too!" If you are only going to remember one thing from this entire part of the method, remember that.

Corporate strategy is the articulation of the company's path forward that the board, CEO, and senior executives identify and align on through objective external and internal assessments. It is the most practical evidence that allows every stakeholder to understand and align on the path to achieving the company's purpose. Moreover, such an articulation allows for optimal deployment of capital to solve the market problem and maximize value creation.

Things To Remember: Corporate Strategy

Corporate strategy is a single overarching decision that articulates what our company will do and will not do based on a comprehensive and cohesive set of strategic choices. Corporate strategy articulates a dovetailed answer to these three questions: 1) Who will we serve? 2) What will we offer? 3) How will we deliver?

It is tempting to whitewash the answers to these questions with obvious responses. A common mistake is to confidently use "Buyer Personas" or "Ideal Customer Profiles" developed in a silo by marketing teams as the answer to our "Who" question.

But selling teams rarely actually use such marketing answers. Productization efforts rarely use these "Buyer Personas" or "Ideal Customer Profiles" to build an offering. Such incongruent efforts don't constitute a cohesive strategy. We must take a more comprehensive approach to ensure we have a single answer to our who-how-what questions.

Strategy development is a triangulation exercise.

When I go through a strategy development exercise, I imagine it is similar to hand painting a landscape on a large oil canvas by an artist who has a clear vision of the image they are trying to produce but doesn't have a step-by-step plan for creating it. We don't start at one end of the canvas and try to perfect it before moving to the next part of the canvas.

Throughout the exercise, we may revisit the same topics, such as analyzing our current offerings or how customers think, because we often learn that our initial hypotheses require revision or that we need more information in specific areas. A simple linear mindset will result in tactics that are incorrectly packaged as strategic choices. Be open-minded about what you will learn through the exercise and revise your hypotheses and assessments.

As you will see in the next three chapters, our principles to answer the who-how-what questions do not take a linear path. They start slightly staggered, but much of the work happens concurrently where we will have to put the paintbrush at the same spots on the canvas multiple times to add depth and colors.

I cannot stress this enough. There are an incomprehensible number of services that package tactics as strategy. The only way to protect our company from being misled is to truly know what strategy is and what "good" looks like.

Principle 3: Leverage a trade-off and choices approach to frame corporate strategy.

We need a framework to translate the complex nature of strategy to a practical and actionable construct that articulates a single answer for our who-how-what questions. My simple framework has three parts.

First, strategy development starts with understanding and articulating how we frame our strategic choices. But it's hard to make one big nebulous decision all in one go.

We can effectively frame a strategic decision using a set of strategic trade-offs. The concept of trade-offs allows us to break down a complex overarching decision about our company's future into mutually exclusive, collectively exhaustive decision blocks. I call these decision blocks **Strategic Trade-offs.**

Things To Remember: Strategic Trade-offs

A strategic trade-off is a decision switch with two, three, or four choices. Each trade-off exhibits the three key aspects that differentiate strategic choices from tactical ones: uniquely significant impact, sizable cost to execute, and unguaranteed probabilistic outcome. Together, these trade-offs answer our who-how-what questions and add up to our overarching strategy.

We must develop a set of strategic trade-offs that comprehensively reflect our operations baseline at the current moment and our current market. A good set of strategic trade-offs is a handful of such switches covering all critical factors that answer our who-how-what questions.

A good rule of thumb is to prioritize between five and ten strategic trade-offs where each has two to four mutually exclusive choices and, collectively, they frame the single answer to our who-how-what question into a tangible decision board. Articulating trade-offs and related choices are critical because it is significantly easier to analyze and decide on a few discrete trade-offs with two or three options than compare ten or fifteen company-level paths, each with many pros and cons.

Think about deciding on our next vacation. We have infinite choices to pick from. Unless we are externally pushed to, we seldom directly choose our next vacation. Instead, subconsciously, we define trade-offs such as type of landscape, which might include choices like beaches, mountains, cities; affordability, which might have choices like low-budget or expensive; length of vacation choices like one week, two weeks, or three weeks; companionship during the vacation choices like solo, with friends, with family, etc. Our final vacation decision is simply an aggregation of our choices for each of these independent trade-offs. The same concept applies while developing corporate strategy.

The crux is that no company can do it all across trade-offs. It is not practical because every company lives within constraints of time, investment, and skill. Higher quality or speed usually implies a higher cost. At the same time, this exercise will also have to ensure that these choices leave us with a large enough market opportunity to meet our company's purpose.

Second, strategy is about making hard choices based on strategic trade-offs and associated choices. That's why people who decisively make strategic choices and risk their reputation and jobs to do so tend to make the big bucks. Identifying the set of strategic trade-offs and the associated choices is important. But it is only practically useful if the board, CEO, and senior executives have the will to make decisions on each trade-off.

Strategic decisions frame what a company will do. But the converse is often ignored and leads to ineffective strategy development. Framing what our company will do also implies it has concretely stated what we will not do. Very few executives are consciously or subconsciously comfortable deciding what we will not do. The option to change our mind is nice, but making strategic decisions comes with the risk that we make a choice that will cost us without the payoff.

A related manifestation is indiscipline. Executives face revenue, cost, and competitor pressure every single day. Being confident in a strategic decision and staying disciplined in executing that decision is not easy, and companies often slip. Once this discipline has slipped, we will not be able to diagnose the real reasons behind why our results are positive or negative.

Third, recall that our company is a Single Market Problem Entity. It has a single corporate strategy, which must be readable as one cohesive sentence, using simple language, limiting any interpretive differences, as illustrated in Figure D2. It must be based on the strategic trade-offs and associated choices, summarizing the company's decision to deploy its investment most efficiently to solve the market problem.

Conversely, corporate strategy is not an aggregation of siloed decisions independently made by executives in a manner that serves the employees reporting to them. This disjointed approach is common yet would invalidate our requirement to create a cohesive, non-conflicting company-level north star.

Figure D2. A company has one strategy.

The CEO must own the single dovetailed corporate strategy, with details crafted by playmakers across the company led by the Congruence Architect. The CEO's leadership enables all executives and the board to rally around the company's north star and stay committed.

Principle 4: Current operations baseline must underpin the hypotheses driving strategy development.

Like any other analytical problem-solving exercise, strategy development hinges on good analyses. The quality of analysis hinges on the quality of the hypothesis, which we introduced in our chapter on data. A motivated data cruncher could prove that aliens live on Earth; but that would be nonsense.

A hypothesis is simply a hunch. There are objective, knowledge-based hunches. Then, there are subjective, self-serving, and poorly informed hunches. The value creators who lead and support strategy development must be good at reality-based hypothesis development. This is not a skill trainable in the short term. Effective hunches come from life experience. Living in the real world and experiencing how people behave and how complexities appear in practice are minimum requirements for a good analyst.

For example, I led the analysis necessary to acquire a commercial signage company. I spent four weeks in deep research and number crunching. But observing store signage in the real world was the only way to ensure that the numbers on my computer screen made any practical sense. The practicality of our strategy development comes from hypotheses based on the real world.

During strategy development, we would assess considerations like which part of the market we could serve best or how we can serve that part of the market best. These hypotheses must be based on the current state of our operations baseline and analysis of data from the execution of our previous strategy and plan.

Corporate strategy development requires a reasonable operations baseline to start from. We must have some real customers who have purchased our offering. Friends, family, and close acquaintances don't count as customers who have objectively purchased our offering. We must also have some semblance of an offering that works. This is critical because we need objective information to develop hypotheses.

Theranos, a healthcare technology company, offers an extreme example to explain the importance of starting from our current baseline. The founding CEO claimed for several years that the company had a breakthrough blood-testing offering that would allow testing for hundreds of ailments by using the company's small testing box, requiring only a small blood draw. The results would be ready in a few minutes.

It was a radically new approach compared to the blood testing methods that we are all familiar with – several vials of blood are drawn from a person, sent to a lab, and the results are available days later. Theranos insiders repeatedly lied to the world and customers and probably themselves for several years. Their box didn't work at all. It was essentially just a front to do traditional testing, except Theranos did even that poorly because they didn't get enough blood from individuals.

I imagine Theranos went through at least one macroevolution cycle. What would have happened if they objectively started a strategy development exercise based on their own history and the market? Basing their efforts to create value on their real capabilities would have anchored them to practical considerations rather than a magic black box that never worked.

Developing strategic trade-offs and choices is a problem-solving exercise seeking insights. Problem-solving implies a vast majority of time goes into problem definition. It is a common mistake to rush to a solution before understanding the problem. A key portion of problem definition is articulating hypotheses. Since corporate strategy development requires some customers and an offering articulated through our operations baseline, it is always the appropriate grounding source for hypotheses.

Principle 5: Avoid antiquated and biased data sources for strategic analysis.

Garbage in; garbage out.

The quality of information created and used to develop insights and frame our trade-offs and choices is as important as the hypotheses we are assessing. Unfortunately, in today's world, information becomes outdated very quickly because the speed with which technology changes markets and the pace at which adoption happens is exponentially higher than in past decades. Change will only accelerate. So, dependence on years of passive experience in the market or what worked in recent years can become more of a liability than an asset.

This speed is a great equalizer, which means every company must stay on its toes. We must renew our hypotheses about changes in our market every cycle, revise our mindset about data elements to capture and analyze, ensure we respect other market participants, reassess how they could have evolved since the past cycle, and so on.

This makes the entire strategy development exercise an open-minded, sprint research program. It involves gathering new and objective data through primary and secondary research.

Primary Research refers to the approach of creating the data we need through our own efforts. The Congruence Architect and the analytical enablement team will have to actively capture qualitative data through structured, documented, and cataloged conversations with various types of customers, partners, and other market participants to test key hypotheses. It also includes actively capturing and analyzing quantifiable measurements of our operations baseline.

We must augment our primary research with **Secondary Research**. This second category refers to externally created information we can buy, borrow, or use freely. There are plenty of studies and research papers written by associations, academics, analysts, and governments in every market that can support our objective analysis efforts.

They are both equally important. But it is easier to know the quality and objectivity of primary sources because we get to account for the data flaws and biases. For instance, using a study about our market published by an association may be misguiding if a company that benefitted from the publication commissioned the study to boost their own business.

Having structured and planned discussions with customers that are unbiased, thorough, and well-documented, along with hypothesis-driven analysis of historical data, is the only path to arrive at the insights we need. Every company should constantly be talking to customers and capturing data objectively. However, to truly understand customers' needs and mindset, we must go well beyond asking superficial questions and work with reality based, unbiased hypotheses about their buying approach and incentives.

Customers are normal human beings; they are often polite, guarded, and very busy. Asking customers unsophisticated questions – such as "will you continue to buy our offerings?" – will allow them to provide ambiguous answers and get back to their lives quickly. Additionally, it is easy to fall prey to biases and capture poor data during primary research with customers. Recall principles from Chapter C.3 to eliminate pitfalls around data flaws and biases.

Whether our current operations baseline is guided by a corporate strategy or not, we can build a new strategy for our next macroevolution cycle with up-to-date and unbiased data. Next, we will explore the levers to build that corporate strategy.

D.2
REBUILD MARKET KNOWLEDGE TO UNCOVER STRATEGIC INCONGRUENCES.

IN our ever-changing world, at least one of our who-how-what trade-offs or associated choices will need to change every macroevolution cycle so that our company stands the best chance to become or maintain its best version. This starts with taking intentional steps each cycle to assess our market and operations baseline. Gaining new insights to shift our north star intentionally will be hard.

Our alternative is to assume that our current path will suffice. The risk is that customer needs, preferences, and environmental factors evolve beyond us, and other players fill the void we leave.

Strategic blunders or lack of strategic focus arise from several factors. These include a shallow understanding of our market, an ineffective definition of the market problem, poor identification of the root causes that need to be solved, and insufficient acknowledgment of the strengths and weaknesses of others in the market. Most strategy development exercises I've been part of had a positive shock-and-awe reaction from the board and executives, especially if they assumed they knew their stakeholders and market well.

Principle 1: Embrace the search for objective insights to counter overconfidence bias.

Donald Rumsfeld's 2002 framing of whether Iraq posed a credible threat with weapons of mass destruction, which eventually led to Iraq's invasion based on incorrect information, is a strategy development lesson for the ages. Our informational universe can be broken into known-knowns, known-unknowns, and unknown-unknowns. Known knowns are things we know we must know and have learned them. Known-unknowns are things we know are important, but we have yet to learn enough about them. This is learnable because we know they are blind spots. The most dangerous bucket is unknown-unknowns. This is a black hole where we don't know what we are missing. This bucket leads to the most strategic blunders. Our goal through market assessment is to reduce the size of our unknown-unknowns and increase the size of known-knowns and known-unknowns.

Remember the Dunning-Kruger Effect? Every struggling entity I've worked with has a loftier perspective about its abilities and understanding of its market and customers than reality. This natural bias bleeds into missing or ignoring the necessary details to solve the market problem and evolve.

As I was kicking off strategy development and strategic planning at a technology company, I informed the CEO of my method, starting with a market study. His response was, "What would you learn? We have already spoken to our customers, and I have the answers we need. So, you can skip that exercise!" This belief permeated across the company because many employees interacted with customers. But it was without an analytical intention.

The company had grown through the sheer wit of a handful of people. But a decade in, new sales proved difficult, operations were highly inefficient, and the company created disjointed solutions, hoping one would change its fortune.

I decided to burn some relationship capital and went ahead anyway. After a few weeks of engaging various market participants, we produced a deeper and more objective set of insights on the market that changed everyone's mind about what we knew. Support grew, and we framed effective trade-offs that changed our path forward. Ultimately, the board approved this new path at the end of the year.

Running a business is a tough job, and it requires self-belief and confidence. But if we believe we know everything there is to understand and deeper market analysis is a waste of time, it will lead to a poor strategy.

It is not uncommon for a CEO to tell me, "I just told you exactly what our market is and what our customers need." In contrast, a customer-facing employee at the same company would tell me, "We are just making things up as we go without a clear direction."

It is easy to get caught up in everyone else's view of our market or take published articles at face value and think we know enough. Few outlets publish information without an underlying bias or agenda, especially regarding companies and markets. Despite my best efforts to be objective, this book will have a skew based on my experiences, and you must apply your critical thinking as you use it.

The world around us changes fast, and our market has evolving needs. An objective and experienced Congruence Architect will ensure that we embrace humility and start strategy development with a learning mindset. We have one company and one market and macro-evolve once a year or less. It's best to do it well!

Principle 2: Commission a market landscape to articulate the market problem comprehensively and objectively.

Strategy development starts with redefining the market problem effectively.

Recall that we introduced the market problem concept earlier as a three-legged stool. It is a combination of non-core activities, voiced pain points, and unvoiced imbalances, as illustrated in Figure D3. Let's dive into how we develop insights around each of these to create a fresh view of our market problem as part of strategy development.

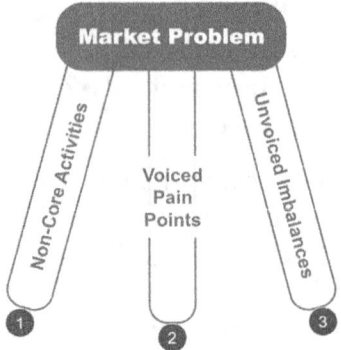

Figure D3. Market problem is a three-legged stool.

Before going further, I repeated the word "market" several times without stating precisely what I meant by it. It is far from a casual concept.

> **Things To Remember: Market**
>
> **A market is an ecosystem with natural boundaries where different players perform various activities to create and extract value.**

The existence of a market ecosystem doesn't imply a fair or equitable flow of value between players. Most markets have poor business models and imbalanced value exchanges between players at any given time. Such imbalances in value exchange imply opportunities for change. Change is good for some players, and not so good for others. We are just one player in our market, which constantly changes.

A mass disruption in any market is predictable based on long periods of imbalanced value flow or low-value creation by players.

An everyday example of such disruption was the entry of ride-sharing applications. For decades, most major US cities operated on a taxi medallion system that created significant value flow gaps. City governments created the medallion system decades ago. Over time, the entities that hold on to medallions squeezed people who drove the taxis while passengers felt they overpaid for poor service. The ride-sharing disruption took advantage of these value gaps and inserted new players and new types of activities.

Most market shifts are far more subtle and gradual, making it even more important to ensure we aren't falling asleep at the wheel. So, how do we understand our market and its problems?

By creating a **market landscape**, we can understand and refresh our view of our market and reframe the market problem.

Things To Remember: Market Landscape

A market landscape articulates our ecosystem with all the relevant players, their activities, and the value flow between them. It identifies potential new opportunities and shifts that our company must address. It also informs us of risks to our current value creation model.

A market landscape frames our market in a single, cohesive view refreshed with the latest insights. It becomes our organization's single source of truth on the market and protects our company from opinions, outdated tribal knowledge, and insight gaps.

Consider these reflection questions to dislodge ourselves from our past when studying our market:

What types of companies or people are involved in our ecosystem? How will we logically group these companies and people?

What activities do each of these groups perform in the ecosystem today? How can we logically group these activities?

Which of these activity groups create value? Which of these activity groups extract value?

Where are the known impediments in the ecosystem? Where are the discrepancies in value flow in this ecosystem? Which players are undertaking activities that are not core to their existence?

How can these insights be dovetailed to frame the market problems key players face?

As we read these questions, let's hold ourselves back from thinking, "I know these answers!" Our goal here is not to have some answers. Remember, it's the unknown-unknowns that will kill us. We want to ensure that the answers are comprehensive and cohesive and reflect our market's evolving reality.

Do not be shy about details. If you do not have an audience for a compelling market landscape, it reflects the organization's management approach, not your work. A quote that the CEO of a struggling company shared with each employee as we conducted 2-on-1 meetings was: "Our challenges come from our headlines culture . . . we need to start reading the details!"

Principle 3: Start with the player groups who create and consume value.

We no longer live in a simple barter system where two parties come to the market to trade with each other. Every trade involves several stakeholders, each with different needs and varying solutions to offer. To understand the whole picture, it is critical to capture all the key players in the ecosystem.

I never miss a chance to learn about companies. Most companies tend to describe themselves as an oversimplified two-player relationship between employees and customers. Unfortunately, this individualistic tendency is in our DNA, which led us to believe in the earth-is-the-center model for millennia.

Our market landscape exercise must break this natural tendency to think that the market revolves around us. We must remove ourselves from the middle and see the market for what it truly is – a multiplayer ecosystem, just like our universe. Our market is an ecosystem that operates with or without us, and there are always several players.

Player groups allow us to understand the whole market in a manageable way.

It is impossible to gather data about all the individuals and companies out there for the research and analyses our market study requires. But we can manage to learn about a few prioritized groups of similar players. Let's call these **Player Groups**.

Things To Remember: Player Groups

A player group is a similar set of individuals or companies that we believe will behave similarly. Each player group is capable of creating a similar value and benefits from a different value created by another player group.

Player groups are a superset of all similar clusters in our ecosystem, including the customer groups we introduced under productization. But in our start-with-a-clean-slate-to-learn mindset, we must assume we don't know our customer groups.

A player group can consist of customers with similar behaviors and needs, companies like ours with a similar operations baseline, or companies that act and look differently from us but add similar value to customer groups. Individuals or companies that our customers serve can form a different player group.

As a rule of thumb, avoid framing players as customers, partners, or competitors at this stage because this presumes that we sit in the middle of our ecosystem. Instead, use value-focused groupings that frame each group's reason to exist by applying the principles we learned in the chapter about company purpose.

For instance, we want to understand our current customers' customers in the eventuality that our current customers create limited value themselves and are largely go-betweens. If we have historically sold to resellers, placing the follow-on value extractors on the landscape is important because who we sell to and how we sell might change.

Consider these design questions to map player groups without placing our company in the center:

Who are the players that gain the most value if their real-world problems in the ecosystem are addressed? Let's call these "primary value extractors."

Are there players who extract a different and small fraction of the value compared to primary value extractors? If so, who are they? Let's call these "auxiliary value extractors."

Who are the players that extract value from the primary value extractors? Consider calling these players "next-level value extractors."

Which players in the market create the most value through real-world problem solving? Let's call them "primary value creators."

Who are the secondary value creators that complement the offerings of the primary players? Let's call them "auxiliary value creators."

Who are the players that the primary value extractors would fall back on if the primary and auxiliary value creators are ineffective? These are "substitutes."

Are there indispensable critical players in our ecosystem? Consider them unavoidable portions of our market, like digital and social advertising or big technology solutions everyone uses. Let's call them "foundational value creators."

Identifying the players in our market is relatively easy. The challenging aspect is finding the discipline and humility to ensure we intentionally include and analyze every relevant player group. Do not succumb to the tendency to obsess over one specific type of player or group and fail to understand the complete picture.

Hubris about discounting the value other entities can create in our market can be our downfall. If our offering is a niche data visualization software, ignoring a group of general software players like Microsoft or Google with raw spreadsheet visualization tools is a desire to tell a story that comforts us.

So, how exactly do we group these players?

Create player groups using externally observable parameters.

The entire goal of our market assessment is to understand how various players behave and what they hope to gain from being part of our ecosystem. So, we must group players according to their behaviors.

The path to grouping players is to develop a set of meaningful parameters with appropriate choices that effectively predict that group's behaviors.

Choose a handful of meaningful parameters and two to four categories for each parameter for each type of player.

If the players in our ecosystem are individual consumers, these parameters describe a human being and their behaviors. These parameters might include:

- *Personal attributes such as age, gender, and ethnicity.*

- *Economic proxies such as employment status or type, residence neighborhood, and property ownership.*

- *Behavioral traits such as frequent traveler or fitness enthusiast.*

- *Relationship traits such as relationship status or parenthood.*

If the players are other companies, these parameters help group companies. Such business traits might include:

- *Size of the company, based on employee count or revenue.*

- *Company's position in the value chain with categories like manufacturer, distributor, or retailer.*

- *Company's business model, like franchising or direct ownership models.*

- *Company's primary capability dimension, like service provider or seller of physical goods.*

- *Company's geographic location by country or other regional categories.*

- *Environment in which companies operate, such as highly regulated or unregulated.*

These examples illustrate how broad our player parameters can be. Strong analytical resources must use their business acumen and analytical prowess to identify optimal parameters for each type of player without rinse-and-repeating parameters from other sources.

Let's formally call these parameters **Externally Observable Parameters**.

Things To Remember: Externally Observable Parameters

Externally observable parameters allow us to group players in our market according to their behaviors, and they must satisfy three conditions: 1) Parameters must have a causal predictive relationship to the group's behaviors, 2) Every single parameter used should be unambiguous and non-interpretive, and 3) Actionable information must be available for every single parameter.

This is one of the most time-consuming steps in our market assessment, and we must expect to iterate because getting these groupings right on the first pass is nearly impossible. Use the three conditions to pressure-test and ensure we choose high-quality parameters.

First, our chosen parameters and categories must have a causal relationship to the activities of that player type. For most companies, vast amounts of data without flaws and biases are not a reality. We must make do with small amounts of carefully selected data, which means we have to start with solid hypotheses on effective parameters and categories that predict the behaviors of different types of players.

Choosing arbitrary parameters and categories with the hope of finding millions of lines of data to analyze is wishful thinking for anyone outside large consumer companies. For instance, an individual's religious affiliation can be a relevant parameter for the right market, but it is a stretch to presume that this parameter predicts exercise habits. Moreover, such arbitrary choices can leave us with confounding insights because we might misinterpret noise in a small data set as meaningful insights.

Second, every single parameter used should be unambiguous and non-interpretive. Different analysts must independently be able to look at players and put them into the same categories for all parameters without ambiguity. For example, suppose I have "value chain position" as a parameter and categorize a player as a "distributor." In that case, my colleagues should categorize that player similarly for the "value chain position" parameter. Ambiguous parameters or underlying categories will lead to misleading takeaways.

Third, actionable information must be available for every parameter, either from an objective data provider or gathered reliably by value creators.

Grouping players is more than an analytical exercise. We must be able to identify all players in the real world based on these parameters. If we choose a specific group as our future customers, we must be able to readily identify all players in that group to sell to without ambiguity.

As we frame our player groups, think about illustrating the outputs of this first step, as shown in Figure D4. This is an opportunity to generate a reasonably accurate count of the number of players that belong to each player group. This key ingredient can help us decide how much effort we should spend on a group. We will use this data to generate our addressable market size, which directly correlates with the value creation opportunity around the market problem and the volume of players who experience it.

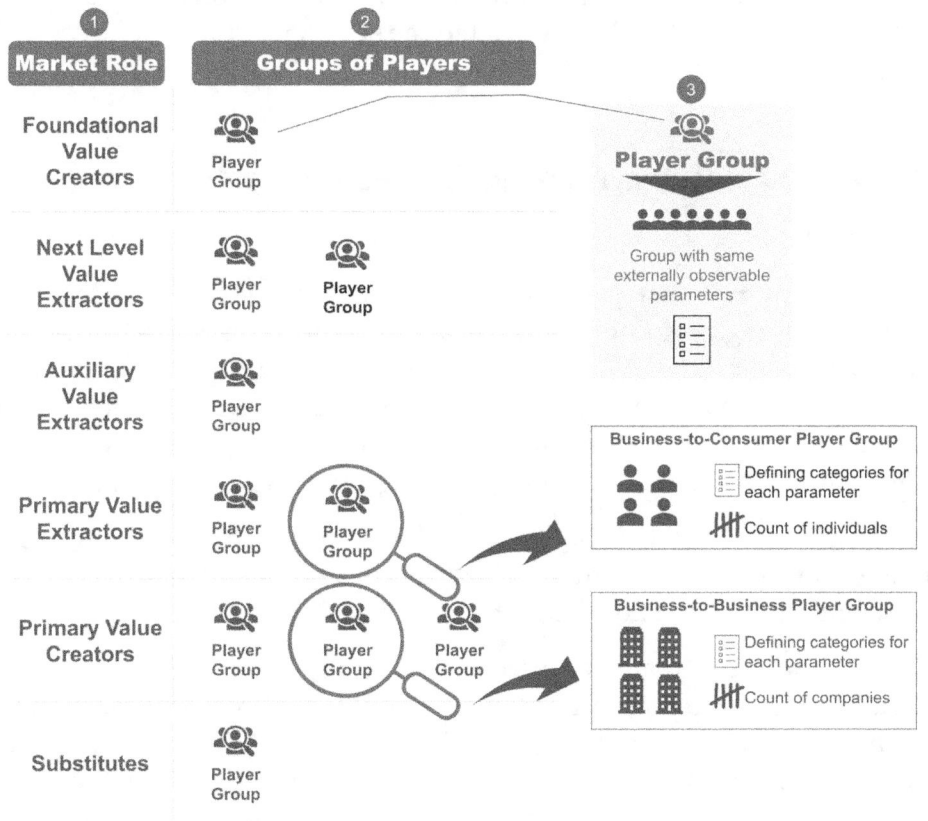

Figure D4. Market landscape unearths all players in the ecosystem.

I led the market landscape assessment for an education solutions client that supported the learning experience for professional certifications using software and services. This client served a broad set of value extractors but had historically not grouped them. Our fresh look allowed us to behaviorally group these significantly different players, including professional certification organizations, industry associations, colleges and universities, training material creators, training material deliverers, and various other types of learners.

The company historically viewed all educators who created professional education content similarly. Through our exercise, we framed educators who created content to teach employees of companies differently from educators who created content for personal professional education in separate player groups. This impacted the strategic trade-offs we framed for strategy development.

Principle 4: Assess player groups' behaviors to identify non-core activities.

Using common industry or functional terms unnecessarily anchors us to history. Imagine going to a large sports facility with basketball courts and volleyball courts. What if our skill is playing tennis and we find one wall in a volleyball court to practice hitting a tennis ball against? Would we say that we are playing volleyball? Are we playing tennis? We aren't doing either. We are just practicing hitting a tennis ball against a wall.

People close to Uber, Lyft, and DoorDash would describe them as a "technology company." They offer transportation solutions through a mobile app, which is more reflective of their profitability struggle.

WeWork was also treated as a technology company. IWG PLC has been around for decades, offering a hoteling concept of workspaces, and has been profitable. These entities can only be seen as office real estate rental outfits. If our goal is intrinsic value and profitability, then we must focus on the underlying activities in our market rather than gimmicks to boost our extrinsic market price.

To do so, we must understand how various player groups we placed on the landscape create and extract value. We must understand these activities, group them logically, and learn which of those activities fall under the strictures of our market.

This must sound familiar. We are applying flow thinking to build journeys for the player groups.

Categorize players' behaviors into logical activity groups.

First, we want to learn the details of the activities that players go through in their hourly, daily, and weekly journeys. We don't know what we don't know, and we need to learn. Changes in one player's activities change other players' activities and relevance.

Companies often take an easy path and source such information from previously published articles. But who publishes these articles and why? Are they marketing? Published information will rarely provide details of how our ecosystem works. We must get our hands dirty to ask objective, critical-thinking questions and gather data to pinpoint changes in activities in our ecosystem across all player groups.

Consider these design questions to build a market landscape:

What are each player group's behavioral characteristics and activities in the context of our ecosystem?

How can we logically categorize these underlying activities into groups?

Focus on what we can learn about each group through behavioral observations without relying solely on what they say they do. We want to build our strategy based on reality instead of marketing messages. Frame these as steps using actionable verbs where possible.

Second, as we learn more, consider whether the definition of each player group changes. In our triangulation approach, we are likely to learn that our perceptions about one or more player groups change after we take the time to understand their activities. This is necessary because our player groups are created based on behavior-predicting parameters.

If the activity groups don't align for players in the same groups, our player groups or our understanding of their activities is likely incorrect.

Hypothetically, if we assume that the shopping activities of students in a specific age group at a particular type of preparatory school are similar, we might be surprised to learn that they are not. Grouping students differently based on their scholarship status may more accurately reflect their activities.

We should expect to learn and iterate.

This effort allows us to minimize our unknown-unknown bucket. But even the simplest of markets can be pretty expansive. We can't successfully learn about every player group and activity group. Just like we drew a boundary around our company with a purpose, we must learn to clearly focus our market study.

Frame a practical market boundary in alignment with company purpose.

Third, strategy development is a series of tough decisions. We cannot address problems around all activities that every player group experiences. Recall the analogy of a village built around a lake that I used to introduce the concept of company purpose. Our purpose-led company exists to benefit specific activities of certain stakeholders, and our market landscape boundary must keep us focused on this task.

Activity groups are the optimal way to define our market boundary. Interestingly, these groups remain thematically similar over decades or even centuries, while the permutations of how various player groups create value around activities often change.

For instance, using a hired vehicle to travel from point A to point B has been a market ecosystem for centuries. The colloquial term "cab" predates automobiles and originally referred to two-wheeled carriages.

In the hypothetical student shopping scenario above, our company's purpose should guide us to focus on activities related to objects like educational materials or nutritious food, services such as cataloging or deliveries, or any other benefits we exist to address.

Consider this design question to build a market landscape:

Which activity groups align with the benefit statements of various stakeholders within our company's purpose? Add two to three adjacent activity groups in each direction to ensure a comprehensive understanding.

Without setting this boundary, we will try to analyze too widely and have few relevant insights to act on. Such a tightened market boundary also limits wishful distractions that creep into strategy development discussions.

Analyze value flow to identify non-core activities.

Fourth, as we learn about the activities of player groups, we must keep a keen eye on our primary task at this stage – identifying non-core activities. They are exactly what they sound like.

Things To Remember: Non-Core Activities

Non-core activities are the first of three parts of our market problem. They are activities that fall outside a player group's core competency or preferred activity, yet they are forced to engage in them due to a lack of options or awareness about comparative advantage. Non-core activities in the ecosystem are optimally solved through a capability that transfers them to another player group that is better at executing or eliminating them.

Businesses that address non-core activities are everywhere. For example, if we consider the ecosystem of groceries for in-home use, imagine a specific player group of primary value extractors with low price consciousness and everyday grocery needs. Transferring groceries from a grocery store shelf to the doorstep can be a non-core activity. Several businesses pegged this non-core activity as the market problem, starting with Peapod over a decade ago and moving to Instacart more recently.

However, another player group in this ecosystem may consider that same activity core to their journey. I belong to a group of primary value extractors who make on-the-fly decisions based on inspecting produce, checking expiry dates, and spotting visual discounts. I have never had my groceries delivered.

Similarly, we must flag non-core activities in the ecosystem associated with specific player groups to highlight obvious value gaps, which is the first leg of our market problem.

Consider this design question to frame non-core activities:

Which activities are performed by specific player groups that do not align with comparative advantage principles?

Figure D5 reflects the use of value flows to learn about our market activities, set our market boundaries, and draft early hypotheses on non-core activities we could address. Remember, strategy development is as much about what we do not do as it is about what we do. So, our hypotheses must also validate non-core activities we will not address.

We fleshed out various player groups' activities at my education solutions client. We further broke out educators who created content for individuals into separate player groups based on mandatory certifications and nice-to-have certifications because their activities were different. This meant that their market problems would also be different. This raised questions during strategy development on whether the company should serve both and how.

Additionally, we identified value flow gaps tied to non-core activities under activity groups like "education content marketing," which hadn't been on the radar prior.

We also set boundaries to focus on the use case of "deep professional learning" based on the company's purpose, which limited distractions. Areas like "education planning" and "education content sourcing" were set out of scope. For these educators, planning around education content was only a small portion of their overall planning activities.

Education content could be effectively sourced through foundational value creators like universities, publishers, and libraries. So, we decided it didn't impact the ecosystem enough to keep inside the boundary.

Without a market boundary, we will be tempted to chase opportunities far and wide, which results in feature-building that doesn't create net positive customer value. As you can see, we can unshackle our company from tribal knowledge while staying connected to our company purpose through the early steps of this exercise.

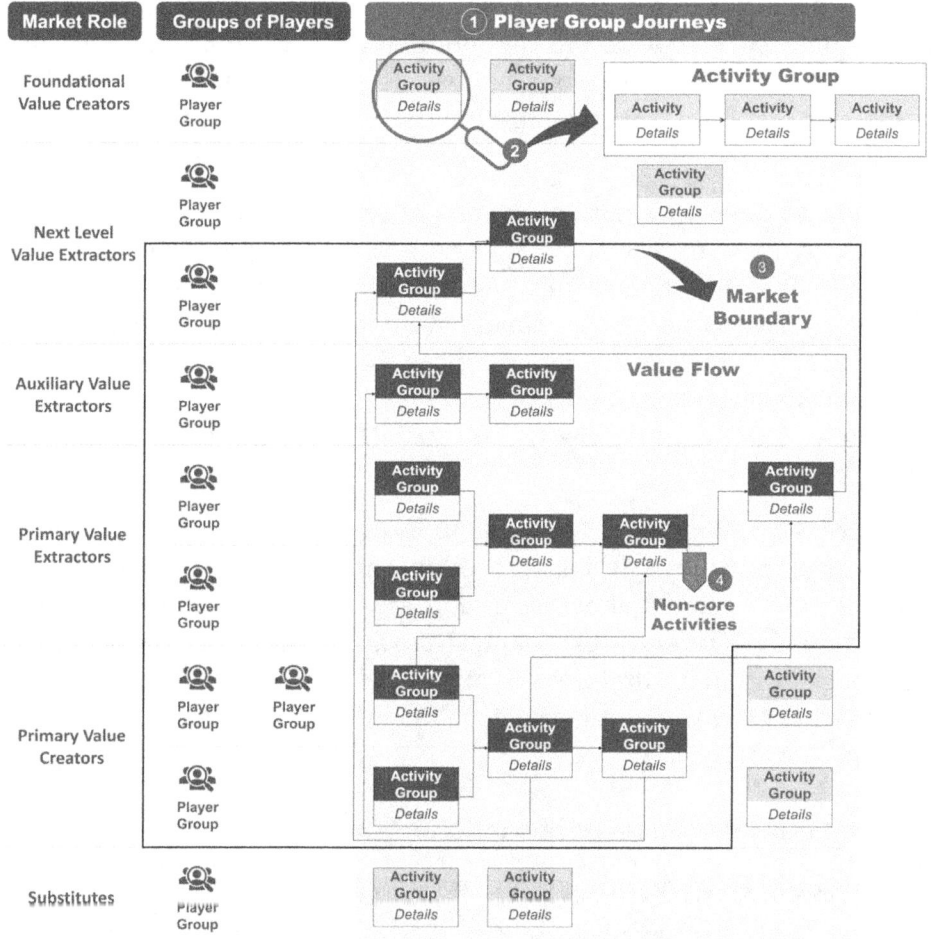

Figure D5. Market landscape articulates journeys of all player groups.

Principle 5: Understand voiced pain points and unvoiced imbalances.

We have already discussed non-core activities that capture untapped potential. We need to assess how effectively value flows between the activity groups we framed and across player groups to understand the effectiveness of existing solutions. This leads us to the second and third legs of the market problem – voiced pain points and unvoiced imbalances.

Is it easy to know the difference between untapped potential and gaps in existing solutions? No. Is it essential to know the difference? No, because they equally contribute to our definition of the market problem. What is important is that we frame our analysis so that we don't miss any of the three legs of our market problem because we didn't ask enough tough questions.

We want to develop hypotheses and gather two types of gaps in value created by existing solutions. They are voiced or perceived gaps and unvoiced or unrecognized gaps. Addressing the former is an act of following, and the latter an act of leading. It matters not whether we intend to solve it all ourselves. We must explore these two aspects for all player groups because we must always find out where opportunities and risks sit. Figure D6 illustrates the type of insights we are working to gather through this exercise.

Interpreting value is an onion-peeling exercise. Our research must use structured interview guides and follow-up questions to probe deeper into the player groups' activities and understand how effectively current activities and solutions create value. Recall the principles we introduced in productization around flow thinking and bidirectional flow of value. Our market assessment must surface the inflow and outflow of value for each player group.

Understand voiced pain points to follow the market.

As a second leg of defining the market problem, we must understand what player groups think and how they feel about value. These are the sentiments of various player groups around their activities, and they will reflect the historical experience of each player group.

Henry Ford, Steve Jobs, and others have famous quotes about the importance of staying ahead of customers or other market players, which is true. But in my experience, most companies aren't changing global behaviors from horses and carriages to automobiles or physical telephone lines to smartphones.

Loss aversion is natural regardless of the scenario. Customers experience loss aversion if they feel we don't consider their obvious voiced pain points. Therefore, we must first address real or perceived sentiments if they exist.

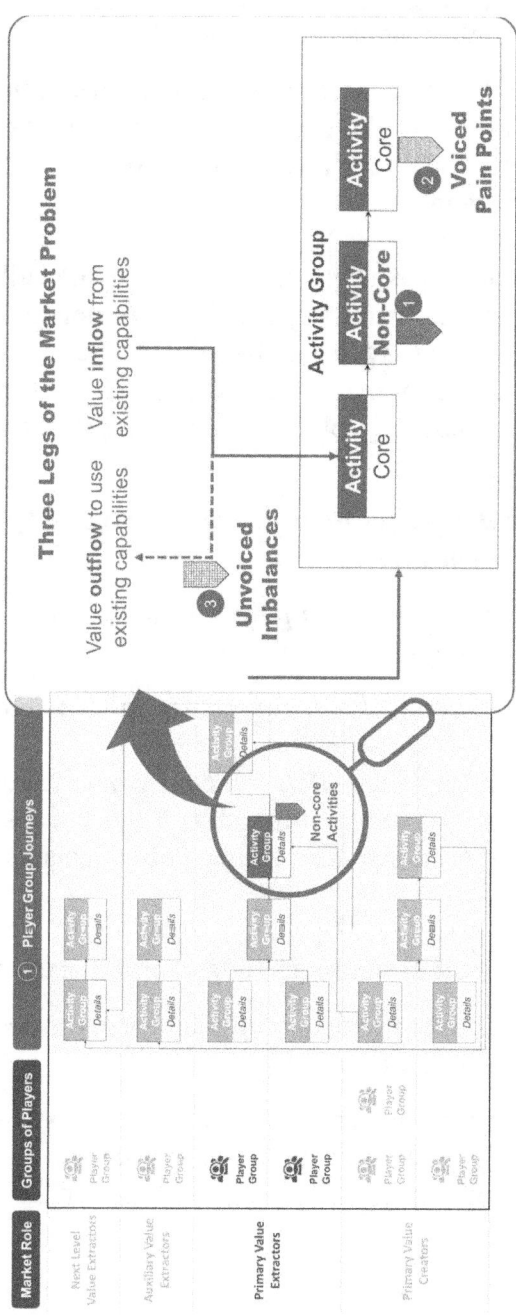

Figure D6. Value flows render three legs of the market problem.

Things To Remember: Voiced Pain Points

Voiced pain points are conscious, real, or perceived sentiments a player group faces. They form the second leg of the market problem. They are often symptoms of root causes that must be addressed via new or improved solutions.

In our grocery shopping ecosystem, players like me will likely find stock outages of certain items frustrating. Another common hurdle is a mismatch between discounts displayed on shelves and actual checkout prices, which I may never recognize and overpay. These symptoms help an observer frame the market problem for my price-sensitive player group's customer journey.

Consider these design questions to frame the voiced pain points leg of the market problem:

What are the pain points each player group feels or experiences for various activity groups?

How effective are current solutions in addressing these voiced pain points?

Before jumping too far, we need to consider what the customer might be missing about their own world. If we only go by what the customer shares with us, we fall into the trap that Henry Ford warns us about designing faster carriages.

Understand unvoiced imbalances to lead and disrupt the market.

Finally, we must identify unvoiced imbalances in the ecosystem to frame the third leg of the market problem.

We are all anchored by our past. Therefore, it is easy to think that inequitable relationships are normal. However, we want to understand such inequities so that we can possibly lead a disruption in our market.

> **Things To Remember: Unvoiced Imbalances**
>
> **Unvoiced imbalances are gaps in value creation that player groups are not consciously aware of or consider the norm due to the ecosystem's historic ineffectiveness. Imbalances often arise because an ecosystem has noncompetitive dynamics due to monopolistic or oligopolistic entities dominating key activities. Solving unvoiced imbalances could lead to market disruption.**

These are opportunities to disrupt the ecosystem where one or more players offer more to the ecosystem than they are getting. Ford and Jobs would likely agree that an external party is more optimally positioned to understand the market needs than the customer due to our vantage point if we have the discipline to learn objectively.

Understanding non-core activities and voiced pain points is a good and necessary start to follow and catch up to our market. But relationships with players in our market cannot only be submissive because we will miss important parts of the picture. Every player in our market has a large spectrum of activities in their life, and our ecosystem likely only intersects with those in a limited way. So, once we understand non-core activities and voiced pain points, we must switch roles and play a dominant one.

Customers and other players live through unvoiced imbalances they don't speak about or recognize themselves. These are significant gaps that a value creator in the ecosystem can close. The longer we focus on playing catch-up via voiced pain points and following the market, the more time we leave our market open for someone else to jump in and solve these inequities, which are typically higher value-creating opportunities.

Consider these design questions to identify unvoiced imbalances:

Within the confines of each activity group, do associated player groups experience unvoiced imbalances due to unfair advantages held by other player groups?

What are the sources of these discrepancies?

As consumers, do we get the best quality on the shelf for the price in our grocery ecosystem? I know a family of beef farmers who decided to forgo the "organic" tag because the bureaucracy and cost were prohibitive. Additionally, marketing is not a core competency for such players. As a result, we are likely to miss out on access to many such high-quality options through our traditional grocery channels. Could someone break the value chain to simplify access blocked by signatories and a handful of large grocery chains? Consumers and farmers can benefit from better trading channels if a player group addresses this inequity. Our goal is to identify and analyze without worrying too much about whether there is a viable solution or not.

The essence of ride-sharing platforms' value creation originated from the recognition that government-originated taxi medallions created inequities for drivers and passengers. Robinhood, primarily a stock trading platform, disrupted its market by offering consumers the ability to trade stocks without incurring fees. This was an unvoiced imbalance everyone lived with and considered a norm because all large traditional trading platforms charged hefty fees for each trade. Traditional trading was forced to follow Robinhood, and trading fees were largely eliminated.

My market assessment effort at the education solutions client also surfaced a potential breakdown in the ecosystem. We can summarize it as follows: "Are there professional educational programs that are not creating educational value for learner groups because such programs exist solely as a tax collection mechanism for traditional accreditors?" The possibility of addressing this unvoiced imbalance presented an opportunity to disrupt the space by not accepting the current terms of trade as good enough.

Assessing the flow of value in our ecosystem helps us create a complete picture of the market problems each player group faces. Additionally, I recommend leveraging the following principle to start documenting insights before exhausting all our planned primary and secondary data gathering and analysis efforts. Remember, strategy development is an iterative exercise. It is advisable to use the latter half of the assessment to validate the insights we draft based on the first half.

Principle 6: Postulate customer and competitor groups, and market problem using market landscape.

Every aspect of strategy development is a tedious exercise. It's similar to handling big weights at the gym. If we use it diligently, the results speak for themselves. We will likely get injured if we do not respect the exercise. The quality of our hypothesis development, qualitative and quantitative data gathering, and objective analyses determine the quality of insights.

In the words of a short-staffed chief strategy officer of a $2 billion revenue company, "We have a lot of field experience on the team, but I need help to move them forward from operating on gut feel. . . . We are barely keeping track of our biggest competitors."

A picture is indeed worth more than a thousand words because there are so many concepts we cannot explain in words without leaving room for subjectivity. Directionality is better shown in a diagram through arrows. We can easily capture the flow of benefits through visual cues such as data, content, or raw materials icons. We can also illustrate a scale of value through size or colors. Sequencing is infinitely more apparent in a visual construct.

Once we comprehensively frame our market into a few cohesive visuals to support our in-depth research and analysis, our company won't be held hostage to potentially biased or outdated tribal knowledge from people who claim market expertise because they have spent years in the space or talked to customers often.

To wrap up our market assessment, we must triangulate and arrive at a few specific insights that we will need to structure the three trade-off questions that form our corporate strategy: 1) Who will we serve? 2) What will we offer? 3) How will we deliver?

First, use player groups to lead us to customer groups and a competitive set. We worked hard to keep ourselves out of the center of our ecosystem to ensure objectivity through the exercise. We learned a significant amount of information about various player groups.

We used externally observable parameters and categories to group the primary and secondary value extractors. Some of them are our likely top customer groups.

We understand the primary and auxiliary value creators and substitutes more deeply, which gives us insights into where threats come from. Our probability of victory in the market depends on who else plays in our ecosystem and their role.

Consider these design questions to shortlist top customer groups and competitors:

Which primary and secondary value extractor player groups do we hypothesize are our short-list of top customer groups?

Which primary value creator, auxiliary value creator, and substitute player groups do we consider competitors?

Second, player groups' journeys are characterized by a visualized market landscape, where their activities are linked by value flows. These player groups include our customer groups. We must validate and memorialize each shortlisted customer group's natural journey and value flow.

Consider this design question to frame the journeys of top player groups:

What is the end-to-end journey, and what are the value inflows and outflows throughout that journey for each significant player group within our market boundary?

Third, hypothesize the market problem for each short-listed customer group, the likely value created for each, and our probability of being the source of that value.

We have identified the non-core activities, voiced pain points, and unvoiced imbalances of player groups. From this, we can derive the essence of the market problem from which each customer group would gain value.

Based on our history and market feedback, we can estimate the probability that a customer group might buy from us. With strong analytical skills, we can assess the value of these market problems quantitatively. The number of other value creators in the ecosystem influences our ability to create value profitably. We will have to share the opportunity to solve the market problem with them.

Consider these design questions to articulate the market problem:

What is our comprehensive and cohesive framing of the market problem for each player group?

What are the estimated odds that each top customer group will buy from a value creator like us?

What estimated value would each customer group gain if that group's market problem were solved comprehensively?

Developing these insights and validating them iteratively allows us to frame the market problem effectively with the most up-to-date research and analysis necessary. The following two chapters will draw upon these insights to answer our three critical who-how-what questions.

D.3
IDENTIFY SWEET SPOT CUSTOMER
TO CHOOSE WHO-TO-SERVE.

SERVING everyone is the same as serving no one. The concept of focusing on and serving one optimal group of beneficiaries is in every business text. We can even go back to the New Testament, which includes an often-quoted verse: "No man can serve two masters. . . . You cannot serve both God and money." Why? Because we will serve both poorly.

When actions align with robust belief systems, we can elevate from basic activities to tangible value creation. We need similar conviction when determining our optimal customers because all companies are resource-constrained. We can only productize certain capabilities and commit to one or two sets of processes, enabling technologies, and data.

Why is focus necessary?

Efficiency, Efficiency, Efficiency. It allows an organization to channel its resources to go after similar customers, those easiest to sell to and have the most to gain from its offerings. Once our company validates that some of its early customers gain value from its offerings, we must take the time to decide the optimal audience for its offerings from among billions of consumers or millions of companies around the world.

Founders and employees are pressured to prove the solution to themselves, early customers, and potential investors during the early stages of existence. Unfortunately, the company also doesn't have much data to rely on to decide who to sell to. So, it is rational to take a broad approach to testing market viability and capturing revenue, as very little reliable information is available.

In this stage, the customers who buy from the company are early adopters who tend to be risk-takers. They are most likely to try new offerings and risk living with some gaps, but this is usually a tiny portion of the market.

As our company grows beyond infancy to a decent number of customers and revenue, it is time to fine-tune how it goes to market. A company's customers can be individual consumers or other companies. Either way, they are different enough that not everyone is equally likely to buy from the company or, even if they buy, unlikely to appreciate its offerings equally well.

Why waste time and resources chasing after customers who are less likely to buy? Why find and serve undesirable customers that cost too much to serve or end up being short-term customers?

There are no rational reasons.

This chapter will discuss the analytical principles for identifying our optimal customer, which addresses the who-to-serve trade-off in our strategy development exercise. It won't be an easy choice to make, but it is a necessary one.

As we go through this chapter, we must view ourselves as protagonists for our entire player group, including our direct competitors. We want to understand who the optimal customer for the best version of our company is without being skewed by our historical mistakes or biases.

First, we will identify our sweet spot customers. **Second**, we will discuss the nuances of the term customer to arm ourselves with the insights necessary to define what we will offer and how we will deliver.

Thematically, we want to define our optimal customer in terms of externally observable parameters we have already developed through our market assessment. A common mistake in strategy development is choosing customers based on interpretive or non-predictive parameters. This defeats the entire purpose because we aim to create actionability and clarity. Therefore, we will frame our optimal customer through this chapter in objective, non-interpretive, and easily observable parameters.

A critical reminder is not to use this customer choice as a branding tactic without the intention of building repeatability and reproducibility into our value engine. Talking about focus is easier than having the discipline to stay focused.

Principle 1: Identify the sweet spot.

As soon as we validate our company's early solution to the market problem through a few good customers in the early months and years, we should focus our efforts on customers who are most likely to buy and discern the most value from our offerings. This shift implies choosing our **Sweet Spot**.

Years ago, a marketing professor compared identifying the sweet spot to finding an ideal life partner. She explained it this way: "Find someone who really appreciates your good qualities and can put up with your bad qualities." Simplistically, this analogy is a good starting point.

Identifying the sweet spot is a highly analytical exercise that involves creating a mold for one or two optimal customer groups to which we must dedicate all our investment. The sweet spot qualifies customers for whom the company proactively creates, sells, and delivers its offerings. Identifying the sweet spot is a best-case scenario analysis in which we must imagine that we will operate as a mature and disciplined company. The reality of our execution weaknesses does not change what our sweet spot is.

> **Things To Remember: Sweet Spot**
>
> **The sweet spot is the combination of common externally observable parameters of customers who genuinely gain value from what we bring to the market. It is important to note that the sweet spot is not the customer itself. Instead, it is the parameters that collectively describe our optimal customers.**

A common misconception is that focusing on our sweet spot precludes us from having other customers. This is misinformation spread by teams that lack discipline. Dedicating our company to serve our sweet spot does not mean customers outside the sweet spot won't buy based on their own volition.

Imagine our company spending $10 million in our next execution cycle.

We should dedicate the entire $10 million to operating and evolving our value engine focused on our sweet spot. We will have resources exclusively focused on designing and building our offerings for the sweet spot. Our digital marketing and branding efforts will exclusively focus on the sweet spot. We hire all new sales reps with experience and focus all their time on the sweet spot. If we apply such a focus, we will dominate our sweet spot.

However, suppose a potential customer we didn't go after with our marketing or actively sell to comes across our company through their own efforts or references and wants to buy from us. In that case, we will absolutely complete that sale if our offerings meet that customer's needs. This also implies that these peripheral customers must adjust their customer journey to use our offering, which is created for our sweet spot. We must not change our focus to make the peripheral customers happy as well. Clarity and discipline on what constitutes our sweet spot are essential for prioritizing which customers and prospects to listen to. Not all potential customers are equal.

As our domination of the sweet spot increases, prospects we never sought out will only increase because we have an ever-more-value-creating offering and reputation. So, ignore the naysayers who dissuade us from identifying and committing to the sweet spot.

I use a simple three-step approach starting with our market landscape hypotheses. The three steps are:

Step 1: Define a short list of customer groups.

Step 2: Analyze and rank customer groups.

Step 3: Extract the sweet spot.

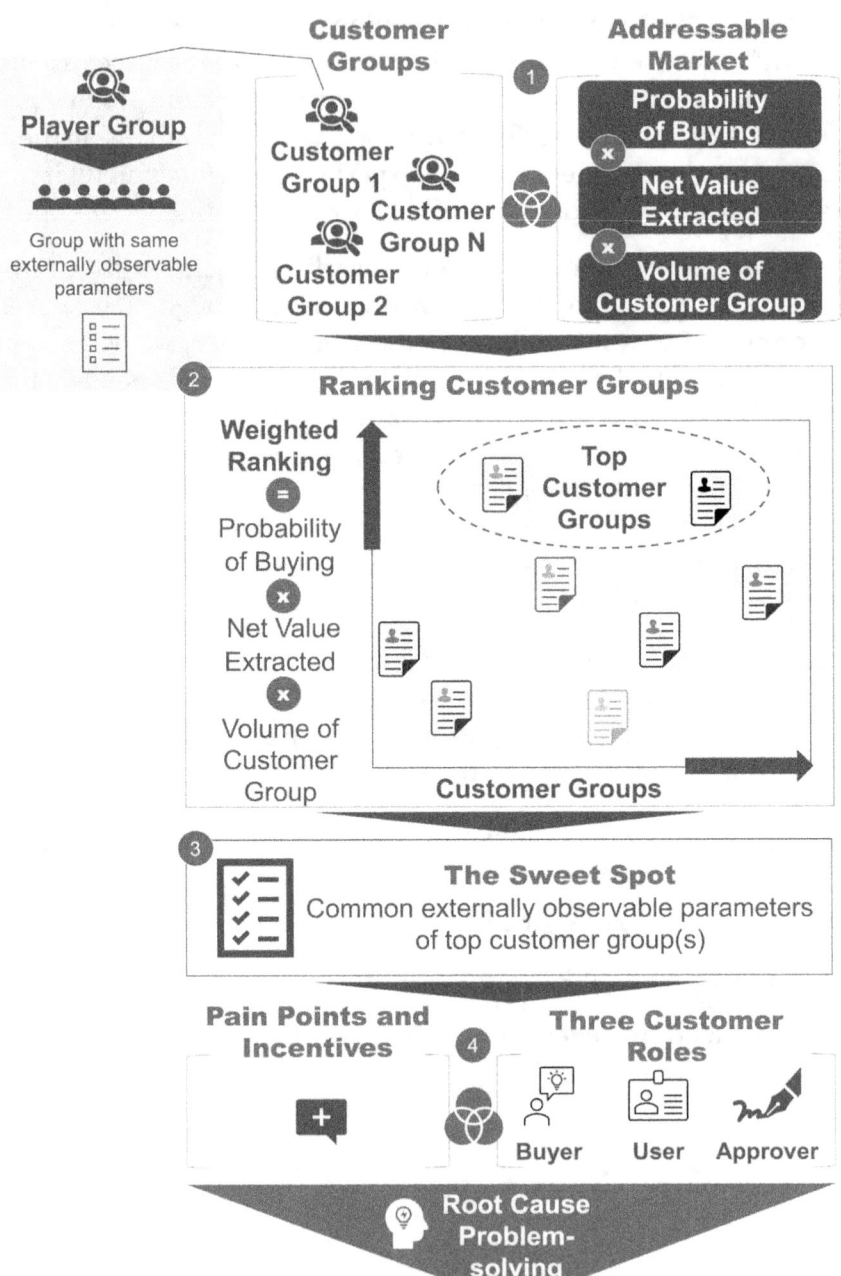

Figure D7. The sweet spot has three customer roles.

Figure D7 illustrates key elements necessary to identify our optimal customer. We framed our market landscape based on our historical experience, data from our operations baseline, and a robust market study. Now, we move to a focused future where the company has an unambiguous definition of its optimal customer. Identifying the sweet spot is one of the most analytical portions of our strategy development exercise. Given its central nature in setting a company's strategy, it's worth the deep dive.

Step 1: Define a short list of customer groups.

Depending on the efficacy of our market landscape insights, we should already have all the necessary ingredients to short-list customer groups. If not, revisit market study principles in Chapter D.2.

To choose our sweet spot effectively, we must start with a broad ecosystem mindset by including as many customer groups as possible. Rethink which value extractor groups could be relevant customer groups. We must cross-validate our market boundary with the current, lost, and prospective customers to ensure we have a comprehensive set of customer groups. I will generically call all of them "customers" for simplicity.

We will also need to know critical information about all these customers. Customers can be described based on externally observable parameters, whether the company operates as a business-to-business (B2B) or business-to-consumer (B2C) entity. These are the same externally observable parameters we used for our player groups in our market landscape.

Over time, I added a personal clarification to my marketing professor's definition of identifying the sweet spot. The world tells us that we should not stereotype. However, defining and using the sweet spot effectively is 100 percent embracing stereotyping.

Grouping customers is a great start. But before we analyze these customer groups, let's validate to ensure our analytical work adds up.

A litmus test for the quality of our customer groups is to ensure that players in each group behave similarly. i.e., are we sure that customers in each group follow the same journey characterized by the activity groups and value inflows and outflows that we defined during the market assessment?

A sound output from this step has three characteristics.

First, we have a handful of customer groups that cover all relevant value extractors in our ecosystem after cross-validation with our current, lost, and prospective customers.

Second, we can tabulate all these customer groups using the same three to five observable parameters, each with a maximum of four categories.

Third, we can validate that each customer group's defining categories predict that group's journey.

Although mathematically, these three conditions could imply many customer groups, effective grouping and removing the long tail of customer groups with limited volume and market problem alignment will allow us to create a compact list. Work towards eight or ten customer groups before moving into Step 2.

Step 2: Analyze and rank customer groups.

I won't downplay it; this second step will require solid analytical muscles and experience. The company must rely on the Congruence Architect and enablement resources with deep critical thinking and thought leadership skills to stack rank the customer groups without reverting to existing biases.

We must base the stack ranking of these customers on three factors.

The **first** factor is the likelihood that customers in each customer group will buy from a company like ours, even if it is another company.

The **second** factor is how much value each customer group gains from the offerings of a company like ours, which essentially determines how much money is really on the table to trade for the value.

The **third** factor is the volume of potential customers in each group, whether individual consumers or companies. It would be a shame to choose a sweet spot that is so small that our return on investment will be low even if we execute flawlessly.

All three factors must be informed by both our market landscape and current operations baseline. Ensure that our current operations baseline does not exclusively guide our strategy development. Relying solely on our operations baseline as a reference for the probability of sale or value delivered will skew us towards mistaking incongruences in our present state as foundational truths. Conversely, using only the market landscape as the single source of truth takes us away from our realistic limitations and might send us on a wild goose chase.

Our sweet spot customers are the ones we can best serve in the future by striving for what is possible while grounding ourselves in our valid limitations. Therefore, besides using past performance data from selling and marketing efforts and customer use of our offering, the playmakers leading strategy development will have to collect and use qualitative and quantitative information gathered through primary and secondary research, as discussed in Chapter D.2.

Let's explore these factors in more detail to set quality guardrails.

The **first** factor is the probability of a customer in a customer group buying from a company like ours but not specifically from us. Here, we must separate the true maturity of our operations baseline from our realistic potential maturity.

Historical sales and revenue data could tell us which customer groups tend to buy more from us than others. However, we must consider the difference in investment that went into selling to and building for each customer group in the past. In other words, we cannot assume that Customer Group A is more likely to buy than Customer Group B because A has more historical sales. What if we had directed much more marketing spend to A? What if our best sales reps focused on A? Is the maturity of our processes high enough that we can rely on historical data? Using spurious or unreliable past data is more likely to lead us astray than help effective decision-making. We are better off avoiding poor historical data if our processes are immature.

Primary research to gather qualitative and quantitative data through interviews with various players during our market analysis can involve objective questions to discern who each customer group might buy from and their underlying reasons. Since each customer group is part of our market landscape, we can preemptively ask these questions as we gather market intelligence.

Carefully conducting secondary research simultaneously can help us find buying decision rationale and data for customer groups. To repeat my warning, secondary research is always a dance with the devil because it is hard to discern between objective, high-quality information, and poor, self-serving data. Therefore, I advise restricting sources to trustworthy publications and always using multiple separate sources to validate each other or using median values across multiple sources.

Exploring such analytical paths will help create an answer around probability. The intention is not to arrive at a numerical probability figure with statistical significance. Creating stratification of the likelihood of buying between different customer groups is enough. We only need granularity that supports objective decision-making.

Consider these design questions to stratify each customer group's likely behavior and probability of purchase:

What is our confidence level that the market problem definition for the customer group is truly value-creating? High = 10 points, Moderate = 5 points, Low = 3 points.

What is the likelihood that the customer group will prioritize this market problem as one that needs to be addressed if there is a solution in the ecosystem? High = 10 points, Moderate = 5 points, Low = 3 points.

How many value creators, including primary, auxiliary, and substitute options within the market boundary, could realistically solve the market problem for the customer group? A higher figure implies fewer customers each gets to serve. High = 3 points, Moderate = 5 points, Low = 10 points.

Such simple questions are much easier to gather data for and analyze than an overarching purchase probability. Starting with such a weighted scoring and stratification approach gives us a strong indication of which customer groups are most likely to buy from a player like us. But please don't skip all analytical work and rely only on your gut feeling to do this. It defeats the whole exercise.

The **second** factor to bake into our analysis is the value a customer group discerns from a company like ours. In our value-centered method, let's not get carried away with placing monetary figures to value discerned as it will be based on history or external reference points. Recall that pricing can be based on cost or competitive comparisons, which are suboptimal references. Value measures the benefits of solving real-world problems. Using past pricing as a measurement of value delivery will likely mislead us.

Most of the information for this second factor can come from our market landscape insights. We have already mapped our customer groups in our market landscape. We already framed the market problem for each customer group. Use what we already learned and augment our market landscape insights if gaps in our data exist.

Value discerned by customers correlates with the market problem's size and scope. Customers are willing to pay for the market problem they experience if it is solved effectively. Does a customer care whether the solution is automation using technology or whether an army of humans sits behind the scenes and replicates the automation manually? Not unless the quality is different. Customers pay for the value created by addressing the market problem.

The value that a customer group discerns tells us how much revenue we might be able to generate from each customer. For example, it could correlate with how often they buy and how long they stay as customers. This second factor helps us understand our likely relationship lifecycle with customers, assuming they buy from us.

The **third** and last factor is the universal size of each customer group. When we choose our perfect customer, we also want to ensure that there are enough such customers to justify our commitment to them.

We touched on developing the size of our player groups as part of our market landscape, and we use it here. Think about market sizing at this stage as a volume check as we choose our perfect customer. Sadly, the most common reason companies size the market is to tell the world that "we have a big market" to boost the company's market price or get investor funding. I understand these motivations, but this is a reason focused on present investors.

The appropriate reason to size our market effectively is to know how many customers we can realistically serve if we focus all our efforts.

It will give us an objective quantification of our likely return on investment. Our strategy development exercise does not aim to show a bloated number that makes us feel like we have a winning formula. Instead, we want to arrive at a reasonable and maybe even conservative size of the customer groups to ensure our return on investment will be high.

The simple outcome for the third factor is a count. If our customer groups are individual consumers because we are a B2C company, we count human beings, households, or similar. If we are a B2B company, we count companies, business units, employees, or a relevant customer-centered volume that our offering may augment.

We must use the observable parameters and categories defined in Step 1 of identifying the sweet spot to conduct research and calculate these counts. All the principles and pitfalls we covered above regarding secondary research also apply here. Embrace objective bottom-up sizing to create a conservative count for each customer group's market volume.

With these three factors on the board, we know how big each customer group is, how likely each group is to buy, and how much value each customer could experience if they buy. By multiplying these three factors directly or through weighted scores, we can create a score for each customer group. This score translates to a stacked ranking of our customer groups. The Congruence Architect must lead experienced and critical-thinking enablement resources to gather the data for these three factors and complete the analysis.

Figure D7 above visualizes the sequence of using these three factors to stack rank our short-listed customer groups. We are seeking the top customer groups in our market here.

Step 3: Extract the sweet spot.

I love it when a good analysis comes to a coasting end because of all the hard work and discipline that went into the early stages. The converse is also true. Imagine speeding through a jigsaw puzzle only to realize we made mistakes along the way. If we execute our market analysis and the first two steps of the sweet spot identification exercise well, Step 3 is relatively easy.

The common observable parameters that characterize our top two or three customer groups are our sweet spot if their behaviors are similar, as reflected through the journey in our market landscape. Both criteria must be true for our approach to be effective. The shared customer journey of the customer groups we choose within our sweet spot also leads us to our optimal use case.

The narrower our sweet spot, the more decisive and focused we are. However, we also want to choose a sweet spot that supports our company's lifecycle stage.

If our company is small or less mature and we only have limited capital to invest, our sweet spot will need to be more niche. We must make the remaining choices mindful of this self-assessment of where we are in our company lifecycle. Regardless, we must always keep at least the top two or three customer groups in play because we want to make a strategic decision that can go beyond the short term. Focusing on a single customer group that does not allow us to scale our operations baseline beyond that group doesn't support sustainable operations. So, here are two rules to frame our sweet spot.

> **Things To Remember: Sweet Spot Rule #1**
>
> **Customers in the sweet spot must have similar customer journeys, especially if we include more than one of our top-ranked groups. Similar customer journeys imply that these customer groups have similar market problems. A shared market problem means we can serve them with a single scalable solution rather than disparate ones.**

Based on this first rule, we must look beyond the simple stack ranking of customer groups to prioritize customer groups with similar journeys. If all our top customer groups have divergent customer journeys, it is critical to reassess the quality of our analysis. It is confounding that our top customers, who are most likely to buy and gain the most value, act very differently in our ecosystem. It is likely because we have misunderstood how value is created and consumed.

Things To Remember: Sweet Spot Rule #2

Ensure that top customer groups chosen for the sweet spot have similar externally observable parameters. The predictive properties that define each customer group also heavily influence how we pursue those customers and work with them, as articulated through The Company Way Processes. Boxing significantly different customer groups into a sweet spot solely because they ranked high will leave us spreading our company resources too thin.

Like the first rule, the second rule focuses on the essence of the analysis rather than robotically picking the top-ranked customer groups without internalizing why or what purpose it would serve. The second rule ensures that we attempt to acquire and deliver to similar customers.

Imagine that one of the vital predictive parameters is age, and our second and third-ranked customer groups fall into the age categories of fifty-somethings and college-aged, respectively. In contrast, the top-ranked group is a high-school-age category. Suppose we need to choose two customer groups. It is significantly more optimal to market, sell, and deliver via our processes to high-school and college students instead of high-school students and fifty-somethings, even if the latter ranked higher. The more similar these customers are, the more repeatable and reproducible our processes can be. The entire aim of developing a sweet spot is capital efficiency and productized value creation.

Figure D8 illustrates the nuances of this final step. The table represents ten customer groups defined using five behavior-predicting parameters. Each parameter has a handful of categories in which the customer groups differ. Effectively, consider each row as the unique identifier for any customer in that group.

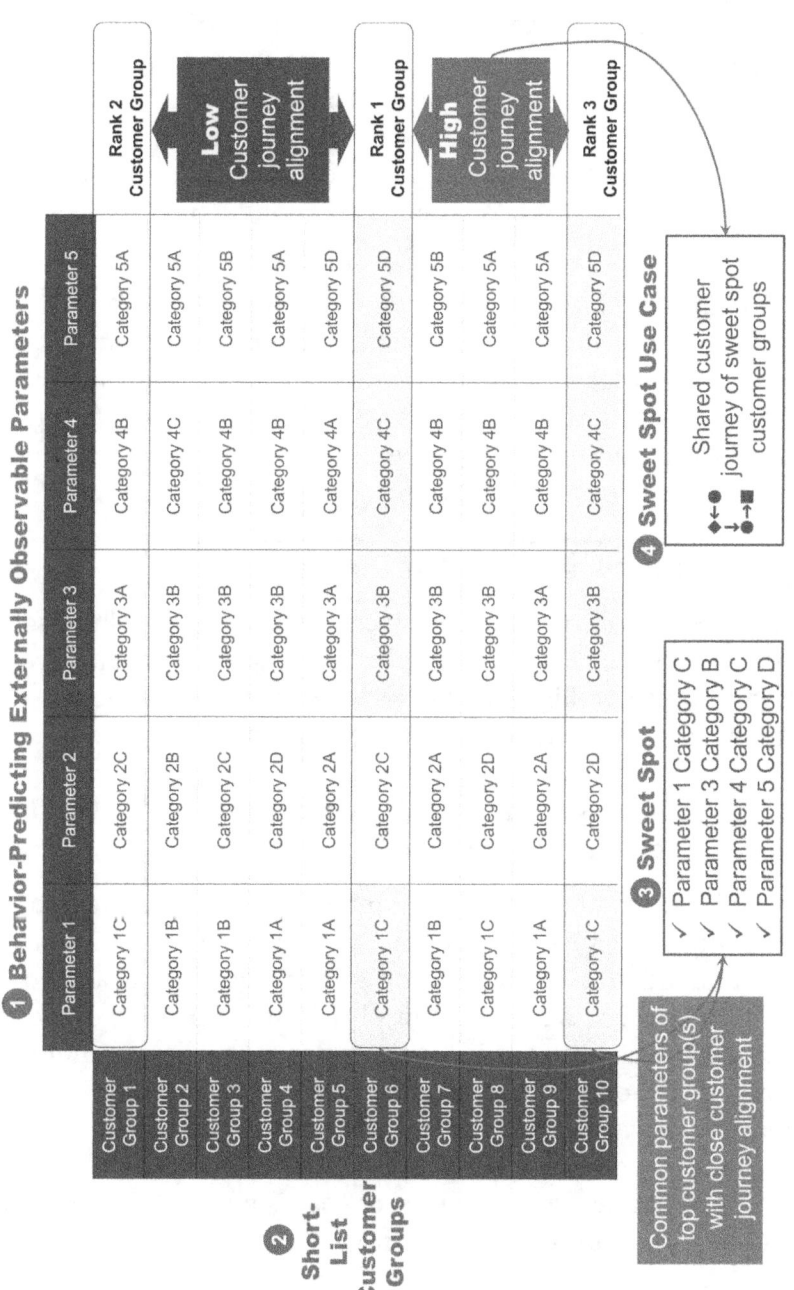

Figure D8. Top customer groups with aligned journeys prescribe sweet spot.

Based on our analysis in Step 2, we ranked Group 6 first. Group 1 came in second, and Group 10 came in third. Although we ranked Group 1 second, the sweet spot is optimal if we choose Group 6 and Group 10 even though they are ranked first and third. The second-ranked Group 1's customer journey is dissimilar to Group 6's. In practice, we must understand why our analysis would result in such a conclusion to ensure the efficacy of our analysis.

Given that Group 6 and Group 10 are ranked highly enough, have very similar customer journeys, and four of the five behavior-predicting parameters match, our analysis is likely correct. The sweet spot is the common parameters across Group 6 and Group 10 because they are relatively similar customers with a similar market problem that we have high confidence we can address.

Things To Remember: Sweet Spot [Refined]

The sweet spot is the set of common categories of externally observable parameters associated with top customer groups, which have close customer journey alignment. The shared customer journey is our optimal use case associated with the sweet spot.

In addition to the sweet spot definition, **Addressable Market Size** is a by-product of this exercise.

We not only learned what the top customer groups are, but we also learned the three ranking factors about them. We know how likely they are to buy, how much value they could gain if their problem was solved, and how many such customers there are. If we multiply the quantification of these three factors, we have the addressable market size for each customer group. If we frame our sweet spot around our top two customer groups and their customer journey, summing the addressable market size for those two customer groups gives us the total addressable market we introduced early on. The market size of our sweet spot is a litmus test for potential sustainability limitations for our company.

As a word of warning, the instinct to show a sizeable addressable market also leads to a temptation to include several customer groups, which breaks our sweet spot definition. This is purely extrinsic motivation and holds no intrinsic benefits.

We must ask ourselves hard questions if we desire to prioritize beyond two or three of our similar and optimal customer groups into others with dissimilar customer journeys.

Do we have a market challenge where our customer groups attribute little value to what companies like us bring to the market? We may have to revisit our market landscape and further iterate on our research to ensure we understand the market well. If we return to this point again, it might be time to raise the flag and ask ourselves whether we have a viable market.

Did we anchor too much on our past performance and give our entire player group a low probability that customers would buy? Remember, we are trying to perform this exercise with an objective mindset and are operating as a spokesperson for our entire player group, including our direct competitors. If customer groups tend to buy from similar players like us at a high probability, we should use that. Our macroevolution cycle intends to improve our operations baseline and catch up and surpass others like us.

I am writing this at a coffee shop across from a candle store. Suppose our company's core capability is to produce scented candles. We can think about many applications for this capability and many selling paths. However, a careful market assessment exercise can help group customers using observable parameters and categories. Examples may include the following.

- *Parameter 1: Size of selling institution. Categories – boutique stores, large nationwide stores.*

- *Parameter 2: Point of sale. Categories – physical retail setting, online setting.*

- *Parameter 3: Selling institution location. Categories – a neighborhood with an average income 50 percent higher than the citywide average, a neighborhood with an average income between the citywide average and 50 percent higher than the citywide average, and a neighborhood with an average income less than the citywide average.*

A candle maker can choose a sweet spot framed as 1) selling candles to boutique stores, 2) in physical retail settings, and 3) within neighborhoods with a median income at least 50 percent higher than the city-wide average income.

Such an articulation of the sweet spot allows this candle manufacturer to tailor its offerings. They can tailor the types of candles, the number of candles in each packet, the type and quality of packaging, the expected number of uses for each candle, and many other considerations to this sweet spot. The choice of sweet spot also drives our commercialization efforts, including packaging and pricing. In addition, the sweet spot dictates how often each end user might buy a candle, the approach to distribute to chosen customers, and several other sales and marketing decisions.

Investing time and mindshare in identifying the sweet spot is critical to deploying our value engine effectively and efficiently. It simplifies and focuses our approach to creating value in the market that aligns with the benefits statements framed in our company's purpose. Once the sweet spot is clear, we must then understand how customers in the sweet spot think and make decisions.

Principle 2: Understand and identify the customer roles in the sweet spot.

We framed our sweet spot, which means we can easily find our optimal customers without ambiguity. But what do we truly mean by "customer"? How does a customer think?

We must internalize that even the perfect customer in the sweet spot has multiple personalities.

Whether we serve individual consumers in a B2C space or companies in a B2B environment, a customer is a complex interplay of incentives. An individual makes decisions based on many factors. Other individuals and their decisions may influence the person we consider a customer. Likewise, a company has many roles, functions, and levels, several of which interplay to decide how value is consumed.

Understanding what constitutes a customer in the sweet spot and how that customer makes decisions is critical before assessing how we might deliver value to the customer.

Identify the customer roles using additional externally observable parameters.

I created a simple construct to break down every customer into three roles, irrespective of the offering or selling approach.

A buying decision is complex regardless of the offering or the type of customer. Whether a company or a consumer, every customer has a **Buyer**, a **User**, and an **Approver** hidden somewhere within. These three roles are not necessarily separate individuals, but designing, building, and selling any offering should consider all three roles and their needs. Although this consideration is more straightforward to grasp where customers are companies and different people occupy each role, the same principle applies when customers are individuals.

Things To Remember: Customer Roles

Every customer is an individual or a company whose collective view of the market problem combines voiced pain points, non-core activities, and unvoiced imbalances of three customer roles - Buyers, Users, and Approvers.

Each of these three roles within a customer will experience the customer journey differently because of their vantage point. A customer's overall market problem is a symbiosis between these three roles' views of the problem. Without identifying and understanding each of these roles individually, we will likely miss a necessary dimension of how the customer thinks. Buyers focus on the effectiveness of value flow and the root causes of the market problem. The user focuses on their individualistic preferences and usually short-term gains. The approver focuses on the commercialization aspects of the customer journey.

It takes more work to dig a layer deeper and understand the incentives of each of these roles within a sweet spot customer. Still, without it, our strategic trade-offs and choices articulating the "what" and "how" questions will remain a shotgun approach.

Once we have framed our sweet spot, we must develop further insights to frame these three roles using additional externally observable parameters that pinpoint each role. The definition of each customer role is a concatenation of chosen categories of parameters that frame the sweet spot and additional categories of parameters that describe each role. Think about our definition of a customer role as a building address with an apartment number where all three roles live in the same building but may live in the same or different apartments, where the building is the sweet spot definition.

So, to complete our optimal customer definition, we must articulate an externally identifiable definition of the buyer, user, and approver role using additional behavior-predicting parameters.

The parameters and categories we use to identify customer roles follow the same principle we used for the sweet spot. As customer roles articulate human incentives, they are always parameters that identify humans in the context of decision-making, regardless of the market.

If the collective customer is a family, a sample parameter is "family role" with categories such as highest income earner, dependent, and family activities manager. If the collective customer is a business, a sample parameter is "people management role" with individual contributor, supervisor, and senior executive categories. Depending on the offering and our sweet spot, we must make these categories specific to articulate each role in the sweet spot.

A CEO with a technical background may gravitate towards a head of technology as the customer. A company can easily mistake the head of the department buying a product as the customer because that person signs the contract. A toy manufacturer can mistake a child for a customer because the child would be playing with that toy. However, these are simply assumptions; every buying decision is complex.

So, let's explore the three roles that apply to any customer in any context.

Customer role 1: Buyer.

The buyer has the most critical role, hands down. The buyer holds most of the cards regarding first-time and ongoing buying decisions. In addition, the buyer is usually responsible and accountable for addressing the specific problem the collective customer is experiencing.

In our market landscape discussion, we described value creation as a problem-solving exercise. Consider the buyer's role as the customer's internal playmaker and decision enabler.

Things To Remember: Customer Role - Buyer

The buyer's role is to make decisions based on the effectiveness with which our offerings address the root cause of the customer's problem and assess the net value flow for the customer as a collective.

Two discerning characteristics frame a buyer.

First, we are unlikely to make a sale or at least prevent a return or cancellation if the buyer is not on board. If we take nothing else away from this segment, remember that.

Second, the buyer is usually responsible for and closest to the problem in question and is best positioned to assess the overall value of solutions. In other words, the buyer is the customer's most capable representative who can discern the actual return on investment over time.

The buyer will be the source of information determining whether the customer will make an initial purchase because this role will have considered all the possibilities. The buyer also constantly thinks about how the purchase is used after the first purchase and will likely decide on future purchases.

Interestingly, and unfortunately, the buyer role is also the most ignored, given their thoughtful nature.

The buyer holds all the soft power and is an analytical personality. This role's objectivity and analytical facets are the most tempting for value creators to avoid or bypass because they ask the most demanding and rational questions. But it is a bridge to nowhere to sidestep this role and try to go after the user or the approver because it will bite back later.

In summary, we must focus on delivering and communicating our offering's comprehensive and quantifiable short-term and long-term value to the buyer.

Customer role 2: User.

The second most important role is the user. This role derives tactical day-to-day value and is directed or permitted to leverage the offering by the buyer. Although the buyer drives buying decisions, the user provides direct feedback to the buyer. Where there are many users, the users' needs and satisfaction become very significant, and the buyer will work to synthesize the users' needs and how much value they are discerning. Two key traits can characterize the user.

First, the user touches or is touched by our offering most often, which also means the user discerns most or all day-to-day value. Our offering's most obvious aspects are designed and delivered to make the user's life easier, happier, faster, or any other applicable measurement.

Second, the user could assess their experience and convey that feedback to the buyer. The user may also demonstrate many subconscious behavioral traits while using the offering that the buyer can observe. Thus, the user strongly influences the first-time and ongoing buying decisions through the buyer.

Although all three roles are important, the user is also the most selfish personality.

Things To Remember: Customer Role – User

The user role focuses on their tactical, day-to-day best interests and expresses their wants. The user has many other priorities or distractions and wants the offering to meet their immediate needs despite the cost or ramifications to the collective customer or in the long term.

It can be tempting for a value creator to bypass the buyer and try to sell to the user. However, even if a company achieves this, this is likely to be a short-term win. Over time, the buyer will learn the user's selfish incentives and block downstream purchases or trigger a return or cancellation.

The commercial approach will have minimal impact on the user. Conversely, the design and delivery of our package and the resulting net value are most attractive to the user. Those are the incentives to understand and win over the user role.

Customer role 3: Approver.

The approver is the role that holds the money bag or the pen to autograph the signature line. However, this role looks to others for a buying recommendation and takes the final step of releasing the finances for the purchase. Usually, the approver is the most senior person in the buying cycle or the budget owner and is often mistakenly considered the most important.

Designers and builders of offerings, sales reps, and marketers often focus heavily on the approver and rely on their perspective to frame the market problem experienced by the customer. This is a mistake because the approver role is not a personality close enough to the user and is not the true problem solver, which is the buyer. Chasing the approver while ignoring the buyer and the user is a path to selling an offering that will likely not get used effectively and thus hurt the length of the relationship with the customer. The approver role's incentives revolve around two aspects.

First, a good approver understands that they are a gatekeeper holding the funds, and the real value will have to be discerned by the user and buyer. Our optimal customer will have an approver who internalizes the importance of the buyer's role and defers to the buyer to offer a recommendation.

Second, the approver wears the hat of the final reviewer or validator. The approver can override the analytical thinking and recommendation of the buyer if the approver feels it's flawed or incomplete. The approver can also control the timing of the decision and the price point at which they strike a deal.

> **Things To Remember: Customer Role – Approver**
>
> **The primary incentive of the approver role is commercial. The approver seeks an optimal deal with reasonable pricing and contractual terms.**

Let's explore a practical example to internalize how the three roles transpire in real life. Consider a B2C scenario about kid's toys, in which my nephew and nieces are the main characters.

This story involves me, my sister, and her three kids. Every visitor appears to bring the kids a new toy, and the kids take on the user role here. They have selfish and short-term preferences. Thoughts about where to store a toy, the best way to use it, or the harm it could cause aren't on their minds.

So, should a toymaker only consider the user?

No, because the children will never have toys unless someone purchases them. If I buy a toy for them, I hold the purse and choose the timing of the purchase. So, I am the approver, but I have no idea what kids like these days or what is safe to handle. I feign interest in what the kids say they want, but guess who I ask what I should get them? My sister is the buyer who might have to pick up after the kids, and she makes me aware of her preference for what the kids should and shouldn't have.

As an approver, I defer to the buyer to tell me the optimal course of action so that all parties are happy. I just have a budget in mind and how to procure the toy with the least amount of effort. Even designing kids' toys and how to sell them can be optimized if we understand the three roles of the customer and their incentives.

The same principles apply in a B2B scenario.

Imagine a company offering a niche operations technology that supports sales and marketing activities. This requires an elaborate process for a complex offering that impacts many stakeholders within a customer organization.

Such an operations technology requires centralized administration, user training, data management, and many other ongoing central activities, which a sales operations resource usually manages.

But this position usually doesn't hold the budget. Still, it will make or break the sale because it is considered the topical expert on process and technology that support related operations. The position is expected to synthesize differing opinions across the organization, prepare the business case after considering many vendors, and recommend the final choice. The same role is also likely to recommend canceling a contract and looking for alternatives if the value is not discerned as expected. In this scenario, this sales operations resource is the buyer.

Marketing resources, sales reps, and sales supervisors use such operations technology daily to do their jobs. Each rep and supervisor will have personal preferences, which will likely be selfish and depend on their unique style. These users will convey their wants to the sales operations resource we established as the buyer. It is critical for the company that offers the operations technology to ensure that it meets these users' day-to-day needs.

The budget to approve this technology frequently sits with a sales or marketing executive who is our approver. However, this sales executive should only be interested in seeing the business case presented by the sales operations position and validating that the collective customer is getting the best deal possible. Therefore, apart from pricing negotiations, the approver will likely delegate all decision-making responsibilities to the sales operations resource.

Unfortunately, I often see companies trying to sell such offerings to executives or sales reps, who are the approver and the user, respectively, because they offer the least resistance. Inevitably, the buyer thwarts these attempts by escalating value-focused challenges, which are likely to be high in the first place because the selling company took the path of least resistance and tried to close a deal with roles not focused on discerning net value.

Through these two examples, I hope you can see the importance of embracing the need to understand and incorporate the incentives of buyers, users, and approvers.

So far, we have used our market landscape and operations baseline to frame the externally observable parameters of our optimal customer and the three customer roles. Before diving into what-to-offer and how-to-deliver for our sweet spot customer roles, let's frame our "who" strategic trade-off choices because making decisive choices is the hardest part of strategy development.

Principle 3: Frame "who" trade-offs and choices based on sweet spot and customer roles.

It is hard work to identify the common parameters of our top customers to form our sweet spot and the three customer roles. However, if we stay disciplined and arrive at congruent answers, one of three outcomes will be true.

Outcome 1: We went through an equally perfect strategic assessment during the last macroevolution cycle and have arrived at precisely the same insights as the previous cycle.

Outcome 2: We went through an equally perfect strategic assessment in the last cycle but have uncovered new insights because time and environmental factors have changed the market.

Outcome 3: Our strategic assessment has matured, and we have arrived at an evolved set of insights that better reflect our changing market ecosystem.

Options 2 or 3 are far more likely. That implies making choices because our understanding of our optimal customer is changing. Therefore, we must frame that possibility as an intentional, strategic trade-off.

For instance, a marketing technology company I worked closely with had a buyer choice dilemma that I framed as a strategic trade-off as part of a strategy development effort. Historically, the company had considered a Chief Marketing Officer (CMO) as the buyer, meaning the offering's data capture and reporting capability was focused on a CMO. Our macroevolution revealed that analytics executives are the ideal buyers. This was a clutch choice because the company would have to tailor the offering and the selling process for a cross-functional analytics executive instead of a CMO. The CMO was identified as the approver role through our work.

Articulating these choices and enabling the company to focus effectively allows us to channel all our investment to customers most likely to buy from us and get the most value from us. It protects us from being distracted and serving no one effectively. So, at this stage, we must draft our "who" trade-offs and choices and make soft decisions, enabling us to explore what-to-offer and how-to-deliver questions more effectively.

Figure D9 is a decision framework that you can use to visualize these choices. Such a representation must have detailed analyses and supporting recommendations for the CEO and senior executives to make effective decisions.

Our analysis identified our top customer groups and their customer journeys.

Our **first** strategic trade-off frames our primary use case. A choice to prioritize a use case is a choice to deprioritize another. We must also include our second and third choices as the options we decide against.

Our **second** who-to-serve strategic trade-off is framing our sweet spot options. For the use case we choose, we will have options on the optimal combinations of customer groups and their parameters and categories that could form our sweet spot. Recall that our sweet spot is a combination of externally observable parameters. Our sweet spot differs depending on which and how many top customer groups we choose for our prioritized use case. This choice set changes our addressable market size and our level of focus. Stage choices between two or three sweet spot definitions and ensure each allows a significant enough market opportunity while also enabling focus.

Our **third**, **fourth**, and **fifth** who-to-serve trade-offs cover our sweet spot customer roles. We must choose from two or three options for the buyer, approver, and user roles. Staging the top two or three choices for each ensures our "who" trade-offs are comprehensive.

If we arrive at single choices for these trade-offs, it likely reflects errors, biases, and blind spots in our analytical efforts to get this far.

Consider these design questions to structure who-to-serve strategic trade-offs:

What are our top two or three options for the primary use case, defined by the shared journeys of top customer groups?

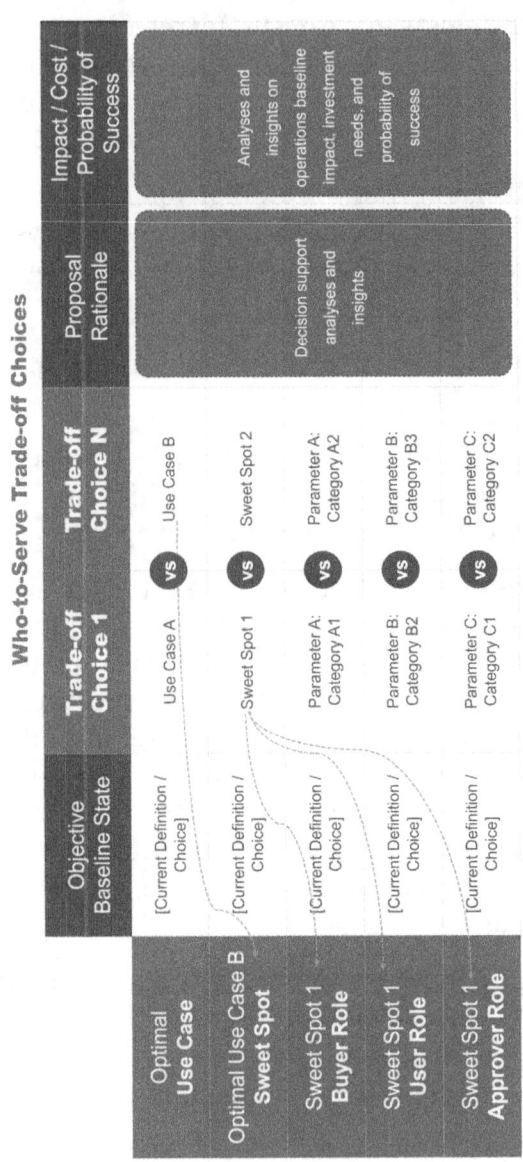

Figure D9. Sweet spot, customer roles, and customer journeys dictate who-to-serve.

What are our top two or three sweet spot customer options that align with the optimal use case chosen above?

What are our top two or three options for the buyer, user, and approver roles within the sweet spot chosen above, defined using externally observable parameter(s) and categories?

We must effectively articulate the impact, cost, and probability of success associated with each trade-off and choice because they are all compelling. The quality and objectivity of analytical steps along the way dictate the quality of our strategic decisions. Framing these strategic trade-offs and choices sets us up to dive into what-to-offer and how-to-deliver for our sweet spot customer and the three roles it comprises.

D.4
ALIGN STRENGTHS WITH MARKET TO DECIDE
WHAT-TO-OFFER, HOW-TO-DELIVER.

WHEN the beat of the music changes, our dance moves must change. We inject incongruence into our company if we keep our productized offering unchanged or do not evolve our processes and management approach when our optimal customer shifts and their customer journey alters.

Our strategic trade-off choices about what-to-offer and how-to-deliver can be represented as a simple game, as shown in Figure D10.

Company Operations Baseline

	Strengths	Weaknesses
Competitors — Weaknesses	**Quadrant 1** Self-aware. Chooses a differentiated advantage to serve sweet spot.	**Quadrant 3** Not self-aware. Misinterprets the market problem.
Competitors — Strengths	**Quadrant 2** Addresses a commoditized market problem. Chooses a suboptimal sweet spot.	**Quadrant 4** Not self-aware. Chooses a suboptimal sweet spot and/or market problem.

Figure D10. Sustainable value creation demands a focus on differentiated strengths.

Quadrant 1 represents our optimal zone. Our likelihood of serving our sweet spot through value delivery is highest if we play to our strengths and our competitors' weaknesses. However, there are no predictable and legal paths to intentionally force our competitors to operate to their weaknesses. So, the strategic trade-off choices that guide our operations baseline must focus on our current or realistic potential strengths. It's simply a bonus if others in the market sabotage themselves.

Quadrant 2 implies that we are operating in a zone where our competitors are also capable value creators. The most obvious reason is that the market problem to be solved is trivial. This is a war of attrition in which our strengths are not differentiated, and it implies that we must ask hard questions about our value creation and profitability prospects. Alternatively, we may have chosen our sweet spot poorly or may not understand its needs effectively, leaving us to mimic competitors.

Quadrants 3 and 4 result from strategic decisions around our operations baseline that do not align with our strengths. Lack of self-awareness or overconfidence in our ability to deliver against the market needs are the most common reasons for this eventuality.

These final levers of strategy development focus on framing critical choices about how to serve our sweet spot. To arrive at these trade-off choices, we must drill down further into the needs of our sweet spot. If we are going to hang the future of our company on a few clutch decisions, it is important to ensure that there are studs behind those spots on the wall.

Through the principles below, we will lay out an objective path to arriving at our corporate strategy by picking up where we left off in the last chapter. Strategy development has a single aim – to evolve our operations baseline to maximize value creation for our sweet spot customers by managing our investment efficiently while staying aligned with our company purpose.

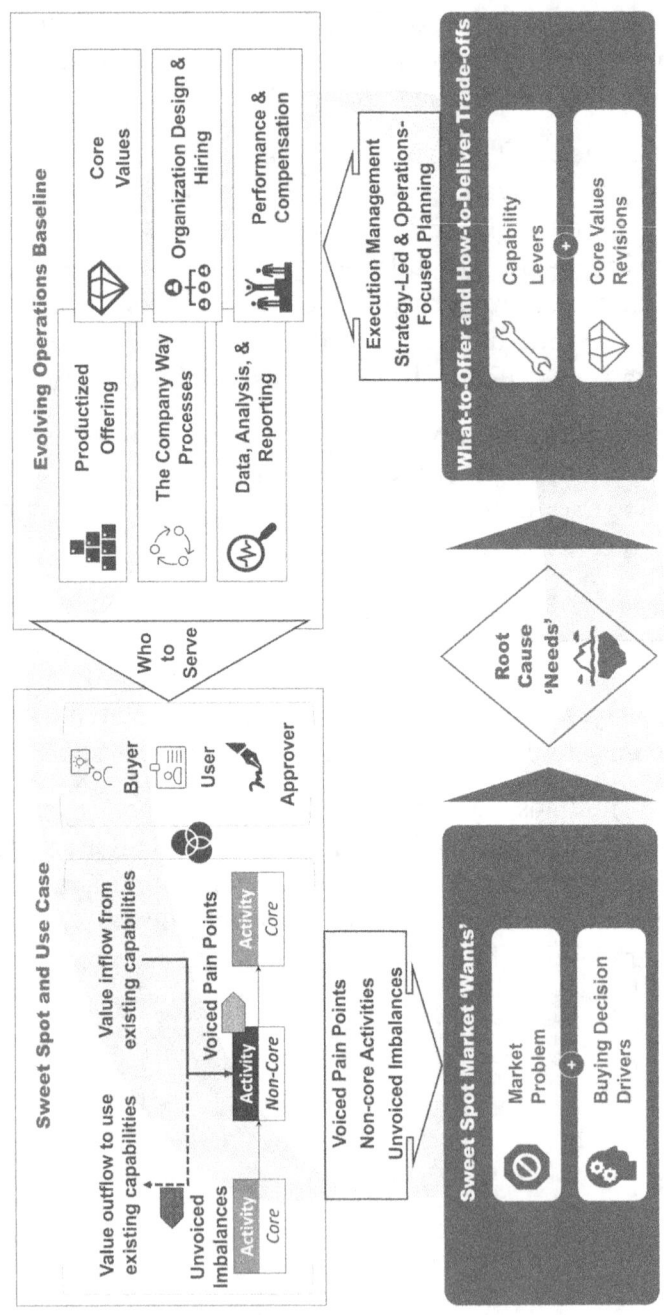

Figure D11. Who-how-what decisions evolve operations baseline.

Figure D11 provides a roadmap for evolving every aspect of our operations baseline, starting from our soft decision on sweet spot customers. Use it as a frame of reference as we go through each principle in this chapter. In the following two parts of our method, we will translate our strategic decisions into a plan to achieve those decisions and execute that plan to evolve our operations baseline while running the business.

Principle 1: Frame buying decision drivers that help customers choose the optimal value creator.

To serve our sweet spot customers, we must understand the three legs of the market problem and create an effective solution. Before discussing how we solve our market problem, let's discuss how customers buy.

Even if we have the most optimal solution to the customers' market problem, how does a customer know that before buying? For customers to extract the value we can deliver, they must buy. Without buying, how will the customer see the value? Once a customer buys, how will a customer know that future buying experiences compare to the past?

Every relationship involves a bidirectional interpretation of behaviors. The same applies to customers and value creators of a company.

First, customers will not have all the necessary tangible information about value creators like us because the use case we focus on is only a small part of their whole life, and we only focus on one part of our chosen use case.

Second, customers do not always think objectively and rationally about their market problems within their customer journey. Like all humans, buyers and approvers in consumer or business buying scenarios are biased and look for shortcuts.

This information gap and lack of objectivity among customers are vital enablers that encourage some market players to disseminate exaggerations and even lie to get customers to buy. But they are unsustainable tactics. To create intrinsic value for customers, how do we fend off others who focus on generating external perceptions that mislead customers? How do we convince customers that we can deliver the value that we are capable of?

Let's understand how customers buy to ensure that our focus on fundamentals reaps its full reward. In addition to objectively assessing the effectiveness of the solutions through trials, customers are also influenced by what I call **Buying Decision Drivers**.

Things To Remember: Buying Decision Driver

A buying decision driver is a framing of conscious and subconscious behavioral proxies used by buyers and approvers to assess, choose, and stay with a value creator in the market, especially in the absence of past experience. Buying decision drivers are stereotypes or decision aids that allow customers to choose optimal value creators. Buying decision drivers heavily depend on the sweet spot, and changing the sweet spot implies changing the buying decision drivers.

We must augment our solution, which we will articulate through the what-to-offer trade-offs, with an impactful delivery path. Our how-to-deliver choices must align with who we serve and their needs. For example, why do the employees at a luxury clothing store dress, talk, and act entirely differently from those who work at more middle-of-the-road ones? The same workers will behave differently when they move from working at Banana Republic, an everyday brand, to Louis Vuitton, a luxury brand. The employee's behavior and appearance are cues for a consumer regarding what is offered. So, we must uncover the behavioral proxies we should build into our operations baseline.

We can learn about the behavioral proxies our sweet spot customers gravitate to through the voiced pain points and activities of buyer and approver roles. Behavioral proxies are observable behaviors that customers expect to see from value creators that promise to address problems in their customer journey.

We are all using this mindset every single day. The same mindset encourages us to dress a certain way for interviews. Investment bankers and consultants dress differently for interviews compared to software developers. Why? The interviewers' buying decision drivers. The interview interactions are just a proxy for our interactions after signing the contract to work together.

Consider these design questions to learn the buying decision drivers of sweet spot customers:

What are the underlying processes, behaviors, and commercialization factors that the buyer and approver roles in the sweet spot use to decide whether a value creator will be a successful one to work with?

How do the buyer and approver interact to finalize a purchase decision?

What are the underlying processes, behaviors, and commercialization factors that the buyer and approver use to decide whether to purchase from a value creator repeatedly?

These are only guiding questions; do not ask customers such direct questions because it is our job to determine the right behaviors through subtle explorations. Instead, we must design situation-specific questions to understand the themes that, in turn, cover these questions. We must also be wary of projecting our perceptions of optimal behaviors on the customer.

Identifying customers' buying behaviors was part of many projects throughout my consulting days. As we shared insights with clients, we always diligently included action plans on how they could augment processes and offerings to accommodate these buying behaviors. Looking back, it is evident that many of these recommendations were not implemented effectively. It took me several years to recognize that the root cause of these implementation gaps was a lack of comprehensive shift in company-wide behaviors.

Where are the root causes of behavioral incongruences around the value engine likely to reside? Core values. The only path to achieving a substantial behavioral shift is through well-operationalized core values.

Principle 2: Leverage core values as a strategic behavioral lever to deliver buying decision drivers.

As promised when we first introduced core values, they have a tremendous role to play as our organization's behavioral guardrails. Core values are powerful and proactive behavioral guardrails that guide our entire operations baseline if we design and operationalize them properly.

The strategic path to learning buying decision drivers and driving their inclusion into our value engine and management approach goes through our core values.

Recall the first layer of our Values Funnel Framework in Chapter B.1. Our key question was, "What behaviors do value extractors most require and demand?" Besides solving the market problem effectively, buying decision drivers are the relationship conduit between our customers and value creators. We don't have to fake the buying decision drivers; we can live them through our core values.

When I say Amazon, what are the stereotypes that come to mind? The first few themes that come to me are "good customer service," "on-time," and "cheap deals." Three of their several leadership values, as Amazon calls core values, are "customer obsession," "insist on the highest standards," and "frugality." When I read the details behind these values and speak to employees I know at the company, I can connect the dots between their core values and my end-user gut feeling about Amazon.

For instance, "frugality" disseminated into a company's offerings, processes, and people agenda categorically reduces the cost of operations. It focuses on developing a solution to the market problem that optimizes cost, which could directly translate to cost savings for customers. In addition, setting such a core value also enables organization design and hiring to attract employees who thrive in such a setting and dissuade employees who prefer an organization that creates a perception that poshness is paramount.

Core values must effectively set the tone for the entire company's behavioral foundation, which must align with our customers' buying decision drivers. This superset of behaviors needs to guide all our actions. In our customer-first mindset, we must not choose behavior traits if they don't align with how we serve our customers.

Given its qualitative, feel-good nature, framing core values can feel effortless. However, identifying buying decision drivers requires strong qualitative analysis and is psychologically and emotionally demanding.

The development of core values requires a methodical approach to ensure their impact. I categorize core values into two groups.

The first is **Value Engine Enablers**.

Things To Remember: Value Engine Enablers

Value engine enablers are core values that directly and dispassionately address customers' buying decision drivers. We can draw a direct line between the themes of such core values and the behavioral properties of our offerings and The Company Way Processes.

We must always start by framing this set of core values. For instance, a sample core value theme can be "best in class," which can directly influence our productization efforts and processes to enable focus on quality rather than cost.

The second is **Management Approach Enablers**.

Things To Remember: Management Approach Enablers

Management approach enablers are value creator-focused prerequisite behaviors that allow us to live by our customer-centric core values.

We have to identify a set of core values that enables us to bat for the value engine enablers. In other words, without such underlying behaviors that primarily impact our management approach, the behaviors we want to build into our value engine are often nonstarters. For instance, a management approach enabler such as "always learning" might be a value creator competency-focused underlying theme that is necessary to enable a value engine enabler such as "best in class."

These two sets of core values are part of our "how" strategic trade-off decision.

Value engine enablers inject buying decision drivers into productization and The Company Way Processes.

Through strategy development, our goal is not to wordsmith or socialize core values. Instead, we want to frame the essence of our company's behavioral themes to align with our sweet spot customers' needs.

First, we want to frame the table-stakes buying decision drivers for our use case as desired behaviors. We must demonstrate these behaviors to have any chance of operating in our market. None of the value creators in our use case will be successful without effectively demonstrating these behaviors. For example, "safety" could be a table-stakes decision driver in domestic or international passenger air travel use cases.

Second, we must incorporate the unique buying decision drivers necessary to ensure our solution stands out in the market. If we have a market-validated solution, we have precedent. Our future solution will likely be an evolution of our past, not a radical shift. Based on our general approach to solving the market problem, what are we learning from our market analysis as differentiating behaviors that make customers choose us over our competitors? For instance, the passenger air travel use case could have a buying decision driver of "luxury" or "cost-effective." Our sweet spot customers likely prefer one or the other depending on their affordability.

Third, we must objectively identify and eliminate existing core values misaligned with our buying decision drivers. Let's put on our critical thinking hat to ensure that we focus on evolution instead of being defensive about our history.

Consider these design questions to set themes for our value engine enablers:

What are the table-stakes buying decision drivers for our use case?

What differentiating buying decision drivers must we embrace to stand out as we address our sweet spot customers' market problem?

Which existing company core values are misaligned with newly identified buying decision driver insights?

Effectively synthesized themes answering the first two questions give us our super-set for our value engine enablers. However, we cannot be good at all behaviors because each has a cost. Therefore, we must answer the third question and eliminate ineffective existing core values.

Define two or three achievable sets of core values, while accounting for ones we would eliminate, which become choices for our value engine enablers trade-off decision. It is optimal to include three to five value engine enablers in each set of core values we put forth.

I led a strategy development exercise for a marketing technology company, and we identified several new buying decision drivers. The theme "buttoned-up" reverberated across all value engine components as a critical buying decision driver. But it was a gap. This gap could be observed in the company's processes, how it launched its offerings, and even the quality of sales proposals presented to customers.

Another theme that customers asked for consistently was "turnkey." It implied that customers were looking for a solution that took all non-core activities away from the customer. However, the company's offering required extensive implementation and ongoing attention. This was also an internally relevant theme because many aspects of execution were half-baked. These two value engine-focused core values were included in a set as a strategic trade-off.

We can move on to management approach enablers once we frame our options for value engine enablers.

Management approach enablers drive foundational behaviors.

Framing the management approach enablers is a considerably easier task because we already know our reason for including them. These themes ensure that the value engine enablers are supported by how our value creators think and act.

We must follow the same thorough analysis to assess the effectiveness of the remaining core values that will support the value engine enablers choices we drafted first.

Consider these design questions to set themes for our management approach enablers:

What foundational behaviors must our value creators embrace and live by to operationalize the value engine enablers?

Which of the existing core values can we eliminate because they do not directly contribute to the value engine enabler options we set forth?

We must frame our optimal collection of supporting values through rigorous qualitative assessments. I recommend a set of two or three management approach enablers for an SMPE.

Core values based on our sweet spot customers' buying decision drivers frame the "how" part of our strategic trade-offs because it articulates the essence of the behaviors we should adopt. Remember, our business exists to create value for customers.

Frame the how-to-deliver trade-offs.

Our buying decision insights, built into our core values, influence how-to-deliver through our value engine and management approach in the future. Therefore, framing the trade-off choices for value engine enablers and management approach enablers is essential. This will also help us decide what-to-offer our sweet spot customers. Figure D12 illustrates how we might represent our how-to-deliver trade-off choices.

Consider these design questions to structure how-to-deliver trade-offs:

What are the two or three sets of value engine enablers, each with three to five core values, that directly achieve our sweet spot's buying decision drivers?

What are the two or three sets of management approach enablers, each with two or three core values, that are essential to operationalizing our value creator behaviors?

These two trade-offs are strategic as we likely couldn't include all the behaviors customers expect. We must evaluate customers' expectations against value creator and senior executive behavioral strengths and weaknesses we explored in the Values Funnel Framework in Chapter B.1. Once we make these two choices on the two core values sets, we can identify the necessary initiatives to implement the chosen ones, which will evolve our value engine and management approach.

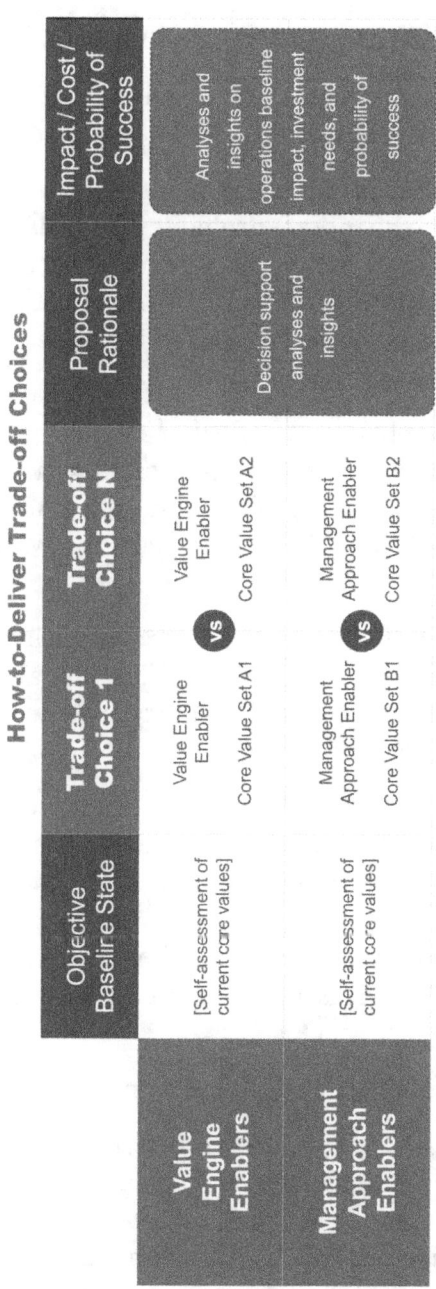

Figure D12. Value engine and management approach enablers constitute how-to-deliver trade-offs.

Principle 3: Formalize the market problem and identify root causes.

Before we can solve our sweet spot customers' needs, we must formalize the market problem and the underlying reasons for it.

First, we need to zoom into the use case associated with our sweet spot customers to validate the market problem. We made a soft choice on a single journey that aligns with customers in our sweet spot. We must validate the value flow analysis we performed through our market assessment with a deeper focus on our sweet spot to increase our understanding of each leg of the market problem.

We will have to test our hypotheses further around buyers' and users' voiced pain points. We must also explore the non-core activities and unvoiced imbalances that aren't at the top of our optimal customers' minds. We learn from sweet spot customers directly by speaking with them or indirectly through data gathered from our value creation interactions.

The deep dive to frame the market problem primarily focuses on the buyer and user roles because we are interested in sustainable value creation and profitability. These roles feel and experience the market problem significantly more than approvers.

Visually illustrate the flow of value within this use case by applying the same six process design elements we use for The Company Way Processes. We must double-click into our use case and understand the details of activities to a point where we can draw each customer role's activities in swim lanes. How can we say we understand our customers if we cannot articulate a day in their lives and their intrinsic motivation to go through these steps?

Second, we must identify the root causes underlying the market problem.

The three legs of the market problem – non-core activities, voiced pain points, and unvoiced imbalances – are symptoms. We want to understand and catalog them, but then we must translate them into root causes that we can solve. An effective strategy development exercise connects symptoms to root causes by relying on a mature problem-solving mindset.

For the hypothetical candle-making company we covered in the last chapter, the sweet spot's voiced pain points or preferences might surround basic properties such as aesthetics or longevity. In a problem-solving mindset, the underlying factors influencing aesthetics and longevity might involve raw material composition, manufacturing processes, or storage methods. We cannot devise the appropriate solution until we truly understand the root cause of the problem.

Root cause analysis is not about finding myriad unrelated shallow reasons. As we learned in productization, that would lead to feature creation and low or negative net customer value. Instead, we want to arrive at a maximum of two or three cohesive and dovetailed root causes that allow us to create comprehensive capabilities.

Consider these design questions to frame the root causes of the market problem:

Why are the user and buyer roles experiencing each voiced pain point?

Why is the sweet spot customer engaged in each non-core activity?

Why is the sweet spot customer experiencing each unvoiced imbalance?

Can we drill down multiple layers into each underlying reason?

Can we follow the common underlying reasons to arrive at two or three synthesized root causes?

Root cause analyses will identify the essence of why the buyer and user roles feel challenges or experience gaps we have identified. These are the root causes of the market problem we need to solve.

At the invoice data software company I mentioned several chapters earlier, one of the persistent impediments customers shared was the lack of visibility into the progress of processing the documents from which the invoice data was extracted. The company had invested in increasingly complex reporting to give customers visibility about where their documents were. Over 30 percent of new investment into offerings went into such reporting efforts. However, customers did not find value in these reports and continued to be dissatisfied.

The root cause of customers lacking visibility was that the company's software didn't effectively track the progress of the documents during processing and had several blind spots. So, how can reports create clarity when the company does not know the processing progress either? The appropriate path was to address the root cause, which was poor internal handling of document processing without excessively focusing on the symptom of "visibility," which resulted in reporting on blind spots.

The "give" of addressing the root causes of the market problem implies applying analytical horsepower. The "get" is that our solutions are significantly more value-generating, lasting, and scalable when applied against root causes instead of symptoms.

Principle 4: Utilize four capability levers to solve the root cause of the market problem.

We paused on solving the root cause of our market problem until we framed our how-to-deliver trade-off using core values because it is an essential input into how we choose what-to-offer.

Similar to framing our core value sets, our goal is not to design all the details of our productized offering. The detailed design will be part of comprehensive enablement initiatives over one or more execution cycles based on priorities we will set during strategic planning. During strategy development, we must focus on the hard choices that impact our entire operations baseline.

Mature productization efforts yield a well-priced package that solves our sweet spot's market problem. That package has one or more capabilities that span the four dimensions we introduced under productization. A mature value engine enables analysis-led ongoing microevolutions to improve the properties of a capability or tweak a package or price while maintaining congruence with the rest of our operations baseline. This is business as usual and doesn't address changes in our market or maturity gaps in our value engine.

A mature strategy development exercise will expose gaps in our historic productization efforts or reveal a shift in the market problem via the three legs, which we must expect to happen in any market at least every couple of years. So, how do we strategically address our new market problem?

There are infinite combinations of ingredients that render solutions to the same root causes of our market problem, each with different effectiveness in value creation, investment efficiency, and alignment to our strengths. A four-lever decision approach frames our optimal pathway to create the most customer value aligned with our strengths.

Capability lever 1: Reconfigure capability dimensions.

Recall our four capability dimensions – action, object, knowledge, and promise. When our market problem shifts, we must comprehensively reassess the balance of our solution across these capability dimensions because subtle changes in the root cause often require a different combination of capability dimensions to frame the solution.

For instance, almost all disruptive companies in the last two decades simply moved solutions from an action dimension to an object dimension using software that became readily accessible on mobile devices. These new enablers allowed companies to address past voiced pain points, unvoiced imbalances, or non-core activities by shifting from an action dimension of unaided activities to a heavier object dimension where technology aids most activities. The essence hasn't changed for activities like getting a taxi or ordering food. It's just a dimensional shift to a software object.

Defining the dimensional balance of an existing or a new capability is not a tactical decision. It is truly a strategic decision to change the composition of our top capability or two along the four dimensions.

The four dimensions around which we can build a capability require very different fundamentals.

Changes to our productized offering via dimensions significantly impact the rest of our value engine and management approach. Many processes and data components exist to support the delivery of our productized offering. Incrementally, dimensional shifts change our organization's design because we require different skills. It could change our compensation models for those impacted roles.

For example, companies that create software solutions, which I categorize in the object dimension, separate the responsibility for selling to new customers from the activity of incremental sales to existing customers. A software solution is expected to sell itself after the first sale because it works well. On the contrary, companies that sell services do not typically separate these duties because the later sales tend to be similar to the first one.

Shifting our capability to include hardware objects implies that our processes must be built around an e-commerce website or physical retail outlets. Such a shift might mean moving from advertising-led sales to people-led sales, which might require an entirely new selling skill set focused on hardware objects.

When I started my entrepreneurial path to provide advisory services to companies, *Congruence™* did not exist. All the structured intellectual property in this book was semi-formed and rattling around in my head, and my primary capability dimension in that early stage was action. Today, I operate in much more of the knowledge dimension, relying heavily on this method to create value. It has completely changed how I sell and deliver value.

Essentially, shifts in these four dimensions encompass the most investment-heavy, high-risk, and high-impact decisions our company will make beyond who-to-serve in the market.

Capability lever 2: Structure capability elements to solve the market problem.

We know that each capability is a multidimensional solution, and our choice among these four dimensions is our first lever. But each capability dimension is not as simple as just an object or an action. Saying that "we are more of a technology company than a services company" is a start, but not enough. Every solution incorporates technology to some extent!

We can only deliver each capability dimension through underlying building blocks, which I call **Capability Elements**.

For instance, an object element in our solution can be hardware or software. It could be petroleum, grains, or anything at all. Depending on the market problem, we might have to consider multiple hardware elements like electronic parts of varying complexity and mechanical housing to complete the hardware object dimension of the offering. Elements can include database coding, end-user-focused coding, or machine learning coding for a software object. Creating value via the action dimension requires different forms of labor, like skilled or commoditized, and further specifics within each.

Creating value via each dimension will require us to commit to one or more underlying capability elements, where the specific choices create a different version of our company. We must choose whether we can confidently commit to a given element that ladders up to solving the root cause of the market problem through a capability. This is our second capability lever.

Things To Remember: Capability Elements

A capability is a comprehensive solution that spans multiple dimensions, each dimension being an aggregation of building blocks called capability elements. Capability elements are single-dimensional Lego blocks that are aggregated to build a comprehensive capability.

Capability elements sit within a single-dimensional silo and contribute directly to the overall value created by the capability. A combination of capability elements forms a comprehensive solution to the market problem. Each capability element requires unique strengths to design, build, market, sell, and deliver.

Think about the market problem as a closed door secured with two or three locks, with each lock being the root cause of the problem. Each lock can be opened with a few keys, and each key is a capability. Capability elements are various potential ridges and notches for a given key. Putting the right combination together creates a functional key. We must choose which ridges and notches we can make based on the tools we have.

Many considerations for capability elements are likely already on the radar in most companies. Our four-lever approach provides a structured framework to pull in internally brainstormed ideas, customer feedback, and newly developed objective options from our market study. Using such inputs, we must formulate hypotheses on the realistic combination of capability elements across the four dimensions that can solve our market problem.

As a **first** rule of thumb, if we cannot come up with at least two practical combinations of capability elements to solve the problem, we haven't considered enough elements and combinations. Remember, decisions require choices.

As a **second** rule of thumb, each capability element must have a significant value contribution to the market problem and have a sizable internal impact on our management approach and value engine. Recall the difference between strategy and tactics. Focus on strategic building blocks without relying on a laundry list of tactical items.

A service dimension always exists in my work with clients. But who performs the actions? Do I? Or do I hire others to do the work? Or do I empower playmakers at companies to self-serve? Choosing one of these capability elements is truly strategic because it completely changes the entire operations baseline of any advisory practice like mine.

Capability lever 3: Define effectiveness vectors for each element in alignment with how-to-deliver trade-offs.

In addition to the dimensional choice of how we build our solution and the underlying elements, we must choose the **quality**, **cost**, **flexibility**, and **speed** associated with each element.

In practice, we can take any single element in each dimension and create it with different levels of quality, speed, flexibility, or cost. To make a strategic decision that is also actionable about what-to-offer, we must expand our definition of a capability even further using these controllable aspects that I call **Effectiveness Vectors**. Our third capability lever is effectiveness vectors, which become part of our what-to-offer trade-off decision.

Things To Remember: Effectiveness Vectors

Each capability element in any given dimension - object, action, knowledge, and promise - has four vectors of effectiveness - speed, quality, flexibility, and cost - from which we have to choose because we can only maximize some of these vectors at the expense of others.

No company can maximize all four effectiveness vectors for a given capability element. For example, offering an object or an action at high speed implies sacrificing flexibility, quality, or cost. Figure D13 illustrates our strategic choices for each capability element with dimensions and vectors.

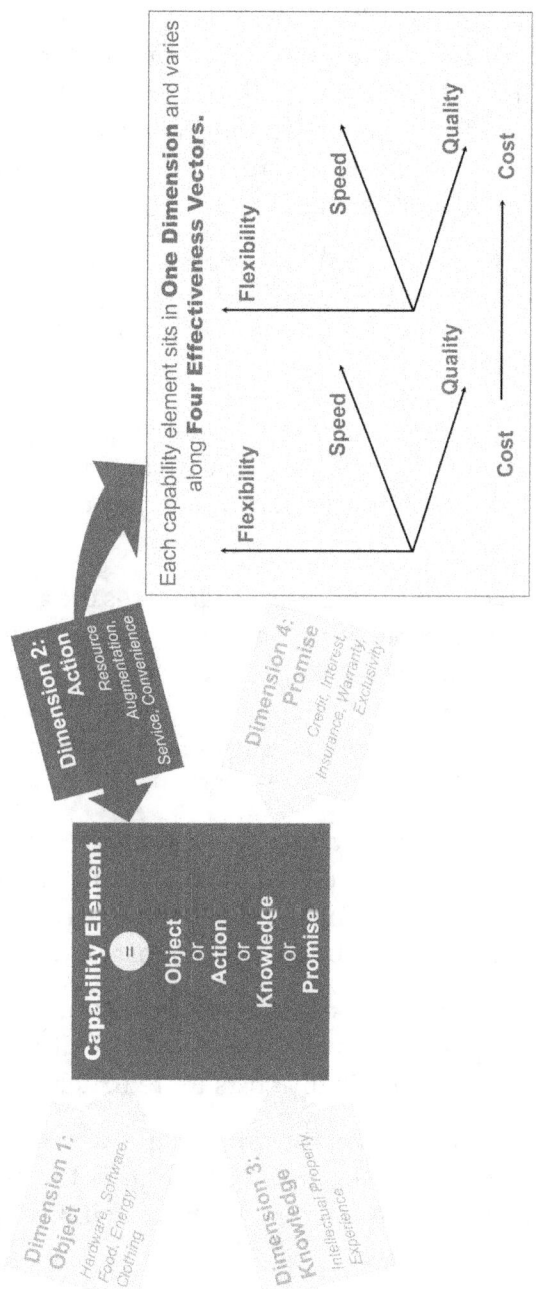

Figure D13. Each capability dimension spans four effectiveness vectors.

Our choices to superimpose these four effectiveness vectors onto the four capability dimensions is core to our productization efforts because offering something of high quality is a very different strength than delivering the same offering with a lot of customization. We must decide which of these effectiveness vectors we must become good at because we also have to choose not to be good at other vectors.

For example, highly customized and expensive Formula 1 race cars are made in machine shops that work on only two or three cars. On the other hand, a road car is mass-produced in large factories with limited variation, quickly and at a fraction of the cost.

Our choice of effectiveness vectors also impacts our processes and our management approach. These four effectiveness vectors apply to the composition of any capability element across any offering, industry, and maturity level.

Flexibility is the first vector. This vector addresses the amount of variation that the company can or needs to incorporate into a part of the solution to optimally meet the precise needs of each unique customer. Customers associate higher value with overall flexibility, which reduces the net value outflow for each customer. Productizing flexibility often implies a low-volume and high-cost environment.

Speed is the second vector. It addresses timing precision by accommodating customers' desire to receive value quickly or at precise moments. Productizing speed implies a higher cost to enable. However, the higher the value created, the higher the pricing opportunities.

Quality is the third vector. This vector addresses the optimal investment in the appropriate quality measure, such as longevity, poshness, or size of impact. Higher quality typically costs more to achieve.

Cost is the fourth and last vector. All other vectors that create value for customers cost money. So, the cost vector is the counterweight to flexibility, speed, and quality vectors. Higher flexibility, speed, or quality implies a higher cost to productize.

Effectiveness vectors are everywhere, and we all come across them in our day-to-day lives. For instance, I was looking to replace tires on my decade-old car. My search results on the online tire retailer's website are a perfect practical example of the use of effectiveness vectors for companies selling a very commoditized and established offering. I can simplify my top three choices as follows:

Offering 1: Mileage warranty = 80,000 miles; Total installed cost = $612

Offering 2: Mileage warranty = 40,000 miles; Total installed cost = $458

Offering 3: Mileage warranty = 0 miles; Total installed cost = $297

Warranty here aligns with the quality vector, and the installed cost is the cost vector. We could imagine why speed and flexibility aren't on the board for an average road car tire. As you can see, we intuitively expect these trade-offs when we say, "You get what you pay for."

Although these four vectors are intuitive and they are largely self-explanatory, their application requires significantly more analysis and discipline. Companies often struggle with objectivity and try to optimize all dimensions and effectiveness vectors, resulting in poor or mediocre performances across all.

First, the root causes of the market problem clue us in on the optimal vectors, which we must index heavily because customers draw different levels of net value from each vector. We must use these indicators from our market study to independently frame the effectiveness vector each capability element must exude.

Second, the value engine enablers we framed as trade-offs articulate thematic behaviors that our customers consciously or subconsciously use to filter value creators like us. We must demonstrate these thematic behaviors through our processes, management approach, and productization efforts. So, these value engine-focused core values set can also inform which of the four effectiveness vectors we must prioritize. For example, Amazon's core value of "frugality" directly points to a focus on optimizing the cost vector.

Let's compare two kitchen cabinet companies. One makes and sells kitchen cabinets through a large retailer like Home Depot, while the other makes and installs custom kitchen cabinets directly for high-end homes. They are entirely different companies.

For the capability element of physically building a cabinet, one offers much more manufacturing flexibility than the other, which must come with a trade-off. The capability element to manufacture the same cabinet design in large volumes quickly focuses on optimizing cost and offers limited flexibility. This is entirely different from a capability element in which a craftsman is hand-making a few cabinets in a machine shop with higher flexibility and cost.

Another capability element could be the design thinking behind the installation of cabinets. The high-volume company's design will require significantly higher quality because it must accommodate a range of consumer tastes and installation challenges in various homes, which comes at a higher cost. Conversely, the custom cabinet maker doesn't have to invest significantly in installation design, given the custom nature of its installations.

Altering the effectiveness vectors can create two very different companies even for the same capability elements because they change all the building blocks in the operations baseline.

So, as a third capability lever, we must diligently choose the optimal balance of effectiveness vectors for each capability element to enable them to collectively solve the market problem while accommodating our core values set as a guidepost for buying decision drivers.

Capability lever 4: Superimpose operations baseline strengths to frame Build vs. Buy vs. Borrow vs. Avoid decisions.

Our fourth capability lever is our choice of whether and how we will acquire a capability element. Creating something ourselves is a very different ball game than using something created by another company.

Let's bring back our Comparative Advantage Ecosystem mindset. We must focus on doing the things we are good at. Irrespective of our market, it's unlikely that we will create our own email platform to communicate within our organization because someone has already built it. The same simple idea translates to any capability element on our design board.

There are three general paths to including a capability element in our solution. We can create it ourselves, buy it from outside, or borrow it from outside. The last alternative is not getting involved in certain capability elements. Understanding and deciding how to realize each capability element is essential to ensuring that our strategic trade-offs around what-to-offer are complete.

It is important to articulate how we plan to acquire each capability element because our strategic plan and execution path diverge based on the acquisition path. So, let's give our build vs. buy vs. borrow vs. avoid path a name – **Capability Element Acquisition Path**.

Things To Remember: Capability Element Acquisition Path

Every company has a choice to build, buy, borrow, or avoid each capability element that is considered an option to create the overall solution. This choice is our Capability Element Acquisition Path.

First, the clutch deciding factors on the Capability Element Acquisition Path are our ability to create the capability element and our ability to manage that capability element. We may be good at one or both or neither.

Second, the level of differentiation or commoditization of each capability element helps finalize our acquisition path. For example, if our ability to create or manage a capability element is unique in the marketplace, we should consider it a differentiation. Conversely, if several companies can spend the same amount of money creating and managing a capability element, we should consider it commoditized.

Consider these design questions to frame our choice around the acquisition path for each capability element:

Would we categorize our ability to successfully create each capability element ourselves as a strength or a weakness?

Would we categorize our ability to successfully manage the capability element ourselves as a strength or a weakness?

Is each capability element differentiated or commoditized? In other words, is the ability to create and manage the capability element unique, or can anyone do it?

Figure D14 shows an optimal decision matrix that summarizes our acquisition pathways using these three questions.

Figure D14. Company's relative strengths and weaknesses inform the Build vs. Buy vs. Borrow vs. Avoid decisions.

Throughout this analysis, strengths and weaknesses imply true potential based on the underlying fundamentals of our operations baseline, not the current performance level illustrated via metrics and market feedback. We want to improve our operations baseline continuously and meet our true potential. Conversely, we must refrain from lying to ourselves and think the improbable is possible. This is an excellent time to embrace our "why us?" principle from Chapter C.1.

When should we **build**? The option to create an element ourselves means we depend on our wits, skills, and experience to create it. We must do so only when we are uniquely good at it. A build option generally implies that we want to create it ourselves because it is our unique strength, and we want to maintain it. If the element is an object, a build option implies designing and building tangible items ourselves. If the element is an action, a build option implies we train our employees effectively to perform the action rather than hire pre-trained employees. For a knowledge element, a build option means we are better at creating the intellectual property ourselves than hiring external experts or licensing others' intellectual property.

Only one of the eight paths in our capability acquisition decision matrix encourages us to build. However, this is the only scenario in which we are creating significant value through the capability elements under consideration.

When should we **buy**? Buying implies we are skipping the creation and focusing on the ongoing management of the capability element. Our optimal path to acquiring a capability element is buying if we are strong at only managing the capability element. We can buy an element from another company and include it in our overall capability. For object elements, think about buying as procuring the object creation source. In our cabinet manufacturer example, buying implies we are acquiring a cabinet production facility that we can manage in the future because creating that facility is not our forte, or it is just as easy for many others to create it. For action elements, hiring fully primed value creators from outside qualifies as buying skills for actions.

We would buy a capability element because it is a necessary building block of the overarching capability, but we aren't optimally placed to create it. Three of the eight scenarios in our decision matrix imply that we are buying.

When do we **borrow**? Borrowing implies limiting our involvement in creating or managing the capability element. The most common form of borrowing is outsourcing the creation and management of objects or the performance of actions. Similarly, software and hardware created and managed by someone else can be white-labeled for our use as a capability element. We borrow when the capability element is a commodity or when our strength is not to create or manage it.

By borrowing a capability element, we are creating no incremental value because another company is creating and managing it for all practical purposes. Two of the eight pathways place us here. The only rational reason to borrow a capability element is that it complements other elements we are building and buying.

Lastly, when do we **avoid** a capability element? If we are not optimally placed to create or manage a capability element that other companies consider a differentiation, including this element in our overarching capability is a recipe for disaster. When there are many permutations to solve a problem, why would a capability be successful if at least one of four to six core elements is our weakness while it's someone else's strength?

Essentially, we must alter the configuration of our overarching capability to eliminate such a capability element from the design.

A consumer-facing people connector company I have worked with had an overarching capability that allowed individuals to get to know each other better through conversations. One necessary underlying capability element was how people connect securely through technology. The company didn't consider this highly secure connectivity element a core strength they should build themselves or buy. However, what they had included in their capability was a unique strength of another company in the market that they decided to borrow through white labeling.

This was a mistake because this single borrowed capability element held all the company's offerings hostage. The correct answer was to supplant the value created via the highly secure technology connectivity with another capability element that creates similar overall value for customers.

Just because a capability element appears effective on paper doesn't mean including it in our overarching capability is appropriate. So, let's summarize the rules of thumb for our acquisition paths.

We must prioritize capability elements that we are uniquely positioned to build because these are differentiated strengths we can create and manage. These capability elements create the most value and fit our strengths.

Buy or borrow one or two capability elements that are essential to complement the capability elements that we choose to build. Limit buying or borrowing to less than one-third of the elements. Without a center of gravity that epitomizes our strengths, our capability is unlikely to truly create value. Storytelling based on several bought or borrowed capabilities is usually just that and rarely sustainable.

Lastly, avoid elements that are our weaknesses and others' unique strengths. For example, suppose we cannot create a cohesive overarching capability when eliminating an element in the "avoid" path. In that case, we must reassess the quality of our problem-solving efforts across the four capability levers.

A services company I worked with was historically focused on resource augmentation and tried to create a software solution for the actions through which the company was creating value in the past. However, productizing software solutions was not the company's strength. The company borrowed and strung together white-labeled software object elements from established vendors that it would have been better off avoiding. The result was a collection of features that didn't dovetail because the company lacked control of any of the borrowed capability elements. Over time, the company gave up on its software capability aspirations and returned to its service roots.

Objectively framing our Capability Element Acquisition Path is necessary because it impacts our strategic plan and execution, our processes, and our management approach. The Capability Element Acquisition Path lever also ensures that we arrive at capability element combinations that can solve the market problem while staying aligned with our strengths.

Now, let's translate this framework into our what-to-offer trade-offs.

Principle 5: Configure four capability levers to frame what-to-offer trade-offs.

Understanding and solving our sweet spot's market problem is often handled with a back-of-the-envelope, "just do it!" attitude. That is not the path to sustainable value creation, investment efficiency, and profitability. Every problem's root cause has many possible solutions, and we have to work within ourselves as a company. Our four capability levers allow us to think beyond technology hype or economic cycles and find a combination that creates optimal value and aligns closest to our strengths, as shown in Figure D15.

Luckily or intentionally, sustainable companies arrive at the proper configuration of capability elements across four dimensions and four effectiveness vectors that align with the company's strengths and optimally solve the root cause of a well-defined market problem.

Methodically moving from framing the root cause of the market problem to structuring solution configurations is a deeply analytical exercise that requires situational awareness and hypothesis-driven analysis. Jumping to a conclusion is the equivalent of hiding from all the other potential options we are not weighing.

Consider these design questions to utilize the four levers of our capability framework:

What are the combinations of capability elements, which are underlying building blocks of a capability along one dimension, that will render a comprehensive market solution? How effectively does each capability element contribute to the overarching capability?

Which capability dimension – object, action, knowledge, or promise – does each element address? Do these elements collectively offer coverage across the dimensions we need to solve the problem?

What is the optimal balance across effectiveness vectors – flexibility, speed, quality, and cost – for each element to create the maximum net customer value as informed by the root causes of our market problem and core value sets?

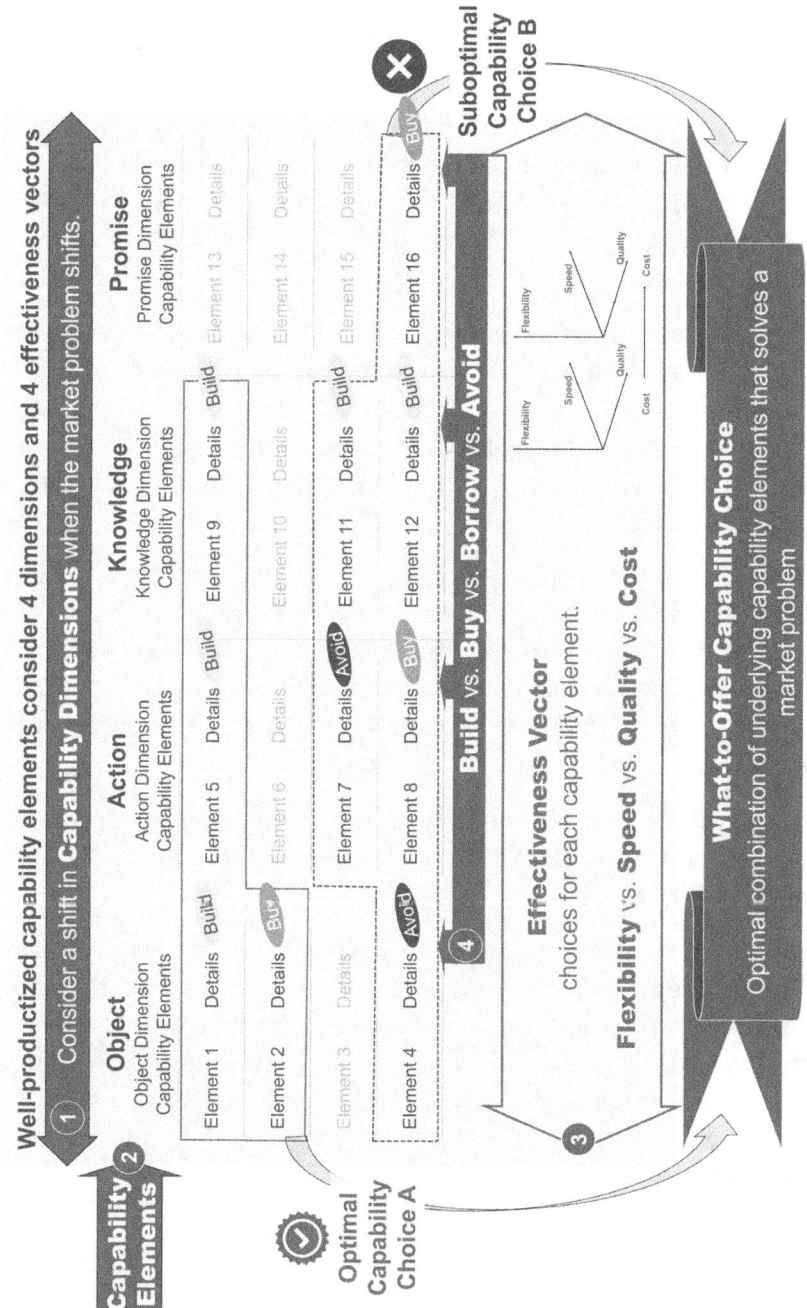

Figure D15. Capability levers framework informs what-to-offer trade-offs.

What is the optimal acquisition path – build, buy, borrow – for each capability element? Which capability elements must we avoid?

A technology-enabled services company that I worked with had customer value creation challenges because it didn't make effective choices along the four capability levers. To replace a predominantly company-performed services capability, the company created a customer self-service technology option.

However, the company didn't consider how the employee knowledge, which complemented the services performed in the past, would be replicated if those actions were to be replaced with a technology. Customers rarely used the technology object because it didn't include built-in user guidance that replicated what the company's service employees subtly provided in the past.

Further, the company struggled to pinpoint its position on the effectiveness vectors. It tried to offer high flexibility, speed, and quality but struggled along all vectors. At the same time, pricing was set as though maximizing flexibility, speed, and quality would come at a low cost. Customers perpetually questioned the offering's value proposition because none of the three value-creating vectors were optimized.

Decisions are hard. Strategic decisions impact the whole company throughout an execution cycle and likely require significant investment, the choice of which implies risk.

How do we choose among all these permutations of options across the four levers? We must pick the configuration that puts us in Quadrant 1, which we framed at the start of this chapter – the zone we operate in within our strengths and, preferably, our competitors' weaknesses. Similar to our "who" and "how" trade-offs, Figure D16 illustrates our what-to-offer trade-offs, where we prioritize the market problem we focus on and choose a congruent path to solving it.

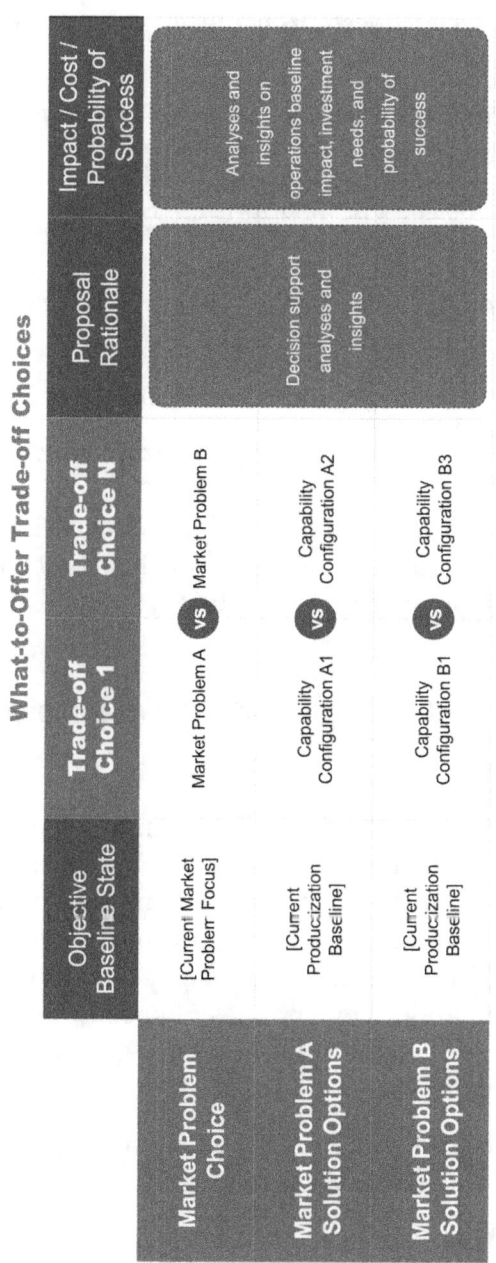

Figure D16. What-to-offer decisions span market problem and capabilities.

Consider these design questions while formalizing the what-to-offer trade-off choices:

What are the structured definitions of the market problems that our sweet spot customers experience?

Which market problem will we prioritize? How long will we prioritize this choice before reevaluating?

What are the optimal configurations of capability elements that form comprehensive solutions to each market problem?

What is each configuration's impact, cost, and probability of success?

Which of these solution configurations is most compelling?

Framing these productized offering-related choices based on our market problem, root causes, and capability levers leads us to our final strategic decision to enable planning and execution.

Principle 6: Frame all strategic trade-offs and choices to decide corporate strategy.

Sticking to the arduous, analytical, and seemingly repetitive yet necessary triangulating approach takes tremendous discipline and confidence. As we go down this path, others in the company may tell us that this is a waste of time, try to use gut-feel-based answers, and create a sense of urgency that makes us feel the need to cut corners. Remain steadfast because our exercise is not about appearances of speed or confidence. Strategy development is about all the things that our gut instincts will miss – the unknown-unknowns!

"It ain't what you don't know that gets you into trouble. It's what you know for sure that just ain't so." – Mark Twain.

To recap, we analyzed our entire market. We took an analytical approach to frame our sweet spot customers and understand their personalities – the buyer, user, and approver.

We went deeper into framing our market problem in the context of our sweet spot customers and their buying decision drivers. Rather than addressing these symptoms, we discussed the importance of analytically understanding the root causes to develop solutions.

We then considered opportunities to reassess and formalize two sets of core values to evolve our organization's behavioral guardrails. The first set directly influences our value engine and thus addresses buying decision drivers. The second enables our management approach and the necessary fundamental behaviors to support those value engine enablers. These two sets of core values are our how-to-deliver trade-off choices.

We discussed four capability levers to frame our what-to-offer strategic choices, which ensure that an effective combination of capability elements addresses our market problem. These elements must cover the relevant capability dimensions while focusing on the right effectiveness levers of flexibility, speed, quality, and cost to solve the problem. We also learned the overall value each capability element would create by considering our acquisition path, which frames the optimal configuration of these elements as a comprehensive solution.

There is no side-stepping the reality that this is a challenging analytical exercise. It is a complex jigsaw puzzle to cast our company's north star. Yet, pursuing this path with discipline gives us the power to articulate our company's future in a single strategic decision.

The strategic trade-off framework allows us to create a single source of our corporate strategy that can be accessible to every investor, board member, executive, employee, and even partner or customer. A cohesive strategy does not contain sensitive information. It helps us align all stakeholders and validate that our path aligns with the purpose we set for multiple years.

The stereotypes of sensitivity about strategy come from individualistic ecosystems where stakeholders are misaligned and uncomfortable sharing information transparently. In a holistic company where we are balancing incentives across stakeholders, what's there to hide?

Some companies take a silo mentality where the "who" questions are tactically answered independently by marketing and sales teams, human resources create core values without balancing the "how" aspects of our company, and "what" decisions are handled independently by teams that manage the offerings. Unfortunately, the result is often incongruent tactics that suit each employee team while customer value and capital efficiency are low. We cannot keep up with our evolving world without a single dovetailed strategy.

Let's wrap up our strategy development effort by packaging the insights and trade-offs into a cohesive and comprehensive corporate strategy. Although I often dissuade templates as they minimize important ideas to tactical box-filling, I use the structure in Figure D17 as a quality guardrail. Let's highlight the five key elements within.

First, consolidate the "who," "how," and "what" trade-offs, choices, insights, and associated soft decisions we have made into a single view. The essence of this step is to make a One Company strategic decision. Every fundamental building block in our company influences each other and must be congruent. To create the best version of our company, we need a singular strategy that enables such congruence.

Second, for each trade-off, we must articulate the current baseline state and propose an optimal evolved choice without ambiguity. Include at least a second choice and possibly a third choice for each trade-off. If we cannot frame compelling competing choices, we should ask whether we have explored our options effectively enough.

Third, the analytical rationale behind each proposed evolved state, and the substantiation for deciding against the remaining choices should be articulated. Senior executives must understand that deciding on a proposed choice is also a decision against the choices we are moving past. This rationale of choosing and not choosing is paramount as we will likely question our strategy on challenging days through the execution cycle. Knowing that we were thorough helps us navigate through storms.

Fourth, articulate the three differentiating factors of a strategic decision for each trade-off – the impact, cost, and probability of success for each choice. It is naïve to imagine that achieving a strategic choice would be easy or guaranteed just because we make a decision.

Fifth, the Congruence Architect must lay up the ball for the CEO to finalize the strategic decision based on the proposed evolved state. It is tempting to

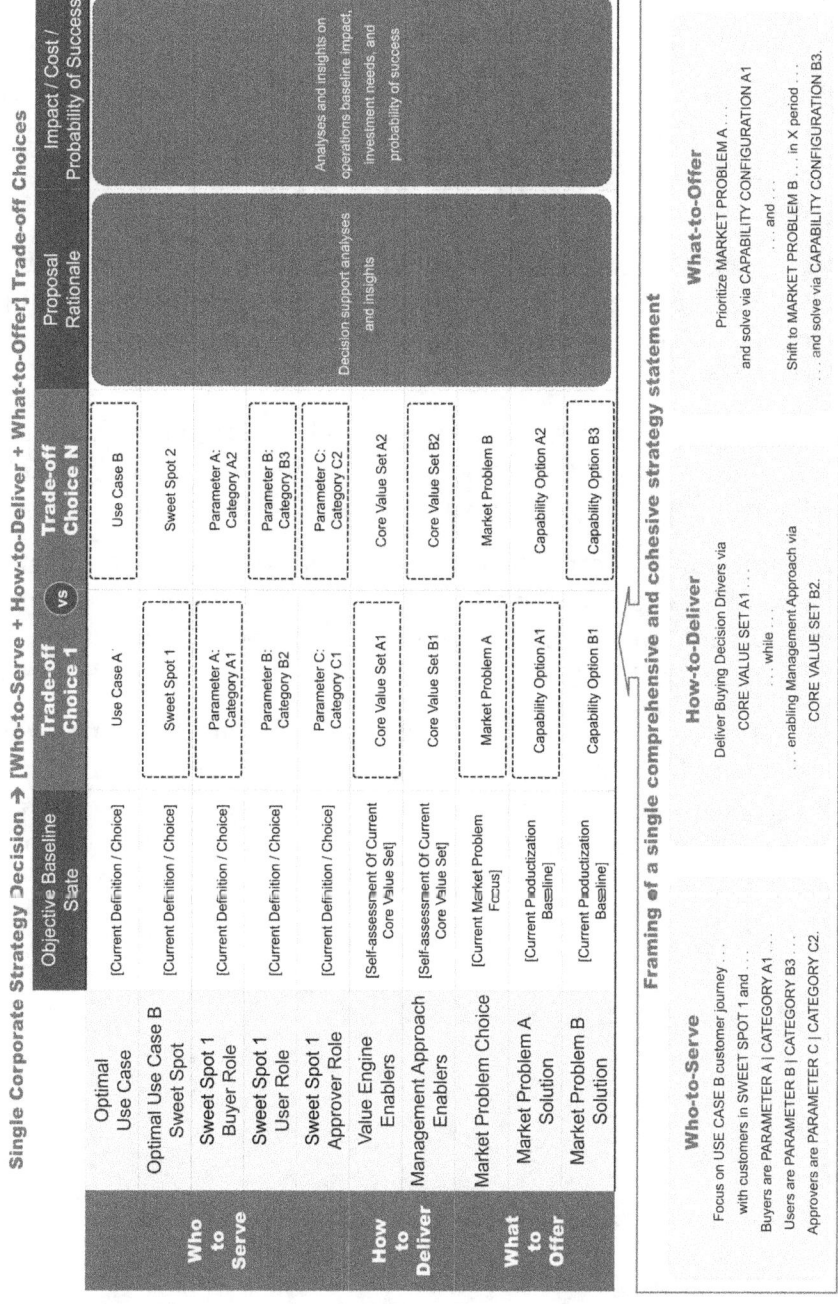

Figure D17. Who-how-what trade-offs form comprehensive and cohesive strategy.

make a couple of easy trade-offs and leave the rest unattended. However, that's why executives make the big bucks – to make tough choices.

Not deciding or a cut-the-baby-in-half mindset are not options. If we cannot forgo a compelling choice on "who" we will serve and then hope that our "how" and "what" trade-off choices will be effective, we are in for a rude awakening when we execute.

Every single strategic trade-off must have a decisive choice. These choices must solve the root cause of our prioritized market problem and address the buying decision drivers for our sweet spot customers. This is our corporate strategy!

Over the last four chapters, we have objectively and insightfully addressed the three incredibly powerful questions of who-to-serve, how-to-deliver, and what-to-offer to macro-evolve our operations baseline.

Many companies choose to guess the answers to these questions. Such a mindset leads to over 50 percent of publicly traded companies in America being unprofitable. Others that go through even less scrutiny aren't likely to fare better.

The power of our methodical strategy development to macro-evolve is that we can address incongruences across our entire company and the impact of scale and environmental changes. A purpose-aligned strategic decision unites the board, investors, executives, employees, customers, and partners.

Now, we must translate the strategy on paper into our operational reality.

PART E

Strategic Planning Dovetails Strategy With Operations.

EVERY company has a plan for the next year and beyond. The question is, is it a good plan? Strategic planning is like other levers. Our only options are developing and operating according to an effective strategic plan or operating in chaos, which is also a plan. A so-called plan in someone's head that changes often is not our intent.

Our operations baseline can self-evolve tactically through objective data analysis on an ongoing basis. But we must comprehensively evolve our entire operations baseline to keep up with the shifting world. We kicked off our macroevolution cycle with corporate strategy, and strategic planning is the second of the three parts. So, what is it?

Things To Remember: Strategic Planning

Strategy is a decision on paper. It's a mental construct. Strategy comes to life through our operations baseline. Strategic planning is the dovetailed and detailed design that translates corporate strategy into real-life operations.

As a mid-career small business entrepreneur, I can attest that translating my strategy into reality through strategic planning is the single tool that allows me to run my business. The anchor and concreteness of an excellent strategic plan protect me from my self-doubt, day-to-day ups and downs, and hype cycles in the broader market that fall outside my purpose. All decision-makers go through such internal turmoil and external influences, and sticking to our path is hard.

Operating a company without a concrete strategic plan is analogous to running blindfolded. We will lose a lot of time and investment stumbling and anxiously course-correcting while living with a low probability of finding the right direction.

Translating strategy into operations requires a mature strategic plan.

A senior executive of an established company recently told me, "I don't think strategic planning is necessary. . . . We just need to focus on growth." A few days later, a vice president who reports to this executive said, "I am sure [the executive] would disagree. . . . But I don't think we have a plan at all. I wish we had one." Even though almost every company dedicates time and effort to planning, a deep internalization of what constitutes an effective strategic plan and belief in its true power is hard to find.

First, a company's strategy must be refined on a cadence to stay ahead of the evolving competitive landscape and customer needs. Staying stagnant strategically is a path to losing customers through deflation of value creation. Translating such a strategy into day-to-day execution requires an effective strategic plan.

Second, operations maturity must evolve to keep up with strategic shifts and our company's scale and lifecycle stage. Skills necessary to execute critical initiatives must mature over time, and operations responsibilities must evolve to accommodate market shifts and our scale. However, making these decisions ad hoc without structure is chaos. Strategic planning provides a structured path to align these evolutionary requirements with corporate strategy.

Third, companies often rely on a linear lifecycle model and rinse-and-repeat tactics that imply investment without maturity. This tactical scaling approach, where we assume more of the same is enough as a company gets bigger, results in the misallocation of investment, as we indicated in our value engine introduction. Strategic planning provides a structured path to reconfigure our operations baseline building blocks to align with the company's lifecycle stage.

Fourth, some owners aspire to sell the company to new private investors or publicly list company shares. Our company's intrinsic value rests with its operations baseline. Increasing our market price for a rational investor implies maturing our operations baseline. Our macroevolution cycle is the only pathway to evolve our management approach and value engine holistically, and this path goes right through an effective strategic plan.

Incrementally, effective planning is also a day-to-day necessity.

Effective strategic planning is the only path to mature execution.

When I was younger, I was an impatient driver, and when I saw traffic, I had the illusion that weaving between lanes allowed me to pick the one that would get me to my destination fastest. This illusion was based on zero rational information to support my choice of which lane to switch to and when. We all do this in different life circumstances. All these lane changes are not getting anyone anywhere any faster. Instead, they're causing chaos or an accident that slowed traffic in the first place.

The board and senior executives face similar challenges as drivers on the highway. Our surroundings make us feel we must move at a certain pace to make observers approve of our company. We use indications equivalent to the road's maximum speed limit to decide how fast we should be going. Companies love to make statements like, "We grew 100 percent last year!" But not every company can or should. In a balanced value exchange ecosystem, our customers may not want to adopt a new solution at that rate.

Setting tangible and realistic expectations allows us not to panic and weave around when the emotional reality of running a business hits us. Effective strategic planning is the magic wand that frames a realistic path to our destination.

A weak strategic plan that sounds exciting but is not reality-based becomes a tool for government-style budgetary approval for the next cycle. However, it does not have the core components to create value or invest efficiently. By the end of the first month of our execution cycle, such a plan will likely get derailed and create a frenzied search for new ways to achieve the unrealistic outcomes that we set ourselves.

This will make our stakeholders feel that our company has no coherent path to our destination. Every stakeholder can feel the motion sickness of a gyrating company, even though they may not know why it is happening.

Without an effective strategic plan, the board and executive team's management will likely reflect a lane-changer in traffic. As exciting as lane changes are for key decision-makers, the remaining stakeholders will feel an imbalanced value exchange around the company.

Strategic Planning Maturity Model.

Strategic planning is like tax season for most executives and analytical value creators. It comes around periodically. We will use the term execution cycle to frame the time window that each strategic planning effort will shape.

Commitment to developing a well-grounded plan enables us to focus solely on delivering flawlessly during the execution cycle without constantly questioning the plan. Conversely, a lack of commitment to planning leads to a lack of confidence in the plan. This results in poor forward momentum and a continuous waste of resources throughout the execution cycle. We will end up perpetually reworking the path forward, even though it could have been well-developed during planning.

The most critical success factor for planning is the intent behind planning. If we use planning as a means to an end that we are already anchored on, it wastes everyone's time. If we embrace that the treasure is truly along the path, strategic planning becomes a powerful part of our evolutionary method.

Figure E1 explains our five-level Strategic Planning Maturity Model. Use it to self-assess your planning maturity. In the following four chapters, we will use this outline to cover how to build an effective strategic plan.

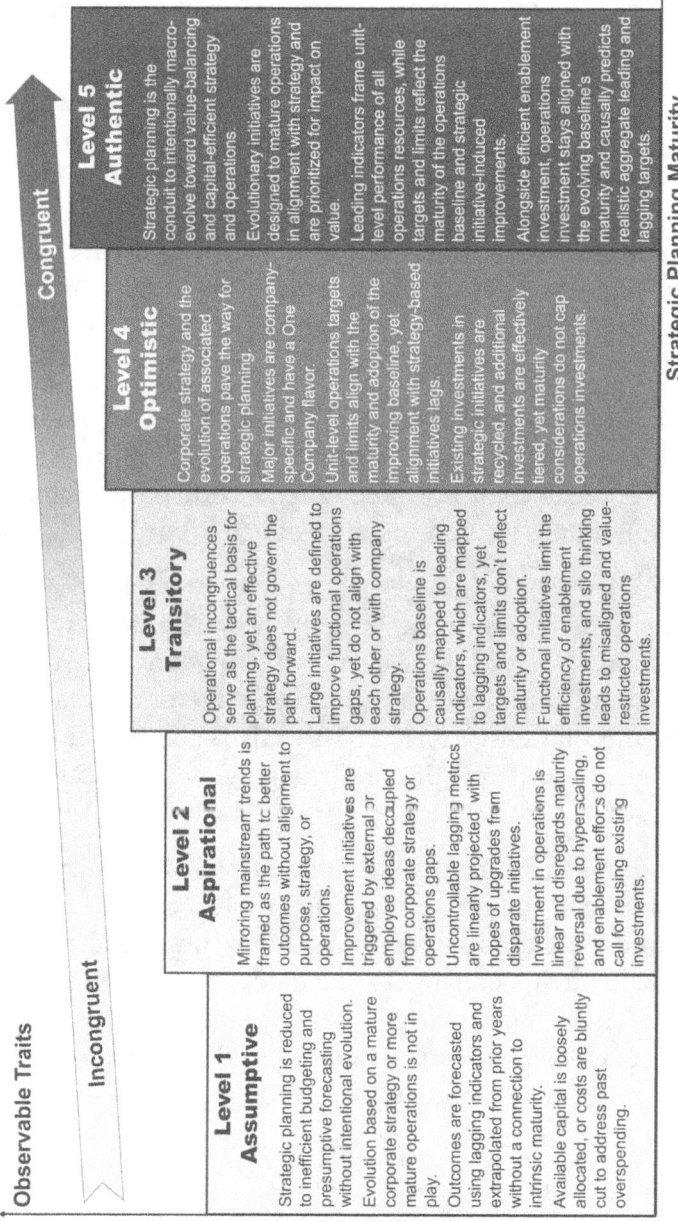

Figure E1. Strategic Planning Maturity Model.

The congruence across other building blocks of our company heavily influences the effectiveness of our strategic planning success.

How mature is our management approach? We will struggle to run an objective and analytical planning exercise if we have an immature management approach. The balance necessary to think as a collective unit while also challenging each other only exists in environments with a mature management approach.

How mature is our value engine? We can't learn from our past if we don't have a customer-focused offering and our processes are in chaos with poor data capture and usage. If we can't operate objectively and analytically on a day-to-day basis, we will likely struggle to do so during planning as well.

How mature is our corporate strategy? If we are in dire straits with our operations baseline maturity in terms of value creation and investment efficiency, we could develop a strategy aligned with our purpose to reinvent our company. But have we developed an effective corporate strategy based on the principles in Part D?

There are no shortcuts unless we somehow get lucky with a magical offering that was a runaway hit, and we can get away with riding that wave. But that only applies to a tiny percentage of companies. The rest have to earn the market victories. With this reality in mind, we want to work on the right-hand side of our Strategic Planning Maturity Model at *Level 5: Authentic.*

Level 1: Assumptive represents a company with no real plan. Strategic planning is reduced to basic budgeting and forecasting without an evolutionary mindset. Lagging indicators are extrapolated from past years without a link to intrinsic maturity. Executive motivation and discussions focus on demonstrating short-term revenue, making the company's plan essentially a performative story. Capital is allocated carelessly, or costs are bluntly cut to revert past overspending.

Moving to the right, *Level 2: Aspirational* represents more structure, yet maturity improvement efforts are sparked by inbound advertisements or employee ideas and largely mirror mainstream themes, disconnected from strategy and operational gaps. Lagging metrics are projected linearly with a hope to hyperscale while ignoring the reality that it is unsustainable. Despite some structure, efforts focus on short-term monetary goals rather than sustainable profitability or alignment with purpose and strategy.

At *Level 3: Transitory*, planning relies heavily on operational gaps, and a cohesive strategy does not guide the path forward. Major efforts are framed to address functional incongruences, but they remain siloed and disconnected. Leading indicators are mapped to company-level results and they connect day-to-day activities with overarching outcomes. But execution targets are not based on operational maturity. Investments are allocated in functional silos, which limit capital efficiency.

Evolutionary efforts are strategy-led and framed in alignment with operational incongruences and a One Company mindset, as the company matures to *Level 4: Optimistic*. Here, the company sets execution targets that match operations baseline maturity, but the alignment with macroevolution improvement efforts lags. Investment in operations resources is also not optimized, which creates the risk of overspending and reversal in operations maturity.

At the highest level, *Level 5: Authentic*, strategic planning is the conduit for intentional macroevolution toward capital-efficient operations and balanced value. Macroevolution focuses on maturing operations in sync with strategy and prioritizes impact on value. Leading indicators govern operations performance, with targets reflecting operational maturity and the improvements expected from macroevolution. Investments in macroevolution and operations execution are optimized to recycle where possible and align with improving maturity.

The following four chapters cover the intricate levers that take months to deploy and build a *Level 5: Authentic* strategic plan.

E.1
PLAN TO ALIGN EXECUTION WITH STRATEGY AND OPERATIONS MATURITY.

S TRATEGIC planning can feel like Groundhog Day. Unfortunately, here is how it often starts.

Revenue-focused CEOs and CFOs kick off the strategic planning season by rallying other senior executives with: "We had some challenges this year. But those were anomalies. . . . We are still a great company. . . . We are the best. . . . Next year will be the best we ever had. . . . Our investors are behind us. . . . Customers love us."

Then comes the ask: "We want you to define your plans to meet our revenue goal of. . . . We already agreed with the board. . . . We want your plans to be strategic. . . . Go!"

Typically, these exercises start without rigorous attention to the levers discussed under Part D: Corporate Strategy. They also end in a collection of disjointed projects that do not achieve their goal or corporate strategy, which is likely missing.

Why does this happen?

Strategic planning is often treated like filing taxes – a chore that involves getting a spending budget approved for the upcoming execution cycle. That's *Level 1: Assumptive* strategic planning.

Most companies do not engage in mature macroevolutions, beginning with strategy development followed by effective strategic planning to implement that strategy. Even many companies that are value-creating and profitable through their first offering and brand do not prepare the company proactively for incongruences that will appear over time, scale, and environment.

Strategic planning intends to frame a realistic path to achieving our corporate strategy. Our purpose-led company's strategy, planning, and operations must align with that purpose. Unless our purpose was to run a pop-up company for a specific period, we must macro-evolve to stay in line with the risk-adjusted benefit statements associated with stakeholders and our company's lifecycle stage.

Imagine we are in the last stage of the company's lifecycle, where the business model has waned, and customer value creation is minimal after several years in business. If we have employees, customers, and partners, we need a strategic plan to wind down the company. So, the principles we are about to discuss are in no way optional for any company.

Principle 1: Strategic planning must hinge on a mature corporate strategy.

The most pivotal principle of strategic planning is that it must always start with a cohesive corporate strategy. Remember the line exercise we used to explain corporate strategy, which articulates our starting and ending points. Drawing the line is execution, which will be discussed in Part F. But how do we draw it? Freehand? Using a ruler as a guide? With what? How fast? Strategic planning is the bridge that takes us from the present to the future.

A mature operations baseline can tactically undergo self-contained micro-evolutions. We can improve each process tactically to address minor unexpected surprises. We can enhance each capability marginally based on objective feedback we gather from customers. However, all such ongoing operations baseline improvements are catching up to our expected reality or marginal. They don't comprehensively move our company closer to our purpose and address the big questions of who-to-serve, what-to-offer, and how-to-deliver.

> **Things To Remember: Strategy-Led Planning**
>
> **Our who-to-serve, what-to-offer, and how-to-deliver trade-off decision triggers the macroevolution of our operations baseline. Corporate strategy is the north star that starts our macroevolution change wave, and strategic planning always follows a mature corporate strategy.**

Starting with a poor strategic decision or ignoring an effective one during planning will leave the company to take Hail Mary shots, hoping for results. Decoupling strategy from planning is also one of the most common paths to incongruence in a company where disconnected individualistic plans take over.

Sadly, most planning efforts attempt a cold start without a strategy. In a strategic vacuum, plans are built on spurious foundations. Outdated tribal intuition, reactive choices to competitor movements, and follow-the-market ideas without analytical backing tend to lead our company astray. Such inputs alone are not cohesive or comprehensive and will leave us questioning our path throughout the execution cycle. Easy come, easy go applies to ideas, too.

A "whale strategy" is a common sales tactic that B2B companies embrace. Its recurrence is predictable, primarily when a company operates in a strategic vacuum.

First, whale hunting is not a strategy; it's a desired outcome. It is a poor sweet spot definition to say that we will go after customers who would bring us considerable revenue, hence the "whale." How could anyone know which specific customers will generate significant revenue unless we are psychic? Companies commit significant resources to such low-probability ocean fishing expeditions because they lack a strategy.

Second, such an outcome-based tactic is chosen due to a lack of confidence in the operations baseline, and the company lacks a congruent purpose beyond making money somehow. The thought process in these circumstances is, "It would be much easier to find one or two big customers who will meet all revenue goals even if we do whatever they want." Usually, it doesn't work at all. Even when one might find a whale without any other qualifying criteria, the company becomes enslaved to that customer's bidding, and any other purpose the company had will evaporate.

To stay true to our company's purpose, we must dedicate significant effort and discipline to arriving at comprehensive and cohesive who-how-what trade-offs and a single overarching strategic decision based on them. Planning must follow that strategic decision.

Principle 2: Strategic planning is not financial forecasting or budgeting.

The chief strategy officer of a publicly traded company recently shared this view on their planning efforts: "The finance team manages the exercise. They call it a strategic plan, but that's just ignorance. . . . All they have is a financial plan." On the same day, the operating partner of a large private equity firm shared the same view about what they wanted to change in their portfolio companies – to focus on a real strategic plan. Sadly, financial forecasting and budgeting are mistaken for strategic planning too often.

A financial outcomes mindset derails strategic planning.

It's hard for a CEO or CFO not to think about the revenue and expense outcomes of the income statement. But worrying too much about the outcome leads us to play poorly. It's like looking too far down the bracket of a knockout tournament.

When CEOs and CFOs set specific revenue or expense goals, they practically undermine objectivity in the planning exercise. Whatever a company's website says, every executive and senior position is constantly trying to prove their effectiveness to keep their jobs.

If a CEO and CFO ask the executive team to devise a plan to reach $75 million in total revenue in the subsequent execution cycle, that's exactly what they will get through planning. Through every single stage in the exercise, every executive will likely come back with projects that magically lead to a total revenue of $75 million. But the plan is a fictional story.

First, anchoring is a bias that skews even the most objective individuals. What is the probability that the CEO's and CFO's asks didn't influence executives to say, "We can get there!"? Very low.

Whether it's building an arbitrary feature, developing a brand-new website, or hiring an entirely new lead generation team, each executive will state that the total output of their projects will help the company reach $75 million. It won't be $70 million or $80 million. There won't be a discussion about whether $75 million is realistic – instead, the exercise anchors everyone to $75 million as if their job depends on it.

Second, herd mentality is another potent bias. Why would anyone put deep thought into the calculations of a math problem if all the focus is on getting to an answer that everyone already knows? When we framed $75 million as the revenue goal, we removed the incentive to focus on the "how." In such financial outcome-focused planning, the plan's details will likely be nebulous and do not dovetail with the company's strategy or operations baseline.

The most important output of a strategic plan is the alignment between strategy and execution – i.e., the path to achieving the strategy and how to measure our progress. Without such strong alignment, a financial forecast is just an aspirational guess or an extrapolation of past performance.

An aspirational or history-based plan will lead to one of two outcomes. We will either miss revenue or expense goals because we didn't develop a tangible and realistic path to execute. Alternatively, we may achieve our arbitrary goals, which understate the company's true potential, and then throw our operations into chaos in our excitement to capture the unexpected upside – ultimately harming the company's prospects.

Things To Remember: Financial Forecasts

Financial forecasts are realistic company-level lagging outcomes derived from well-developed strategy-led and operations-focused planning deliverables. They are not intended to be set based on the company's history or patterns outside the company's borders, as that would lead to incongruence during execution.

Financial outcomes and financial sustainability are critical matters and are the responsibility of the board, the CEO, and the CFO. When framing our company purpose, we must balance stakeholder benefits with risk, including financial risk. We practically enact this risk management by ensuring that financial outcomes and risks that align with our purpose dictate our boundary for the company's investment and how much revenue that investment brings.

Beyond these purpose-aligned financial thresholds, letting extrinsic outcomes influence the strategic plan is suboptimal. Customers don't care or know whether our revenue and expenses went up or down. Although every employee should know the financial details of their company, most don't and focus on their day-to-day. Partners care about our financial outcomes to a point where they are comfortable with the payment terms they give us or a long-term partnership they might invest in.

Planning must lay a strategy-led, practical path to create value and use investment effectively to achieve outcomes that keep us within those purpose-aligned financial thresholds. If an objective, well-defined strategic plan places our company outside those financial thresholds, we must question whether our purpose-level expectations are realistic and reframe a realistic purpose. Trying to force-fit our strategy, plan, and operations to an unrealistic purpose results in the incongruent and dysfunctional ecosystems I mentioned on the very first page of this book.

A budgeting mindset is ineffective.

A major organization design pitfall we discussed under the management approach was empire-building. I observed this tendency early in my career and told myself I would always be an objective team builder. Several years later, I fell into the same individualistic trap of wanting to add more people to my team. It's a human tendency to fortify our environment and build kingdoms.

This human tendency kicks into high gear during strategic planning when we make investment decisions for the upcoming execution cycle. It is tempting to make a land grab for investment to hire additional employees or buy a popular new technology. Such ideas are only worth investing in if they are objectively correct, align with our strategy, and how we plan to mature our operations baseline. Otherwise, these are just random ideas that are spurious reasons to divide the budget.

When we described the "whale strategy" earlier, what could be the subconscious thought process of such a team? It is not driving a maturity shift in the operations baseline. It is a wrapper for approving a budget to make investments and hoping for the best. It allows the team to keep people and assets and potentially spend more without a real strategy or a plan.

We must avoid allocating investment to unvetted channels that distract from creating value, investing efficiently, and operating profitably. A friend who advises venture capital-backed companies on marketing topics told me about turning down clients because she wanted to work with companies that understand their investment decisions. One specific example was: "Two founders want to immediately spend $30K to $50K monthly on advertising because they got $2 million in early-stage funding. I just feel uncomfortable agreeing to this. I don't think they realize this will be a waste."

Strategic planning can waste organizational resources if the primary output is a budget allocation for another year of business-as-usual execution that hopes for desired outcomes. It often implies deploying investment toward non-value-creating tactics and empire-building where individualism and short-termism supersede congruent decisions.

Principle 3: Operations focus effectively translates investment into outcomes.

Strategic planning must focus on how we will achieve our strategy.

The world constantly measures and discusses extrinsic outcomes. They are preferred not because they are better but because they are easier. If we are watching a football game, anyone can look at the scoreboard on the screen and tell who is ahead or likely to win.

But what if we didn't have a scoreboard on the screen? Can most people look at the state of play and say who is winning? Some can. It takes a keen observer who looks at how the players are walking and talking, their energy level, urgency, confidence, and the tactics deployed to know who is likely ahead and who has the momentum.

The same principle applies to a company. Anyone can look at past revenue or profitability trends and say whether a company did well or not in the past. However, past outcomes are not an indicator of future outcomes.

Present and future incentives, actions, and decisions are the only predictors of future outcomes.

Things To Remember: Operations-Focused Planning

Operations-focused planning frames the incentives, actions, and decisions that accurately predict future outcomes. Extrapolating past outcomes does not reflect the company's realistic potential over time and as scale and environment change.

We can predict our outcomes if we know the quality and quantity of our incentives, actions, and decisions. Taking a lap around the office one afternoon can tell us far more about our company's operations than employee engagement surveys.

An executive described his recently failed turnaround experience as: "There are six of us in the office after 4:00 p.m. on Fridays consistently with the remaining 1500 people having packed up and gone. . . . Meanwhile, we were still bleeding revenue every quarter." Talking points don't influence our outcomes; value creators' actions and decisions do.

So, our strategic plan must focus on how we operate. Connecting intrinsic behaviors to extrinsic outcomes is complicated, and it requires discipline and analytical skills, but it is necessary.

Let's think about our whole company as one giant process flow. A process is a black box that converts inputs to outputs. Any output depends on two aspects: the process and the inputs.

From a strategic planning perspective, our company-level outcomes form the output. We must frame extrinsic outcomes such as revenue and profitability as an outcome that ladders up from how we run our company.

The input is our total investment into the company. However, stating how much we can afford or want to invest is not enough. That's just our investment threshold. So, what does this investment go into?

The process that converts the investment inputs to outcomes is our ever-maturing operations baseline. The hardest part of strategic planning is articulating the improvement and performance of this black box. What evolution do we want to drive across various building blocks of our operations baseline? How will it perform during execution as we evolve it? The key differentiating factor of high value companies is not the inputs and outputs. The real magic sits with the ever-evolving black box that efficiently converts investment into value and sustainable profit.

Figure E2 illustrates this input-process-output model of our company.

Thematically, our planning approach will primarily focus on four aspects.

First, we will focus on improving the maturity and alignment of our operations baseline with our corporate strategy. We define time-bound enablement initiatives through planning to achieve this. I think of our collective enablement efforts as a cocoon enveloping our current operations baseline and transforming it into a more mature and congruent one.

Second, driving this macroevolution via enablement initiatives requires investment, which we will call **Enablement Investment**.

Third, we will also focus on the maturing metrics and targets of our productized offering, processes, data gathering and usage, and management approach, which collectively reflects our evolving operations baseline and its performance.

Fourth, the operations baseline requires investment to run, which we will call **Operations Investment**. Through planning, we will optimize this investment, not necessarily increase it.

Together, these four aspects result in the financial outcomes we desire.

This will be challenging because we will likely feel pulled into revenue and expense discussions often, how many employees we can hire, or constructing aspirational stories about the company's market price. Planning requires analytical thought leaders to lead it with the support of executives who can withstand these tendencies and focus on our operations baseline, which is the only path to value creation.

Principle 4: Disciplined, analytical thought leadership is a planning prerequisite.

A company's investment in the planning exercise is people and skills,

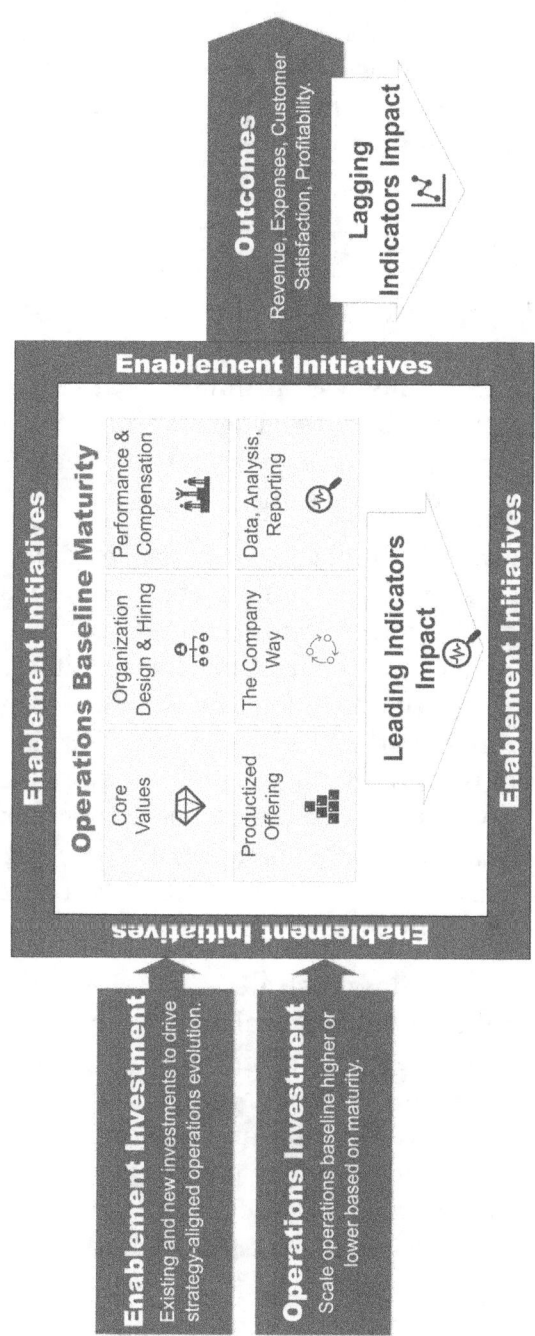

Figure E2. Frame the company as an input-process-output strategic planning model.

which employees or partners can bring. Putting the right people – those with an objective and analytical mindset – on the task is the only path to success. Proposing a one-size-fits-all planning team structure wouldn't be optimal. Instead, planning requires a few critical roles and specific responsibilities.

Role 1: Strategic planning architect.

Strategic planning requires a true playmaker to take the helm. The Congruence Architect is the ideal role to take on this responsibility. The CEO must delegate this responsibility because it requires serious attention to strategic and operational details and analysis. However, this role must have the complete backing of the CEO. The planning architect must demonstrate two essential skills.

First, the planning architect must have an analytical mind, strong business acumen, and a keen understanding of how a company fits together across all functions. The role must also know the pitfalls of poor strategy development, planning, and execution. The architect must also have experience running strategic planning efforts, without which the company risks its time, resources, and future on someone learning on the job. The planning architect is accountable for defining the planning approach tailored to the company's lifecycle stage, choosing the correct individuals required throughout the various planning phases, and moderating all problem-solving, reviews, and decision-making to ensure the plan is comprehensive and cohesive.

Second, this role must demonstrate leadership. Strategic planning exerts a heavy emotional toll and analytical complexity, and ineffective leaders resort to democratic decision-making to ease these demands. Planning can lead to poor results that range from tactical ideas cobbled together on the ineffective end to a land grab for the budget by various teams on the harmful end. Strategic planning will not make everyone happy because it is intended to be a disciplined trade-off exercise. The path to making choices cannot be a split-the-pie-evenly or a command-and-control approach.

The planning architect should be an independent thought leader who can stand firm and balance all the available information to arrive at the most optimal outcomes using dependable frameworks. The architect should seek depth of rationale and details on all critical building blocks of the plan.

Role 2: Executive sponsor.

The CEO is accountable to the board for the company's strategy and plan. The CFO is accountable for the company's financial forecast and management against that forecast. Both aspects are outcomes of strategic planning. The board is accountable for ensuring that these aspects align with the company's purpose. The executive sponsor is the dispassionate referee who speaks for all three parties. This may be the CEO or a delegate.

The executive sponsor must stay fully engaged by consuming and understanding all relevant analyses and findings and actively monitor all participants for objectivity. The role must also bring holistic perspectives around market dynamics and investor interests. Lastly, the sponsor must strongly advocate for the importance of staying focused on the corporate strategy and building a plan that focuses on the operations baseline.

If the executive sponsor is not fully engaged, decisive about making decisions based on objective findings, and advocating adherence to the planning approach, the exercise risks devolving into a financial forecasting and budgeting effort.

Role 3: Analyst.

An analyst does not imply someone who robotically slices and dices data. This role must have a firm handle on our productized offering, processes, and data usage and is responsible for objective analysis and insight generation throughout planning. This role remains joined at the hip with and executes on direction from the planning architect.

Role 4: Objective functional representatives with a One Company mindset.

This is the most challenging role to fill. During strategic planning, we need functional operators to take on the same congruent value exchange mindset we embraced at the company stakeholder level. It requires a team that can put the One Company hat on.

However, many employees and executives spend most of their careers in one function and are not cross-functional thinkers. How does a fan who roots for one team throughout the season objectively help decide what's best for all teams? It's not easy. With that in mind, we must staff the planning effort with executives and thought leaders who can solve for all the colors of a Rubik's cube, not just the color each person likes.

This role is also the all-important conduit between the strategic plan and the rest of the company. These individuals will help develop initiatives to improve the maturity of our operations baseline. They will support the identification of metrics that monitor the maturity and execution of our operations. They must also think critically about investment trade-offs to develop a plan that aligns with all stakeholder needs. Beyond planning, this role must evangelize our One Company plan when it's time to execute.

None of the responsibilities above are functionally focused. Strategic planning cannot be along functional silos.

Companies often swing between extremes of over-inclusion or under-representation. Many include key players from every team responsible for any topic impacted by strategic planning. Other executive sponsors might try a command-and-control approach by only including a minimal group based on seniority or organizational position. Neither extreme is optimal.

A planning exercise I led recently involved a company that brought together every department lead into the effort. However, only one executive asked hard questions, challenged groupthink, and instilled a prove-it-to-me attitude. Others were disengaged until it was their turn to talk about their functions. They mainly spoke about their spending plans with limited details on how they would improve congruence with other parts of the company or achieve an overarching strategy. The quality of the plan suffered.

We must apply our CAE mindset to create a work-based staffing model for the planning team. We need a relatively small, hands-on SWAT team staffed with individuals who can influence up, down, and across an organization and bring a critical thinking and analytical mindset to the exercise. Unless senior executives are hands-on with designing and performing analyses and ideating and detailing enablement initiatives, they are better off delegating to others who can. Planning is a complex exercise requiring the core team to be comfortable with details.

In summary, staffing for planning is more about quality than quantity. A few carefully chosen, objective, and influential playmakers are the most optimal candidates for the four critical planning roles.

Principle 5: Leverage a three-phased strategic planning approach.

Strategic planning follows the same triangulation theme as corporate strategy.

Astronomers could state the expected path of the Earth around the sun if there were only two objects. But the moment we add in the moon or any other planets, it's no longer a simple formula to determine its path due to the interdependencies of gravity and position.

As we go through the critical levers of strategic planning, we will discuss related concepts together. But it is essential to understand that every principle is like an object in the universe. Their mass and position affect all the others. It is an iterative triangulation effort. Nothing we discuss will be a drafted-once-and-done effort. We will have to revise and reconfigure every aspect to get to a plan that gets us closest to our corporate strategy and desired overarching outcomes.

Tailor approach to our planning maturity.

Like many concepts in our method, the planning approach is not a one-size-fits-all answer. Our planning history anchors our approach.

Consider these design questions to develop a realistic planning approach:

Have we performed a structured strategic planning exercise recently?

Was the strategy development, evolutionary efforts, and execution cycle effective and aligned with the plan?

How mature is our value engine, particularly processes and data?

These self-assessment questions provide a litmus test on the prerequisite steps we must take before starting a planning exercise and optimally well before the cycle.

First, past annual budgeting exercises don't count as planning experience.

Second, suppose past efforts resulted in forecasts and budgets or an effective plan was abandoned during the execution cycle. In these cases, we are likely starting with a weak management approach that thwarts evolution and maturity.

Third, being positioned on the immature end of the Value Engine Maturity Model implies significantly more pre-work requirements, including manual data gathering and insight generation.

The planning team must internalize the current maturity level of the management approach and value engine and embrace the importance of being open-minded and objective about hearing and sharing difficult messages about the company's level of congruence, maturity of building blocks, execution performance, and needs for improvement.

Figure E3 illustrates the core components of a comprehensive strategic planning exercise. Regardless of our historic planning maturity, we must go through all these components. However, based on questions and considerations of our present reality, we must only chew off what we can swallow. If we try to jump from the Strategic Planning Maturity Model's left side to the very right side, our team will be ill-equipped to handle the exercise and necessary follow-throughs.

Use three strategy-led and operations-focused strategic planning phases.

The *Congruence™* method's strategic planning approach has three phases.

The first phase is **Enablement Planning**. Here, we decide how to evolve from the current operations baseline. We want to transform our operations to one that is congruent with our strategic trade-off choices while maturing the fundamental building blocks to enable higher performance.

Why is this "change" mindset necessary? Just because we made a strategic decision one evening at the end of the strategy development effort doesn't mean our operations align with that decision and associated performance when we arrive at work the following day. Our operations baseline is

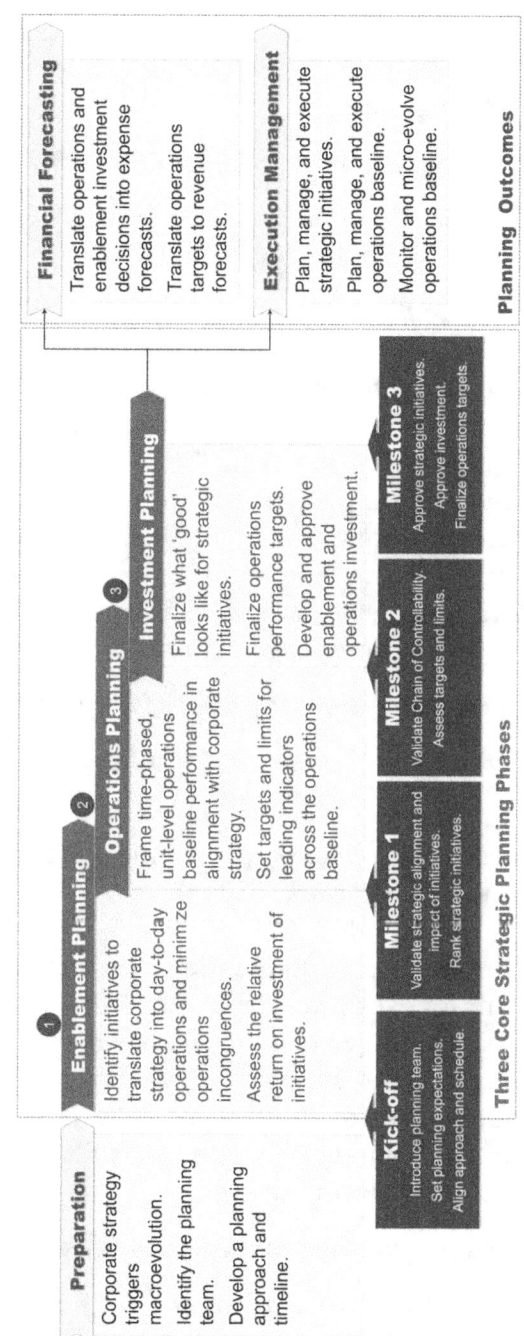

Figure E3. Use a maturity-aligned three-phased strategic planning approach.

precisely where it was the prior day. It will take Herculean efforts to plan and execute to reach our evolved state, where our strategic choices are part of our day-to-day operations.

Consider these design questions to prepare for enablement planning:

What meaningful efforts will increase the maturity of our operations baseline to align with corporate strategy?

How will we prioritize these efforts?

The second phase is **Operations Planning**. Here, we will outline exactly how our operations baseline will perform from the start through the end of our subsequent execution cycle. This is not trivial because our operations baseline is a living and ever-improving entity. As we improve our alignment with our corporate strategy, the performance of various operations baseline building blocks will hopefully improve; however, such improvements are rarely guaranteed or smooth. These anticipated improvements impact our company outcomes.

Consider these design questions to prepare for operations planning:

How will we characterize the current performance of our operations baseline?

How will our operations baseline perform over time as various enablement initiatives improve building blocks within?

The third phase is **Investment Planning**. Here, we prepare our enablement and operations plans for execution. Saying something is a lot harder than doing it. Beyond planning, we will engage our company's enablement and operations resources to execute our strategic plan. That requires investment decisions. Investment planning dictates how we deploy our capital against our enablement plan and operations plan to maximize value creation while maintaining efficiency.

Consider these design questions to prepare for investment planning:

What are our investment considerations and decisions for enablement initiatives and ongoing operations?

What are the expected aggregate operations targets and likely outcomes based on our investment decisions?

These three phases build a bridge from our current operations baseline to one that aligns with our corporate strategy. We will define marching orders for the enablement resources to work on major initiatives. We will set operations targets and adjust them over time for all operations resources.

Leverage milestones as accountability guardrails.

The amount of work required for planning will differ based on the planning team's experience, the gap between the company's strategy and current operations baseline, and investment availability or constraints. Regardless, it is important to make incremental progress, collectively align on progress, and challenge conventional and subjective thinking.

The optimal collaborative approach depends on the planning team composition, geographical and time zone spread, and similar logistical aspects. Historically, planning meetings were elaborate multi-day affairs. Milestone reviews can involve broadly attended conferences with fun kick-offs and icebreakers.

Conversely, the core planning team can get together in a room for a few tedious and intense hours to review key deliverables and dismiss the meeting to iterate deliverables offline. As we increasingly work remotely and globally, we learn to collaborate with others in more constrained circumstances.

Beyond these stylistic considerations, the more important part is ensuring that every planning team member is well-prepared to lead insightful and objective discussions. Most of the effort must go into structuring critical questions to answer and tailoring frameworks that help us arrive at objective decisions.

Optimally, at least three milestones are thematically included in our approach to ensure that our three phases effectively push us toward a strong plan. The planning architect must lead milestone meetings objectively and in a structured manner to discourage a herd mentality.

First, begin with a formal planning kick-off to set expectations. Use this opportunity to state our corporate strategy to guide our planning exercise. The executive sponsor and planning architect must outline the planning approach and specific roles and responsibilities.

Second, the first progress checkpoint should be used to pressure-test initiatives that further align the operations baseline with our strategy. Utilize this session for preliminary prioritization of our enablement initiatives for the next cycle. The discussions and feedback will lead to rework and improvement of initiatives.

Third, by the second progress checkpoint, we should have a firm handle on how our initiatives impact our operations baseline. We will also have set realistic and predictive targets for our operational performance for the next cycle.

Fourth, a final approval checkpoint ensures the planning team collectively approves the success factors for initiatives and operations performance targets. The final strategic plan also aligns the planning team on the investment to evolve and run our company.

Combining our three-phased approach with an iterative, milestone-based review-and-improve mindset is a minimum requirement to stay true to the essence of our treasure-is-in-the-path planning approach.

Derive financial forecasts from strategic planning outputs.

We can derive the financial forecast from the planning outputs. Operations targets directly translate to revenue outcomes, and investment decisions translate to expenses and cash flow decisions. The forecasts that help the CFO manage the company's financial health can be easily extracted based on the outputs of a well-run strategic planning effort.

As discussed earlier, anchoring planning with financial outcomes is the most common strategic planning mistake. Attempting to start with aspirational goals and force-fitting strategy and operations into such goals is equivalent to putting the cart before the horse.

Planning must lay out a comprehensive strategy-led and operations-focused evolutionary path. The planning roles we listed above should take responsibility for creating all deliverables outside the financial forecast, which the CFO and finance team will build as the final portion of the strategic plan. Developing a strong foundationally dovetailed plan ensures that we achieve our true intent – value creation aligned with our strategy and purpose. As a natural side effect, it simplifies the creation of realistic financial forecasts for board alignment and approval.

Now, let's dive into *Phase 1: Enablement Planning*.

E.2
TRIGGER OPERATIONS EVOLUTION
WITH ENABLEMENT PLANNING.

ENABLEMENT planning defines how we evolve our operations baseline at a macro level to ingrain our corporate strategy into our company's operations. A shift in our strategy requires a change in our management approach, productized offering, processes, and data acquisition and usage. These four parts of our operations baseline are symbiotic and influence each other heavily.

Things To Remember: Enablement Planning

Enablement planning is the first stage of strategic planning, where we define an optimal path to ingrain our corporate strategy decision into our operations baseline and address existing operations incongruences.

Incorporating the who-to-serve, what-to-offer, and how-to-deliver strategic trade-offs into our operations baseline is required to evolve it intentionally and proactively to meet increasing customer and investor value expectations, serve more customers, and address environmental shifts.

At the same time, it is essential to distinguish enablement planning from identifying quick wins, which is a subset of microevolutions. In a recent strategic planning readout, a sales function presented the first draft of their enablement plan, which can be summarized as: "Define Ideal Customer Profile; Source market knowledge; Ensure sales and marketing wins; Use contextualized product demos." A few flags went off in my head.

Are these items technically incorrect? *Unclear.*

Are these specific to that company? *No.*

Is this detailed enough? *No.*

Did this align with the company's strategy? *No.*

Planning requires details, depth of problem-solving, and alignment with strategy. Enablement planning has three steps.

First, we must clearly frame our current operations baseline maturity and how far our leap to the evolved state, which reflects our strategy, needs to be. To build a bridge, we have to know the state of the ground on both sides of the river and its span. This first step is a gap assessment. Setting off toward our evolved state without an effective gap assessment is akin to planning to build a bridge without internalizing the lay of the land.

The **second** principle covers the development of **Strategic Initiatives**, which we also refer to as enablement initiatives. Once we know where we are, where we need to be, and the distance we need to cross, we need to lay out the specific packages of work that can get us there. If our corporate strategy has changed materially from prior years or our past efforts to evolve fell short, this may not be a small leap accomplishable in one simple initiative. To reach our evolved state, we may have to define and dovetail several initiatives covering various building blocks of our operations baseline.

Things To Remember: Strategic Initiatives

Strategic initiatives are comprehensive transformational efforts that evolve our operations baseline. They inject our corporate strategy and greater congruence into our operations execution. They dictate how we make investment decisions and the realistic, measurable outcomes we can achieve over time.

Third, our world is built with constraints, and we always have to prioritize. We decided on a strategy with a visionary timeline of one, two, or three years. However, we did not pinpoint how long it would take to achieve the strategy and did not consider what it would cost us to get there. This falls into strategic planning. So, as the last step, we must prioritize the most impactful efforts within our available or appropriate investment thresholds for the next execution cycle. This step of enablement planning prioritizes strategic initiatives and shapes one of our key inputs in our process-model view of our company – enablement investment.

Principle 1: Close operations baseline gaps to achieve strategy and maximize congruence.

Three aspects dictate our current operations baseline: The cohesiveness of our past strategy, the effectiveness of converting that strategy into reality through dovetailed building blocks, and our past efforts to create a company-wide system. We can't change our past, and the present is our starting point.

Our future operations baseline must reflect two facets. First, it must reflect the new strategy we framed through our who, how, and what trade-off choices. Secondly, our operations baseline building blocks must also dovetail and minimize incongruences.

We must figure out how to make the leap from today's operations baseline to our evolved operations baseline. The framework for this comparison has five elements, as illustrated in Figure E4.

The **first** element is our strategic trade-off decisions. Let's place these decisions on the left side of our framework. Anchoring our framework with the trade-off decisions ensures that our enablement planning efforts align with our new corporate strategy. Even when we have effectively framed a corporate strategy, planning and executing that strategy is far from a foregone conclusion.

The **second** element of the framework is the introduction of functions. Throughout our method, we intentionally avoided the concept of functions. Success factors in a company are cross-functional and apply to everyone equally. Our One Company mindset breaks down silos and ensures that the same principles and rigor apply across the board.

However, during execution, individuals do the work. Strategic planning connects our company-wide strategy with every employee and asset, and they are grouped inside functions for convenience.

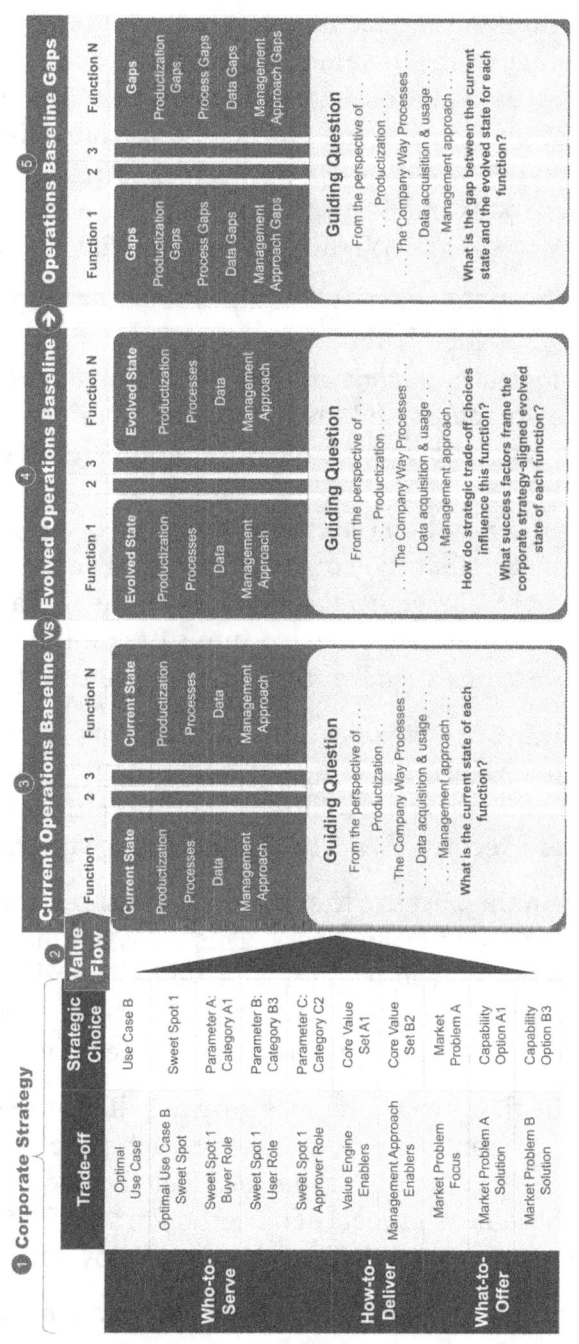

Figure E4. Enablement planning starts with operations gap assessment.

Let's recall flow thinking and focus on how we create value for customers each day. Groupings from our value creation flow become our functions. This focus on effective value creation flow articulated by our processes is essential because planning for the future based on our existing reporting structures reflects our past hiring patterns. It's best to assume it's not perfect – it never is. In our value-focused ecosystem, we want to continuously shift our company to align with the flow of work that creates value.

> **Things To Remember: Functions**
>
> **Functions are logical groupings of roles in The Company Way Processes, and operations resources fill them. Functions are optimally defined using value creation flow as the basis for grouping roles.**

For instance, lead generation is a crucial function. Lead generation roles and processes ensure that the company effectively attracts prospective customers. But we rarely see "lead generation" framed as a function. This critical function is often piecemealed into sales and marketing teams, even though these teams are never the same between any two companies.

So, why do we always use the sales and marketing buckets? Convenience! If lead generation is a critical value-creating function, we want to call it out as such, even if the responsibilities today are split between sales and marketing senior executives. Maybe that reporting structure isn't ideal.

With this flow thinking, list five to seven of the most relevant functions as the second element of the framework. This list is optimal if it correlates with our processes instead of groups of humans and their reporting structure today. The reverse will backfire. We want to identify our gaps based on how we create value, not how we hire people.

Once we have the first two elements set up as pillars, the **third** element is assessing the current state of affairs for each function across every component of the operations baseline. Recollect the intertwined nature of our operations baseline – aspects of our productized offering, processes, data usage, and management approach must all dovetail.

Consider these design questions to frame the current state:

What is the current state of each function from the perspective of 1) productized offering, 2) processes, 3) data acquisition and usage, and 4) management approach?

What are the most prevalent symptoms and root causes that hinder the building blocks of our operations baseline from efficiently creating and delivering the expected customer value?

Understanding our current state implies having an insightful grasp of existing processes and data collection effectiveness. For the illustrative lead generation function, we may explore the quality of advertising that creates inbound interest, proactive outreaches to start selling efforts, and related data gathering and reporting. Our current state assessment may also evaluate the effectiveness of our productized offering's pricing and packaging and how we present it to prospects, along with organization design, hiring for roles, and incentive compensation around lead generation roles.

Our insightful takeaways from these questions for each function, through effective analyses, highlight current incongruences and influence the scale of the macroevolution that awaits us.

We must also explore whether a strategy guides our current operations baseline. Suppose we start from an immature and chaotic operations baseline that isn't strategy-led. A significantly higher change management effort will be required than beginning from a mature strategy-led environment that internalizes macroevolution. The latter company's system has the muscle memory to macro-evolve and operate with strategic discipline.

The **fourth** element is to draft what "good" looks like for our evolved state of the operations baseline. The future state must articulate how our new strategy is enabled through each function, along with the improvements and alignment necessary across that function's building blocks.

To compare the current and evolved states, we need to articulate essential success factors in the evolved future state. Conversely, challenges in the current state, which are always symptoms of incongruence between fundamental building blocks, must be identified as success factors in the company's better future.

Consider these design questions to frame our evolved state:

How do our strategic trade-off decisions influence each function from the perspective of productized offering, processes, data acquisition and usage, and management approach?

What are three or four of the most relevant incongruences across fundamental building blocks that we want to see addressed in the future state?

Staying with our lead generation example, we want to state the general parameters of our evolved processes and data capture. We want to frame the optimal lead generation skills required and related incentive compensation, along with highlighting obsolete staff skills in the current state. The same goes for the commercialization aspects of our offering.

At this stage, we aim to set guardrails on success factors that allow us to develop the specific initiatives that will enable our strategy. We can leverage analytical details from our strategy development exercise to draw a rough picture of our evolved state for each function. For example, we already know which capability elements to build, buy, or borrow. We know the essence of the behaviors expected via our processes and the skills we must demonstrate based on our deep exploration into buying decision drivers. Superimposing these onto functional building blocks allows us to frame our future state. We will continue to build depth of detail and revise the current and evolved state definitions throughout strategic planning.

However, it is paramount that we don't use preconceived opinions as the evolved state. Ignoring our strategy and operations baseline's objective realities means operating with an "I hear your well-vetted analysis, but I am going to do what I want anyway" mindset.

The **fifth** and final element is to frame our **Operations Baseline Gaps** as a direct result of comparing the current and evolved state.

> **Things To Remember: Operations Baseline Gaps**
>
> Operations baseline gaps refer to the spaces between the realities of the current state and the desired evolved state of the operations baseline. They pinpoint improvements necessary for each function – framed in terms of management approach, productized offering, processes, and data usage – to facilitate the transition from the current state to a future state that incorporates the new corporate strategy and addresses incongruences that cause value limitations and capital inefficiencies.

Think of operations baseline gaps as our shopping list to define our evolutionary efforts. If our investment threshold allows, we will identify the initiatives that can help us cover as many of these gaps as possible. Figure E4 offers a high-level visual structure to build this gap assessment.

Consider this design question to frame operations baseline gaps:

> *What are the gaps between each function's current and evolved states from the perspective of productized offering, processes, data acquisition and usage, and management approach?*

Although we must perform this gap assessment for each function, consider this a preliminary information-gathering step. Silos destroy cohesive and comprehensive problem-solving and execution. Our path to addressing these gaps must embrace a One Company mindset.

A typical enablement planning mistake is asking each senior executive's team what projects they will do. This is akin to operating without a corporate strategy. The answers will be incongruent blocks of ideas that fit in a silo and are formed based on instinct without directly connecting to our corporate strategy.

This brings us to the development of company-wide, cross-functional strategic initiatives.

Principle 2: Company-wide strategic initiatives close operations baseline gaps.

How do we enable our corporate strategy and move our operations baseline for each function from its current state to the evolved future state? We develop and execute strategic initiatives to close the gaps we identified.

Things To Remember: Strategic Initiatives [Refined]

Strategic initiatives are comprehensive, cohesive, and mutually exclusive efforts that evolve our operations baseline to reflect corporate strategy and improve cohesion between fundamental building blocks.

A mature operations baseline implies that work moves through and between functions seamlessly without interruption. Maturing any building block of our operations baseline, whether our management approach, productization, processes, or data usage, doesn't just sit in a single function. This means it's ineffective to independently evolve each function, like lead generation, from the current state to the future evolved state. For instance, changes to lead generation processes will have to dovetail heavily with changes to selling to a prospect, which will impact how we manage a customer we have successfully sold to.

Cross-functional problem-solving is the only path to congruence.

First, attempting to box projects into reporting hierarchies inevitably leads to operating with an individualistic mentality, where we miss continuity and dependency between related efforts across functions.

Second, planning and executing closely related efforts across functions create significant economies of scale by limiting duplication and conflicts in work. This creates better accountability by keeping related efforts under a single owner.

Third, no company can drive progress on many initiatives without fatigue. An optimal number, say between eight and twelve cross-functional and comprehensive initiatives, is reasonable. The scope of these initiatives will be broader as a company gets bigger, but the volume shouldn't.

We shouldn't mature each function independently because hand-offs and dependencies exist across functions. Strategic initiatives allow us to achieve meaningful shifts from the present state to our evolved future state across multiple functions and closely related strategic trade-off decisions.

Most strategic initiatives will address more than one operations baseline building block based on the gaps we articulated in Principle 1.

Set three quality guardrails for effective strategic initiatives.

It's too much of a simplification to say strategic initiatives achieve our desired state. A founding CEO once asked me how often I see successful projects. My tongue-in-cheek response was, "80 percent of projects fail. . . ." But there is a lot of truth to this. I have been part of several large, failed initiatives, some costing over $100 million. The COO of a different company quipped, "I don't think I have been part of a major successful change effort if I were to be objective. . . ." So, we need to align on a "good" strategic initiative.

First, effective strategic initiatives are uniquely tailored to achieve our company's strategy by evolving our operations baseline. Half a strategy is no strategy at all. We want to ensure that strategic initiatives translate all strategic trade-off choices into our operations baseline.

This single attribute alone justifies why a One Company-minded Congruence Architect must own planning. Breaking silos is hard. Ensuring we address every building block and trade-off decision across all functions requires immense discipline and thought leadership. One person must be accountable for ensuring that the strategic initiatives collectively achieve our evolved state for all functions in alignment with our strategic trade-offs.

This also means these initiatives will always differ from company to company because operations baseline starting and ending points are different across companies – don't rinse and repeat what other companies are doing.

During one of my client partnerships to lead strategic planning, the company hired several new executives just beforehand. It was one of the situations where the "whale strategy" came up. The new sales executive came from another company's sales group, which exclusively sold to large customers, and brought along the "whale strategy." Assuming the same tactic would work in an unrelated market and at a company in a different lifecycle stage was incorrect. As a planning architect, I also failed to prevent the excitement behind this rinse-and-repeat idea, which was disconnected from the company's strategy. Months after our partnership, the executive team shared that the "whale strategy" failed during the execution cycle.

Second, strategic initiatives must always be defined to address operations baseline gaps. We must define a comprehensive set of strategic initiatives to ensure that, collectively, they take us to our evolved operations baseline, which requires focusing on closing our operations baseline gaps.

During the planning effort above, the marketing executive proposed a single bucket of spending with an initiative that replicated a popular marketing approach called account-based marketing. This would have accounted for a 200 percent increase in marketing investment. However, we considered the following: What is the operations baseline gap this new marketing approach addresses? Why is this specific initiative important in achieving the company's strategy? Asking these probing questions changed the image of this proposal during enablement planning.

The **third** quality guardrail is a comprehensiveness check. Visually place the strategic initiatives on a grid with our trade-offs and functions to ensure that every operations baseline gap is covered. Ensure that the lack of strategic initiatives across trade-offs, functions, and operations baseline building blocks is a proactive choice to maintain the current state.

Consider these design questions as a litmus test for the quality of drafted initiatives:

Does the roster of proposed strategic initiatives effectively cover all the strategic trade-off decisions across all functions?

Do the proposed strategic initiatives collectively cover all operations baseline gaps to their intent?

Does a lack of strategic initiatives at intersections of strategic trade-offs, functions, and operations baseline building blocks imply a purposeful choice not to evolve?

Figure E5 illustrates how we can comprehensively define and map cross-functional strategic initiatives. Our goal through this planning phase is to place all the relevant efforts on the board so that we can prioritize the initiatives we will focus on during the next execution cycle.

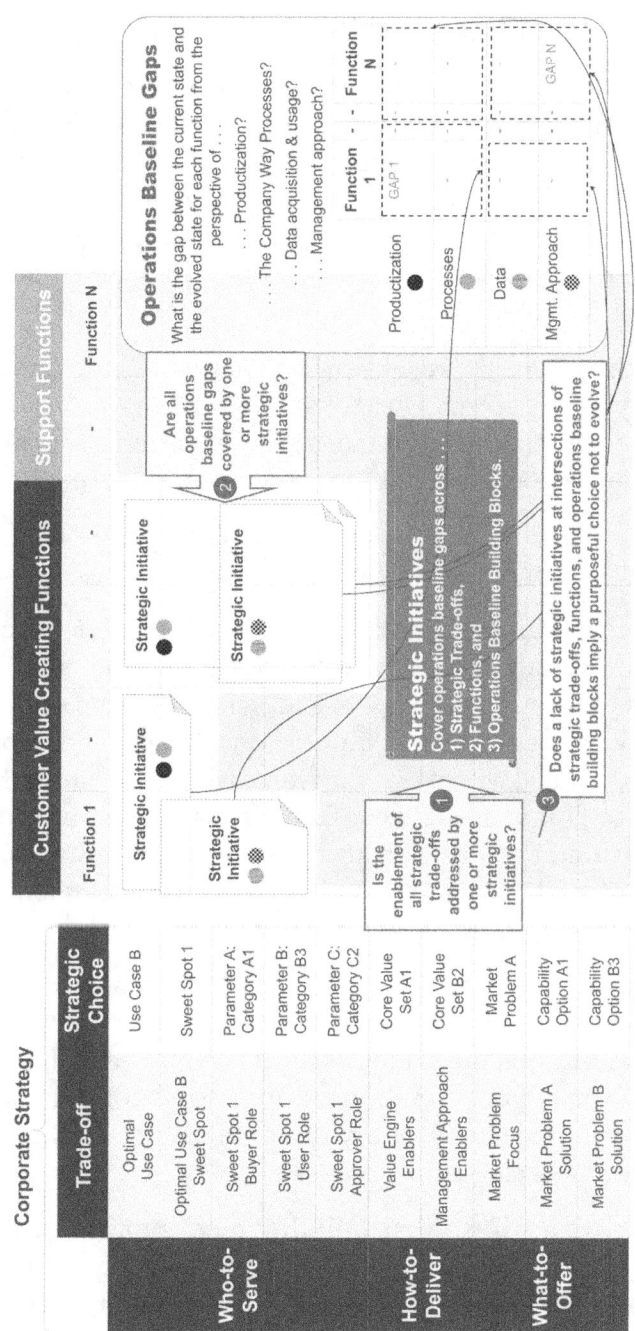

Figure E5. Strategic Initiatives Map enables effective enablement planning.

Draft strategic initiatives using four rules of thumb.

Developing strategic initiatives from our gap assessment is an analytical exercise. We started with two sets of inputs. One set is each function's current state and the corresponding evolved state that accommodates our strategic trade-off decisions. The second set is building blocks that require evolution for each function, whether it is the management approach, productization, processes, or data. Together, this formed our operations baseline gaps.

With discipline, drafting early versions of our strategic initiatives can be a relatively simple grouping exercise. We group our operations baseline gaps to create meaningful strategic initiatives. Given our goal of breaking down functional silos, the planning architect must manage this exercise.

Leverage the following rules to transform our operations baseline gaps into the first draft of our strategic initiatives.

First, group gaps with most interdependencies together. Problem-solving is optimal if the same people solve interconnected problems. For instance, we will likely have to address gaps in lead generation and sales functions to improve our alignment with our who-to-serve trade-off decision. These are also highly dovetailed with delivering value to those customers because we set expectations for value delivery through lead generation and sales. So, why solve customer acquisition and retention gaps around who-to-serve trade-offs separately? These answers depend on each other, and they are optimally solved together.

This example represents one of the most common incongruences in companies. Customers are attracted by a lead generation function that sets early expectations that the sales efforts may not align with. Furthermore, the sales efforts set certain expectations to encourage customers to buy, but what if the value delivery function cannot deliver accordingly? Individualistic silos cause this outcome.

Second, group gaps in similar building blocks together. For instance, process changes are easier to resolve together because it is a niche skill being deployed. Evolving half of one process and improving some aspects of compensation by a person who isn't highly skilled at either is suboptimal, all else being equal. Addressing each specific building block requires unique skills and experience, and we significantly increase the probability of successfully executing a strategic initiative by bucketing similar work together.

Third, create groups requiring roughly similar completion efforts. We don't want to devise strategic initiatives requiring significantly different workloads. Prioritizing and managing these initiatives can become messy if they are not reasonably similar in size and complexity. Resourcing and attention during execution can be a challenge.

The **fourth** rule is that our strategic initiatives are distinct. Overlapping strategic initiatives implies duplication of efforts and conflicting points of view that become hard to resolve downstream. Consider this attribute a soft rule at this stage because it is essential to be comprehensive first. We will further flesh out strategic initiatives through various planning and execution phases and have opportunities to improve their definitions.

These four rules of thumb give us a fair start for framing our strategic initiatives. Use the three guardrails in Figure E5 and these rules of thumb. This is our opening bid to move from our current state to our evolved state. Once our planning team has our evolutionary path laid out, prioritizing is essential.

Principle 3: Rank strategic initiatives to prioritize.

Our goal for the first strategic planning milestone is to arrive at a prioritized set of strategic initiatives. We want to pressure test the quality of initiatives and focus on the more impactful and cost-effective ones. Consider this principle as preparatory activities, key outcomes, and follow-through actions leading up to the first planning milestone to arrive at our initial prioritized strategic initiatives.

We need meat on the bones for each strategic initiative to compare and prioritize them. Over my years of leading planning, I learned that even key planning team members might not understand the implications of our strategic choices to create a purposeful design for our company. Although a Congruence Architect can lead these efforts, senior executives and supervisors must embrace the One Company mindset and dive into the details to frame and choose effective strategic initiatives.

A skilled and engaged planning team can use a thoughtful and methodical return-on-investment approach to prioritize strategic initiatives.

Once we validate the completeness of our strategic initiatives, this prioritization exercise offers a formal assessment of their efficacy. A return-on-investment approach allows us to pressure test and fine-tune our strategic initiatives before prioritizing them.

Further, stack ranking is a powerful tool. Slotting initiatives one above the other forces clarity and analytical rigor. It will inject much-needed debate and discussion into a planning exercise.

Return of a strategic initiative is its impact on operations.

To stack rank our proposed strategic initiatives, we must know their impact. Attempt to stack rank our proposed initiatives from *high* to *low* based on their impact on the operations baseline. This impact is how well a strategic initiative addresses operations baseline gaps. This is the vertical axis in the prioritization framework in Figure E6.

Consider this design question to explore impact of strategic initiatives:

What is the comprehensive impact of each strategic initiative according to how well each addresses operations baseline gaps?

Before we finalize the strategic plan, we must be able to quantify the impact of strategic initiatives on our operations baseline via leading indicators, even if it's zero. Some strategic initiatives are necessary to lay a foundation for other initiatives. Regardless, we must internalize each initiative's impact. This is a tedious, analytical exercise that we will save for *Phase 2 – Operations Planning because* we only want to do this for the prioritized initiatives.

However, we will never be able to **quantitatively** compare the impact of initiatives on various parts of our operations baseline because each leading indicator metric is different. This is precisely why folks often use monetary measures in return-on-investment calculations. But this is a significant folly through false precision. Attempts to use revenue or cost impact are usually quantification-for-the-sake-of-quantification. There is always a many-to-one relationship between fundamental drivers such as strategic initiatives and operations performance and lagging indicators such as revenue and expense. The drivers of these lagging monetary indicators are so interdependent that narrowing the likely impact source will always be confounded.

Our best path to comparing the impact of strategic initiatives is weighted scoring, which relies on our understanding of the **qualitative** impact on our operations baseline. A strong planning team can devise a ranking method tailored to the planning cycle's needs. Consider these three sample ranking variables to develop a weighted impact score.

First, an initiative's impact correlates with the number of strategic trade-offs it addresses across functions. For example, count the number of grid spots in Figure E5 that each strategic initiative covers. The higher the number of grid spots covered, the higher the impact score.

Second, count how many other proposed strategic initiatives depend on this single initiative. The higher this number, the higher the foundational impact score will be.

Third, in addition to the breadth of coverage, we want to consider the comprehensiveness of that coverage. How many operations baseline building blocks does each initiative address? Addressing improvements along productization, process, data, and management approach is far more impactful than just addressing data usage evolution, thus, a higher score.

Consider these design questions to create variables to stack rank impact of initiatives:

On a scale of 1 to 5, 5 being the highest, how broad is the coverage of each initiative across strategic trade-offs and functions?

On a scale of 1 to 5, 5 being the highest, how foundationally prerequisite is each initiative to enable other initiatives?

On a scale of 1 to 5, 5 being the highest, what is the depth of impact of each strategic initiative across operations baseline building blocks?

We can multiply or average such individual impact scores to develop weighted scores at the initiative level. This is our numerator for a return-on-investment comparison.

Relative cost of impact enables weighted investment comparison.

The cost of completing an initiative is the denominator to assess return on investment. We do not need to finalize specific investment requirements during enablement planning. Assessing the exact cost of each initiative is an arduous task that we only want to take on during *Phase 3: Investment Planning* for fewer prioritized initiatives. In this phase, we aim to prioritize the most critical initiatives and eliminate poorly defined ones. To do so, we need to weigh the investment across initiatives in a relative manner.

To assess the investment needs of each initiative, we want to have a reasonable early understanding of the path to completing the effort. Like impact scoring, our goal is to stack rank initiatives in terms of investment. Consider these three variables as a guide to develop a weighted cost score.

First, approximate the initiative execution cost by estimating the number of enablement resources and supporting infrastructure required for each initiative. The higher the execution cost, the higher the initiative's cost score.

Second, changes to our organization are costly as they distract operations resources from their primary focus of creating customer value. Therefore, a higher estimated disruption implies a higher initiative cost score.

Third, every initiative takes time for impact; a longer estimated time to impact implies a higher opportunity cost score due to this initiative.

Consider these design questions to create variables to stack rank the relative cost of initiatives:

On a scale of 1 to 5, 5 being the highest, how high is the execution cost for this initiative compared to others?

On a scale of 1 to 5, 5 being the highest, how significant is this initiative's operational and mindshare disruption?

On a scale of 1 to 5, 5 being the highest, how long will it take for the strategic initiative to impact the operations baseline?

Like our impact scores, we can multiply or average these individual cost scores to determine a weighted investment score for each initiative for comparison purposes.

Prioritize strategic initiatives as a soft choice.

Together, these scores allow us to create a stack ranking of our strategic initiatives as illustrated on the grid in Figure E6. We want to work on initiatives with the highest impact and require the lowest investment. Conversely, we will be best served by deprioritizing initiatives with the lowest impact and high investment needs.

Consider grouping the initiatives in each of the four quadrants – high impact low investment, high impact high investment, low impact low investment, and low impact high investment – as a preliminary prioritization for the remainder of our planning efforts. As we will see in the following two chapters, we must have a firm grip on the strategic initiatives we prioritize and their impact on operations to evolve our company intentionally.

Our takeaway from this prioritization effort is the soft choices of initiatives that form our enablement plan. The enablement plan is a prioritized set of strategic initiatives that we know we can afford to invest in and will help us evolve our operations baseline to align with our corporate strategy. Imagine drawing a bold line between the initiatives we will build the rest of the strategic plan around and those we do not believe are plausible or affordable, as shown in Figure E6.

Similar to making strategic trade-off choices, stack ranking and prioritizing allow focus and actionability and are significantly more important than the perfection of the exact rank. Once we place initiatives into the four quadrants, it doesn't matter whether an initiative was third or fourth if it is both in the first quadrant and at the top of our priority list.

Translating our corporate strategy to the tangible evolution of behaviors on the ground is difficult and emotionally taxing. Formal, structured, and tangible strategic initiatives help us achieve this transformation.

I partnered with a data services company attempting to turn around its performance trajectory. The company wanted to move from a service-focused

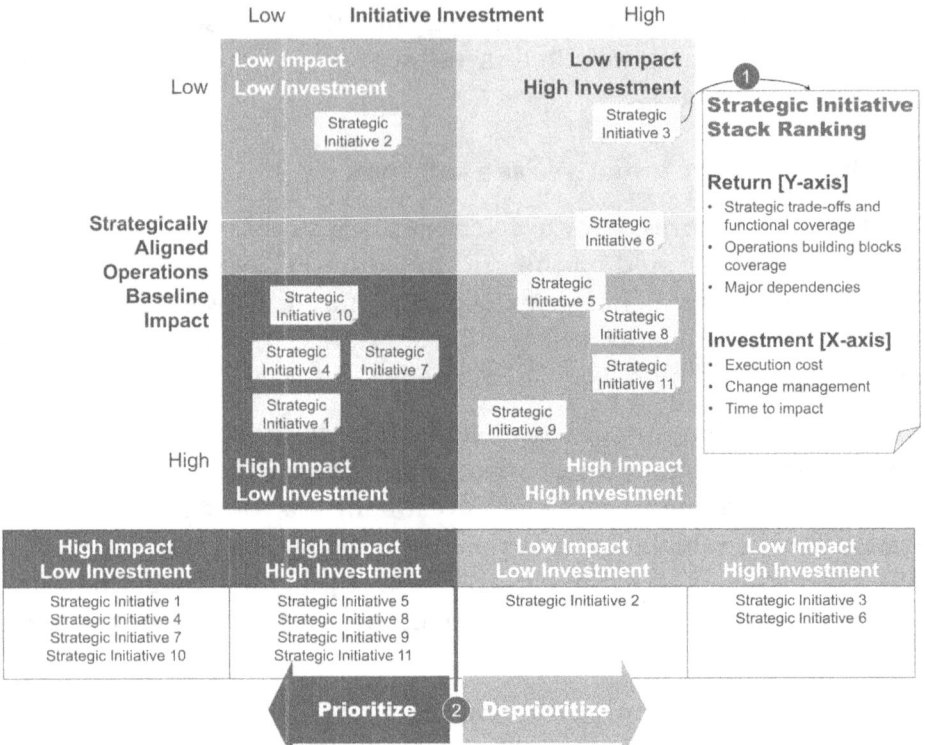

Figure E6. Strategic Initiative Prioritization Framework enables stack ranking.

offering to an object-based offering, leveraging technology. The board agreed to the strategic change because new customer acquisition had stalled, and customer satisfaction for services delivered was low.

One of the necessary changes was how the company sold its offering. However, no strategic initiatives were defined or executed to transform the operations baseline components around the sales function. The company's tenured sales team continued to sell services even after the CEO and the board had agreed to a shift to a technology-focused solution. Over several quarters, the sales function continued to sell an increasing variety of service packages the company had never done before while other employees focused on enabling the strategic shift. The company could not reconcile between solo activities from long-term employees and a strategic change. The company's trajectory did not improve.

An initiative prioritization exercise can be the difference between an effective strategy on paper and an effective strategy implemented. This prioritization effort of our strategic initiatives wraps up the enablement planning phase and kicks off the planning of operations performance through our execution cycle.

E.3
UTILIZE OPERATIONS PLANNING TO PREDICT UNIT PERFORMANCE.

THE performance of our entire company is the additive output of operations baseline building blocks across all functions. Executing each portion of our operations baseline creates tangible value directly for our customers or indirectly to support activities that create value for customers.

The overall outcomes produced by our operations baseline are a simple multiplication of two factors – the outputs generated by each value creator or asset in our operations baseline and the volume of those value creators or assets. We will refer to the concept of framing outcomes generated by each value creator or asset as **Unit Performance**. It reflects the true maturity and execution effectiveness of our operations baseline.

Things To Remember: Unit Performance

Unit performance measures the maturity and execution effectiveness of every relevant part of our operations baseline at the lowest controllable unit, which could be an employee or partner, a machine or asset, or a portion of their time.

Through strategic planning, we need to formalize our company's expected evolving performance throughout our next execution cycle. Operations planning is the interim step towards arriving at such an overall prediction. Operations planning frames the intrinsic performance potential of our management approach and value engine.

We will arrive at the expected performance or output of each operations resource – a person, machine, or asset – we use in our processes. We want to know what we can achieve at the unit level without conflating the volume of resources contributing to a given process. Our goal is to be capital-efficient.

Things To Remember: Operations Planning

Operations planning creates a unit-level performance blueprint for our management approach and value engine. It focuses on maturity, not scale, and allows us the flexibility to scale the volume of resources up or down through investment decisions.

Operations planning helps us answer questions like: What is the expected performance of an average resource in each role in a specific part of our operations baseline? How many widgets can a given machine produce? What is the expected value created for an average customer by a particular capability in our offering?

Our operations plan will remain the same whether we have twenty or twenty-five sales reps because all baseline components will remain the same regardless of the exact staffing counts.

This is important because we are more interested in the fundamentals and have a value-centric approach. Throughout our execution cycle, we will have scale variability due to value creator churn or volatility in the volume of other assets. Therefore, it is essential to know what we can expect from our operations baseline on a per-unit basis at any given point in time. This is so we can delineate maturity gaps, execution problems, and scale limitations.

Using this backdrop, let's discuss the core operations planning principles we must embrace during the second strategic planning phase.

Principle 1: Embrace the Chain of Controllability.

Our company's performance reflects the congruence of our operations baseline, which must stay aligned with our strategy and purpose, along with its effective execution. This is all we can control. Our operations baseline directly influences our aggregate revenue and expenses, which are compounded and lagging measurements, as we will learn. This focus on fundamentals is the difference between our planning method and typical financial forecasting, which jumps to conclusions that are disconnected from the "how."

In physics, a fulcrum is part of a force transference system that allows us to apply only a reasonable amount of force to an accessible position and transfer a significantly higher impact to a distant or less accessible point. We use this concept every day in our lives.

We can use the same force transference mental model to design our company's future. In line with our core philosophy of fundamentals focus, we want to address the portions of the operations baseline we can genuinely influence so that they can, in turn, create the desired lagging outcomes that we can't directly control. We apply force in certain places and measure the outcomes elsewhere. I call this model the **Chain of Controllability**.

Things To Remember: Chain of Controllability

The Chain of Controllability is the structured path to translate meaningful enablement efforts into impact on outcomes measured via lagging indicators. This structured path starts with the prioritized enablement initiatives and goes through our evolving operations baseline, which is measured via leading indicators.

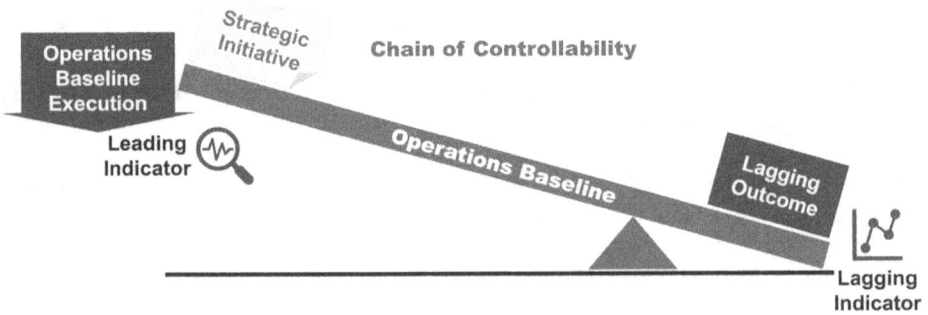

Figure E7. Chain of Controllability enables a predictive
and actionable operations plan.

The Chain of Controllability focuses on designing a system to predict our future outcomes based on what we can influence. Nothing about this concept is particularly new from what we have already discussed. It's a matter of applying it to planning our future. We must focus operations planning efforts on internalizing the importance and power of the relationship between the four elements that form our Chain of Controllability. These four elements are:

1. *Strategic initiatives that evolve the operations baseline.*

2. *The adoption and execution of our ever-evolving operations baseline.*

3. *The performance measurement of our operations baseline via leading indicators.*

4. *The overarching outcomes measured via lagging indicators.*

Figure E7 shows the relationship between these four elements. Before we take any actions, let's internalize how the Chain of Controllability works.

The **first** link is the injection of operations baseline maturity from strategic initiatives.

Our company's future performance will reflect the impact that our prioritized strategic initiatives can inject into our offerings, processes, data, and management approach. These initiatives are our first controllable because they impact our work to create value. They are intended to evolve our operations baseline, not directly impact outcomes.

Consider this design question to create the first link in the Chain of Controllability:

What direct improvements will prioritized strategic initiatives have on our operations baseline?

The **second** link in the chain is to predict the relationship between the actual maturity of our operations baseline and the adoption and execution compared to that optimal state. A strong sports team doesn't always mean that results on a given day or during a season align with the team's true potential. Execution matters.

For this reason, we will dedicate the entirety of the next part of our method to execution management. Through strategic planning, we must understand and slate the difference between the true potential of our operations baseline and the realistic likely execution expectation. If we do not know the difference between the two, we might blame execution for systemic problems or systemic problems for poor execution.

Consider this design question to enable the second link in the Chain of Controllability:

How effectively will the ever-evolving operations baseline maturity be adopted for operations execution?

The **third** link is our ability to measure and delineate between the maturity and execution of our operations baseline using leading indicators during the execution cycle. Recall that leading indicators measure our operations baseline at the specific spot where work gets done. They measure our execution via our productized offerings, processes, and the enabling management approach.

Through operations planning, we will have to define or validate the set of leading indicators that can quantify the maturity and execution effectiveness of our operations baseline.

Consider this design question to create the third link in the Chain of Controllability:

What objective measurements can convey the maturity level of various parts of the operations baseline and simultaneously delineate execution strengths and weaknesses from the true potential of the operations baseline?

The **fourth** link in our Chain of Controllability is translating leading indicators to externally relevant lagging indicators. The relationship between leading indicators and overarching company outcomes is the same as the relationship between root causes and symptoms.

Lagging indicators are always a compound measurement of an eventual outcome. We achieve optimal overarching outcomes by executing various building blocks of our operations baseline as intended. Therefore, we can never directly impact a lagging indicator.

Consider this design question to build the fourth link in the Chain of Controllability:

How do we translate leading indicators that measure the work we do daily to results that articulate the overarching success or failure of the company?

If we wanted to gain 10 lbs. of muscle weight, would a rational fitness regimen suggest that we check our weight daily or tally the number of good push-ups we can do daily? Obviously, the second. Our push-up count directly triggers muscle growth and weight to appear weeks or months later.

The fitness regimen is our strategic initiative; push-ups are one building block of our operations baseline, and another might involve our food habits. Push-up counts are a leading indicator we can influence. Our muscle weight and image are things we cannot directly influence and are our lagging indicators. As simple as the Chain of Controllability is, it is surprising how often companies try to improve muscle weight by . . . improving muscle weight.

Our approach focuses on creating an operations plan based on leading indicators that measure our work. Our Chain of Controllability enables causality, and our work results in predictable monetary outcomes, which are lagging indicators. Permutations of revenue and expense measures that investors care about are our lagging indicators. But investors don't do day-to-day work in our operations baseline, and our operations plan isn't built for them. The benefits are twofold.

The **first** is **controllability**. We exert all our efforts to influence the aspects we control, which are the components of the operations baseline. We have no direct control over revenue or expenses because they are always multiple degrees separated from tangible actions.

The **second** is **predictability**. Focusing on measurements of our operations baseline implies we can predict our lagging indicators well before the actual events. The whole purpose of planning is to know what will happen in the future – literally! If we can only say with confidence that we will miss our revenue or expense goals after we slide behind on actual revenue or expense performance, what was the point of planning in the first place? Sadly, this is where most companies live.

Leading indicators that measure our operations baseline give us predictive powers to alter our course.

My amateur beach volleyball team wanted to win games despite our poor skills. We had a single measurement to determine our likelihood of success – how well we handled serves. Since volleys don't last long in amateur games, our plan was simple: send a very high percentage of serves over the net while serving and send the ball back over immediately when receiving. Our serve-handling measurement was the single most effective indicator and predictor of our overall scores in our early playing days.

Similarly, our goal through operations planning is to effectively create or refine the Chain of Controllability across all operations baseline building blocks and functions.

Savants can often go from A to D without going through B and C. Unfortunately, most of us must work through problems. It is tempting to jump to predictions, but we might be confusing confidence with competence.

The mental gymnastics necessary to build a predictive and controllable chain from strategic initiatives to outcomes are high. These principles will test the planning team's objectivity and analytical skills.

Principle 2: Map operations to leading indicators and lagging indicators.

Enablement initiatives are intended to further mature our operations baseline building blocks to align with our new strategy, thereby improving our leading metrics and lagging indicators. This is our proactive, predictable, and systematic macroevolution path. The first step of operations planning is to codify the impact of our prioritized enablement initiatives.

Define leading indicators that measure maturity and execution across functions.

We must apply the principles discussed under Part C: Value Engine to measure our operations baseline processes and steps using leading indicators throughout the execution cycle. Recall Process-Data Symbiosis. Remember that The Company Way Processes dovetail with the management approach, our productized offerings, and how we deliver those offerings to customers. It is the only path to gather and use data effectively.

We might choose a single leading indicator to articulate the performance of an entire process or use more than one leading indicator to convey the performance of a crucial step. We make these decisions situationally as we design and routinely micro-evolve our operations baseline. Strategic planning allows us to validate the efficacy of these definitions collectively.

Figure E8 illustrates a small portion of our operations baseline. Let's stay with our lead generation function from the last chapter. One of the common ways for companies to generate leads is to perform outreach to prospective customers. A simple leading indicator could be the number of outreaches performed. Conducting more outreaches will positively impact our overall company outcomes, such as the number of customers and revenue.

The performance of every process involves complexities, and the design of our leading indicators must accommodate the incentives of the roles performing each process or process step. Could outreaches be executed poorly? Absolutely. Some employees may not be motivated enough to understand the prospect well before performing the outreach, even if our process execution guidelines set specific expectations. We may have to consider a secondary leading indicator around the execution effectiveness of outreaches, such as time spent on preparation.

Similarly, we can measure a productized capability with one or more leading indicators. For instance, measuring whether a customer uses our offering as part of their journey is a powerful predictor of whether they will continue to buy in the future.

A leading indicator is a simple measurement or ratio that directly measures either or both the maturity and execution of a portion of our operations baseline. Conversely, they are not complex measurements with several factors in the numerator and denominator. Instead, they measure what one value creator or a group in the same role might do. They measure how effectively a specific portion of our productized offering creates value. The more confounding a measurement is, the more uncontrollable it is.

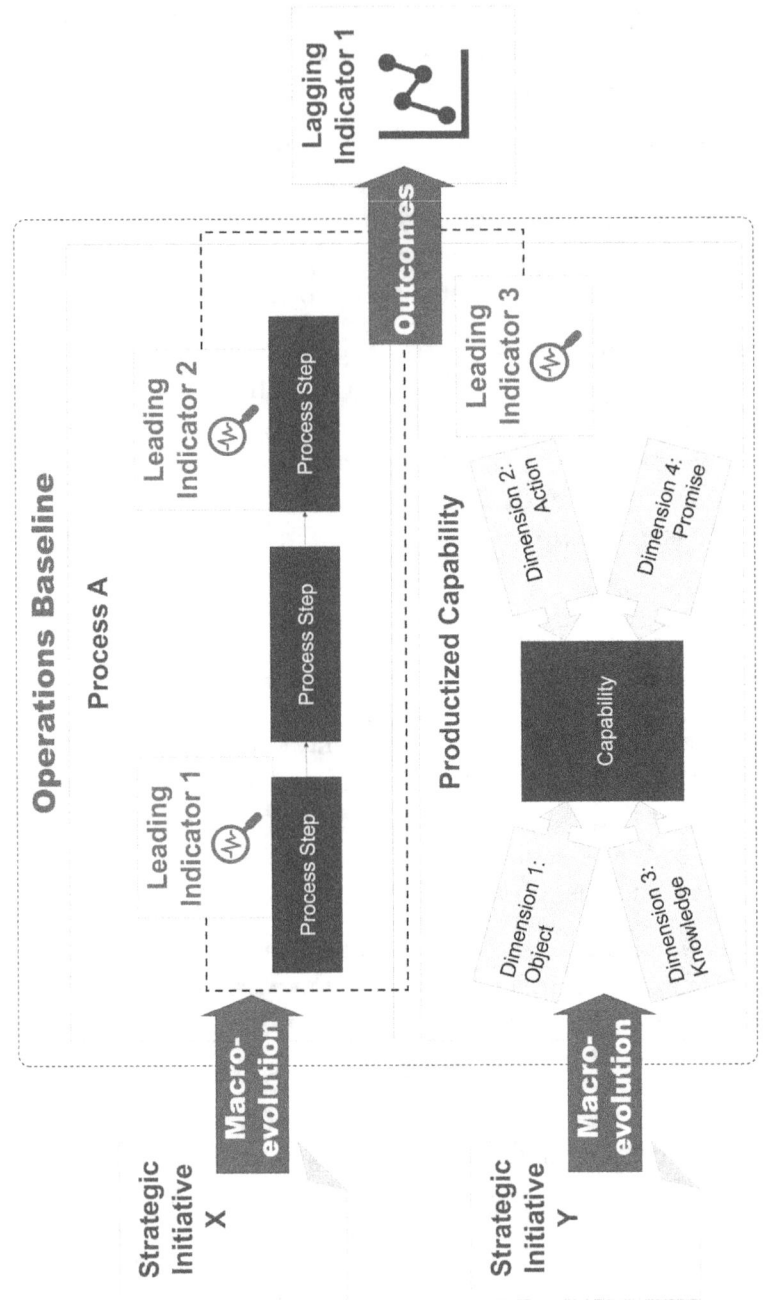

Figure E8. Leading indicators measure operations maturity and execution.

Think about our operations baseline's maturity and execution effectiveness as a flowing liquid. Our choice of leading indicators must contain the liquid that prefers to flow in the path of least resistance. So, how many walls do we have to build to contain the liquid? That's how we think about choosing and defining our leading indicators. We want to select the optimal set of leading indicators that can help us understand the maturity of our entire operations baseline and the behaviors that determine its execution effectiveness.

Figure E9 illustrates my framework for defining leading indicators. Consider all the building blocks of our operations baseline – productized offerings, processes, data, and management approach – across all functions. The choice of leading indicators must consider all our functions. The choice of leading indicators can stay within a single function, span multiple functions, or involve a hand-off between two functions.

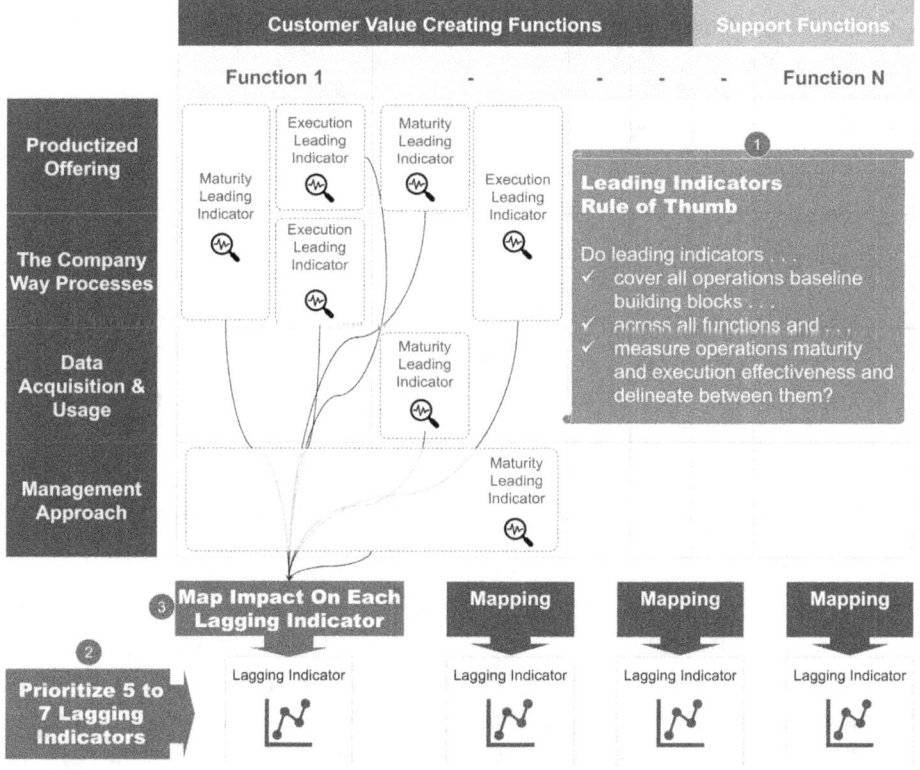

Figure E9. Leading and lagging indicators have a many-to-many relationship.

The planning team must be able to identify the circumstances in which multiple indicators are needed to frame our operations baseline's maturity and execution effectiveness. The choice depends on current maturity and execution effectiveness. It also depends on whether we have slated a strategic initiative that is expected to shift maturity and require its adoption in the next cycle, which implies we must measure execution effectiveness.

Are you worried about too many leading indicators? Don't be – effective target setting and reporting, which we will discuss in Principle 4, ensure these require no work unless we cross reporting thresholds. If we have leading indicators that breach thresholds, we really should have been monitoring them anyway.

Consider these design questions while assessing and refining leading indicators:

What simple measurements can set expectations and monitor our work to create value through every management approach and value engine building block?

Do these chosen measurements cover all functions comprehensively?

Do they collectively measure both maturity and execution effectiveness, especially in areas where our corporate strategy will shift the maturity of our operations via strategic initiatives?

Defining these leading indicators is a starting point. We will iterate them as we map them to lagging indicators, set targets, and create our execution plans, because a critical-thinking planning team will refine the quality of the strategic plan throughout.

Map leading indicators to lagging indicators for external use and storytelling.

Revenue and expenses are compound measurements determined using standard accounting rules, and they reflect real-world actions and decisions weeks, months, or years ago. Measurements such as "churn," which states the total revenue we lost because we lost customers, are complex, and they never tell us why the measurement is what it is. We must undertake a situational root cause analysis to understand why such measurements went up or down.

Additionally, accounting for revenue and expenses is unique to each company because the underlying operations always differ between companies and over time. The result is that benchmarking lagging indicators across companies doesn't tell us anything actionable.

Such lagging indicators have a use, and we must choose five to seven for our company. They are ideally suited to share our company's story for reporting to investors who want to know how our company is performing without being involved in the details or helping us achieve results.

However, this same interest in lagging indicators from non-day-to-day stakeholders creates a tendency for executives and supervisors to operate and manage the business exclusively using lagging indicators. This is problematic.

Lagging indicators are very tempting. They require very little work to define because they measure outcomes. It's like looking at ourselves in the mirror to assess fitness – easy but not actionable. If our management approach is immature, lagging indicators are tempting because they can be used as a stick to manage supervisors, employees, or partners without giving them a specific path to achieve associated outcomes. In our lead generation example above, it would be easy for a supervisor to demand more high-quality leads from employees who work hard to find them. Demanding results is easy. The hard part is to design a way that makes it possible.

The relationship between each lagging indicator and influencing leading indicators is complex. This relationship is multi-variable calculus. Every lagging indicator has a one-to-many relationship with several leading indicators. A lagging indicator usually only improves once multiple leading indicators collectively improve. The impact of each leading indicator on a lagging indicator may also not be linear.

A major challenge at a company I partnered with was the rift between the marketing and sales teams. A standard lagging indicator sales teams use is "pipeline," which reflects likely revenue based on prospects actively worked on by the sales teams. However, at this company, the sales reps attributed little value to the leads handed to them by marketing lead generation resources and worked on only the leads they self-generated. So, the lagging pipeline measure would remain unchanged regardless of the number or quality of marketing leads created. As we planned and executed strategic initiatives to improve the hand-off steps between sales and marketing teams, we used leading indicators to measure hand-offs and improvements in marketing lead generation activities. Improvement in lagging indicators, such as the sales pipeline, becomes evident months later.

We need to understand an approximate relationship between our leading indicators, which we can directly control, and the resulting lagging indicators. Fretting too much about exact future measurements of lagging indicators is not a good use of resources because that's a management philosophy not focused on value.

Figure E8 illustrates this relationship between our work to create value through processes and offerings, measuring them using leading indicators and relating them to downstream outcomes measured via lagging indicators. Use the tabular framework in Figure E9 to comprehensively map the many-to-one relationship between leading and lagging indicators.

Consider these design questions to map leading indicators to lagging indicators effectively:

What are the top five to seven lagging indicators our external stakeholders are interested in?

Which of our drafted leading indicators directly impact these five to seven lagging indicators?

What is the approximate level of impact (direct correlation, partial correlation, etc.) that each leading indicator has on the lagging indicators?

What are the dependencies amongst leading indicators for strategic initiative-driven improvements to be observable via each lagging indicator?

Using these guiding questions, we must operate our company with a causal mapping between leading indicators and their estimated impact on extrinsically relevant outcomes such as customer satisfaction, number of customers, new revenue, revenue retention, or cost of goods sold.

This mapping helps the CFO and CEO translate the controllable reality of our operations baseline to investor-friendly outcomes. Based on our Chain of Controllability, this conversion is always the optimal mindset for measurements.

Principle 3: Timeline of strategic initiative impact predicts leading and lagging indicator measurements.

So far, we have discussed the level of impact of strategic initiatives through our Chain of Controllability. But "when" such an impact will manifest is equally important. To predict the performance of our operations baseline, we must internalize when our strategic initiatives drive improvements into our operations baseline. Let's incorporate how strategic initiatives, operations baseline, leading indicators, and lagging indicators relate over time.

Consider these design questions to build an operations plan that accurately reflects macroevolution as we move through the next execution cycle:

When will strategic initiatives trigger improvements in the operations baseline measured via maturity-focused leading indicators?

When will operations resources adopt improvements and realistically demonstrate improvements measured via execution-focused leading indicators?

What is the time-sequenced impact of operations baseline improvements on overarching outcomes measured through lagging indicators?

Every sports team starts each season with enthusiasm and excitement. But are they playing at their best at the start of the season? Typically, no. If we normalize psychological breakdowns, injuries, and similar setbacks, we expect a team to learn more and play better as the season progresses. The same maturity growth trend applies to our business. Our maturity growth comes from our effectively executed and adopted strategic initiatives.

Effective maturity growth via our strategic initiatives implies that our leading indicators will improve through our execution cycle as we implement more initiatives. Lagging outcomes will eventually reflect these improvements. We wouldn't know whether our strategic initiatives are effective without predicting the timing.

Enablement roadmap conveys timeline of operations baseline improvements.

At the start of each execution cycle, we are exactly where we finished the previous cycle. Without injecting maturity shifts into our operations baseline, we must assume that the next cycle's starting performance is the same as the ending performance of the current cycle.

Under this scenario, the best we can do as a company is short-term tactical scaling with more of the same. For example, we can hire more sales reps to sell the same way and with the same offering. We could offer the same capability without increasing the value created. However, scaling up and down isn't creating the best version of our company.

We would be sacrificing sustainability because more sales reps would become unwieldy to manage without maturity improvements. In addition, the same offering has less net value for customers over time because value experiences inflation, just like currency. The hiring and layoff cycles companies undergo are characteristic of being frozen from a maturity improvement perspective.

So, we choose our maturity and congruence-focused path.

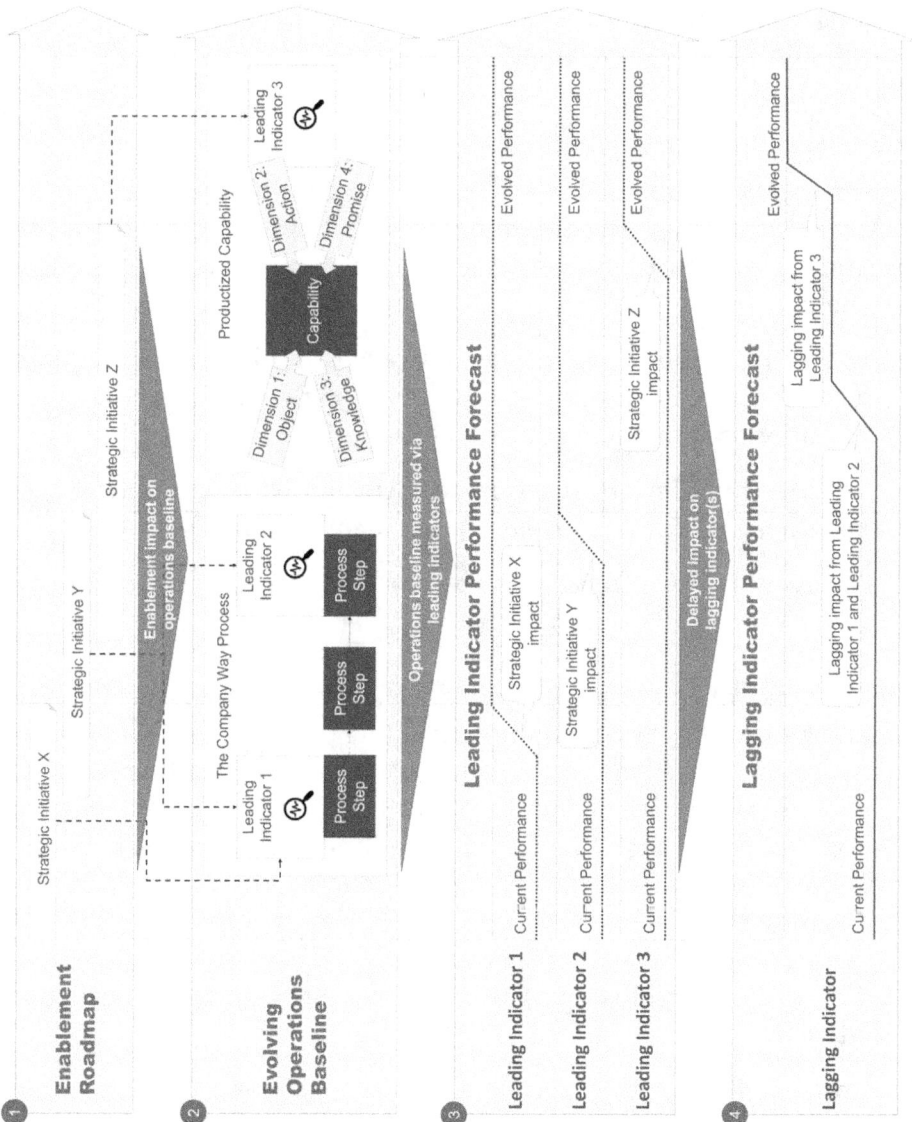

Figure E10. Strategic initiative timelines predict leading and lagging indicator performance improvements.

We must create a tentative timeline for our prioritized strategic initiatives, which we will call our **Enablement Roadmap**. Let's begin the roadmap as a simple construct where we add a start date and an end date for each initiative. The following chapters will further detail our initiatives and bolster our enablement roadmap.

We cannot work on all our prioritized initiatives simultaneously. Nothing will get done. We must stage-gate our strategic initiatives based on their dependencies. We might have to complete some before others, and we should consider practicality around enablement investments because the same resources might have to work on one initiative after another is complete.

In Figure E10, element 1 illustrates how we can think about the phased approach to strategic initiatives. It builds from the preliminary initiative prioritization we conducted during Phase 1 of planning.

Consider this design question to draft our strategic initiative execution timeline to start our enablement roadmap:

What is our high-level timeline to start, execute, complete, and transition each prioritized strategic initiative?

The left side of Figure E10 illustrates the starting point of our execution cycle. Let's simplify our company to just one capability and one process, measured via three leading indicators. These three leading indicators reflect the performance of our operations baseline at the start of our cycle. However much we wish that our lagging indicators perform at a higher level, it will always be a trailing aggregation of the three contributing leading indicators.

Leading indicators closely track improvements injected by strategic initiatives.

As strategic initiatives improve our value engine and management approach, the measurements of our leading indicators will ramp up as operations resources adopt these improvements. The impact timeline depends not only on the successful completion of strategic initiatives to drive improvements but also on their adoption by operations resources. It is important to note that our operations performance ramp reflects both maturity improvement and execution alignment to the new maturity level.

Our operations performance improves as we complete various stages of each maturity-injecting strategic initiative. Each improvement is a crucial time stamp for our operations-focused plan. This is one of the critical payoffs of embracing leading indicators. We will know early on whether our enablement investments are working without hoping and waiting for company-level outcomes to show improvements.

Consider these design questions to frame the impact timeline on leading indicators:

When will each leading indicator show maturity improvements triggered by the successful completion of strategic initiatives?

What is the reasonable adoption timeline for operations resources to embrace improvements created by strategic initiatives?

In our lead generation example, a hypothetical enablement initiative that aligns with the how-to-deliver trade-off could be to change how we find leads. Let's shift from active outbound outreaches to inbound advertising-driven lead generation. A leading indicator like "percent of sweet spot leads from advertising as a ratio of the total" will immediately show the uptick when our strategic initiative progresses without waiting for company-level outcomes such as new sales revenue.

Lagging indicator measurements will improve later than operations baseline improvements.

No one in the world will disagree with the importance of leading indicators. Unfortunately, in my experience, lagging indicators have a nicotine-like addictive effect on many executives and let themselves and the company run ragged with efforts to influence outcomes directly.

The mathematical truth that lagging indicators will always show a significantly delayed uptick from our strategy development, strategic initiatives, and operations improvements demonstrable via leading indicators should be obvious. Lagging indicators are also compound metrics, and it's never apparent why they go up and down just by looking at them.

But most people are quick to credit or blame a president or CEO for current positive or negative outcomes when many results during their tenure are lagging impacts of their predecessor's decisions or actions. Operations planning helps us avoid judging today's operational reality based on the lagging numbers we see.

The chart at the bottom of Figure E10 illustrates this delay and compounding nature of lagging indicators. In our operations-focused planning, we will learn no new information from lagging indicators that we cannot learn from leading indicators. However, we must understand and incorporate the impact timelines of lagging indicators.

Why? When investors or the board ask about outcomes, we will feel pressure to give them good news. If we lack clarity on when our controllable aspects – strategic initiatives and operations baseline execution – will impact our lagging indicators, we will likely feel the need to act irrationally and take knee-jerk actions to alter outcomes directly to share good news.

If irrational reactions set in, it drives executives and key resources to deviate from our well-laid-out plans. This is the equivalent of operating without a plan.

I used to work closely with a revenue executive who loved saying, "The long term is important, but we just need results now!" My response was typically, "How do you suggest we do that?" Unfortunately, this executive limited the company's opportunities to create more value and operate more efficiently.

Consider this design question to build a credible relationship between leading and lagging indicators:

When will the compounded impact of improving leading indicators be observable in our five to seven lagging indicators?

To summarize, we must iteratively triangulate towards a high-level timeline for our strategic initiatives at this stage in our planning efforts. We must also understand at what points in time our planned strategic initiatives will impact our operations baseline and demonstrate improvement in our leading indicators, as well as when we expect to see those improvements reflected in our lagging indicators.

Use the framework in Figure E10 to define a realistic timeline for strategic initiatives. Predict their impact on the operations baseline and realistic expected measurements via leading and lagging indicators.

Principle 4: Leading indicator targets anchor operations baseline performance.

We prioritized enablement initiatives to mature our operations baseline at the closest access point in our Chain of Controllability. We linked our strategic initiatives to leading indicators and lagging outcomes and set when improvements will appear throughout the chain.

How much will our operations improve? We must set targets. Setting analysis-backed targets enables us to set expectations on how our operations baseline will perform throughout the execution cycle. This is our operations plan.

A common pitfall is for teams to volunteer for unachievable targets. Senior executives or supervisors often feel that future performance can be significantly better than past performance because they are involved. This is a form of optimism bias. It's the human tendency to think, "This time, it will be different!" In a poor planning approach, this optimism is based on spurious rationales such as hiring a new senior executive or subjective feeling that we won't repeat past mistakes. But these aren't evolutionary.

Even individuals will struggle to shift personal behaviors without a tangible enabler. For example, how many substance abusers say that they quit every so often? Going through a rehabilitation program and associated accountabilities is a tangible enabler. Similarly, our improved future targets will require directly related enablers.

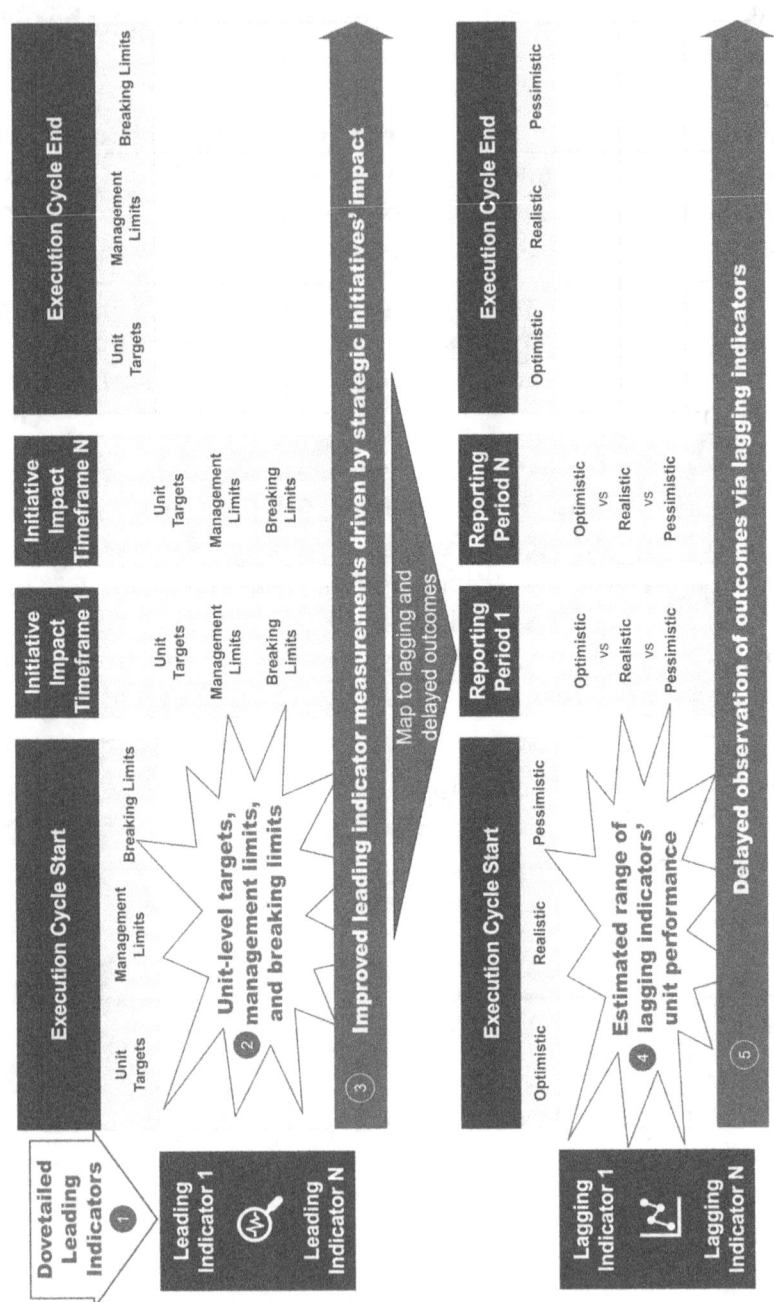

Figure E11. Operations plan forecasts unit-level performance.

Recall our principles from Chapter C.3 to set guardrails for effective targets for our operations metrics. Figure E11 summarizes the elements we must create for a viable operations plan. The four guardrails below highlight the critical parts of implementing this framework to formalize an operations plan.

Guardrail 1: Comprehensive set of leading indicators ensures company-wide coverage.

The spine of our operations plan is the comprehensive set of leading indicators that we developed and validated using the principles above. Operations plans speak to every value creator and executive. Operations resources live and breathe the building blocks of our operations baseline, and their performance is set and measured using our leading indicators.

The left side of our framework above illustrates this guardrail, which ensures that our operations plan covers our entire operations baseline. Measurement gaps often act like the slope in the bathroom floor, attracting all the water flow, which is an undesirable behavior in this analogy. Failure points via maturity gaps and execution ineffectiveness congregate around these blind spots.

Guardrail 2: Leading indicators require targets, management limits, and breaking limits.

We must know how we will perform on each leading indicator at any time. The measurements that we can hit for our metrics should not be defined in a vacuum or based on desired outcomes. We must leverage mature analyses to set operational performance expectations. The targets must reflect reasonable performance expectations based on maturity at any given time.

Recall our discussion about creating effective reporting. Reporting is a robust risk management tool if we set optimal targets and limits. This is the most opportune moment in our macroevolution cycle to reevaluate and reset targets that can help us repeatably and reproducibly achieve necessary performance levels for each component of the operations baseline across all functions.

We must also set appropriate management limits for each leading indicator, which trigger corrective actions and supervisory intervention when breached during execution.

Imagine trying to monitor a comprehensive set of leading indicators without effective thresholds! It will be akin to finding someone we don't know visual details of by looking at feeds from several security cameras showing hundreds of people. Robust reporting with management limits is like knowing this person's face and having facial recognition software. Without it, we will likely pick an arbitrarily interesting and incorrect person, not the correct person. Therefore, setting management limits for leading indicators is a necessity.

The breaking limits for our leading indicators, which identify situations where our operations baseline is at risk of an unanticipated breakdown, are also critical to reassess and reset throughout our operations planning effort. As our operations baseline matures, the expected worst-case performance gets more stringent.

Guardrail 3: Targets, management limits, and breaking limits will evolve over time with operations baseline improvements.

The impact of our strategic initiatives must lift our performance expectations for leading indicators and their targets, management limits, and breaking limits. Precision is pertinent here. We want to be realistic about our impact timeline.

If we are too optimistic, we have set ourselves up for failure. If we sandbag, we are poorly allocating investment to protect ourselves from the risk of failure at everyone else's expense. As we highlighted under Principle 2, the planning architect must devise objective analyses to quantify the impact of each strategic initiative on portions of the operations baseline.

One practical approach to arrive at reasonable figures is to estimate optimistic, realistic, and pessimistic scenarios for each leading indicator. Triangulating from three such figures often renders a reasonably precise target and management limit.

Our starting performance as we ring in the next execution cycle must equal our performance when we finish the current cycle unless we finish a present strategic initiative at the turn of the cycle. Wishful thinking must not convince us to set elevated performance targets. Instead, establish the expected performance targets and limits that align with enablement initiatives' completion timelines. The third guardrail is this time-based adjustment of operations performance targets and limits triggered by maturity improvements from strategic initiatives.

Additionally, we must consider dependencies in our operations baseline and enablement initiatives. In our lead generation example, what if we trained our lead generation resources to deliver incremental leads, but our efforts to generate interest in the market via advertising spend or branding efforts are not complete? Target setting must be dovetailed across leading indicators to ensure dependencies are accounted for, especially time lags.

Adhering to these three guardrails will help us translate all the inputs we have developed thus far into a single plan that articulates what our company will do operationally.

Easy, right? On paper, yes. However, lagging indicators will always tempt us to abandon discipline and skip using leading indicators. So, we must adopt a fourth guardrail to ensure that we can predict our operations' lagging performance at a unit level.

Guardrail 4: Frame unit-level lagging outcomes.

Our goal through operations planning is to set an operations blueprint for our organization. However, we are always tempted to deal in outcome-focused conversations about revenue, expenses, and growth rates. The best way to stay focused on aspects we can control is to effectively answer all frequently asked questions about how the factors we can control will influence aspects we cannot directly control.

Like making performance predictions for leading indicators, our goal is not to predict aggregate outcomes. Instead, we want to predict lagging outcomes while staying with our unit performance mindset as we approach the second strategic planning milestone.

Using our causal mapping between leading and lagging indicators and the estimated impact timeframe of our improving leading indicators, we must create a simple mathematical model that estimates the outcomes we can observe in our prioritized five to seven lagging indicators. We only need to estimate optimistic, realistic, and pessimistic scenarios for each chosen lagging indicator for critical moments in time through our execution cycle. False precision is not our goal. These key points can be the turn of fiscal quarters or months and when we expect impact from strategic initiatives.

For a lagging financial metric like "new sweet spot revenue from the existing offering," we can predict the "number of new sweet spot customers trialing existing offering for an average sales representative." This is based on a strategic initiative to train existing sales reps to find customers in our new sweet spot. Through operations planning, we are interested in lagging unit performance measures like the number of new sweet spot customers one average sales rep can attract.

The aggregate company-level revenue from selling our existing offering to new sweet spot customers is influenced by factors like the number of sales reps, lead generation resources, and advertising spending. These factors are investment decisions that will be part of the final planning phase and directly build on the maturity level articulated by our operations plan.

I have included this fourth guardrail in Figure E11 to complete the minimum set of answers that we must draft as our operations plan. A second planning milestone will bring together the planning team to vet and iterate the Chain of Controllability and resulting operations plan, which spans the operations baseline, prioritized strategic initiatives, and their impact on leading and lagging indicators.

The concepts we discussed aren't complex. But getting them right under the pressures of time, priorities, and personalities can be extremely difficult. Committed leadership and the maturity level of the company's management approach will determine our success.

E.4
OPTIMIZE CAPITAL EFFICIENCY AND SCALE THROUGH INVESTMENT PLANNING.

To make money, we must spend money. Every dollar we spend on our operations and enablement efforts is our investment. But what is the right amount to spend? In our holistic company mindset, we don't believe that careless investing will help us sustain profitability.

There are two simple guardrails for any investment decision: affordability and the tangible impact of the investment.

Affordability is the upper threshold for investment.

Affordability implies our ability to invest without risking our company's financial health. We want to remain in a relatively stress-free cash position as a company where we can pay our partners' bills, keep our employees, and serve our customers effectively even if we face some headwinds. It implies only taking on interest-bearing debt that we can afford without being consumed by the risk of default. Affordability is the CFO's realm.

If we are running anywhere close to the best version of our company, we have profits. If we are running at a loss, we need funding from an investor or a bank to keep our operations going. If we have profits, what is the correct share of profits to reinvest during the next execution cycle? As our affordability police, the CFO will work with the CEO and the board to identify relevant investment thresholds for our next execution cycle.

Impact is the second guardrail, and it is the realm of the board and the CEO. What can each dollar we spend get us in intrinsic maturity improvement, operational value creation, and resulting extrinsic outcomes?

We divide all company expenses into two categories: operations and enablement. For the execution cycle, we must formalize our investment decisions in both these categories through strategic planning, and these decisions must depend on the impact of the items we invest in.

The impact must consider the maturity improvement we can realistically drive in our operations baseline through enablement initiatives and the scale of our operations baseline that our present maturity level can support. There are realistic limitations to the impact of investment.

Our planning impact assessment must be realistic about how fast we can execute enablement initiatives due to dependencies, availability of decision-makers, and other company-level constraints. Additionally, we should scale our operations investment only to the point where further increases would lead to a regression in performance. Beyond this point, we will undermine the unit performance of our operations plan as a result of a decline in our operations maturity. The ceiling created by these impact thresholds could be well within our affordability, so we must stay prudent and not overspend.

Improving net positive value creation as a sustainably profitable company requires us to commit to our methodical corporate strategy and planning approach. Skipping our macroevolution and investing in the existing maturity of the operations baseline will lead us away from the needs of our sweet spot customers and result in increasing inefficiency. Investing in an immature operations baseline is akin to pouring high-quality wine into a perpetually unwashed glass.

The final planning stage is **investment planning**, and it involves three deliverables.

> **Things To Remember: Investment Planning**
>
> **Investment planning is the third and final phase of an iterative strategic planning exercise. In this phase, we finalize both enablement and operations investments and formalize forecasts for company-level lagging indicators.**

First, strategic initiatives are difficult to execute and derive maturity from because we are trying to change our company, and change is challenging.

So, as we formalize and approve investment in our initiatives to begin execution, we must agree on what "good" looks like for each strategic initiative.

Second, we need to formalize our investment in resources and assets contributing to our processes to achieve the unit-level leading indicators we laid out in our operations plan. Operations investment is an optimal scale decision. In other words, we must decide when and how much we will scale a specific portion of our operations baseline and what maturity improvement will trigger each scaling investment.

Third, we must finalize our target for leading indicators based on the impact of our strategic initiatives and associated enablement investment. Superimposing our operations investment decision on top of the finalized unit-level operations plan gives us the aggregate measurements of our operations baseline performance.

These deliverables provide the CFO with the inputs necessary to create a detailed financial plan that forecasts revenue, expenses, and cash flow. These core outcomes also give our fundamentals-focused company a predictive and practical plan to execute effectively in the next cycle.

Consider these design questions to build a checklist for investment planning deliverables:

What does "good" look like for each strategic initiative that will translate our new strategy into our future operations?

What will be our enablement investment to support our strategic initiatives?

What will be our operations investment to deliver customer value through our operations baseline?

What will our lagging company-level outcomes be, based on our finalized operations plan and operations investment?

We must decide our total enablement and operations investments in a manner that optimally balances these two categories. We want to invest in enablement efforts to mature our operations baseline before scaling too much because size demands more maturity. Conversely, we do not want to overinvest in enablement where our operations sophistication far exceeds our company's scale. This is also an investment misallocation. We must strike a balance between operations and enablement investment.

The planning architect can work with the CFO and the finance team to ensure that the strategic plan stays within the guardrails of total investment and cash flow constraints without compromising our primary focus on investment impact.

Principle 1: Finalize strategic initiative impact via steady state definition.

The first step of the investment planning phase is to nail down what "good" looks like for our prioritized strategic initiatives.

How would we consider our decision to sign up for a running race? First, we want to know whether it's a marathon or a 5K. Next, we'd like to know which city and time of year the race is because elevation changes and temperature impact it. Our list will include factors that determine our success on race day.

Similarly, we must frame what "good" looks like for all our strategic initiatives during investment planning to ensure that we are crystal clear on the expected impact and investment requirements before finalizing our plan.

The impact of strategic initiatives is far from guaranteed.

Recall that strategic initiatives are enablement efforts that macro-evolve the maturity of our operations and move our company closer to achieving the new corporate strategy. They don't just start and end. An unsophisticated "get it done" tactical mindset is a common path to failure.

After running many transformation projects over the years, I have realized that most initiatives fail if we objectively measure outcomes and don't try to spin the outcome as a success. Failures take two forms.

The **first** type of failure is when initiatives fizzle out and do not achieve the objective and measurable outcome that was their original intended essence. This often happens due to a lack of clarity on their intended improvements.

Many strategic initiatives start by intending to achieve nebulous outcomes that the people involved don't agree on or understand, and eventually, they fail due to disharmony.

The **second** type of failure is regression. Even among the initiatives that demonstrate improvements early on by completing the execution phase, many fail to maintain those improvements over time. Strategic initiatives can achieve the desired improvement in the near term due to intense attention and investment, but the performance can slip back after the initial excitement.

Gravity is a practical reality. What goes up will come down unless the necessary energy is spent to fight gravity and keep the object at a higher state. Executing strategic initiatives to improve company-wide congruence has a similar constraint. Imagine training for that running race, and we get ourselves to a pace that makes us proud. What if we stop running for the next six months? Our running speed likely drops back to what it was before we trained for our race. Maintaining operations baseline maturity requires the equivalent of continuous training.

The root cause of these failures is a lack of clarity about what "good" looks like for strategic initiatives and an internalization that maintaining that "good" state requires work. I call this articulation of "good" the **Steady State**.

The steady state definition articulates strategic initiative success factors.

Figure E12 illustrates the maturity trends for well-run and poorly executed initiatives. Poorly run initiatives look for quick improvements without dedicating the effort to truly mature fundamentals. They are what we colloquially call duct tape fixes. The dotted line represents the trajectory of such doomed efforts.

For example, companies often invest in a strategic initiative to automate and streamline sales and marketing processes using the latest software as the number of employees increases. It's the right choice. But what if we dilute the initiative by buying a software solution off the shelf and quickly turning it on without effective design to ensure it aligns with mature processes or has strong governance?

Yes, we can get value creators to use it very quickly. They might even appreciate it for a few weeks. But without proper design, governance, and training, the software will soon become the Wild West. It will regress our execution because the new software allows bad data and individualistic styles to supersede efficient operations and customer value. Where do we end up? We lost our investment in an initiative that devolved after the initial appearance of success. This storyline is a near guarantee for any strategic initiative execution that does not embrace the steady state concept.

Things To Remember: Steady State

Strategic initiatives go through a heavy-lifting execution phase to complete certain tasks and deliverables that improve current operations performance and achieve the new company strategy. Then, the evolved state must be embraced and maintained. This evolved state that requires perpetual maintenance is called the steady state.

An initiative moves into a steady state when we achieve the desired, measurable maturity improvements and transition the responsibilities from enablement execution resources to long-term operations execution resources. I illustrate this trajectory with the bold line in Figure E12. This is our desired execution path for each strategic initiative with three benefits.

First, the end does justify the means. A clearly articulated desired state allows strategic planning to predict each initiative's realistic investment needs and impact. In addition, an accurate depiction of the steady state is necessary to firm up the targets and limits we drafted as part of *Phase 2: Operations Planning*.

Second, we all tend to rationalize and put a convenient spin on situations when conditions turn sour. For example, execution can take longer than expected, or high quality may be harder to achieve than anticipated. Unless a steady state is well articulated ahead of time, there is a strong likelihood that we will settle for "good enough" results far from the original intent as deadlines slide and unanticipated obstacles arise. Starting with a strong articulation of the steady state helps the company and

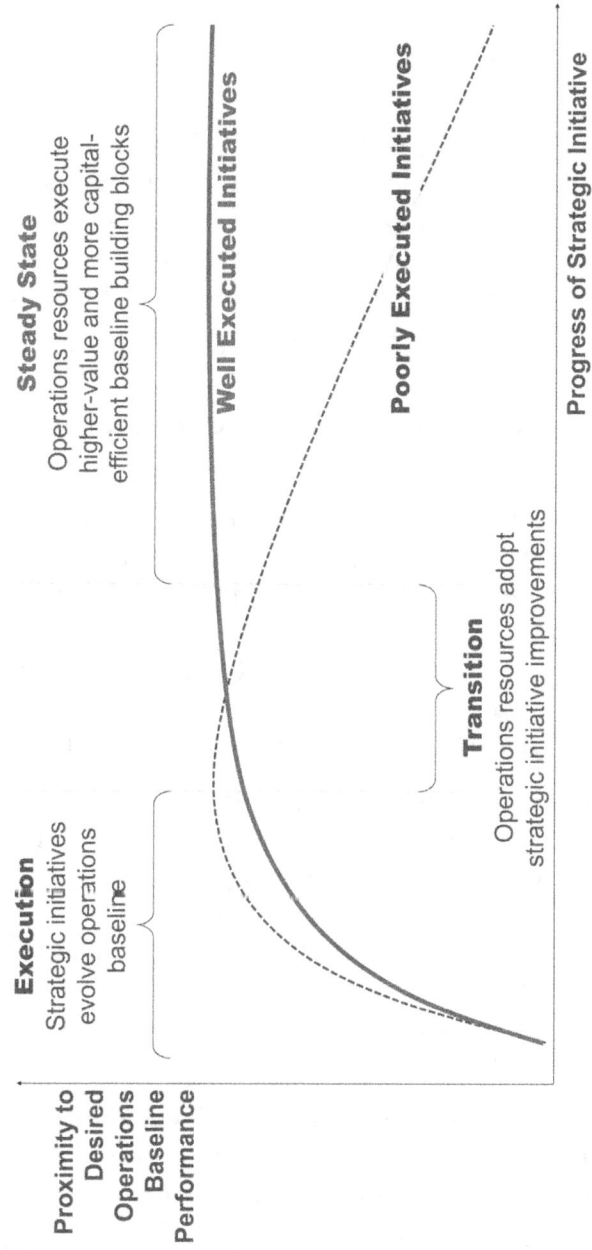

**Figure E12. Strategic initiative steady state definition
dictates sustainability of macroevolution.**

individuals involved hold themselves and each other accountable to achieve the essence of each strategic initiative.

Third, the idea of maintenance of maturity is not evident in most operational settings. Over the years, I shifted to the new term – steady state – to highlight the importance of perpetual maintenance instead of an abrupt end state. Formalizing the steady state of enablement initiatives drives clarity as we go through planning, design, and building through the "execution" phase and push for organizational adoption during the "transition" phase, where responsibilities are handed to day-to-day operations resources.

> *Consider this design question to prepare enablement plans for execution:*
>
> *What is the impact of each prioritized strategic initiative on the operations baseline we want to hold ourselves accountable for through qualitative maturity improvements and leading quantitative indicators?*

Now, what does a "good" steady state definition look like?

Formalize and approve strategic initiative impact on operations baseline.

In previous planning phases, we developed high-level impact and timeline details as part of the prioritization of enablement initiatives and the development of the enablement roadmap. But we need to get deeper as we progress to the tail end of strategic planning. Documentation, debate, and decision-making are often underrated. Strategic planning is more than just an opportunity to think and talk about what we will do. It is a time to formally write down what we will do so we can hold ourselves and the organization accountable for our promises.

> *Consider these design questions to detail each initiative's impact on processes and data, productized offerings and related pricing and packaging, and management approach:*
>
> *What are the expected qualitative improvements in processes and data?*
>
> *Which operations roles must embrace improvements?*
>
> *How will adoption and improvements be measured and monitored?*

Which leading indicators will quantify process improvements, and by how much?

What value-creating capability improvements will be delivered?

How will these improvements be evidenced via pricing and packaging?

Which leading indicators will quantify productization maturity improvements, and by how much?

What are the expected organization design, hiring, performance management, and compensation model improvements?

What new skills are required to execute the improved processes, capture or use higher quality data, or deliver value through evolved offerings?

The quality of these answers dictates our ability to hold ourselves accountable through the next execution cycle. Note that only some people want to be held accountable, which is precisely why our planning team must be staffed with thought leaders who embrace maturity growth and a One Company mindset.

Additionally, these answers also flow directly into finalizing our strategic initiatives' impact on our leading indicators. Without knowing what we will achieve and when, how can we frame what it would cost to achieve it? Framing concrete answers to the questions above forms a business case for whether and when we must allocate investment for each prioritized strategic initiative.

Such a precise framing of the steady state allows us to start execution management of enablement initiatives with confidence and clarity.

Imagine a group of executives going through a planning effort and framing a major nebulous initiative with few specifics. . . . The initiatives are then presented to the board and even the whole company as critical to a maturity shift. Then, we hire an enablement resource to manage that initiative. Would we want to be that enablement resource? No! This person is set up to fail. This pattern is all too common, and we want to avoid it.

Our diligence at this stage ensures that we are effectively planning and readying our enablement initiatives for execution.

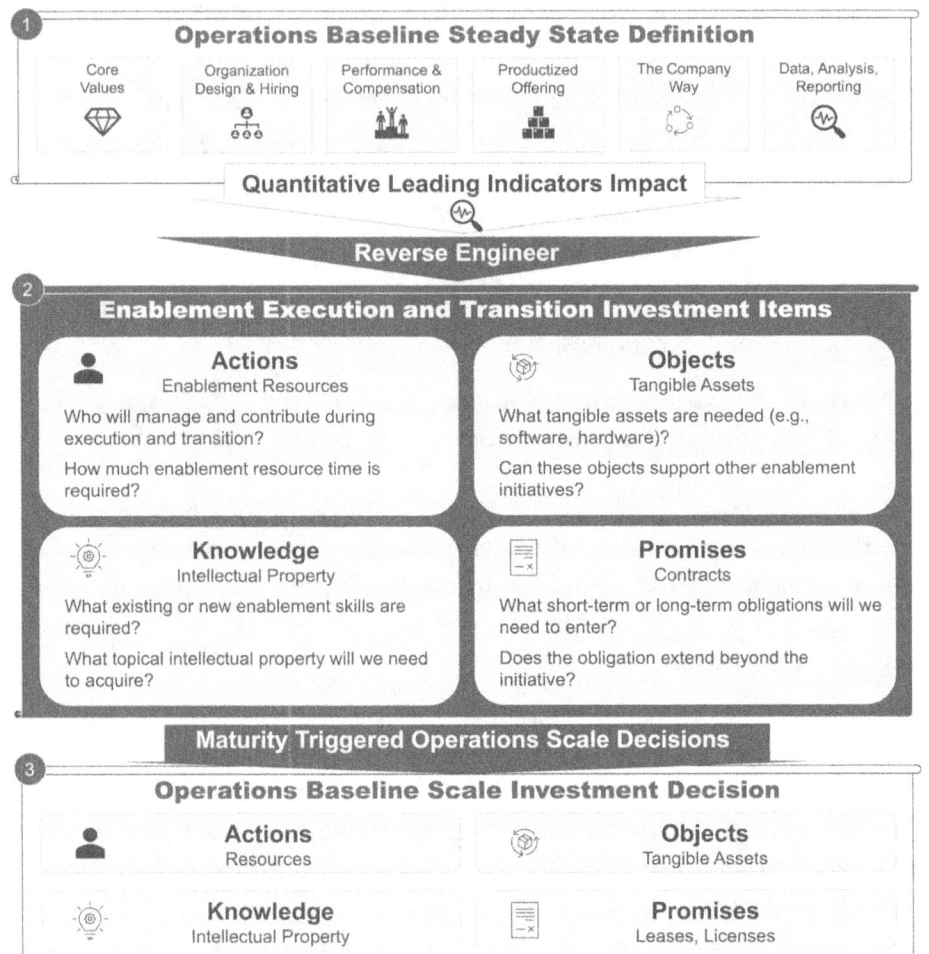

Figure E13. Strategic initiative steady state definition enables investment decisions.

Figure E13 visualizes the pivotal role of defining the steady state for strategic initiatives. Effectively articulating what "good" looks like ensures that we are ready for effective execution after planning. Without effectively framing the steady state for each initiative, we will make emotional and subjective investment decisions.

Principle 2: Formalize enablement investment for strategic initiatives.

The first half of our company's investment decision is dedicated to evolving our operations baseline. Enablement initiatives require a short-term investment that does not become a perpetual cost burden. Because of this short-term aspect, enablement investment planning must be managed surgically. We want to execute our initiatives without investing beyond the time horizon at which we optimally need them.

One could easily add names and dates to initiatives and call it a plan. But often, these are throw-away, lazy efforts that give planning a lousy brand. The truth is that we can predict most aspects of how an initiative will play out if we reserve some thoughtful time to ask more profound questions and identify answers.

> **Things To Remember: Enablement Investment**
>
> **Enablement investment is the time-bound allocation of finances to execute and adopt prioritized strategic initiatives until the transition to steady state operations.**

The following three guardrails will help formalize enablement investment.

Guardrail 1: Frame enablement investment items for each initiative using four capability dimensions.

Each enablement initiative implies an investment. We started by defining the steady state for each initiative. Now, let's reverse engineer from that vision of where we want to be and identify the cost to achieve that steady state.

The cost must cover the complete staffing of enablement resources and all technology, infrastructure, and knowledge support needed to run those initiatives. Most enablement investment goes into people for asset-light markets such as software. Asset-heavy markets such as energy or manufacturing may require machinery, land, or buildings investment.

Recall the four dimensions of capabilities we used for productization and what-to-offer trade-offs in Chapters C.1 and D.4, respectively. We must use the same four-dimensional capability framework to state our investment needs for enablement initiatives.

First, consider all the actions we will have to take to accomplish each initiative. This approach helps us firm up our investment in the number of enablement resources, the share of time we will need from each resource, and the role each will play. If we do not know this ahead of time, how will we know whether an initiative we have prioritized can be executed?

Consider these design questions for each strategic initiative:

Who will manage and contribute during execution and transition?

How much enablement resource time is required?

Second, we must consider all the object dimension requirements necessary to execute each initiative. For example, we might need existing or new software, hardware, or other tangible assets, especially if such a thing is either hard to find or cost-prohibitive. It is also essential to consider whether such an investment can benefit other initiatives so that we can share the investment burden across initiatives.

Consider these design questions for each strategic initiative:

What existing or new tangible objects or assets will we need (e.g., software, hardware)?

Can these objects support other initiatives to ease the overall investment burden?

Third, we might need special knowledge or skills to evolve our operations baseline. We must acknowledge this even if current employees or partners possess it so that we can intentionally choose to keep them. For instance, we might have to invest in a partner who can support employees who do not have experience in a niche topic.

Consider these design questions for each strategic initiative:

What niche enablement skills are required?

What topical intellectual property will we need to acquire?

Fourth, we live in a world of obligations through contracts and informal expectations. This is the least prevalent dimension for an enablement investment, but it is essential to consider whether a unique situation calls for it.

For example, we might have to enter into an informal agreement with our large customers in which they are willing to test our new capability as we design and build it in exchange for offering it to them for free. This delivery beyond testing will have a cost without sales revenue, and that cost is part of enabling the initiative to mature that capability. It is essential to consider such hidden costs as we finalize the expected cost of each strategic initiative.

Consider these design questions for each strategic initiative:

What short-term or long-term obligations must we enter for the success of each initiative?

What is the opportunity cost of extending the obligation beyond the execution stages of the enablement initiative?

Our four capability dimensions help us formalize all the items needed for each initiative. As part of the investment planning phase milestone reviews, the planning team must document, discuss, iterate, and align on an execution plan, including investment requirements, for each enablement initiative. If we approve the initiative, we can build on these plans during execution management.

Consider this design question as an overarching guardrail for each strategic initiative during investment planning:

What are the investment items – considering object, action, knowledge, and promise dimensions – necessary to plan, execute, and transition to a steady state for each initiative?

We must consider the investment needs across all dimensions because one dimension without another may prove a waste. For instance, assigning enablement employees to manage an initiative without investing in knowledge gaps in the form of niche advice from a partner might render our initiative ineffective. Once we have defined initiative-specific investments, it's time to make our overarching enablement investment decision.

Guardrail 2: Leverage three tiers of enablement investment to guide prioritization.

Every company has investment constraints. Whether we have significant profits or have the luxury of spending significantly more than we earn because of new investments or loans, we must practice constraints. Having cash in the bank doesn't mean we have to spend it, especially if we know that the return on investment is limited. Diminishing returns is a real phenomenon.

In the late 2000s, there were a slew of reports about highly paid athletes living in financial distress. Over 75 percent of professional American football players were in financial distress by their fifth year of retirement. Over 60 percent of professional basketball players in the US were in the same situation. If we simplify all their reasons, it all comes down to poor investment choices that arise from the sudden influx of spending power.

Companies are the same. Every company that contacts us to sell something when news about a funding round or public listing comes out is no different from obscure relatives suddenly contacting someone who came into new money.

Here is another truth to embrace. Regardless of the size of the company and the amount of investment we can afford, we can only juggle a certain number of major initiatives that have a relevant impact. Maturity improvements must become embedded into our DNA before investing in additional related initiatives. Otherwise, maturity improvements are a few tough days away from regression.

Deciding whether an initiative is worth the investment in a vacuum is hard. So, we must combine the Strategic Initiative Prioritization Framework in Figure E6 with the enablement execution investment items we framed in Figure E13. Beyond this impact-focused information, our CFO sets the upper investment threshold. I recommend using three investment threshold tiers, where the specific monetary figures come from the CFO based on the company's financial health.

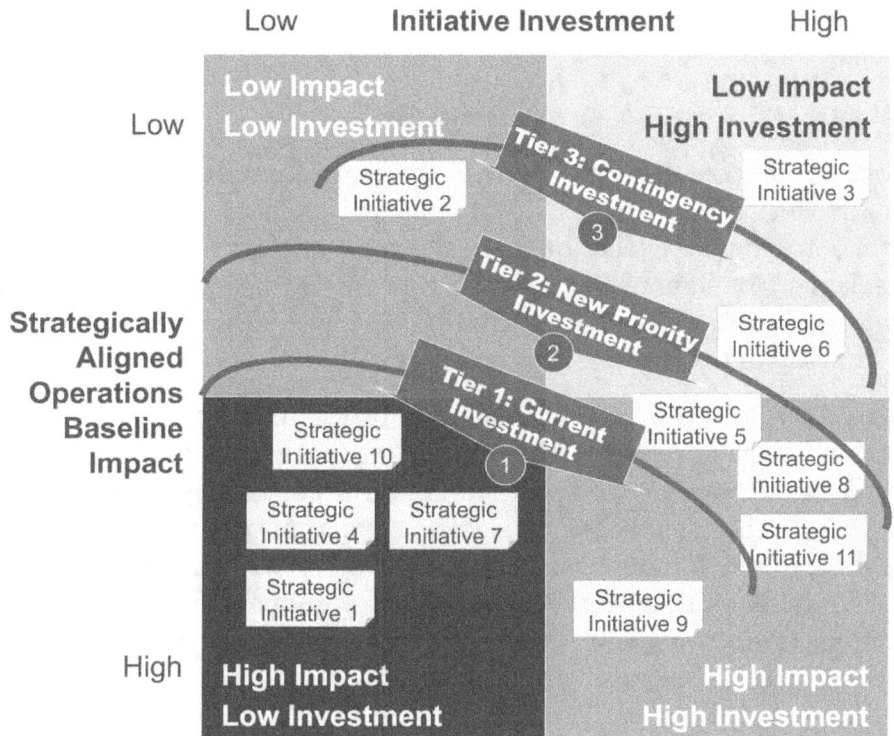

Figure E14. Investment tiers enable efficient enablement investment decisions.

A tiered decision-making approach removes initiative-specific biases from influencing our decisions. Figure E14 illustrates the three conceptual tiers overlayed on our Strategic Initiative Prioritization Framework.

The first tier of enablement investment is the current investment. Unlike perpetual operations efforts, enablement efforts are time-bound. Therefore, we will always have enablement investment that is available to recycle. Given its time-bound nature, current investment can and must be reused. Since we are likely already investing in time-bound enablement efforts, we must address it first. Thus, it is **Tier 1: Current Investment**.

Existing enablement efforts must transition to a steady state by the time we are ready to begin our next execution cycle. So, it is essential to ask whether the current enablement initiatives align with our new corporate strategy. If they do not, should they continue? They are part of our new strategic initiative priorities if they do. If not, we must stop investing in them.

We must avoid two Tier 1 investment pitfalls.

First, companies often fall prey to the equivalent of growing plaque around Tier 1 investment. Environments with an immature management approach and poor execution management tend not to redeploy existing enablement investment. This stagnation results in a stale Tier 1 investment. When companies raise external funds, it is tempting to avoid addressing the efficacy of the existing investment.

Second, as our company grows, we must further mature existing enablement investment. As our initiatives become more sophisticated, as more customers, employees, and partners are involved, we may have to train or hire new skills instead of existing ones. We may have to upgrade existing technologies or tangible assets to handle the increasing sophistication of the initiatives. If existing resources cannot support increasing sophistication, reallocating this investment to new value creators or assets is necessary.

As an extension of these two reasons, if we have invested too much in enablement in the past, this current investment may need to be cut.

Consider these design questions to assess Tier 1: Current Investment:

What is the total Tier 1: Current Investment?

Which of the four dimensions and initiatives are these investments allocated to?

Should the company at least maintain existing Tier 1 investment, or should it be reduced?

Can we effectively redeploy 100 percent of our Tier 1 investment? (We must be able to understand and address reasons we cannot.)

The second tier of enablement investment is **Tier 2: Priority New Investment.** This is incremental to our current investment. Only some companies have this luxury, and so it's a duty to use it well. We may tap into incremental investment if our new strategy and operations gaps require us to execute certain costly enablement initiatives. Incremental investment ideally comes from our profits. However, this investment can also come from new funds raised from investors or banks.

The enactment of Tier 2 enablement investment must be contingent on the effective use of Tier 1 investment. Throwing good money after bad makes matters worse because we end up with a larger, poorly managed company that is more challenging to fix than a smaller, poorly managed one.

Consider this design question to guide Tier 2: New Priority Investment decision:

What is the total incremental enablement investment the company can afford and must unlock without conditions to achieve corporate strategy or address operations gaps?

The translation is that Tier 2 investment is approved to drive incremental maturity through strategic planning.

The third tier of enablement investment is **Tier 3: New Contingency Investment**. There are many reasons to split new investment into a readily approved bucket and a contingent bucket that gets unlocked when positive execution performance reveals itself in the future.

Investing in too many efforts simultaneously usually results in limited progress on any of them. All strategic initiatives have dependencies, and we must internalize the optimal sequencing of initiatives. One condition for unlocking Tier 3 investment can be hitting key milestones of other dependent initiatives.

Another condition is leading or lagging indicator performance. We could set a new contingency investment, which triggers a $10 investment to buy and implement new software if our sales go up from $100 to $120.

Consider these design questions to prioritize stack-ranked strategic initiatives into three tiers:

If we need to invest beyond Tier 2, what is a realistic Tier 3: Contingency Investment we can allocate to strategic initiatives?

What enablement or operations execution and performance triggers should unlock Tier 3 investment?

As the **first** rule of thumb, we must leverage our Tier 1: Current Investment to perform the "high impact" and "low investment" efforts, which are our top priorities. If we continuously recycle our Tier 1 investment effectively, prioritization will automatically approve these initiatives.

The **second** rule is to skew our prioritization to include "high impact" and "high investment" instead of "low impact" and "low investment" efforts. The slant of our tiers in Figure E14 is emblematic of this proactive choice. Higher fundamental maturity and alignment with strategy are worth the investment.

As a **third** rule, approximately 10 to 20 percent of the least favorable strategic initiatives identified should be eliminated. Poor ideas are always floating around; it's unavoidable. The few initiatives we ranked at the bottom are unlikely to be effective even if we prioritize them.

Guardrail 3: Leverage Initiative Investment Map to optimize total enablement investment.

Guardrail 1 and guardrail 2 allow us to define a relatively precise investment requirement for each initiative and the total investment that our company can afford through the three tiers. But we must take one final step to ensure that our final enablement investment decision aligns with all our work through the three planning phases. Why?

Multiple companies I have worked closely with have fallen prey to the athlete-financial management challenge. Year after year, increasing Tier 1 investment flies under the radar without effective redeployment through maturity improvement in skills and effective execution management. Through annual budgeting, companies add Tier 2 new enablement investment on top of a poorly leveraged Tier 1. As a result, the impact of Tier 2 is often just as low because it is only possible to hold Tier 2 investment accountable if we can hold Tier 1 accountable. The result is increased enablement investment and decreased maturity improvement and operations performance for each dollar spent.

I recommend using the **Initiative Investment Map** framework in Figure E15 to ensure that we have a single dovetailed and verifiable enablement investment decision.

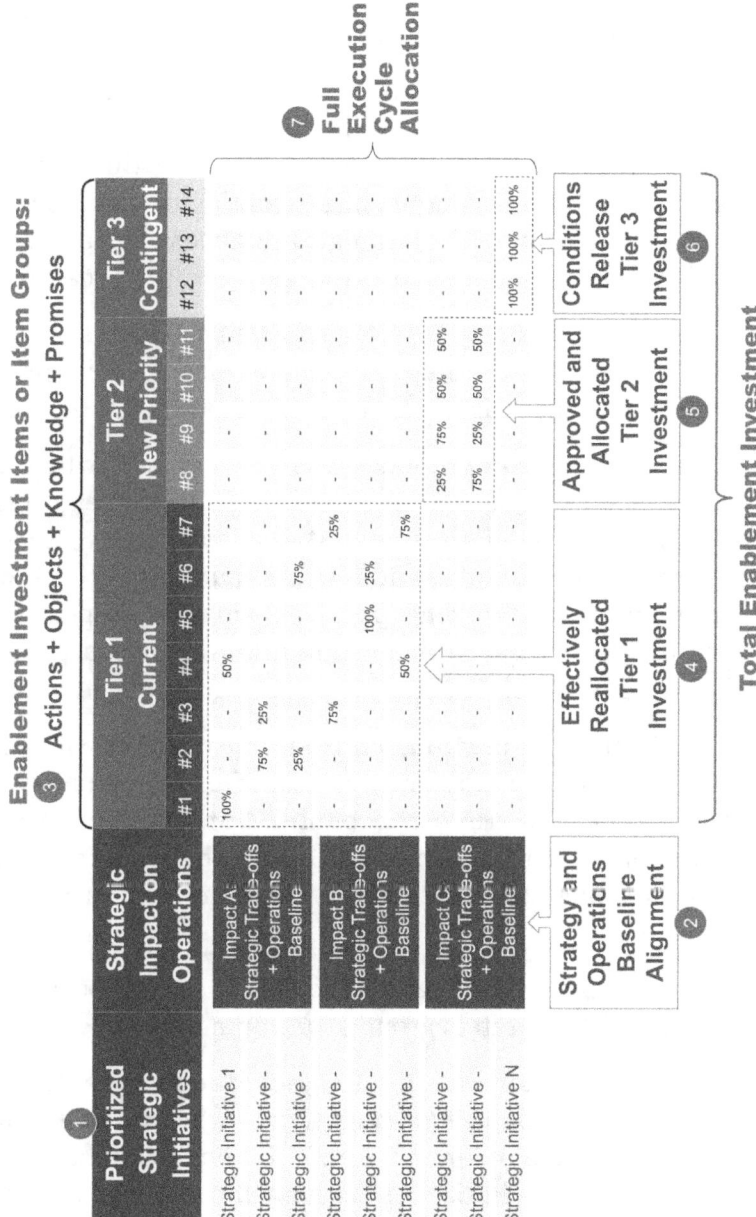

Figure E15. Initiative Investment Map optimizes allocation of enablement investment.

The **first** element of this framework is our prioritized strategic initiatives, which require no additional context.

The **second** element is mapping our strategic initiatives to our strategic trade-offs and operations baseline building blocks. As we wrap up strategic planning, we must ensure that we haven't lost our way through weeks of discussions, debates, and iterations. It is essential to ask ourselves: "Do the steady state definitions of the strategic initiatives align and cover the strategic trade-offs and operations baseline gaps we used to define them?"

If we have lost our way and our strategic initiatives do not produce the desired impact, we must take a step back and revisit our earlier principles. Sadly, individualistic agendas often break this link.

The **third** element is the comprehensive listing of all our critical enablement investment items across all four dimensions and strategic initiatives as columns. The Initiative Investment Map allows us to connect rows of initiatives to columns of investment items spanning actions, objects, knowledge, and promises. We must put all existing and proposed enablement investment items for all strategic initiatives on the board, including niche and commoditized skills, critical assets, and intellectual property.

For a small company, a column might include one resource with a specific skill. For a larger one, we may group similar items, such as people or assets, into the same item group in a column. Our Congruence Architect can make these situational adjustments to ensure that relevant investment items are reflected adequately and make the framework easy to use.

The **fourth** element is mapping the utilization of each Tier 1: Current Investment item to specific strategic initiatives. We must allocate the share of each enablement item or item group to one or more strategic initiatives.

Planning is the perfect opportunity to assess the need to mature current enablement investment. For example, do we have an enablement resource that we invested in for a past initiative but do not have the skills to contribute to any future initiatives? Leaving the mapping for this niche enablement resource as 0 percent across all initiatives helps us objectively assess how to leverage this resource. Misallocating this resource to an initiative may fail both the resource and the initiative.

Yes, planning for an entire company is an emotionally taxing and sensitive exercise.

Similarly, we must perform the same exercise with proposed new enablement items via Tier 2 and Tier 3 investments. The framework's **fifth** and **sixth** elements map Tier 2 and Tier 3 enablement items to strategic initiatives. We must diligently perform the same exercise of mapping utilization to the best of our knowledge based on all the planning analyses we have conducted.

Consider these design questions to map enablement investment items to strategic initiatives:

How effectively can we evolve our operations baseline via strategic initiatives with only Tier 1 investment if we stagger the initiatives and recycle our investment optimally?

How effectively can we evolve our operations baseline by adding Tier 2 investment?

Which initiatives can we place under Tier 3?

Which initiatives will we deprioritize?

The **seventh** element of this framework is accounting for ebbs and flows of utilization of proposed investment items throughout our execution cycle. We must assess the allocation of every enablement investment item throughout the execution cycle rather than at the highest utilization points. We aim to approve only enablement elements slated for close to 100 percent utilization.

If a proposed investment item is a highly niche and expensive skill set that we need exclusively for one strategic initiative that lasts three months, the utilization over a year-long execution cycle is only 25 percent. This indicates that this skill is optimally borrowed from a partner for three months rather than hired as an employee. Borrowing skills or assets is a more investment-efficient path to value creation rather than hiring employees or buying assets in such situations.

Through this systematic approach, we can avoid overstaffing and padding middle layers with supervisors or acquiring equipment and technology with a low return on investment. The Initiative Investment Map provides a rational and structured approach to ensuring the company remains lean and efficient.

Once all seven elements are incorporated and vetted, the Initiative Investment Map forecasts the total enablement investment for our next execution cycle. It feeds the expense side of the financial forecast after overlaying the market price for these enablement investment items. The CFO and finance team can develop expense forecasts by incorporating the market price of the enablement investment items, such as the fully loaded cost for compensation, technology licensing cost, and equipment purchase cost.

Formalizing the impact of strategic initiatives and associated enablement investment allows us to move forward and finalize operations investment decisions.

Principle 3: Formalize operations investments as efficient scaling decisions.

The second half of our company's investment decision is the outlay that goes into running our ever-evolving operations baseline to create value for customers.

Imagine pointing a flashlight at an object and observing the shadow behind it. Our unit-level operations plan is analogous to the object, while the operations investment decision represents the angle at which we shine the light. The shadow reflects the total performance of the operations baseline. The goal of the operations investment decision is to optimize the size of the shadow without making it fuzzy. If the shadow becomes fuzzy, it implies too much or too little operations investment.

There are many similarities between our considerations for making enablement investment and operations investment. Regardless of the reason, all investment is channeled into one or more of our four capability dimensions. Operations and enablement require efficiency considerations where we want to reassess our past investment choices. They both require effective allocation; we must allocate enablement investments to enablement initiatives and operations investments to specific parts of our operations baseline.

The most significant difference between operations and enablement investment is that each specific operations investment decision is perpetual. In contrast, enablement investment is time-bound and recycled when the enablement initiative transitions to steady state.

Things To Remember: Operations Investment

Operations investment is the perpetual capital allocation to scale up or scale down specific building blocks of our operations baseline without introducing incongruences due to excessive or insufficient investment. Operations investment decisions are approximations and must accommodate real-life variances in translating these allocations into expense forecasts.

The following five guardrails will help us develop our operations investment decision. The **Operations Investment Map** in Figure E16 is a comprehensive framework to ensure that our operations investment decisions objectively incorporate these five guardrails.

Guardrail 1: Operations investments must directly link to operations baseline building blocks and functions.

The simplest things can be the hardest. It is important to start operations investment discussions by internalizing "why" we are investing. Operations investment decisions often go wrong because we focus on "what" we are investing in before knowing "why."

Why are we making operations investments?

Operations investment must be directly channeled into the operations baseline building blocks –productized offering, processes, data usage, and management approach – within the core functions that we defined in enablement planning using our flow thinking.

We have all bought something that we saw on TV or the internet because it seemed exciting at the time, but we never ended up using it because we never thought about the application. We have the right to do this with

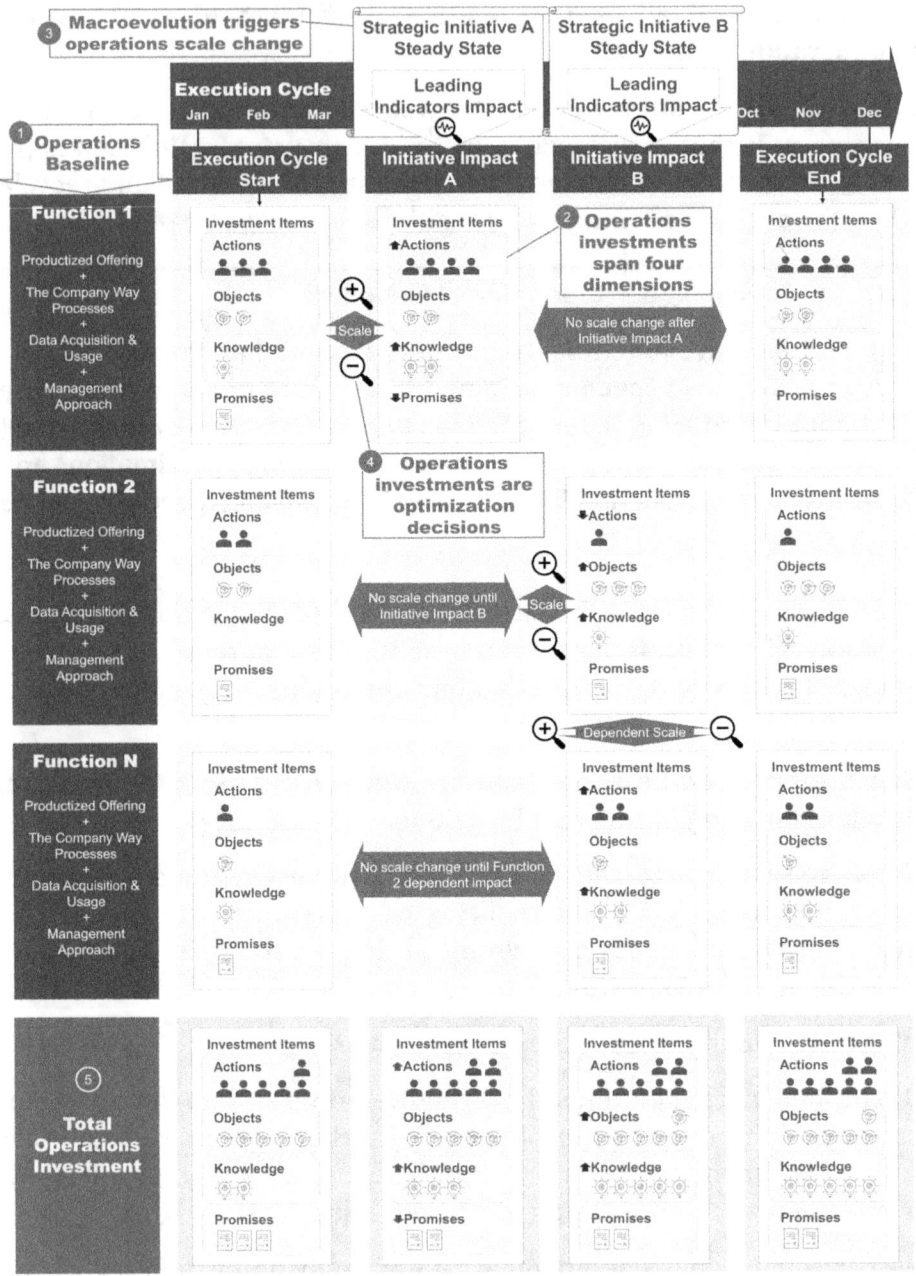

Figure E16. Operations Investment Map enables scale optimization.

personal funds. But it's unacceptable with communal funds, which is what operations investment is.

Starting with decisions such as the number of employees or assets focuses on the "what," not the "why." The context of the investment channels is vital to ensure that our natural biases on what we invest in do not lead us astray. In our framework above, we positioned this guardrail on the left side as an anchor to ensure that every operation's decision is based on a specific reason.

Before putting investment options on the map, we want to understand the function within which investment would sit using our flow thinking rather than historical organizational charts. We must also ensure that every operations investment item ties back to each function's mature operations baseline building blocks. This "why" guardrail alone could have prevented the massive post-COVID excessive hiring followed by layoffs across privately funded technology companies.

Operations investment must be allocated to productized capabilities that create significant and sustainable net positive customer value. Similarly, we need to ensure that operations investment is channeled into mature functional processes or allocated only once processes have evolved.

We want to ensure that data management-related operations investments are tangible ongoing needs instead of solving a short-term tactical challenge. Short-term needs must be part of an enablement initiative in the first place.

From a management approach perspective, we might invest in software for managers and employees to enhance performance management and coaching or a solution that creates ongoing clarity on incentive compensation for each function.

Consider these design questions to relate operations investment to our operations baseline functions and building blocks:

Using flow thinking and focusing on value, what function will the investment item sit in?

How will this investment directly create customer value through our productized offering within each function?

Which processes will this investment be part of within each function?

What data capture and reporting aspects will this investment contribute to in perpetuity within each function?

How will this investment perpetually support or enhance our management approach components within each function?

To prevent creating a bloated organization, we need a robust answer to all these questions to ensure we do not confuse a short-term need for a perpetual one. Moreover, it ensures that our operations investment truly dovetails with the company we are running instead of spending on random ideas we believe might work.

I partnered with a marketing solutions company, where I led strategic planning, among other things. The company believed that its crucial challenge was a need for leads to drive more sales. The sales executive proposed hiring a sales development representative (SDR) manager and a team of SDRs who would create sufficient leads for the sales reps.

It is a plausible idea, and many companies deploy such a lead generation tactic. But beyond that, the proposal lacked an answer to the question: Why would this work at our company? The what-focused investment proposal didn't tie back to existing operations or improvement plans. After several grueling discussions about the importance of framing a strategic initiative that connects the investment and existing operations, the proposal was included in the final operations investment.

After several months of hiring and staffing, this SDR team proved ineffective at creating leads, and eventually, the company terminated those newly hired employees. The reason for this failed investment and heartache for many was that it focused on what the investment was rather than why it was the right investment. In addition, it didn't tie to the company's existing functions or processes. Nor was there an enablement initiative to evolve processes to accommodate the new operations investment.

We want to avoid such a pitfall in our operations investment decision. So, always start by framing our maturing operations baseline building blocks across functions as the first guardrail. Our operations baseline is the reason for our investment, not shiny ideas pulled from thin air.

Guardrail 2: Operations investments span all four capability dimensions.

The second guardrail ensures that "what" we invest in is comprehensive and cohesive. All operations investment items, like enablement investment, fall within our four capability dimensions.

What operations elements will we invest in?

Operations investment falls into four dimensions – actions performed via resources, objects we buy or borrow, knowledge we acquire, or promises we make with external parties. Effective operations investment implies that every investment choice is impactful because they are synergistic and address all necessary dimensions. So, we must catalog the critical operations investment items across functions just like we did for enablement investment.

Consider this design question to frame investment needs across capability dimensions:

What are the specific investment items – actions, objects, knowledge, and promises – necessary for each function to execute optimally across all operations baseline building blocks?

These items must be sourced from documentation of our operations baseline building blocks and strategic initiative steady state definitions that inject improvements during the upcoming cycle. The best version of our company always requires good documentation and adoption of all building blocks and underlying principles. It's likely not mature or well executed if it's not written down, and hence, it's not an optimal item to invest in.

Multiple capability dimensions of the four are likely necessary for each function and building block; other dimensions will prove ineffective without all the required dimensions. To ensure our investment catalog is complete, it is essential to consider the dependency between investment items. A decision to scale in one dimension, such as resources, typically implies that we must also scale in other dimensions to support that first one.

Operations resources for a specific process, such as sales, customer support, or value delivery services, imply operations investment items along the action dimension. Hiring more operations resources in one role implies they perform more actions. However, performing more actions in one role often impacts other roles, such as the supervisory layer for that role, tools or raw materials that might be needed, or information that we might have to invest in complementarily.

Once we have our "why" and "what" constructs in place, we can consider the timing of "when" we need to make operations investments.

Guardrail 3: Operations investments must be triggered by maturity changes.

The timing around investment is the most significant difference between operations and enablement investment.

When will we trigger operations investment?

Operations investments must demonstrate two key timing factors. First, they must be perpetual, not time-bound. Second, operations investment changes must always align with shifts in maturity in the operations baseline triggered by strategic initiatives.

The **first** aspect aligns with the themes throughout our method. We must base our operations investment decisions on the understanding that it is perpetual. Operations investment backfires when we confuse a poorly defined, time-bound enablement effort as ongoing operations or make overly optimistic choices to rely on immature building blocks that create limited intrinsic value. Avoid perpetual investment items that do not have a concrete longer-term rationale.

The **second** aspect around timing is alignment with operations maturity improvements.

Imagine playing a video game where leveling up gets us extra tokens to acquire more potent tools or weapons, allowing us to play a higher standard of the game. More tokens are analogous to unlocking more operations investment to create more value for customers and engage more value creators. Earning the right to play at a higher level in the game is the evolved maturity of our operations baseline via our initiatives, which we must earn.

Scaling without maturity is a house of cards that will crumble. The planning team must agree on the specific maturity improvements that need to be demonstrated by leading indicators in our operations plan to trigger the operations investment changes. Think back to the timing principle of our Chain of Controllability under operations planning. These are the same points in time that our leading indicators tick up in performance when strategic initiatives drive improvements.

Say we want to increase the number of sales reps from five to fifteen because we intend to launch a new capability. The timing of this investment must carefully align with the capability launch. The operations investment must consider potential delays in the launch or changes in expectations of the capability's value close to launch. Hiring and training reps too far ahead can be a poor investment.

Additionally, scaling the number of resources in a role by three times is a maturity requirement game changer. Such a hiring investment must align with the completion of enablement efforts around our sales processes. Too often, companies assume that a scale shift will produce more outcomes, only to fall backward into a management approach and process nightmare. Having ten more reps acting without direction will result in little incremental lagging outcomes and a poor investment.

These decision triggers are illustrated via the vertical columns in our Operations Investment Map framework. As we move from left to right, strategic initiatives are completed, and various parts of our operations baseline are evolving.

The next execution cycle starts exactly where our current execution cycle ends. So, always reserve the first column of our framework for our starting point, which is our current operations investment in our operations baseline.

The remaining columns are our operations investment triggers, which must align with our enablement initiative impact timeline. These triggers directly flow from our operations plans, where we set leading indicator targets and limits and the timeline of impact. Our operations investment triggers align with our operations baseline performance upticks, which we can measure via our leading indicators.

Guardrail 3 allows us to align the impact of strategic initiatives on the operations baseline with the timing of related investment choices.

Consider this design question to set timing guardrails for operations investment:

What are the time triggers to dial up or down our operations investment items in alignment with our strategic initiative impact on our operations baseline?

We do not need to be robotic to remain disciplined. Hiring more sales reps in the example above takes time and requires flexibility. We must be prudent and align an investment, like tripling the number of sales reps, with strategic initiatives that mature management approach and value engine building blocks. A contributing strategic initiative may also include the time-consuming act of hiring and training new sales reps.

Guardrail 4: Operations investments are maturity-based optimization decisions.

Our disciplined, systematic approach using these guardrails will pay off because our investment proposals will not be guesses.

How will we invest? This is our fourth guardrail.

Operations investment decisions are optimization decisions; investing in poor operations is terrible management. So, we must vet operations investments to ensure that each item is allocated to high-value, high-efficiency portions of our operations baseline.

This involves reconsidering existing expenses on the operations baseline that don't need to exist as we mature. Companies often think about cost-cutting as a separate effort compared to investment decisions, which is an immature mindset. Cost-cutting will never be required if our investments are proactively efficient and value-centric.

We developed a unit performance-focused operations plan in Phase 2 precisely for this reason. We want to invest more in mature and high-productivity parts of our operations baseline and limit investment in immature or unnecessary parts. Maturity improvement of our operations baseline is not only an opportunity to add more fuel to the fire but also an opportunity to remove too much wood that is stifling the fire from burning well.

A common requirement for scale rationalization is dimensional changes in our operations due to evolution. Investing more or maturity improvements in one dimension might allow us to scale down on another. Suppose we have evolved our manufacturing processes and want to invest more in objects like automation robots and software. It might also be an opportunity to scale down operations investment in the action dimension by reducing the value creators who perform those actions today.

My recent strategic planning partnership provides a good example. A director who managed a customer onboarding team proposed investing in project managers due to historic value delivery challenges. However, this function already had several technical resources trying to do this work with lower-than-desired effectiveness. The director wanted to hold on to them while investing in project managers. The rationalization of "they are already working too much" didn't address the reality that the hard work highlighted poor processes and misaligned skills. If we approved hiring project managers, we needed to repurpose the poorly utilized investment in technical onboarding resources.

Strategic planning must encourage such emotionally taxing but necessary discussions. Our operations investment items must propose the optimal scale, which may be higher or lower than the present state.

Consider this design question to scale operations investment optimally:

What is the 1) optimal, 2) maximum, and 3) minimum scale for each operations investment item within a function, considering all four dimensions of outlays – actions, objects, knowledge, and promises – and in alignment with the optimal investment timing trigger?

Operating at the optimal and realistic scale ensures that our operations can deliver the leading indicator performance targets we set via operations planning. This answer can be zero for poor or outdated existing investment items, allowing us to recycle investment.

Framing the maximum scale for each item tells us how far we can dial up each without compromising the maturity of our operations baseline. Setting this upper threshold protects us from compromising the unit-level performance in our operations plans.

Lastly, the minimum threshold tells us how far we can dial down on each investment element without wrecking the unit-level performance targets and limits that we set in our operations plans. It considers dependencies on other parts of our operations.

In our solid object and its shadow analogy at the start of this principle, we want to shine the light firmly within a range where the shadow isn't too big and blurry or too small and unrecognizable.

Leveraging this framework keeps us accountable for looking at operations investment as an optimal scale decision instead of a perpetually incremental investment or last-ditch cost-cutting decision. Strategic planning offers a critical juncture to make proactive value-centered operations investment decisions. Companies that go through mass layoffs or major cost cuts likely evaded this scale optimization guardrail over several planning cycles.

I partnered with a company that had purchased software that allowed customer-facing resources to find nice-to-have customer information. However, there were no processes around its application, and it was rarely used. A million dollars sounds like nothing these days, but tiny drops of water fill an ocean. We identified this wasted operations investment item during strategic planning. However, that waste could have been avoided altogether if it had been vetted and deprioritized when initially proposed.

We can build a tabular format of the Operations Investment Map framework that states the optimal, maximum, and minimum scale for each operations investment item. It will connect each investment item to functions and mature operations building blocks, covering all four dimensions. In addition, it will align with strategic initiative impact timing. Then, the CFO and the finance team can directly translate these investment decisions to monetary operations expense figures, just like we did with enablement investment.

Guardrail 5: Company's investment threshold provides a ceiling for operations investments.

Our operations investment decision must be constrained to maintain our company's financial health, just as we did for enablement investments. The CFO owns and manages the company's overall affordability threshold.

In Guardrail 4, we identified a scale range from maximum to optimal to minimum for each investment item. The operations baseline performance can stay true to its maturity and unit-level targets of leading indicators within this range.

To cap our operations investment decision, we must dial each item up or down while remaining within the acceptable range, and we must ensure our total operations investment is kept below the company-wide investment threshold. The Operations Investment Map allows this iterative refinement cycle with the finance team to align on a total operations investment decision.

Operations investment prioritization is different from enablement prioritization. Every relevant operations investment item is critical if it meets guardrails 1 through 4; we only get to dial each up or down. Cutting out any relevant operations item could stall an entire process. For enablement initiatives, we didn't spread investment across all proposed ones. We chose the most impactful and affordable initiatives and cut out the rest because half-initiatives don't improve maturity.

These five guardrails allow us to develop an optimized total operations investment decision that aligns with our strategy, evolving operations baseline, enablement initiatives, and the company's investment thresholds.

Principle 4: Optimally scaled operations baseline completes the strategic plan.

Superimposing our operations investment decision on top of our unit performance-focused operations plan gives us aggregate performance expectations. This leading indicator performance prediction is the company's **Aggregate Operations Plan**. These are the performance predictions required to measure our functions and operations baseline building blocks throughout the execution cycle.

Illustratively, the unit performance operations plan may have framed that an average lead generation resource could find ten leads. If we set the associated operations investment item to ten resources, the company's aggregate operations plan will expect one hundred leads. The practicality of this aggregate number relies entirely on the rigor with which we use our strategic planning principles. A history-based projection could show the same expectation. The difference in our method is its grounding in reality.

> **Things To Remember: Aggregate Operations Plan**
>
> **The aggregate operations plan predicts our operations baseline performance for the upcoming execution cycle. It combines the impact of strategic initiatives on the operations baseline, leading indicators of operations performance, unit-level targets and limits for leading indicators that account for maturity improvements and associated timeline, and operations investment changes over time.**

Creating the aggregate operations plan is necessary because it can be used to manage execution. It articulates each of the elements listed in the definition above. That's all executives, supervisors, and individual value creators require to keep themselves and each other accountable.

This aggregate operations plan is a simple multiplication of each measurement in the unit-level operations plan and the optimal scale figures we land on through our operations investment decision. To visualize the aggregate operations plan in Figure E16, we can build on the unit performance operations plan framework in Figure E11 from Chapter E.3. We superimpose scale decisions from operations investment, resulting in the aggregate operations plan.

Our finalized plan wraps up our strategy-led and operations-focused planning effort. These are the targets to which we will hold ourselves accountable during execution.

Our prioritized strategic initiatives and their corresponding steady states empowered by enablement investment are the driving belts of our operations baseline's macroevolution. The operations investment decision informs how we optimally scale our maturing operations baseline. Leading indicators and associated targets and limits based on the realities of our strategy and operations baseline complete our strategic plan. The CFO can use these strategic planning outputs to create a realistic financial plan.

Principle 5: Strategy-led, operations-focused strategic plan renders a practical financial plan.

In our value-centric mindset, it is essential to understand that money metrics such as revenue and related permutations are not strategic or operational. Calculating revenue is challenging if we consider accounting rules. Recall that it is also notoriously hard to decipher because it is a lagging measurement.

I partnered with a company where executives felt they didn't have a meaningful execution management approach and lost most of their time to perpetual reactiveness. The company relied exclusively on revenue measurements, which were spread across the entire customer relationship length. When the largest customer informed the company that they would not renew for the following year, the revenue metrics showed no change for several upcoming months until the new year started. No reports nosedived even when the largest customer canceled, and value creators didn't feel any urgency to change behavior. Operational measurements were nonexistent. I had to build an operational measurement system from the ground to help this company. We cannot manage execution with financial metrics.

Financial metrics can also create incentive challenges. Imagine a big customer signing a three-year contract, then canceling six months later because the customer wasn't getting what they expected. What if the sales rep blames the offerings and the employees responsible for value delivery services? What if the delivery services-focused employees blame the sales rep for over-promising? Who is accountable for this revenue? There is no good answer because thinking in revenue is a mess, strategically and operationally.

If we live by financial measurements, executives, supervisors, and operations resources will live with this ongoing strife. A company going through an outsized success phase may not feel this measurement strife because monetary measurements going up are always a cause for celebration. At the same time, operations gaps fly under the radar. However, that phase will end when the company outgrows that particular lifecycle stage. Then, living and breathing financial outcomes will backfire for them, too.

Having said that, we need to forecast and track lagging extrinsic outcomes for two reasons – financial management of our company by the CFO and informing investors, especially passive ones who do not wield influence through the board, regarding the company's health. We want to predict how much money will come in and out of the company each day, week, month, and year because we should fund much of our investment with revenue.

In addition to revenue metrics, we likely want to forecast other lagging outcomes such as customer counts, revenue per customer, or customer satisfaction. Using our operations planning approach, all such lagging metrics have one or more leading indicators that give us predictability and controllability.

Forecasting financial outcomes becomes seamless if we use the strategic planning levers we discussed. We can forecast revenue directly from our aggregate operations plan, which is powered by the underlying unit-level operations plan and the scale choices associated with investment items. Our expense forecast flows directly from our enablement and operations investment decisions. This simple but predictive connection between the strategic plan and a financial plan is the silver lining of our persistent focus on the fundamentals we built through the past four chapters.

Poor strategic planning results in limited valuable inputs for the finance team, who will then plan a future based on history, not our strategy or operations maturity. Then, when the company misses those forecasts on the high or low end, there is little clarity on the root cause.

A forecast built on the company's fundamentals avoids this unpredictable and reactive future because we have created a plan anchored on controllable aspects. Isn't it better to put in the extra thinking and analysis ahead of time? A mature operations baseline and planning exercise ensure that performance expectations are practical and predictable before the execution cycle starts. They also protect us from predictable reactivity once execution starts.

Apart from the CFO's cash management and investor reporting needs, we can manage the entire company's execution using our aggregate operations plan, strategic initiative steady state definitions, enablement investment decision, and operations investment decision. Revenue and other extrinsic outcomes will be stellar if we execute these four planning outcomes effectively. If they are not, we can easily trace back to where our maturity changes or execution failed us.

As we wrap up strategic planning, it is worth remembering that we have yet to play the real game – execution.

PART F

Execution Management Aligns Strategy, Operations To Outcomes.

OUR pre-season preparation is now complete. It's time to play.

Any sports team's execution through a season is like an annual execution cycle for a company. Top racing outfits invest in preparing every minute until the lights go off and the first race starts. Such teams have the right drivers, pit crew, top-of-the-line car, and race tactics to execute flawlessly during the season.

Figure F1 reflects this focus shift and pivots the *Congruence*™ method to put execution management in the crosshairs.

Execution management covers two aspects. We complete our macro-evolutionary cycle by executing enablement initiatives to improve our operations baseline. We also effectively execute our ever-improving operations baseline to create customer value.

Through our past execution cycles, we have established a management approach that dictates our people agenda. We also have our value engine, which is how we serve customers. It articulates our customer offering and how to deliver that offering. Together, this forms our operations baseline.

But we can't stop with what we have. We must evolve our operations baseline every execution cycle. We reframed our corporate strategy and

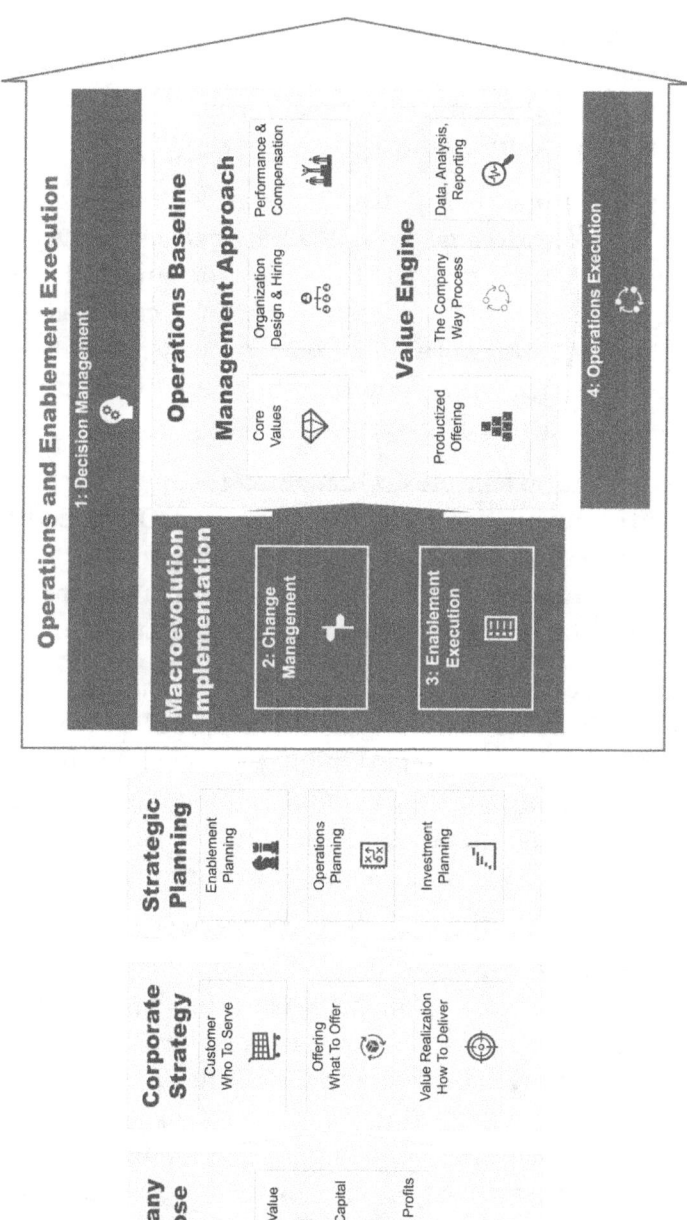

Figure F1. Execution management realizes strategy and operations baseline outcomes.

created a strategic plan to guide our path. Recall that our strategic planning efforts culminated in initiatives to improve the level of congruence in our operations baseline, along with an aggregate operations plan designed to guide the execution of that evolving baseline.

When I was a Six Sigma Black Belt at General Electric, we classified projects into Six Sigma or Nike projects. We followed a structured Six Sigma framework for important efforts. The systematic approach was worth all the mistakes we avoided. But we classified one-off tactical tasks differently. Per the Nike motto, those were "Just Do It!" projects. Evolutionary efforts to improve congruence within our operations and with our strategy and purpose fall in the former bucket.

What makes execution complex is that our company is constantly changing. If we aren't evolving, we are sliding backward. Our execution cycle is our opportunity to climb another level of organizational maturity. It allows us to further evolve our offerings, processes, and management approach, capture incremental customers, and create more value for them.

In our racing season analogy, using the same engine and chassis design from last season is much easier because it requires less work and implies fewer risks. A newly designed engine might have reliability problems; a new aerodynamic design might create unanticipated balance issues. But we have to push our design parameters forward. We can comfortably drive around the track with last year's car, but our competitors will likely be much faster. So, evolutionary change is not optional.

There is one significant difference between a racing season and our company's execution cycle. A racing season runs only nine months. All sports teams have an off-season to recalibrate before the following season. However, our company execution cycle runs all year, and we don't get to stop our value engine at any point. We start each execution cycle with the management approach and value engine that we finished the previous cycle with. So, we must accept the challenge of upgrading our operations baseline seamlessly as the execution cycle progresses.

This reality that we don't get to pause our execution to evolve is the core reason for companies to abandon an evolutionary mindset. If we succumb, the only changes come from reactions to events that hurt the company.

Unfortunately, those reactions are often shortsighted and decoupled from an effective corporate strategy.

Does this mean that we never get to mature rationally and proactively? No! Our macroevolution cycle enables the forethought and discipline to achieve it. Think about execution management as refueling an airplane in mid-air. It is possible with the right approach, skills, and tools.

Let's start by framing what "good" execution management looks like.

Execution Management Maturity Model.

Figure F2 shows our Execution Management Maturity Model. Study the details and consider where your company is on this spectrum.

The last four chapters of the *Congruence*™ method frame execution management levers that we can use to create the value we intended through our strategy, plan, and operations baseline.

The final chapter covers the levers that allow meticulous execution of our ever-evolving operations baseline starting on Day 1 of our execution cycle. This is to achieve the targets we have set through strategic planning.

Prior to that, we will discuss how to execute our strategic enablement initiatives, which will inject improvements into our operations baseline. As the execution cycle progresses, we set more challenging targets because we are counting on improvements to feed in from our enablement initiatives.

We will also cover fundamental levers that allow us to manage execution effectively. We will discuss the importance of effective decision-making at all levels to support execution. Enablement initiatives drive change, and change is difficult. We need a framework to manage change.

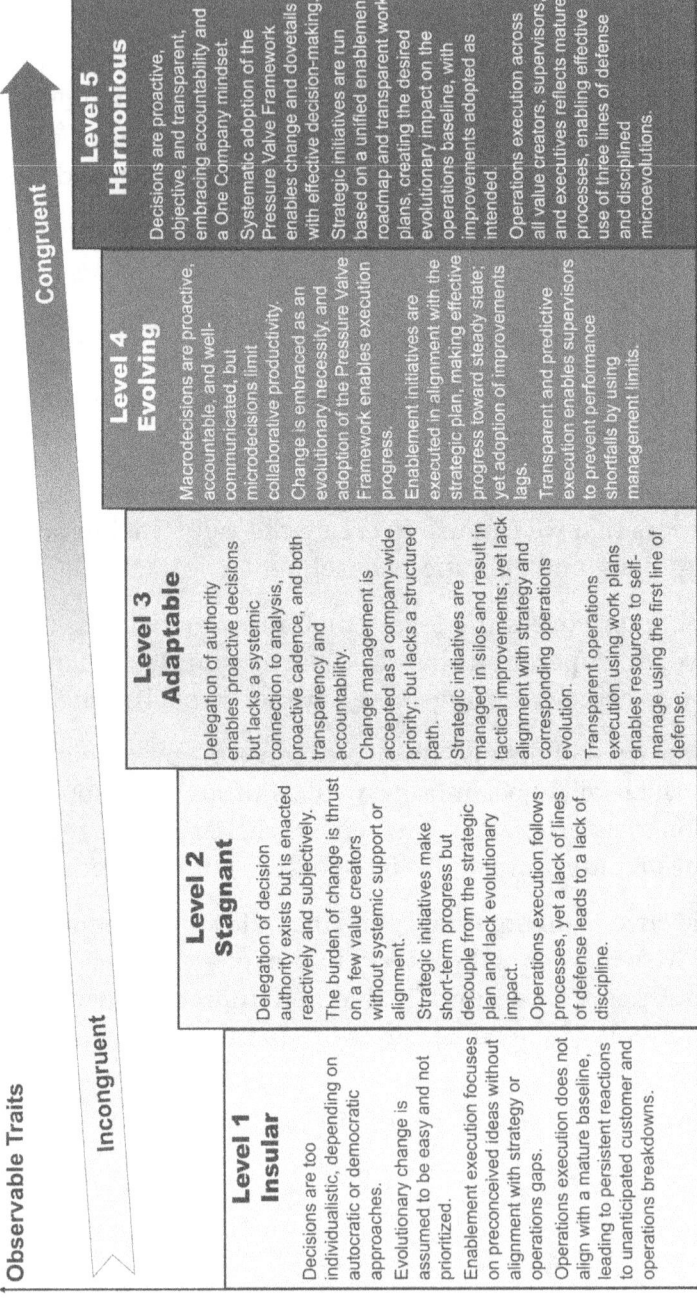

Figure F2. Execution Management Maturity Model.

The left side of our maturity model, *Level 1: Insular,* reflects a company where decision-making remains concentrated among a few individuals. Macroevolution is considered a foregone conclusion and, thus, not prioritized, while enablement efforts revolve around preconceived ideas rather than actual strategy or operations gaps. Operations resources perpetually firefight to resolve unforeseen customer and operational issues without reliance on a mature operations baseline.

As we move to *Level 2: Stagnant,* decision-making authority is delegated to some extent but remains reactive and inconsistent. Responsibility to enact transformational change is unfairly placed on a few top performers without broader systemic support. Strategic initiatives show short-term gains but stray from a cohesive strategic plan and do not drive meaningful maturity improvements. Although process execution is embraced, a lack of operational lines of defense results in persistent performance gaps.

At *Level 3: Adaptable,* forward-looking decisions are made by value creators who are granted the authority. However, systemic gaps limit objectivity and transparency. Although evolution is accepted as an existential requirement, the lack of a formal structure and a silo mindset limits the impact of strategic initiatives. Operations resources execute processes transparently using work plans, which provide a first line of defense for them to self-manage.

By *Level 4: Evolving,* major decisions are proactive, well-communicated, and accountable, though day-to-day decisions that enable effective collaboration are not optimal. Change becomes systematically integral and is supported by a comprehensive framework that enables transformation and adoption. Enablement initiatives align with the strategic plan, yet adoption of improvements remains suboptimal. At this level, supervisors are able to oversee predictive operations execution and address performance gaps using effective management limits.

Reaching *Level 5: Harmonious* allows us to capitalize on proactive, objective, and transparent decisions, with a unified One Company mindset. Systemic change management levers enable the adoption of evolutionary efforts and complement sound decision-making. Implementation of strategic initiatives stays in lockstep with an effective strategic plan and injects the intended evolutionary impact into the operations baseline. Operations execution follows a mature baseline, and effective use of a complete suite of lines of defense optimizes value creation and capital efficiency.

Execution management implies bringing all our value creators onto the field. Recall that a value creator may be an employee or a partner. Enablement and operations resources may be employees or partners, and that choice is coded into our organization design and processes based on our strategy, strategic plan, and strategic initiatives.

Under Part B: Management Approach, we covered the importance of two resource types – enablement and operations resources. Throughout execution management, we will see the importance of delineating between these two groups, whether they are people or assets. Value creators who own and execute enablement initiatives must think and work differently from those who manage and execute our operations. Without this differentiation, our enablement initiatives will likely fail to evolve our operations baseline, and our operations baseline will suffer from a lack of execution discipline.

The concept of improving our operations baseline via our enablement initiatives is simple. But achieving it is always challenging. It requires discipline and change management expertise from our Congruence Architect and all enablement resources.

Operations resources, supervisors, and senior executives must be disciplined and execute according to the spirit of our operations baseline. They must also embrace a change mindset and support the enablement resources in injecting improvements into the operations baseline. The board, CEO, Congruence Architect, and senior executives must enable a system that promotes effective decision-making and embraces evolutionary changes.

With these responsibilities in mind, let's dive into the first component of Part F: Execution Management.

F.1
SYSTEMATIZE DECISION MANAGEMENT TO TURBOCHARGE PRODUCTIVITY.

EVERYTHING we do professionally is either an action or a decision. There is nothing else. Actions lead to decisions, and decisions lead to actions. Actions intertwined with decisions help us reach outcomes. Without coherent decisions, actions won't lead to desired outcomes. Every execution cycle involves thousands of small and big decisions. Some decisions lead to new actions, and others do not.

Consider these reflection questions to internalize the importance of decision frameworks:

Are we relying on a few overpowering personalities to make all our decisions?

Are our small and large decisions competing and conflicting with each other, resulting in a cacophony of unproductive actions?

To enable mature and coherent actions throughout the company, our decisions must be congruent, for which a systemic decision management approach is a prerequisite.

A robust decision-making approach builds trust and objectivity while saving eons of lost time and investment in circular discussions and disjointed actions. It drives productivity of every dollar we invest and creates positive outcomes. The success of our enablement and operations actions depends on the effectiveness of our decision-making.

In our era of tools, many help us access and share information quickly. Others give us reminders to act. But we are also bombarded by notifications.

We stare at gadgets and perform digital activities for many hours of the day. "Smombies" is a word coined to describe our obsession with tools. It is short for "smartphone zombies."

Are these tools making our actions more decision-ready? Some are, and some are not. It depends on how we use them.

Management experts will tell us to shut off emails and focus. Successful business leaders boast about never attending meetings. We wouldn't disagree with these sentiments. But mere mortals boast obscure measures like, "I have two hundred unread emails!" "I respond to messages within the hour!" or "My meeting calendar is full for the rest of the week!"

There is a disconnect between conventional wisdom and what happens in real life.

Slack, a popular messaging platform, frames its mission as "Make work life simpler, more pleasant and more productive." Sure, Slack is easy and fun to use. We can share an incredible volume of information. But what happens to the words, pictures, and files that we share? Is there any evidence of tangible collective productivity improvements? Are we piling more information onto each other? Most senior executives and supervisors I have spoken to find such channels distracting. Why the disconnect?

Actions do not constitute outcomes. Regardless of how many meetings we attend or emails we write, it is meaningless if those actions don't result in relevant outcomes. The path to outcomes involves decisions.

Work environments face significant inefficiencies, starting with never-ending meetings. A lack of decision-making and ownership structures usually worsens matters, leading to more meetings. When do we do actual work, such as thinking, reading, and writing? Endless discussions without progress stifle strategic and operational maturity.

Strong decision-making attains outcomes with fewer actions. It eliminates red tape and perpetual revisiting of the same topics, which causes discussion fatigue and a sense of hopelessness. A well-implemented decision-making system that allows the company to self-manage seamlessly is a game-changer. It simplifies day-to-day decision-making and rules of engagement.

Both enablement resources that run time-bound initiatives and operations resources that execute on our operations baseline need systemic support via decision management tools. Inefficiencies in both groups are often a symptom of a lack of rules of engagement.

We will cover four levers that collectively create a holistic decision-making structure to drive better outcomes. The four levers are 1) delegation of authority, 2) formal one-on-ones, 3) decision and communication ladder, and 4) collaboration technique. We must use these levers to systematize decision-making.

Principle 1: Embrace delegation of authority as decision empowerment.

In line with our Comparative Advantage Ecosystem mindset, outcomes are most easily achieved if experts make decisions.

Delegation of Authority describes allocating permissions to make decisions based on predefined criteria. A company that doesn't empower experts remains autocratic or democratic and thus unproductive. The intent is not to exclude individuals or force inclusiveness but to formalize the lowest threshold of expertise necessary to decide on topics and, therefore, improve efficiency.

> **Things To Remember: Delegation of Authority**
>
> **Delegation of authority creates zones where different experts have unilateral permission to make decisions based on topical expertise and accountability.**

Such zones and allocation of authority are unique to each company and must be framed based on the skills built into our mature organization design. CEOs won't be successful if all decisions go through them. Likewise, senior executives won't be successful if all decisions go through their peers or the CEO. Many topics could stay out of a CEO's or other executives' zone to empower other experts.

A CEO can delegate hiring decisions around skill-based roles. A Comparative

Advantage Ecosystem and mature hiring will lean on skills interviews and depth of experience. Supervisors and senior executives can handle this. A mature performance management approach must tackle personnel decisions without escalation at every turn. The system self-manages performance if an objective human resources executive and Congruence Architect have developed a robust performance management approach.

While a CEO is a great asset to manage top customer relationships, getting involved with customer relationships too often isn't optimal. Depending on the company's size, the CEO or sales executive's micromanagement of customers beyond the top few reflects a lack of confidence in sales and account management value creators and revenue-generating operations roles.

A CEO owns the corporate strategy but needs to delegate the development of corporate strategy and planning to the Congruence Architect and other playmakers. Delegating the development stages enables the CEO to own the strategy instead of trying to contribute analytical components and even risking injecting bias due to investor pressure.

A company will always have several significant initiatives. Once initiatives are defined and scoped as part of strategic planning, we must delegate the decision during execution to appropriate senior executives and supervisors.

Through such proactive allocation of decision authority, we align the quality of decisions with skills and expertise and transparently map accountability of decisions to specific roles and individuals. Incrementally, decisions range from company-level strategic trade-offs to day-to-day value creation choices. The efficiency of operations and enablement resources depend on their empowerment to string together actions without involving superiors too often.

For instance, each enablement initiative has an owner and a few stakeholders we identified through strategic planning. We delegated this group of value creators the authority to plan and execute the initiative while being held accountable for its completion.

Similarly, operations resources, supervisors, and senior executives involved in process execution must leverage the authority granted to them via process design. For example, if a sales rep wants to send a heavily discounted proposal to a customer, it may require approval from a supervisor. Conversely, we incentivize smaller discounts and streamline operations by empowering the sales rep to discount the sale price minimally without approval.

Consider these design questions to enable effective and productive decisions via delegation of authority:

What are the expertise and accountability zones of senior executives and supervisors where they are empowered to make unilateral decisions?

What are the day-to-day decisions that enablement and operations resources are empowered to make on their enablement initiatives and processes, respectively?

Delegation of authority is necessary to drive decision-making. However, all value creators need effective coaching and issue-resolution support to harness their authority. Formal one-on-ones address this.

Principle 2: Formal one-on-ones double-up as a decision forum.

We introduced formal one-on-ones in Chapter B.4 as a lever to manage performance expectations and ongoing evaluations. Decision management is the second application of formal one-on-ones.

Value creators interact with superiors often, whether in person or virtually. Some interactions involve workers asking clarification questions or for tactical help. Others involve coaching on skills and offering advice on role-specific challenges. But these are typically ad hoc and insufficient to drive decisions and outcomes. Instead, value creators and supervisors must leverage structured, cadence-based formal interactions called one-on-ones to optimize decision-making.

Informal one-on-ones are popular because they require no work. Unfortunately, they often become glorified venting sessions to talk poorly about customers or other individuals because they are treated as personal conversations rather than professional ones. It is a missed opportunity that could be an intentional decision forum that moves the company in a positive direction.

Cadence-based, structured, documented one-on-ones serve as bottleneck relievers and opportunities for escalations. It allows employees or partners to plan and prepare to highlight significant challenges they cannot solve or require help with. Value creators must prepare and present options and demand decisions from supervisors or executives.

We must design formal one-on-ones to readily identify outstanding future decisions, which may otherwise be ignored until it's too late. One-on-ones force value creators to use the forum as a deadline to present decision options. These discussions do not happen naturally in most companies; structured one-on-ones enable them.

Structured one-on-ones also give value creators predictability and control over their time. Supervisors shouldn't use ad hoc interactions to change priorities. In alignment with our performance management approach, changing goalposts too often leads to an unproductive environment where value creators are always reactive.

Consider this design question to structure formal one-on-ones:

Has the organization built a systemic decision forum of at least one documented and forward-looking monthly vertical check-in between every value creator and supervisor to support issue resolution and decisions?

Additionally, we must avoid two common mistakes.

First, ensure that one-on-one check-ins don't devolve into backward-looking progress discussions. Execution environments that lack work tracking dilute one-on-ones into reactive and ineffective work progress conversations. Instead, we should cover such details through the normal course of executing strategic initiatives or operational processes.

Second, a common misconception or excuse to circumvent this formal forum is the mindset that "it is unnecessary to wait for such formal one-on-ones to discuss major challenges or make key decisions." On the contrary, the lack of structured, forward-looking decision-making that formal one-on-ones enable creates an illusion that reactive problem-solving is the only option. In these cases, one-on-ones likely already degraded into informal conversations.

One-on-ones complement other decision levers and reduce reactive and unprepared decision discussions. They encourage enablement and operations resources to proactively seek advice or approval on decisions to drive outcomes efficiently.

Decisions made during one-on-ones need to be communicated or may require further escalation. A decision and communication ladder offers an organizational forum to address that.

Principle 3: Decision and communication ladder enables transparency.

Have you been part of an organization where senior executives and supervisors spend significant time preparing for one big meeting after another? Senior executives may be unavailable for forward-looking decisions several weeks before a board meeting. Other internal executive meetings and all-employee meetings also require preparations. These meetings are essential.

However, the availability of critical decision-makers to run the business is also important. Therefore, every company must build an efficient decision-making and communication cadence that minimally involves three engagement types.

First, even with effective delegation of authority, many decisions cross the zones of delegated authority and need multiple decision-makers to collaborate. Every company needs a core group of decision enablers to make complex and multi-zonal decisions. This group includes key personnel with delegated authority and many key contributors involved in strategy development and planning. Too small a group implies that we are not delegating and inclusive enough. Too large a group suggests that we have passengers with limited authority in a practical sense.

These decision enablers must be hands-on and participate in a periodic, structured session to assess the company's ongoing purpose, strategy, and operations alignment. The optimal owner of this forum is the Congruence

Architect. If well executed, this executive decision meeting becomes a year-round recalibration that connects strategy development and planning with execution throughout the year. Such a decision meeting allows the group to assess the progress of strategic enablement initiatives, assess continued alignment with strategy, and escalate and resolve operations breakdowns.

Like formal one-on-ones, this forum enables proactive decision-making and communication at a company level. These cadence-based meetings are not intended to be tactical and retrospective conversations. In this age of ubiquitous access to information, decision enablers must independently review operations and financial reports. A good executive decision meeting requires prior problem-solving and insight generation, where decision options are prepared ahead of live conversations. The Congruence Architect must moderate preparation, execution, and follow-through. Unstructured, on-the-fly discussions are counterproductive.

Second, every company has a board of directors. Independence and expertise characterize its effectiveness, as we articulated in Part A. An effective board will offer the CEO and senior executives the necessary thought partnership to make difficult decisions and provide a constructive accountability forum. Before formalizing decisions that pertain to the alignment of purpose, strategy, and operations, executives must engage the board for constructive feedback. Interacting with the board using a mindset of "share the best version of the good news and hide everything else" implies an imbalance in stakeholder incentives.

Third, all-hands engagements are an excellent opportunity to communicate major decisions broadly and transparently. In a congruent ecosystem, such information is equally consumable by investors, customers, and partners. Feedback from all stakeholders only leads to better decisions and actions. We want to instill awareness about progress and challenges transparently without spin. Remember that employees work on all the details; they already know. Partners run their own companies and work closely with employees. Customers can sense the reverberations of our company's realities through the value they consume. Small investors are privy to the same information as large investors on the board. Transparency about options and decisions is always optimal.

All stages of this engagement sequence cover the same topics and require similar information tailored to different audiences. Too often, these events are scheduled around key personnel's individual conveniences or ad hoc external events such as conferences. This peppers these highly time-consuming events all over the yearly calendar. Whether it's financial data, the status of strategic initiatives, or analyses to support decisions, each event requires the latest information. Scattering them across the calendar makes preparation activities a perpetual time and mind-share consumption for decision-makers. It also limits the quality of problem-solving and related decision-making due to fatigue from these repetitive events.

Effective decision-making requires us to create a ladder for such events where we set a purposeful and firm cadence to lead from one to the next in quick succession. This allows us to create an information ladder and limit redundant meeting preparation. Figure F3 illustrates a decision ladder using the levers in this chapter.

Such a coordinated and intentional approach reduces the time between these decision-making and communication events, allowing us to focus more on problem-solving and structuring decisions for each ladder of meetings.

Operations reporting, related analyses, strategic initiative status reviews, and escalations should ladder up from formal one-on-ones, where we make individual-level decisions. The executive decision meetings enable discussions that require higher authority and visibility. Beyond that, board meetings offer a higher decision layer. Finally, we can share key decisions and insights more broadly.

We can schedule each ladder over a three-week period each quarter. Then, for the remaining two months of a quarter, formal one-on-ones can lead directly to monthly executive decision meetings, where we focus on enablement, operations execution, and connectivity with strategy.

Consider this design question to develop a mature decision and communication ladder:

What is our streamlined and effective decision-making and communications ladder, from one-on-one meetings to executive problem-solving and decision meetings to a board-level meeting culminating in employee, partner, investor, and customer communication?

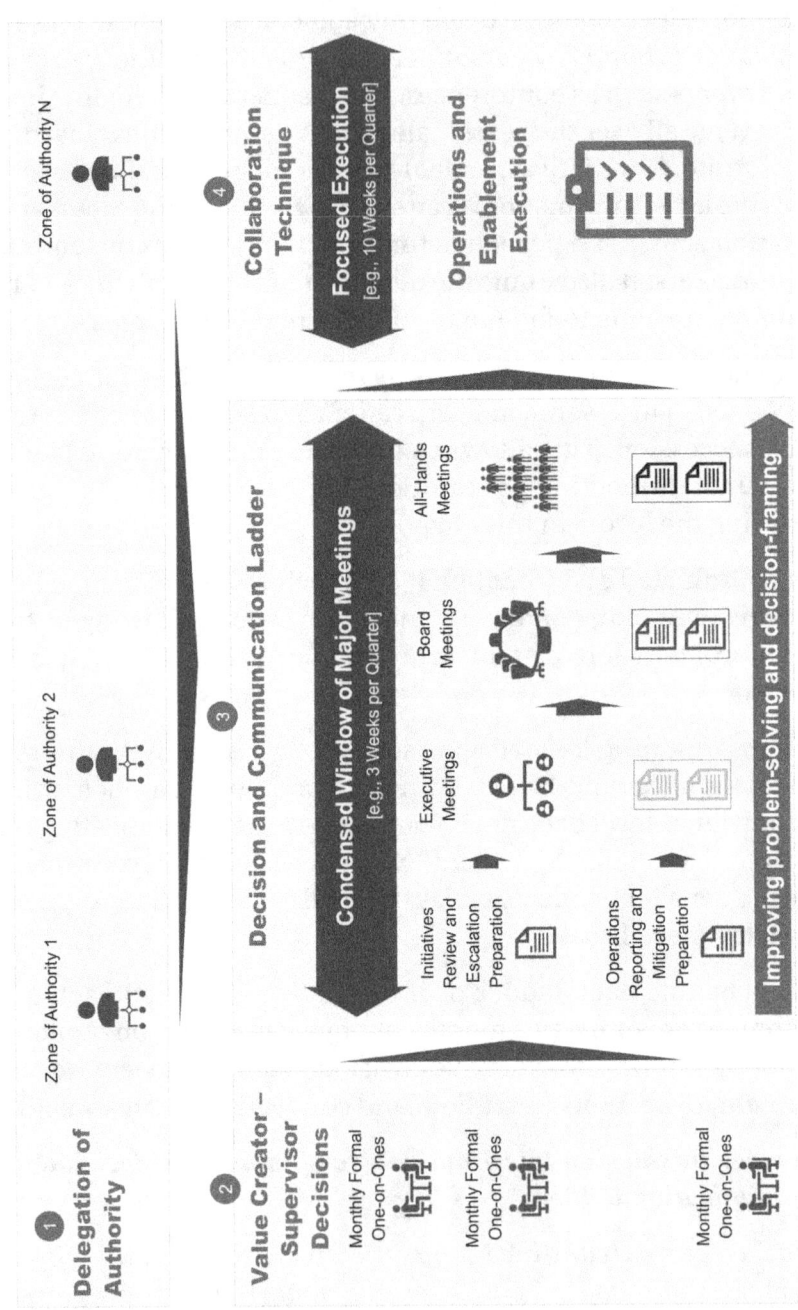

Figure F3. Decision management levers enable productive execution.

Such a cadence quarantines all major meetings into a small window of time and avoids the perpetual rework of the same information. This also allows all resources to use the remaining time to focus on execution, which drives operational momentum, sharpens our problem-solving and decision-making, and improves productivity at all levels.

Principle 4: Collaboration techniques differentiate productive organizations.

The first three levers enable structured, formal decisions. To frame structured decisions that supervisors and executives can choose from, ongoing daily activities must progress. We need to set guardrails around how value creators interact in day-to-day work, which includes a myriad of microdecisions. I call this lever the **Collaboration Technique**.

Conventionally, presenteeism implies that an employee could be at work without performing productively due to sickness, exhaustion, personal reasons, or lack of motivation. This is not optimal, and this challenge has risen to the top of productivity concerns in post-COVID virtual work settings. In our method, management approach levers address motivation concerns.

What if the ailment is a lack of organizational governance, where value creators are present, attend meetings, and respond to emails without tangible work products? We can stretch presenteeism to cover situations where face time and unproductive activities are proxies for work quality. This version of presenteeism can affect all value creators. It leads to an ecosystem heavy on activities but low on outcomes.

Collaboration must lead to effective decisions to move initiatives and operations forward. We must minimally embrace two collaboration techniques: memorializing actions and decisions and adopting a SWAT team mentality. These techniques become even more important as we increasingly work with employees who don't physically sit beside us.

Memorialization is the first collaboration technique.

A head of strategy whom I partnered with described their core challenge in one phrase: "lack of memorialization." Many of the company's discussions and decisions lacked any documentation trail. Unfortunately, "documentation" often evokes the same emotion as "taxes" in the modern workplace. Such environments usually dedicate minimal effort to framing foundational decisions and choices. This tendency frequently leads to revisiting the same decisions and discussions with little forward momentum because we forget undocumented history. Repeating past discussions costs us exponentially more time and resources than a few minutes to write conversations down.

Ecosystems that don't set firm expectations on written preparation for interactions and substantiation of analyses and recommendations limit individual and collective productivity. The same unpreparedness creeps into all activities, including customer value creation.

So, we must set company-wide expectations around documentation quality and behaviors that precede and follow all collaboration events. Collaboration always seeks to arrive at large or small decisions and requires prepared inputs. We might solve a problem, agree on a plan, or address potential risks. The collaboration may not be necessary if we aren't committed to documenting the before, during, and after.

We may choose any one of the hundreds of tools available today. The critical part is the quality and comprehensiveness of the ideas, how they relate to each other, and how well they allow us to solve problems and enable decisions.

Consider these design questions to set memorialization expectations for all value creators:

What are the minimal inputs to each collaboration event?

How do we memorialize the collaboration event to avoid losing value from the interaction?

How does each collaboration arrive at decisions?

Who should memorialize decisions and discussions?

How must decisions and follow-through actions be managed?

How long must critical decisions hold before we revisit them?

Bureaucracy is not our goal. We want to drive deeper thinking and analysis and limit poor ideas and indiscipline from consuming resources. We wish to avoid decision paralysis due to a lack of structure and preparation. In addition to memorialization, we must use our resources efficiently.

A SWAT team mentality is the second collaboration technique.

It's never optimal to have too many cooks in the kitchen. Value creators must discuss critical problems and effectively make decisions without big gatherings. This implies operating in small groups without drawing too many resources because roles are skill-based in our Comparative Advantage Ecosystem.

The first decision-management tool delegates authority. Similarly, only necessary experts must collaborate to make decisions without a committee of observers. If done effectively, this will drastically reduce meetings and limit democratic tendencies, resulting in more objective decisions.

However, small groups must not operate in a vacuum either, staying true to our One Company mindset. SWAT teams must communicate decisions and discussions broadly in a format that others can consume and contribute to, which circles back to the criticality of memorialization. Otherwise, small groups making fast decisions is akin to going rogue or operating in a silo. We must allow the rest of the company to stay aligned without verbal debriefs. If we resort to communicating progress verbally, we create another meeting, which invalidates the entire purpose of a SWAT team mentality.

If we are remodeling our house, we want the owners to design and plan it without involving the neighbors in all discussions. But we want to ensure the neighbors are on board with noise issues and blocked streets. As simple as this analogy is, workplace collaboration typically veers to one extreme or the other. We want to balance the efficient use of resources, which requires effective communication of decisions to enable others to operate efficiently.

Our four fundamental decision management levers are necessary to move beyond an early company's lifecycle stage, where founders make all decisions. We must enable value creators to seamlessly make and contribute to decisions in order to successfully execute increasingly complex enablement initiatives and sophisticated operations.

However, no two people have the same worldview. Such diversity in thought makes decision-making and alignment difficult, especially around enablement initiatives that drive evolutionary change. So, let's discuss change management.

F.2
EMBRACE CHANGE TO ENABLE
MACROEVOLUTIONS, MICROEVOLUTIONS.

IN this final part of our method, we enable and manage all value creators to execute the enablement initiatives and operations activities for which they are responsible. Change management is the backbone that imprints enablement efforts into operations execution so that our company can stay on the evolutionary path.

As our company grows and a broader spectrum of employees and partners are involved, the incentives of value creators also broaden. Additionally, our value engine will need to serve more customers and their increasingly divergent needs. Supporting diverse incentives and needs through maturity improvements in our offerings and operations requires systemic guardrails to ensure the company can move toward its strategy and purpose.

Through strategic initiatives, we will fundamentally improve our operations baseline. Process governance, analysis, and reporting will also trigger microevolutions that inject improvements. Our operations resources embrace those improvements to execute at higher productivity, quality, transparency, or other relevant qualifiers. These macroevolutions improve congruence across our operations and with our strategy and purpose.

The catch is human beings don't just embrace improvements created by others. We tend to be stubborn and stuck in our ways. Some human beings are motivated to self-evolve towards a greater purpose. Others prefer the comfort of the current state. Yet others prefer to evolve in the direction of their own choice. Some might like to evolve things so much that nothing can take root before the next idea comes up. In short, our evolutionary agenda is habitually challenging in an ecosystem with divergent personal incentives.

To evolve, we must change. Our evolutionary mindset will always be challenging because change is hard. To embrace big and small changes and move together collectively, we must set expectations and build structures that enable change intentionally. That's **Change Management**.

Forward-looking evolution is significantly easier than fixing past sins.

My entire career has been a kaleidoscope of change programs, and it's incredible how often change efforts fail despite honest intentions from all parties involved. The primary reason is that most change programs are reactive and too late, accumulating too much improvement debt. Change efforts prove too little too late.

I have performed several challenging company-level surgeries over the years, and a turnaround is nearly unachievable. By the time a company is in a turnaround mindset, the fundamentals have been left unattended for far too long. The biggest reason for the disintegration of fundamentals is the failure to embrace an evolutionary change mindset early on.

Companies in these situations choose to fix obvious symptoms far too long while deep wounds fester and incongruences continue to build. Gluing together a broken vase is a theoretical possibility; in my experience, it is just too many shards to reassemble. I have tried enough times to strongly advise a proactive evolutionary mindset from the get-go. To build the best version of our company, we must choose the path of evolution that improves alignment between building blocks across the company as quickly as possible, regardless of the discomfort that comes with change.

Principle 1: Set expectations using the Pressure Valve Framework.

After racking my brain for years to figure out how change programs can be effective, I arrived at a framework to drive change in any scenario. The framework builds on two ideas of change. The first is that hardship is necessary to enable change, and embracing hardship helps us set the right expectations around change. The second is that change's effectiveness always correlates with the weakest portions of the effort.

Hardship is the core enabler of change.

Of the three forms of rocks on earth, igneous and sedimentary rocks are the original forms. The third type is metamorphic rocks. The dictionary definition of metamorphism is "alteration of the composition or structure of a rock by heat, pressure, or other natural agency." These evolved rocks are formed through the transformation of igneous and sedimentary rocks with the natural application of extreme pressure and temperature.

The evolution of living organisms follows the same theme. Demanding environments allow an organism to become better at adapting to that environment.

Every fitness instructor I have taken classes from would say, "Pain is gain," "If you aren't uncomfortable, you might not be using a large enough weight," and "Don't stop now; change is happening just when you want to stop!"

This all seems obvious. But then, why do most companies assume that change efforts will sail smoothly to the end and everyone will be holding hands and singing throughout?

Take any major policy issue that any country has kicked around for decades with many charismatic politicians promising results. Unfortunately, most politicians fail to make changes stick because they pander and do not communicate that change requires discomfort and compromise.

The good thing is that a company is not a democracy, as we framed through the Comparative Advantage Ecosystem mindset in Chapter B.2. Topical experts and delegation of authority enable decision-making and accountability. Effective communication of expectations is necessary for a corporate setting to ensure that behaviors align despite divergent incentives.

It took me a decade and a half of intensive transformational experiences to internalize and evangelize the mindset necessary to drive change. Until then, I was ashamed to admit that change was difficult because I was trained to think otherwise, and that difficulties reflected my weaknesses. In order to make progress with our evolutionary mindset, we must embrace the reality that hardship is the core enabler of change. A counterargument is just naiveté.

Change impact correlates with the weakest portions of enablement efforts.

My second core epiphany around change management is that the impact of change always correlates with the least effective part of the strategic initiative. Conversely, the most effective execution portions have a limited effect on the quality and adoption of the change.

Does this mean that if we work hard and perfect our responsibility in a change effort, the quality of change may not correlate with our work? Yes. If a single other portion of the initiative is poorly run, the impact of the overall change correlates with that weaker portion.

Early in my career, I led the operations design portion of an enormous transformation effort at a large wholesale distribution conglomerate. My firm had several teams like mine on the ground. First, my team spent months redesigning the company's processes and roles. Then, we worked with software-focused resources to build that design into new software intended for thousands of employees. The entire design and build were reviewed and approved many times by many stakeholders.

There was one last step left – let the client employees use what scores of value creators collaborated to create. My firm's security access team was also part of this strategic initiative. Despite weeks of rational discussions, the security access team decided that the best way to let clients start using the new software was to give all of them full access. Unfortunately, this team didn't internalize the concept of roles, as we covered in Chapter C.2. The introduction to the client was complete chaos. Many employees and supervisors were confused about why they could use all the options they saw on screen. Others started using all the bells and whistles, breaching the publicly traded company's financial controls.

One very narrow set of decisions and actions by a small group of individuals resulted in the client questioning the entire initiative. This is a typical example of how change programs fall apart; the least effective portions dictate impact.

I arrived at the Pressure Valve Framework when I internalized that hardship is the core enabler of a change and that change impact correlates with the weakest portion of enablement efforts. The Pressure Valve Framework is a practical concept I developed to prepare CEOs and executives for the seriousness and complexity of successfully achieving change.

The Pressure Valve Framework.

It may be the engineer in me. My mental model about change management is a water management apparatus illustrated in Figure F4. This simple view encapsulates the three core elements of a change management effort.

Water is the ubiquitous source of our lives and is as fluid as human emotions and incentives. It flows to wherever gravity allows it or other external pressures direct it. We have all experienced a water leak to know that there is little controlling its flow unless it's well contained. Human behavior is not very different. It needs to be channeled for collective benefit. The levers we covered under Part B: Management Approach and Part C: Value Engine does so at a company level.

Each strategic initiative we framed through planning is intended to close the associated operations baseline gaps, which achieves a steady state that reduces incongruences between building blocks and improves alignment with strategy. This improvement is akin to an increase in the water level in the tall vertical portion of our apparatus, and the desired level mark is the expected steady state. This change in water level is the **first** element – the change impact.

Since strategic initiatives are intended to enable much more significant improvements and, thus, changes, we will discuss them throughout this chapter. However, the same principles apply at a smaller scale when microevolutions are initiated through process breakdowns or analytical findings around operations execution, as we will see in Chapter F.4.

The **second** element is the change effort, which includes a detailed execution plan for the enablement initiative and its flawless execution. The piston on the right side of our visual symbolizes this effort. The water

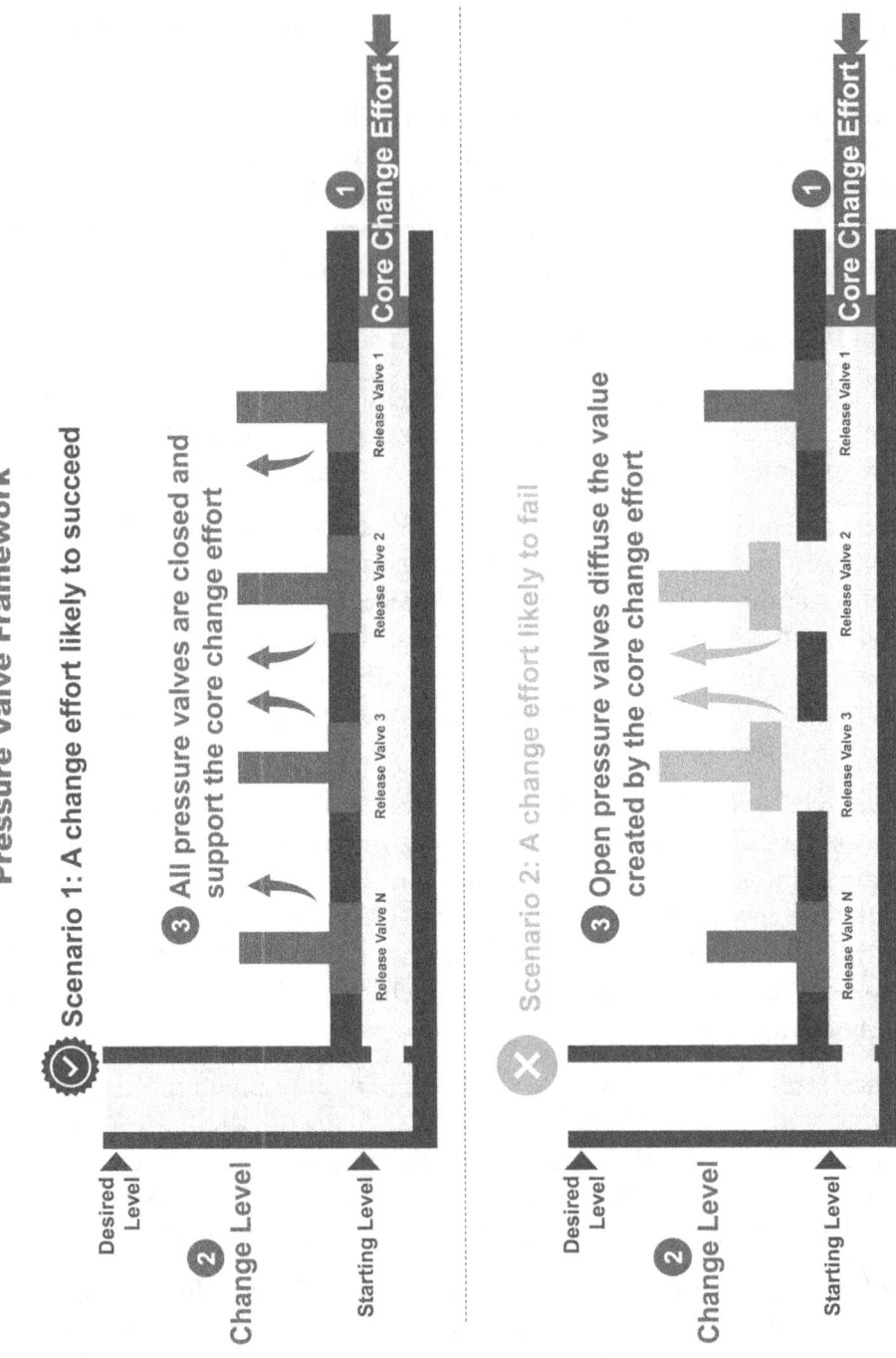

Figure F4. Pressure Valve Framework empowers change management.

level in our apparatus or the resulting steady state of our initiative doesn't happen because we wish it would or because someone announced it is the new normal. There is always work that needs to be done to enable that steady state.

In the next chapter, we will dive into how to manage an effective enablement initiative. For now, let's say that a poorly run enablement initiative will imply that the overall change will not take effect and that we are unlikely to reach the desired state. Think of this scenario as a piston that doesn't apply enough pressure to push the water higher in our apparatus. Regardless of any other factors, poor management and execution are common potential failure points.

The **third** element of change management is pressure valves. Pressure valves are catastrophic risks in achieving the steady state of our strategic initiatives. Over the years, I have noticed that the word risk is often watered down and not very actionable. They also do not relay our second change expectation – impact correlates with the lowest impact portion of the initiative.

So, I insist that we use pressure valves as a more actionable way of thinking about how an initiative can fail. In our water apparatus, each pressure valve becomes an escape route that releases all the pressure our enablement initiative creates to move the water level.

Any given pressure valve has the power to negate all of our change efforts. The list of potential pressure valves spans all the topics in this book. Through the next few principles, we will internalize the importance of pressure valves and how to address them to ensure the highest likelihood of success for each enablement initiative or microevolution effort.

Principle 2: Genuine alignment on steady state definition is the first pressure valve.

The first pressure valve for any change effort is the clarity and depth of the steady state definition and the level of alignment on that definition. In other words, a change program's most common failure point is the lack of clarity and alignment around the steady state.

First, categorizing a change effort as a success or failure requires an objective definition of the steady state. Most projects lack a clear articulation of what a "good" steady state looks like, and this often muddies the reality of whether the desired change is ever realized. It might result in a "mission accomplished" claim without any accompanying tangible impact.

Even though this chapter is situated at the end of the book, I drafted it early in my overall manuscript. Why? If I can firm up the ending of this narrative, I have set myself strong guardrails on how I want to explain various topics that help us communicate effectively to reach the end. Running an enablement initiative that is driving operations changes follows the same logic.

This is also why preparing, debating, and prioritizing an initiative's definition during strategic planning is paramount. Why bother prioritizing an initiative that folks disagree on afterward when the details are more apparent?

Second, before we start driving change, aligning on the steady state with the appropriate individuals is essential. Lack of such alignment is a near guarantee that change efforts will derail. But who needs to be aligned?

Like our delegation of authority decision lever, each strategic initiative requires a SWAT team of decision-makers. This small group represents impacted individuals across the company, like lawmakers representing constituents. Attempting to change the hearts and minds of every impacted person across the company will fail. These decision-makers are framed as we define the steady state. Let's name this group the **Change Committee**.

The specific tactics to align the change committee are situational. They depend on the level of change the initiative is driving, the sensitivity around the operations baseline building blocks we are changing, the current maturity of the management approach that influences skill and performance, and, most importantly, the incentives of the committee and the people they represent. We must write down and illustrate our steady state definition. Then, we can conduct one-on-one or group discussions. We may even ask the committee to sign off on their alignment formally.

The reality is that I have royally failed at getting through a change program after such a committee boisterously supported the change multiple times.

Conversely, I have successfully driven changes with well-aligned change committees with nothing more than an email to share the steady state view.

The wrinkle is that people don't usually publicly share their thoughts and privately act in their individual interests. If we understand genuine incentives, the alignment level indicates our success probability. So, alignment is a behavioral analysis exercise rather than tactical vote counting.

Consider these design questions to assess alignment on change:

Do we believe that the change committee is genuinely engaged?

Do we believe that the change committee has aligned incentives, internalizes the importance of congruence across the company, and does not prioritize conflicting individualistic motivations?

Are they the correct experts to support the initiative, keeping with our Comparative Advantage Ecosystem mindset? In other words, do they understand what is going on?

Are we convinced that they are not passively aligned but actively misaligned?

I recommend being a realist and considering these questions before jumping to the next success factor. A "no" answer to any of these questions implies that we are carrying an open pressure valve – a misaligned change committee – into our enablement effort. Document the answers and articulate the nuances around the alignment gaps. Ensure this pressure valve is visible to the Congruence Architect and executive decision meeting participants and is escalated and addressed via the executive decision meeting.

It's unfair to put the weight of improbable outcomes solely on each initiative's owners. Incentive gaps must be addressed systemically.

Principle 3: The price of change is the second pressure valve.

In alignment with our Comparative Advantage Ecosystem mindset, companies aren't democracies. Even in a democracy, we choose lawmakers who write policies that sometimes benefit us and other times only others. A weak management approach triggers a common change management failure point, creating an illusion that every impacted individual must agree with the steady state for a change to be the right or necessary course of action.

Change events typically require alterations in the behaviors of some or all employees, partners, and sometimes even customers. Change requires discomfort. That is the pressure in our Pressure Valve Framework.

The first law of thermodynamics, also known as the Law of Conservation of Energy, states that energy can neither be created nor destroyed; energy can only be transferred or changed from one form to another. In plain English, this means we can't have something for nothing.

It is shocking how often company representatives feel or speak as though we can break natural laws and achieve change without sacrificing much. As simple as this pressure valve is, it is worth placing it on our checklist, given the frequency of this misconception. There is always a price to pay for change to take hold, and that price always includes discomfort.

I once led an enablement initiative to mature a sales prospecting function. The sales reps worked based on individual preferences, which resulted in them selling to the same prospects, creating diminishing returns. Although the change committee was on board with the necessity for a maturity shift, the sales executive and supervisor insisted that formal prospecting lists would impede the sales reps' freedoms. Their refusal to communicate with the impacted reps that a small compromise was necessary to improve the company's operations performance diluted the initiative.

If anyone says that change can come without sacrifice, they impose unfair expectations on the change initiative owner. So, let's always embrace the simple principle that achieving higher maturity and congruence requires some sacrifice.

But that price isn't spending more money, especially if we are a well-funded company. Regardless of how much we spend on fitness coaches and gyms, higher fitness levels imply going through physical discomfort ourselves.

Consider these design questions to highlight the price of change:

What is the price that impacted individuals will experience due to the change?

Have we effectively communicated this price using our decision and communication ladder and process training?

It can be tempting to shield impacted individuals from the reality of evolution. That's just delaying the inevitable. Set the appropriate expectations and communicate broadly upfront to avoid surprises. The human desire for arbitrage is the second pressure valve we must manage.

Principle 4: Unilateral support for the strategic initiative owner is the third pressure valve.

However large or small, every enablement initiative needs an owner. We slate this owner as we approved the initiative during strategic planning. This owner is responsible for detailing the enablement initiative's steady state and aligning the organization about the price to pay. The owner will only be successful with the unilateral public and private support of the CEO, board, executives, and supervisors.

Workplace politics has escalated over the decades as more value creators sit at desks, and an average value creator's work is increasingly intangible. People often don't attack other individuals in company settings because it's impolite. Instead, we consciously or subconsciously attack what they do, undermining their credibility and work effectiveness.

A strategic initiative has the same effect on a company as a significant policy bill does on a country. The price of change often creates enough consternation that people resist or fight back. Inertia is natural.

It is also a human tendency to offload risk onto others. The adage about finding someone slower than us when chased by a bear reflects our human tendency to let someone else take the heat when uncomfortable situations arise.

As an enablement initiative picks up speed and moves closer to the steady state, the price to be paid starts coming due. In the early stages of an enablement initiative, the onus falls on the change owner and the core resources to do the groundwork necessary. Only in the later stages do the change committee and impacted individuals start to feel the pressure to change. This is the stage when the impacted audience begins looking for pressure valves. The CEO, senior executives, supervisors, and vocal employees become paths to relieve the pressure of the change.

An easily accessible pressure valve is to empathize with the impacted audience and question the initiative's efficacy or the owner's competence. In weak change systems, such a subtle shift in focus is easy and stalls change.

The time to challenge an enablement initiative is not during the tail end of the execution or change management phase. An enablement initiative is in the execution management stage for one reason only – it was framed as a path to achieving the company strategy and prioritized over other strategic initiatives.

Consider these design questions to maintain focus on the objective reasons to sustain progress on strategic initiatives and avoid politicking:

Does the strategic initiative's desired steady state still align with the company strategy or address incongruences across the operations baseline? If yes, stay focused.

Has a mature and objective performance evaluation changed the role of the strategic initiative owner? If not, refrain from politics and focus on the problem.

Change requires all relevant stakeholders to pull in the same direction in intent and actions. Company-wide change efforts must be treated like an orchestra performance rather than a linear relay race.

Principle 5: Accountability structure to protect against rationalization is the fourth pressure valve.

Regardless of the best intentions and efforts of the CEO, senior executives, and initiative owner, successfully completing an enablement initiative can prove unnerving at clutch moments. A less aligned and less effective steady state will tempt us because it reduces the pressure for change felt by our impacted individuals.

Humans naturally tend to rationalize, also known as choice-supportive bias. Rationalization is a cognitive bias where we create unsubstantiated reasons for why a specific choice or outcome makes sense. In the context of driving enablement initiatives, the initiative owner and the organization are likely to feel tempted to avoid the discomfort around change and conjure up irrational excuses to support a suboptimal steady state. The familiar aphorism, "Don't let good get in the way of great!" often appears when people want to avoid feeling the necessary pressure associated with change. As you will see in Chapter F.3, there is a vast difference between taking reasonable bites of what we can chew and not eating enough. We want to avoid the latter.

How do we counter this? The simple answer is to create accountability structures. We all tend to deliver more and with higher quality when held accountable. It limits our natural tendency to rationalize subpar outcomes. The same applies to our strategic initiatives. Let's discuss three lines of defense for this.

The **first line of defense** is performance management. Every strategic initiative's steady state must be an expected performance outcome for the initiative's owner. This creates a direct incentive for the owner to drive initiatives to the intent of the steady state articulated in the strategic plan. The enablement owner's supervisor can leverage formal one-on-ones to coach and support decision-making to ensure progress and closure of pressure valves.

The **second line of defense** is our executive decision meeting, where we must review strategic initiatives. It offers an accountability forum to assess our progress toward the steady state. The forum also provides an opportunity to escalate pressure valves and drive decisions to close those pressure valves.

The **third line of defense** is the company's board of directors. Every company has this built-in accountability partner. An operationally minded and engaged board offers a cadence-based opportunity to collectively assess the progress and challenges around strategic initiatives, which are critical evolutionary changes that the board must oversee.

All three lines of defense are necessary, and none must be circumvented. A symbolic use of these three lines of defense will not be enough.

The key success factor for these accountability partnerships to serve their purpose is objectivity and transparency. As we move from the first line of defense to the third, the audience in the accountability forum is further removed from the details of the enablement initiative.

Human beings try to fix a broken situation privately before admitting difficulties. If we read the newspaper regularly, most corporate issues metastasize and blow up before the involved parties own up to the existence of a problem.

I have overseen strategic initiatives at the company level over multiple execution cycles, during which I created and managed these three lines of defense. There is a strong correlation between the impact delivered by initiatives and the level of objectivity and transparency with which we manage them. For initiatives that are laggards and fizzle out over time, the initiative owners' openness to share intricate details of progress and leverage the support of the whole company is typically low. So, embrace the accountability structures because they exist to help.

Consider these design questions to assess the effective use of accountability structures:

How effectively are enablement initiatives built into performance management expectations of owners and change committee members?

How effectively are decision management levers used to support change initiatives?

How objective and transparent are the CEO and executives in engaging the board on initiatives enabling necessary changes?

Embracing these five principles allows us to enable systemic support for the enablement initiative owner to drive change. However, change efforts can also fail when initiative-specific pressure valves are open.

Principle 6: Identify and manage initiative-specific pressure valves.

The enablement initiative owner's role is not that of a project manager who is checking off boxes. The #1 quality of an enablement initiative owner is conviction. The owner must genuinely commit to driving the change because the pressure created by the change will always look for a release path. The change owner must dedicate a significant effort to identifying and closing initiative-specific pressure valves. Outside of the four organizational pressure valves discussed above, an enablement initiative's success depends on closing topic-specific release points.

The enablement initiative owner must identify, monitor, and escalate any potential failure point. In a robust system, responsible experts can help the enablement owner close each valve tightly to support the change. The ability to receive support from other skilled resources is critical. This is precisely why we are discussing execution management at this late stage in our method. The maturity necessary to support change doesn't materialize overnight. We need a mature management approach and value engine to drive effective change.

Consider this design question to identify the pressure valves that can derail each change effort:

Given the current maturity of our management approach and value engine, what are the realistic impediments that moderately or strongly limit the effectiveness of the desired change?

The closure of these topic-specific pressure valves must be part of our enablement initiative scope. Therefore, we must plan and manage their closure during the initiative's execution. The initiative owner may take responsibility for some of them, and other experts may own and tighten the remaining pressure valves. We must enter the critical enablement execution phase with a firm understanding of how likely our initiative will be to fail.

If we believe one or more pressure release valves will remain open despite our execution efforts, STOP! It is tempting to think that we can push through against all odds. But believe me, if one pressure valve is open, we will likely fail. It's irrational to commit significant resources to an initiative that we know will fail unless our three lines of defense accountability structure commits to helping close all initiative-specific pressure valves.

These principles, which build on our Pressure Valve Framework, allow us to integrate effective change management into our company's system to close pressure valves that could stand in the way of our evolutionary enablement initiatives.

A recent conversation with the CEO of a 100-year-old insurance company sums up this chapter. The CEO took over about five years ago and successfully revitalized the company's stagnant trajectory in the established industry. When I asked this CEO why the transformation succeeded, he quickly replied, "We have a clear vision, and we are determined not to let anything get in the way!"

We always have a choice between embracing the significant pressure to evolve or the relative comfort of maintaining the status quo. However, this choice must be congruent with our company's purpose, corporate strategy, strategic plan, and the maturity of our management approach and value engine.

If we are happy with our value creation and profits, then the enablement initiatives in our strategic plan are likely less demanding. Thus, very little pressure is necessary to drive the initiatives forward. This purpose and associated trade-off decisions and execution can be congruent.

Conversely, a purpose to pursue greater value creation for a large share of the addressable market will require significant change through macroevolutions. Companies often attempt overhauls and dedicate little time and mindshare to ensuring those changes stick. The funny thing about change management is that it is less about what we do; it's more about what we don't do. Everything we don't do becomes a pressure valve that can undermine all the good work we put into macroevolution.

F.3
REALIZE ENABLEMENT INITIATIVES TO
INJECT STRATEGY INTO OPERATIONS.

W E exhaustively discussed the importance of ensuring that our strategic enablement initiatives dovetail with our strategy and evolve our operations. Every strategic enablement initiative has a single goal – to evolve and harmonize one or more building blocks of the management approach and value engine, closing specific gaps that we defined during strategic planning. If we do not achieve the desired steady state intended for each initiative, we will fail to achieve our strategy or will live with incongruences in our operations.

Enablement resources are dedicated to planning and implementing these strategic initiatives. Strategic initiatives can range from short sprints that involve limited enablement investment to significant efforts that consume the company's attention for months.

Executing slated efforts and successfully maturing our operations is a tall order, and we covered some of those difficulties in the previous chapter on change management. What else makes it hard to perform seemingly straightforward tasks based on a plan to achieve relatively achievable organizational maturity and productivity improvements? A lack of connectivity between strategy and operations.

I spent the early part of my career trying to piece together how to dovetail strategy and operations. Although a lot of literature is available about strategy and operations improvement, much of it confuses strategy with tactics and operations with activities. The evidence from my exploratory career indicates that highly congruent systems are a rarity because companies tend to direct investment toward work and economic activity disconnected from strategy, which does not result in constructive operations improvements.

I have spent years on large transformation projects that cost clients tens of millions. Despite the incredible organizational investment and change management efforts, the value realized is often spurious. Similarly, I have worked on incredibly insightful strategic efforts that never made their way into operations impact even years later.

Internalizing the integral requirement that enablement execution must connect strategy with operations is one of the triggers that began my *Congruence*™ journey.

Things To Remember: Strategy and Operations Connectivity

Strategic initiatives are the enablement efforts that link strategy to operations. Strategy is a decision. Operations is the real-world translation of strategy. Strategic initiatives stitch them together. The strategic initiatives identified and prioritized through planning are the magic keys that evolve and improve the operations baseline in alignment with our strategy.

The connectivity of strategy and operations is a necessary alignment that epitomizes our One Company philosophy. Executing strategic initiatives should not be a pursuit of shiny objects – it must perfectly align with our corporate strategy to avoid wasting precious resources. Strategic initiatives decoupled from tangible operational evolution are meaningless. With that in mind, let's dive into enablement execution and start with pitfalls to avoid.

Principle 1: Internalize common manifestations of enablement execution failures.

A strategic initiative will likely miss the mark if we do not effectively develop the steady state definition. We touched on this criticality to enable change, but there is more. Even if these plans are well developed, implementing initiatives can be troublesome. Before we address the principles to maximize our probability of success, it is good to internalize the general themes that trigger failure.

Change of priorities.

"Change of priority" is generally a code for, "We are admitting defeat without saying so!" Initiatives often start strong with kick-off meetings and forward momentum for the first month or so. After that, however, senior executives often change their minds about commitment to the initiative or what it should achieve based on limited new information. This mindset usually happens due to two reasons.

First, the initiative may not have a comprehensive rationale, which becomes evident when the tires are kicked in the first few weeks. This implies that the preceding strategic planning effort that birthed the initiatives was poorly managed or that the commitment to our corporate strategy is weak.

Second, strategic initiative outcomes will always lag behind implementation efforts. Improvements do not appear overnight. Senior executives must internalize this time lag and have the discipline to stay the course on strategic initiatives and see them through to the end regardless of discomfort due to the pressure created by change or unsubstantiated wishes to have a quick impact.

Change of personnel.

Senior executives may change, and enablement resources implementing initiatives may resign. Such personnel changes are par for the course at any company. However, companies tend to mothball existing plans or change directions because new individuals are on the playing field. Personnel changes are not a good enough reason by itself to change course. We must rely on our robust system, which includes our corporate strategy and associated strategic plan. Our plan to implement an initiative should only change if we reframe our corporate strategy comprehensively and then our associated strategic plan.

Another symptom of this manifestation is passing the responsibility of the same initiative to different owners over time with limited real progress in the desired outcomes. This is a practical version of stalling an initiative without drawing attention by killing it. These are symptomatic of the company not effectively leveraging our decision management tools.

Check-the-box outcomes.

Another indicator of an initiative failure is a declaration of victory without demonstrating measurable improvement in our operations baseline or disclosing tangible deliverables that objectively lead to productivity or maturity impact. Such symptoms imply that these initiatives have fizzled into a check-the-box exercise during execution. This indicates ineffective use of management approach and decision management levers to drive accountability.

It is easier to avoid difficult conversations in the short term than face the truth of execution challenges. But as a collective, the company will suffer. Therefore, we must keep these symptoms in mind as we implement enablement initiatives.

Principle 2: Balance purpose-strategy-operations alignment with execution feedback adjustments.

Waterfall is a project management approach with strengths around long-term planning and execution. It was commonly used in larger companies with established project managers and large-budget projects with many resources. Over time, many jobs and certifications grew around Waterfall, and project managers became a staple in most execution environments. However, Waterfall usage went too far, to the point where projects started failing because poor practitioners didn't adapt to new information and changes in the projects' environment.

The world has all but shunned the Waterfall mindset. When the poor use of Waterfall started to demonstrate stodginess and a lack of flexibility, the proponents of Agile saw the opportunity to propose the importance of being adaptable and nimble.

Agile is a project management framework primarily created by software developers for the software development space. Its usage has expanded widely, and even large companies have embraced it as an improvement over Waterfall.

The funny thing about humans is that we are exceptionally good at taking amazing ideas too far! Misuse of Agile has manifested into modern-day operational short-termism in companies.

Agile now has a similar misuse issue as Waterfall. Agile users tend to focus so much on the short term and flexibility that they lose sight of the big picture. Agile is intended to enable reasonable adjustments to the path forward. It does not mean that we lack a vision or clarity on the path forward or that we change the vision or path on a whim.

But history tends to repeat itself for a good reason. Overreliance on Agile has led to poor execution management behaviors. Agile never intended to encourage us to execute in a fast-and-loose manner or operate without a comprehensive plan.

The 2024 CrowdStrike software update that caused a worldwide computer outage is a practical example of overextending the well-intentioned Agile method too far. The root cause was too many actions too fast. As customers, we regularly experience microtremors caused by poor execution, whether it's software glitches or service frustrations. Companies overspend to patch over these microissues, which distracts from solving real problems.

I used to work with an executive who insisted on using the word "agile" as an excuse to operate in a world of firefighting. Work was limited to tactical emails or conversations based on Post-it notes, and every endeavor was watered down into tactical actions. Such a short-term, task-based mindset is not enough to evolve a company strategically.

An optimal approach to execution management is in the middle. Strength of frameworks like Waterfall lie in its focus on laying out the big picture and connecting the execution details to that big picture. Frameworks like Agile incorporate good practices to inject new learnings and adapt the details to reach the desired outcome without being too strict about the path forward.

Our enablement execution must focus on congruence between our purpose, strategy, and plan and practical impact on operations evidenced through leading indicators. We must work with a crystal-clear vision of the steady state and a well-laid-out plan to achieve that steady state while managing the execution to incorporate objective new information into the plan and the steady state.

For enablement initiatives to have an impact, they must be driven by an overarching steady state view, a strong work plan, and an adaptive approach to iterate the steady state view and the work plan when relevant information is found through proactive means.

Principle 3: Organize initiatives centrally using a comprehensive enablement roadmap.

The first step of enablement execution beyond systemic empowerment via effective decision and change management is to build on the **Enablement Roadmap** drafted during strategic planning. It addresses resource constraints, dependencies, and communication of enablement efforts at a company level.

You may think that a roadmap as a tool is cliché. We have all been frequently disappointed by the broken promises made by roadmaps. But we can't blame an English word or a practically useful lever for its poor usage.

> **Things To Remember: Enablement Roadmap**
>
> **An enablement roadmap is a living timeline that comprehensively frames strategic initiatives in a visual format with time on the X-axis.**

Any Gantt chart or a timeline is a roadmap. There is nothing complex about it. Unfortunately, that also makes it dangerous because anyone can create one in a few minutes, and it is hard to know whether it is effective.

Roadmaps that seem good but do not deliver or don't seem cohesive have the same underlying root causes. They may not be based on an effective overarching corporate strategy, may not have cohesive enablement initiatives that dovetail with the corporate strategy, or may not be realistic because the execution team lacks the skills and experience to deliver on strategic initiatives.

Inherently, a roadmap must never contain new information. Every single detail on a roadmap comes from our strategic plan. Use this as a rule of thumb: if our roadmap has information that does not perfectly jive with our strategic plan, our roadmap will fail. We drafted our enablement roadmap during enablement planning and formalized all necessary inputs during investment planning.

An enablement roadmap articulates dependencies very well. An effective roadmap offers a single tool to validate that our top-of-the-house strategic initiatives meet the bottom-of-the-house actions and that nothing is amiss. A good roadmap offers connectivity between our prioritized strategic initiatives and detailed executable plans, which we will discuss soon. It allows all value creators to understand and act while enabling us to monitor progress.

A strong enablement roadmap is also a compelling communication and alignment tool, assuming that we are good at delivering against it. A critical aspect of preparing for change through an enablement initiative and managing that change is to share our path forward with stakeholders across our company.

Have you played billiards at a bar? Any competitive opponent would ask us to "call the shot" before we take a turn. Execution must be predictable and transparent so that we can inject accountability and take corrective action early on if we go off track.

Anyone in our company must have access to understand our macroevolution and microevolution efforts. Every employee and partner wants to know how their actions each hour of the day add up to the big picture. Customers want to know the future of their partnership with us because it is a determining factor in their choice of an offering. Rational investors need to gauge the likelihood of future profits based on our evolutionary efforts.

Only a few key decision-makers, including the board, executives, Congruence Architect, and a few other playmakers, may be privy to the complete details of our strategy and strategic plan. So, we need a consistent way to communicate our path with a broader audience. An enablement roadmap allows this.

What does a "good" roadmap look like?

Given the throwaway rate of roadmaps, it is worth getting into the specifics of what constitutes an effective one. We can look for four rules as signs of a good roadmap.

The **first rule** of a roadmap is that a growth-phase company has one cohesive roadmap that covers all functions. Roadmaps often originate in functional silos, the most common being a "product roadmap." However, a function is only part of a company, and a functional roadmap is thus incomplete. If our roadmap is a comprehensive validation and communication tool, how can it be effective with only part of the picture?

For instance, to take an offering to market, we may evolve commercial aspects through org design, hiring management, and compensation design improvements. In addition, some enablement initiatives may also evolve value engine building blocks around the commercial processes, which will have to dovetail with the offering that we are selling and delivering. These all sit within a single roadmap. Stitching together a sales road-map, a marketing roadmap, an HR roadmap, and so on results in more incongruences and overlapping wasteful investments.

The **second rule** of an enablement roadmap is that it includes all strategic initiatives and only strategic initiatives. A roadmap must be comprehensive for each strategic planning and execution cycle.

Suppose we feel that a strategic initiative prioritized during planning is not worth its space on a roadmap. That means our enablement planning efforts were politicized, and we likely slipped in one or more enablement initiatives that do not align with our strategy.

Additionally, slipping in unplanned new efforts is a common way to fail enablement execution. If we feel compelled to include an effort that didn't seem relevant during planning, we must ask ourselves why it is relevant during execution. Did we make a mistake during planning?

If so, we must go back and include the initiative in the strategic plan and rework the resourcing, timelines, and related investment decisions. If we do not, we are essentially breaking our entire plan. How do we know this new addition doesn't distract from everything else we planned to work on? How do we know this new initiative is more important than another one we had prioritized?

"The CEO or the board said so!" is a lazy answer. Pulling rank isn't symbolic of a robust decision-making system. Our strategic plan is intended to be congruent within itself. We might need to revisit the entire plan if we need to add a relevant strategic initiative during the execution cycle.

This is not to say that we cannot simplify or articulate our strategic initiatives in layperson's terms on a roadmap. But if a stakeholder inquires about an initiative on a roadmap, it must relate to our planning efforts without ambiguity.

The **third rule** of a roadmap is that the book-ending parameters of each strategic initiative must align with the operations and investment planning details we developed through levers in Part E. For instance, if we framed an initiative to be executed and adopted in three months, we must reflect that time window on the roadmap. That must be the same timespan we use to detail how we execute each initiative.

Misalignments will imply that the real-world impact of strategic initiatives decouples from the timing and amount by which we expect our leading and lagging indicators to move. Our aggregate operations plan is built on those expectations. Essentially, we'd break our Chain of Controllability.

The **fourth rule** is that every strategic initiative on a roadmap must comprehensively reflect four phases. Although enablement initiatives are time-bound, they do not simply start and end. Every strategic initiative goes through four stages: planning, execution, adoption, and monitoring.

Our detailed work plan for each strategic initiative must address the activities and deliverables associated with these four stages. We will describe the considerations for each of these stages in Principle 5. It is critical to frame the entire lifecycle of a strategic initiative on a roadmap.

Refrain from giving in to the temptation to build obscurity and flexibility into the enablement roadmap to give ourselves a backdoor if execution lags. This would be selfish. Everyone in our company is on the same side, and there is no need to create obscurity in a company with a mature management approach and decision management system.

Consider these design questions as guardrails to manage an effective enablement roadmap:

Does the enablement roadmap comprehensively span the entire company's macroevolution?

Does the enablement roadmap show all and only prioritized strategic initiatives?

Do each initiative's details reflect the parameters approved through strategic planning?

Does each initiative cover all four enablement execution stages – planning, execution, adoption, and monitoring?

With these rules in mind, the CEO and Congruence Architect must develop and manage a comprehensive roadmap that reflects our strategic plan and all the enablement work slated for the present execution cycle. The CEO's ownership and the Congruence Architect's independence will be necessary to dovetail our roadmap with both our corporate strategy and details of the enablement initiative execution.

Principle 4: Use enablement work plans as leading indicators for enablement execution.

In a system-centered execution, we don't have heroes. None of our company stakeholders are interested in seeing magic tricks from us when we execute an enablement initiative. No one wants to be shocked by how we took an idea and got it done. Everyone prefers a well-defined path without surprises on when and what will happen. To successfully translate an enablement initiative into incremental maturity of our management approach and value engine, we must execute with transparency and predictability.

As our working environments become more digitized and employees increasingly work remotely, the need to create transparency and predictability around execution will increase exponentially. We want to manage our enablement initiatives with predictability and transparency. Well-defined **Enablement Work Plans** achieve this.

> **Things To Remember: Enablement Work Plans**
>
> **Enablement Work Plans frame the detailed and comprehensive execution path of a strategic initiative and span planning, execution, adoption, and monitoring.**

Let's cover the success factors to include in enablement work plans because work plans are often poorly created, rendering them non-executable and unmeasurable. We should intend for our work plans and associated elements to create accountability for the enablement initiative owner, the change committee, other supporting experts, and for the impacted individuals' level of adoption.

Success factor 1: Milestones.

Strategic initiatives are significant, impactful efforts that span weeks or months. So, all decision-makers, contributors, and impacted individuals must have visibility into progress throughout. However, they all have other responsibilities and likely won't have the mindshare to pay attention to execution details. So, we must choose a few tangible checkpoints along the way to demonstrate progress. These are our milestones. We must articulate milestones well enough to limit misinterpretation of its intent and enable accountability.

All key decision-makers in a company must internalize that enablement initiatives do not progress linearly. As a simple example, if we rebrand our company and need to rework our entire website, the externally facing website will remain unchanged until we transition to a steady state. However, many checkpoints along the way, such as alignment on brand themes, current webpage rationalization, new content inventory, and content creation and review, can be used as milestones. Such milestones form the leading indicators to demonstrate progress for strategic initiatives.

Consider these design questions to develop milestones for an enablement work plan:

Is the strategic initiative broken down into five to eight reasonable interim checkpoints we can use as milestones?

Is every milestone articulated effectively to ensure downstream accountability?

Success factor 2: Deliverables.

Milestones must be meaningful. How do we know if we met a milestone, especially if enablement initiatives do not progress linearly and most outcomes are only observable at the end? We all want to trust each other, but after dozens of companies, I am confident that accountability only exists in environments where individuals are actually held accountable. The correlation between internalizing the importance of deliverables and the level of accountability is uncanny.

Accountability for each milestone implies creating evidence to demonstrate the achievement of the milestone. Deliverables are evidence in a documented format that shows that the responsible party genuinely met the milestone. It serves the same purpose as legal evidence in a courtroom, without which there is no case.

Deliverables are a fantastic way to drive accountability and ensure that we have made the progress we have set ourselves or others have set for us. We must become comfortable with the reality that we are in a professional environment regardless of the market we serve or our lifecycle stage and get accustomed to saying, "Don't tell me; show me!" Talking our way through our accomplishments is too squishy to be considered effective management. I have always found myself stretching the extra distance regarding quality, completeness, or timeliness if I set myself a formal deliverable as a requirement to complete a milestone. The same goes for people who have worked with or for me over the years.

Consider these design questions to frame effective deliverables for milestones:

Does every milestone have a tangible and verifiable output that demonstrates the milestone has been achieved?

Are deliverables for each milestone incremental to previous ones to ensure the intent of each milestone is being met?

Success factor 3: Actionable steps.

Milestones are also outcomes, just interim outcomes. We need to frame the actions and decisions that move us toward milestones and the overarching steady state. These are the portions of work that need to be completed by individuals contributing to our initiative.

One of the most important aspects of a work plan is that it is actionable. However, the inability to frame an actionable path is also a common execution weakness. So, always frame every action step with an active verb such as "prepare," "review," "schedule," or "send." This helps us to close our eyes and imagine performing each step.

Additionally, it is important to ensure that each action step is relatively easy for one person to accomplish in a reasonable time window. If multiple people are involved in an action step, it implies transitions between them, and those details would be lost in our work plan if we combined those actions. Our process design hand-off principle applies to enablement efforts as well. Hand-offs are the most common failure point in execution.

Suppose one person is working on a single step for an extended time. It would be unclear to anyone else whether they could perform this step faster or whether they made progress in the interim. It is optimal to break up such work into smaller action steps. Be bold about details because execution goes wrong in the details.

Consider these design questions to frame action steps and chart a path to milestones and deliverables:

If we complete the action steps and take no other actions, will we be able to achieve the milestones and the overarching steady state?

Does every step in our action plan start with a verb?

Can each step be completed in a reasonable period, say four or eight hours?

Success factor 4: Single point of accountability.

Accountability requires a single owner. Without ambiguity, every action step must have one individual expected to execute that step. For example, even if an action step is to conduct a meeting to review a design element associated with the enablement initiative, a single owner must ensure that the meeting succeeds regardless of the number of attendees.

Additionally, accountability also requires time constraints. Every milestone and action step must have realistic, unambiguous timelines that ensure forward momentum.

Avoid the tendency to pad the timeframes as this often leads to filling space with unvetted, ad hoc priorities that could expand, become all-consuming, and derail planned activities. Chaos during execution starts from such small cracks. Think about it like water freezing and expanding inside a crack, eventually breaking the object. If critical work is unassigned, escalate to vet and prioritize through decision meetings. It must be part of our strategic plan before someone works on it.

Although this is an elementary success factor to internalize, work plans often leave out names of individuals and realistic timeframes. Not everyone is comfortable with accountability.

Consider these design questions to assess accountability level in enablement work plans:

Does each action step have a single owner who will execute its original intent?

Does each action step have a realistic accountability timeframe?

Success factor 5: Hand-off.

Lastly, work plans fail when breakdowns that stall progress are unanticipated. Moving from one action step to the next must feel like passing the ball in a free-flowing soccer game. If the steps in a work plan are disjointed, where one doesn't lead to the next and hand-offs are missing, then our execution is in jeopardy. Similar to process design, consider whether subsequent action steps with different owners clearly articulate how responsibilities are transitioned between those owners. Our cross-functional Congruence Architect must review enablement work plans for all strategic initiatives and assess whether this success factor and others are incorporated.

Consider this design question to evaluate work plans for hand-offs:

Does every action step seamlessly lead to the next one in a logical flow?

Building these five success factors into enablement work plans is paramount in creating transparency and predictability for strategic initiatives during execution.

Principle 5: Manage all strategic initiatives across four stages.

Now that we have framed the success factors to plan each enablement initiative, let's cover the four stages that each initiative must include. Regardless of scope, these stages are 1) Work Planning and Alignment, 2) Design and Build, 3) Rollout and Adoption, and 4) Monitoring. Figure F5 shows the minimal considerations to plan and execute an impactful enablement initiative.

The four stages are not a linear progression from one to the next; rather, they are overlapping and incrementally progressive stages. Including the concepts in these four stages will ensure comprehensive and impactful enablement work plans and execution.

Stage 1: Work planning and alignment.

Creating the work plans discussed in the last principle takes time and mindshare. Before the enablement initiative owner starts working on the details, we must allocate time to build and socialize a work plan for alignment. Each initiative's owner and change committee must align on the details with the Congruence Architect and executive decision meeting participants.

Ideally, this alignment occurs before we adjourn strategic planning at the end of the year. The next realistic opportunity to revisit this topic could be an executive decision meeting a month later when 10 percent of a yearly execution cycle has already passed. So, set aside time upfront and consider the work plan itself as a deliverable.

As with strategic planning, work planning is also not a one-and-done effort. Enablement work plans are living tools that allow us to manage an

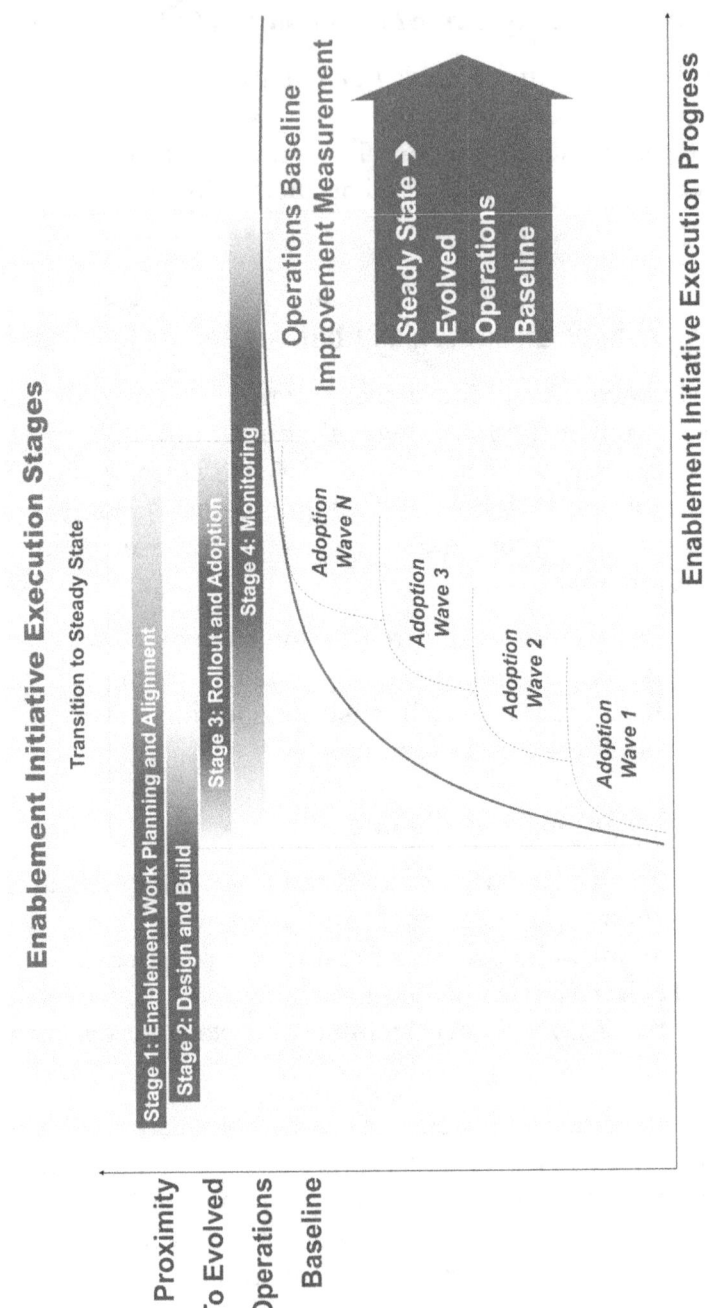

Figure F5. Strategic initiatives require multistage execution and adoption waves.

entire initiative through the steady state. As we learn new information, improving our work plan to reflect the reality of the path forward is essential. Plan details are our leading indicators, and without a good plan, we cannot know where we are headed, and we cannot hold ourselves or others accountable.

Stage 2: Design and build.

As the name suggests, the second stage covers the solution aspects of the enablement initiative. Enablement initiatives will not have the desired impact if they do not follow a problem-solving mentality. If we execute with a ready-fire attitude, we will likely miss the essence of our desired steady state.

Like our market problem-solving discussions, one of the most common reasons enablement initiatives fail is the symptom-solving of operations baseline gaps. Observable gaps identified during enablement planning are often not the root causes. However, a critical thinking initiative owner, supported by the Congruence Architect, will determine the actual root causes and address those.

A strong problem-solving framework allows us to do that. All problem-solving frameworks follow a logical and predictable pattern. The various levers in the *Congruence*™ method cover essential elements required to solve problems.

However, there is no substitute for practical experience in real-world situations. So, enablement initiatives require skilled problem-solvers to contribute. We hired specialized skills in our enablement resources to take on such problem-solving challenges in a manner that fits the problem.

At this stage, we have already done the hardest part of problem-solving: articulating the steady state, which is similar to stating the market problem from a strategy perspective. Now, we need to actualize that steady state. The specific steps to problem-solving and solution development will be unique to each enablement initiative, not to mention unique between companies.

From an enablement resource capacity perspective, the design and build stage will likely be the meatiest. We must plan to progress through this stage with multiple iterations of problem-solving. Work planning is only effective if it is realistic. No initiative owner will likely get to the most optimal design or build the first time and will need to iterate based on feedback from impacted individuals and the change committee.

Stage 3: Rollout and adoption.

Once we have designed and built a solution, we must validate that it works. Once we iron out the kinks iteratively, we need to inject the solution into our value engine and management approach so that operations resources can create higher value more efficiently. Execution of an enablement initiative is not done when we have created a solution.

First, we must validate that our solution works in practice. We have to include steps to test and learn the effectiveness of improving our operations baseline. These responsibilities continue to sit with the enablement initiative owner.

Second, once we have confirmed the effectiveness of our solution through iterative validation, we engage our impacted value creators and customers to begin adopting the improvements, which may involve changes to any combination of building blocks across the company.

We must convince the impacted individuals to embrace the maturity shift during adoption. Our work plan must include the steps to enable impacted individuals to move to the steady state. This might include documentation, training, and ongoing audits to transition to the evolved state.

We dedicated an entire chapter to change management because enablement initiatives often break down at this stage – adoption. We must predict the detailed steps necessary to address all our pressure valves and include steps to close each valve.

A "wave mindset" is optimal for adoption. Waves are our way of biting off what we can chew at a given moment, but also eating well. It prepares us to have incremental success instead of achieving all changes overnight, which is unrealistic. It also limits the tendency to rationalize and settle for a small improvement because it is easier to adopt. We must plan and execute communication, training, and ramping behaviors to the steady state. Figure F5 illustrates the wave mindset to adoption.

Consider these design questions to build the "wave mindset" into adoption steps:

How many adoption waves are appropriate for each initiative to reach the steady state?

Are adoption waves best structured based on the individuals, roles, or entities that we are impacting, the scope of changes that the entire impacted group would adopt, or a combination of both?

Which individuals, roles, or entities will be part of each wave? What scope of changes will be part of each wave?

What specific actions need to be taken to enable each adoption wave?

If we plan and execute meaningful adoption waves, we optimize our probability of success in implementing change and ingraining the desired steady state into the operations baseline.

Stage 4: Monitoring.

The "end" of our enablement initiative is not characterized by completing our work plan steps. Checking off the action steps in our work plan is an excellent leading indicator for enablement execution. The steps in the first three stages keep us on track. However, it isn't very meaningful without improving the maturity of the operations baseline as scoped in each initiative.

As a fourth stage, we must measure adoption to ensure we hold ourselves accountable for achieving maturity improvements. Each initiative's steady state definition already lays out the corresponding leading indicators we must impact and associated targets. We must meticulously measure these leading indicators through adoption and the steady state.

Adoption is rarely single-directional. Recall that improvements towards the desired steady state can regress after early success. The impacted stakeholders may adopt changes in the short term but then revert to past behaviors when the excitement dies down. We can make a New Year's resolution to exercise more and fall back into our sloppy old habits by spring.

Incrementally, adoption can also be artificial. Depending on the maturity of our management approach, operations resources may adopt changes with a check-the-box mindset without adopting the essence of the change. In our New Year's resolution, we could also get a membership to a fancy gym and visit the spa there without exercising, yet give ourselves credit for "going to the gym." Adoption of enablement initiatives can cause similar unintended behaviors.

We must consider the essence of the impact we require and devise measurements that address behavioral skews that the change effort might create. An unidentified or unmeasured behavior skew can become a pressure valve for our initiative.

The measurements we monitor during the transition to the steady state can differ from the steady state leading indicators in our strategic plan. We can devise interim operations measurements to support our transition to the steady state, and these can be decommissioned when we are confident about adoption. For example, we might create a metric that uses manually collected data periodically, observations through audits, or cadence-based surveys to track progress toward the steady state.

Consider these design questions to monitor the adoption of enablement initiative solutions:

What are the success factors for each adoption wave? How will we measure these success factors? Who will measure these success factors?

What are our contingency plans if our measurements reveal adoption challenges for each wave?

What are the potential behavioral skews the change effort might cause? What are the interim measurements to monitor these skews?

What measurement thresholds must be satisfied before we confidently consider adoption has reached the steady state?

The gradual docking of our monitoring measurements with the steady state leading indicators in our aggregate operations plan will signify that we have accomplished our evolution. Effective enablement work plans framed across these four stages give us the leading indicators to manage all our enablement initiatives transparently and predictably.

Principle 6: Leverage systemic thinking to manage enablement execution.

Managing and executing enablement initiatives requires discipline and objectivity and can be easy if we embrace a system mindset. Conversely, every attempt to work individually or in silos creates a potential failure point throughout the execution cycle.

First, work plans for enablement initiatives are created to be followed. They are our easily measurable leading indicators. Work plans include names and dates. Stick to them. Stay accountable and leave deadlines unchanged, even in the case of delays. Optimize work plans only when objectively relevant new information is available. Perpetually kicking the can down the road is a sign of accountability failure.

Second, we can purchase work management software at a modest cost to store and manage our work plans. Such centralized document and status management complements a good work plan. It allows owners to track progress and every stakeholder to assess progress against actionable steps, review deliverables associated with milestones, and view measurements that demonstrate progress towards the steady state.

We can measure progress by reporting on actionable steps completed as a share of the total actionable steps. We can automate escalations through a centralized reporting of all missed milestones. Deliverables can be stored in such software to support broad communication and audits to assess completion risk. The Congruence Architect and decision enablers can support initiative owners by using the broadly accessible work plans as the single source of truth on initiatives' progress towards the steady state.

Third, use our mature performance management approach to drive execution accountability. Supervisors must map enablement initiatives to performance management expectations set for enablement resources. This linkage would be evident in a mature management approach. Not using this accountability structure is a missed opportunity.

The milestones and deliverables of enablement initiatives are the performance management outcomes we must set for our enablement resources. However, we cannot attribute the success or failure of achieving the steady state improvement solely to an initiative owner, as it also relies on the robustness of the company's system to support owners.

Fourth, our decision management levers will help us manage initiatives effectively. Delegation of authority allows the enablement initiative owner to engage the key contributors of the initiative as the SWAT team to drive progress and decisions. Supervisors must leverage formal one-on-ones to track progress against work plans and inject coaching and issue resolution into initiative execution management. Our decision and communication ladder allows enablement initiative owners and supervisors to escalate and disseminate decision requirements and critical change communications. Mature company-wide collaboration techniques empower initiative owners and their supervisors to get work done efficiently and decisively.

Fifth, the Pressure Valve Framework empowers the enablement owner to identify likely failure points and seek help. Although the steps to address pressure valves are included in our work plans, company-wide awareness of their hazards is paramount.

Leverage all these systemic aspects to manage initiatives without succumbing to individualized, ad hoc approaches. Execution delays, modifications to the work plans, and decisions can all be handled through our company-wide systemic enablers. While we move through the four stages of the initiatives to implement change, we must ensure that our initiative has the intended maturity impact we slated during strategic planning.

Principle 7: Harmoniously inject improvements into operations baseline.

Our clarity of the steady state, the quality of our work plan, and the contingencies we build into our work plan can get us far. But we cannot trivialize the complexity of the last two stages of enablement execution – rollout and adoption, and monitoring. The final piece of complexity is maintaining or improving congruence.

During the latter execution stages, we attempt to improve and align multiple building blocks of our management approach and value engine.

Each enablement initiative or various initiatives in concert will address our operations baseline's symbiotic and intertwined nature.

Regardless of our market and offering, every enablement initiative will impact our processes. When we change our processes, we must consider how we leverage technology to support those processes. The way we look at data changes when our processes evolve. We will trigger data collection flaws if we do not address how process changes impact our data collection. We must address the impact of our process changes from our enablement initiative on our data, related reporting, and how we might use that data for any future analysis.

Conversely, when we change our offerings or introduce new capabilities, we change how customers use our offerings or the associated processes that value creators perform. We may need to enable impacted parties through training and formal one-on-one coaching.

Changes in our offering, processes, or use of data can significantly impact roles. We must augment our organization design if we add significant responsibilities to one or more roles. We can't just tack on more responsibilities, especially if new skills are required. Changes to the organization design also imply that we reconsider our compensation design for that role and similar roles.

Enablement initiatives might impact our people agenda across the entire company or specific roles. We might have upgraded our offering significantly, which must increase each seller's revenue expectations. Alternatively, we might have matured our organization design that changes the commission plan for all customer-facing resources.

That is congruence. Our company is a Rubik's cube. We cannot conveniently nudge a single cubie without impacting others. To change the state of one cubie, we almost always have to rearrange several of them. This is the only path to maximize value creation and optimize capital efficiency.

The initiative owner must ensure that dependencies across the management approach and value engine components across all functions are already baked into our steady state definition and execution work plans. Identifying dependencies like the need for a new role or compensation design changes during adoption would be a shame. This further underlines the importance of dovetailing the strategic plan with enablement work plans throughout the execution cycle.

As an example, a real-world enablement effort that I led epitomizes the complexities of evolution. As a turnaround partner, I implemented account planning, which is a common practice that allows companies to manage customer relationships methodically.

I developed and rolled out tailored processes and tools to the customer-facing team and their supervisors. Then, I invested a significant amount of time around adoption through group training, information sessions, one-on-one coaching, and managing the process in a hands-on manner until most individuals got the hang of it. Finally, I used the wave mindset by driving early adoption only among the top customers before moving to the rest.

To monitor adoption, I set up three interim measurements.

The **first** was to assess basic adoption using work management software that I had incorporated into the process design. It demonstrated whether we had completed key process steps for specific customers, offering a basic litmus test for adoption.

The **second** measurement was manual quality review via audits, feedback summaries, and one-on-one coaching for the first three account plans created by every customer-facing resource. These audits ensured that each individual understood the essence of a "good" account plan.

The **third** was a steady state leading indicator that validated ongoing process adherence. This included hands-on process oversight by attending customer meetings, where we reviewed the account plans.

This in-depth adoption monitoring was essential to prevent regression. For example, we identified one team using old customer-meeting documents that didn't meet the newly set criteria, renaming the documents as "account plans" to avoid creating new ones. This predictable behavioral skew was identified through the second measurement of quality reviews.

The simple truth is that there will always be resistance movements to changes driven by enablement initiatives, whether conscious or subconscious. Therefore, it is crucial to monitor whether abnormal influences shift the operations in unintended directions even beyond an adoption phase.

This account planning enablement initiative changed the company's processes and implied an evolution of the management approach. The company never considered account management a specialized skill. As a result, the company's organization design had to evolve, leading to hiring more specialized skills and optimizing compensation design for all customer-facing roles. Changing compensation for one role often implies reassessing compensation for other roles.

In summary, we must begin our execution cycle by translating our strategic plan into our enablement roadmap and initiative-specific enablement work plans that minimally leverage the five success factors and the four execution stages we covered.

In addition to deploying these execution management levers effectively, iterative learning must be part of our psyche. If we learn that an initiative that we had intended to get to the steady state in three months will now take four months, update the strategic plan to assess whether the change impacts our ability to complete all approved initiatives. For example, if we had prioritized eight initiatives, this shift in the execution window might mean that we can only execute six or seven initiatives, holding enablement investment constant.

New information is not good or bad. It is reality. However, we must revisit and update our strategic plan and trickle down the impact on our enablement work plans. We must manage our living enablement roadmap to reflect any revisions in our strategic plan. This allows us to collectively internalize that our new execution goal is to drive fewer enablement initiatives, which influences the value creation and capital efficiency we can achieve during the execution cycle. This may imply revising to set lower leading indicator targets in our aggregate operations plan. It is in the company's best interest to predict that we will likely hit lower lagging metrics such as revenue. It avoids reactivity and firefighting as we will discuss in the next chapter.

The reverse scenario might also occur, where we overestimate our commitment to executing a strategic initiative. Our approach doesn't change;

we must maintain the connectivity between our strategic plan and day-to-day activities. Otherwise, the controllability and transparency we built through our macroevolution components will break. Being agile through execution is not about being unplanned; it's about proactively planning and incorporating new information into our plans in a thoughtful and disciplined manner.

Enablement execution is a challenging undertaking. We can only measure success by the evolutionary shift in our operations baseline that moves it closer to our corporate strategy and greater harmony. Anything short of that implies we lost connectivity between our strategy and operations along the way. Once we inject evolutionary improvements into our operations, we enable operations resources to perform at a higher level to achieve the targets we set in our aggregate operations plan.

F.4
ACTIVATE PREDICTIVE, PREVENTATIVE, PROACTIVE OPERATIONS EXECUTION.

IT'S January 2. We are starting a new execution cycle. How does our company perform day-to-day work to market, sell, create offerings, deliver them, manage people, and all the efforts that result in customer value and eventually profits for investors?

Throughout our journey, we insisted on embracing a system mindset to empower employees and partners to operate methodically. A system mindset avoids the onus of each value creator independently solving the complex puzzle that our company is. If we deploy our fundamental levers thus far effectively, our operations resources will be well-enabled via our ever-evolving management approach and value engine.

Conversely, no sports team ever won a season by throwing Hail Marys. That is the summary theme of our final chapter. We will not consistently create value or use capital efficiently if each individual around a company operates at their discretion. At best, we can do that for a day, a week, or a month.

This final chapter will cover how operations resources work. The aim of operations execution is to stay disciplined and deliver to the system we have built over past and current macroevolution cycles.

Things To Remember: Operations Execution

Operations resources, including employees or partners and owned or borrowed assets, iteratively execute the operations baseline building blocks. All such efforts comprise operations execution.

If our past enablement efforts matured our management approach and value engine to the right side of the respective maturity models, operations resources would achieve optimal outcomes by executing our highly congruent operations baseline. If our management approach and value engine have significant incongruences, the correct path forward is to recognize and address it. The only path to high value creation and capital efficiency is to rely on our macroevolutionary cycle and improve the maturity of the operations baseline.

Executing our operations baseline is like setting off a domino. A well-designed domino is an incredible sight when we set it off. However, a poorly staged one won't progress, and we will constantly jump in and try to keep the domino moving. This is called firefighting. We could think that moments of firefighting are never predictable or avoidable. However, the maturity of our operations baseline and the effectiveness with which we execute against it predicts our level of firefighting.

Think about our operations baseline as a baking recipe that's meant to be used with precision. If we know our recipe is bad, we must inject improvements through our macroevolution cycle. Regardless, our company only has one recipe. Our operations resources must execute it as intended, while enablement resources improve it along the way.

Principle 1: Aggregate operations plan dictates activity and output expectations.

We all want to know how much work we are expected to do and how much output we are expected to produce. Our strategic planning exercise set leading indicator targets for our execution cycle. These are the measures that our operations resources are working towards.

Each operations resource must meet the unit performance targets set for their role, and collectively, the company must meet the aggregate operations plan target. Overperforming or underperforming are both bad. Yes, overperforming unpredictably usually backfires.

First, if our operations are genuinely capable of beating targets significantly, our strategy and plan are off, and we don't have a firm handle on the market or our operations baseline. Did our competitors set themselves on fire? Did the market somehow turn in our favor more than we expected?

Outperforming our own goals might feel comforting. But it should actually concern us that we couldn't anticipate it. Most companies create marginally incremental value in the market and do not drive a holistic market disruption. A market-disrupting artificial intelligence chip maker or a pioneering electric car manufacturer may come along every decade or two.

But the rest of the companies work in the realm of marginal progress, which is predictable. If we don't understand our present trajectory, we might as well prepare for a reversal of fortune in the next execution cycle.

Even if we are truly capable of surpassing our targets in our execution cycle, it often results in incongruence. Our operations baseline is a finely tuned system quantified via our aggregate operations plan across the company. We can't perform unpredictably well in one function and expect the system to stay balanced.

Imagine an execution cycle in which we land twice as many new customers as expected. This is fantastic because we can generate more sales revenue. But it also means we must serve twice as many new customers as planned. Do we have the skilled operations resources to do that? Can our offering support that unexpected influx? Does our need to be reactive stall our enablement initiatives?

Peloton, the in-home exercise solution provider, was one of the major beneficiaries of COVID lockdowns that triggered unanticipated demand for its exercise bikes and treadmills. The company's ill-conceived reaction to scale manufacturing, expecting the COVID-related demand spike to persist, eventually cost the founding CEO his job and led to company-wide lay-offs because the demand spike proved an aberration.

Even a good thing can hurt sustainability if it pushes our execution into reactivity and forces us to make up our path forward on the fly.

Second, purposeful sandbagging during planning can also result in the appearance of overperformance during execution. Low-balling strategic planning targets with a primary aim to show that "we beat targets" is a sign of an imbalance in incentives between executives and the board.

Such tactics arise from a lack of trust between senior executives, value creators, and the board. A lack of confidence in the operations baseline's maturity can also lead to the same aberration. Essentially, executives make unrealistic demands of value creators, hoping that getting close to those expectations will meet the targets communicated to or demanded by the board. However, this breaks all the planning levers we learned.

The company may maintain multiple financial and operations targets in these situations. The lowest set of targets is board expectation. The highest group of targets is set for value creators to strive for independently. The third and middle one is executive hope.

Tracking and managing one set of strategic plan targets is hard enough. Monitoring multiple targets creates a heavy burden. These are signs of incongruence that pit individuals and groups in a company against each other.

We aim to achieve well-defined strategic planning targets via disciplined execution. Even if we are overshooting our targets unpredictably, revisiting our strategic plan and reworking our aggregate operations plan is the only path to maintaining congruence in our operations baseline. An unplanned good year of outcomes that pushes our operations into chaos will likely result in a reversal in fortunes soon after.

Principle 2: Embrace management approach and value engine as execution mandates.

At a microscopic level, operations execution usually appears easy – people doing everyday things. Unfortunately, that apparent ease drives complacency and can leave us with complexity in the form of broken operations execution.

The actions performed by each operations resource to keep our offering up and running or deliver value to customers might appear trivial. As a result, we might get tempted to let each of them operate as independent islands because it's easier to give individuals complete freedom. However, when we have several resources to execute perceivably trivial actions in a divergent manner, our overall operations will involve many permutations of actions and decisions, which is the definition of anarchy.

Similarly, each sales rep might use independent tactics to find and convince customers to buy our offerings. It may feel easier for supervisors and senior executives to allow each sales resource freedom to sell in their own way. But it gets complex quickly when they start selling to the same customers, sell to customers outside our sweet spot, or promise value that deviates from our offerings.

Even if we start with a strong operations baseline, it can all go wrong without discipline. Deviating from our operations baseline has enormous ramifications. If our actions do not reflect the building blocks we set in place, we no longer know whether they are effective because our data do not reflect them.

Senior executives must lead commitment to the operations baseline.

Senior executive roles demand the skills to withstand pressure to conform and appease, see the bigger picture, see further into the future than other employees, and make difficult choices. That is *leadership*. I have refrained from using the term "leadership" often intentionally because its modern-day application has diluted it to mean appeasement, not the essence described above.

A senior executive must be a leader and lead by example to demonstrate that operations execution is not a free-for-all or a passion-driven subject. It is a proven science with centuries of history. Every executive must internalize the operations execution principles we covered and demonstrate their commitment daily. It's not easy, but that's the price of leadership. Operations discipline will not take root if senior executives waver in their commitment to it, especially if other value creators do not internalize its necessity and challenge it along the way.

Operations resources must focus on their skills and deliver to the operations baseline.

Understandably, every human being prefers to do things in their own way. But working for a company is a team sport. Perceived high performers may have their personal style, and they should be able to maintain it as long as their style doesn't conflict with our operations baseline. Effective operations baseline execution has two characteristics.

The **first** is the unwavering adherence to our management approach and value engine building blocks. Our company invested heavily in these. Use them! Why reinvent the wheel or break a comprehensive foundation for personal ego? All operations resources must play within our operations baseline.

Amazon's core value epitomizes this mindset: "Have Backbone; Disagree and Commit." It is essential to share our ideas and sentiments or hypotheses and analyses. But at a certain point, it is crucial to commit to either playing on the team or leaving the team. This applies to everyone in any company, but it is more critical for operations resources because they execute against a predefined baseline.

We must resist the temptation to allow perceived top performers to circumvent our operations baseline. Robust process design does not hinder top performers. Processes must be reproducible to be effective, and strong processes help performers at all levels optimize outcomes. Senior executives and supervisors must ensure that top, mid-tier, and low performers adopt and execute processes consistently.

Adherence to the operations baseline is also necessary to ensure that perceived high performers are not hitting or exceeding their targets at others' expense. Almost every sales function will have at least one example of a sales rep who brings in significant revenue but sets customer expectations that are misaligned with the company's offerings. In this situation, the account managers or teams that develop and deliver our offerings are cleaning up after a seemingly high-performing sales rep, while falling behind in their own expected contributions. Similarly, an overzealous account manager can maintain high customer satisfaction for a short period by overpromising to customers and leaving the company at risk of losing revenue months later. So, adherence to our operations baseline is non-negotiable.

The **second** characteristic focuses on the specialized skills associated with operations roles. Resources in these roles must possess the necessary skills and desire to leverage those skills.

Most reasons for confusion among operations resources stem from poor organization designs with ineffective role definitions or laissez-faire and biased hiring. These put individuals with misaligned skills and incentives in the wrong roles. In addition, weak performance management approaches that do not address gaps caused by organization design and hiring challenges aggravate such situations.

As our organization scales, each operations role will require several experts and supervisors. These roles require very specific skills and experience, without which we cannot meet the targets we set.

For instance, we must have a mature productized offering regardless of our market. Therefore, we need an associated capability management process that allows issue identification, root cause problem-solving, escalation paths, prioritization, and work management. The maturity of this process allows us to set an expectation floor for how we maintain the quality of our offering. However, a role that executes such a process to manage offerings will require skilled problem-solvers to translate unique customer issues into underlying root causes and manage solutions to address those causes.

Every operations role requires role-specific expertise. The effectiveness of our operations baseline execution to hit the planning targets is predicated on operations resources focusing on excelling in role-specific skills and delivering to the operations baseline with discipline.

Operations supervisors must have skills to oversee adoption of the operations baseline.

Operations supervisors are necessary oversight roles to support each individual value creator through execution. But they are difficult to staff effectively.

First, highly skilled operations resources are hard to acquire, and our performance and compensation management approach must incentivize and reward them exponentially well. This means we might have sales reps or designers and builders of our offering who deserve very high compensation. The complication is that their supervisor's primary skill required is to coach and guide them. This might demand a lower compensation than the highest performers in the operations resource roles.

Using the sporting world as a comparison, a significant share of the players on top teams are compensated more than the coach. The same may apply to operations resources at a company with an effective management approach. A supervisor must be staffed based on skill to coach instead of a natural progression via promotions.

Rarely has the same person been a great player and great coach. But average players have become amazing coaches, and great players consistently prove to be average coaches.

Second, a dedicated operations supervisor must embrace their primary responsibility to enable their team's operations skills through coaching, ongoing decision-enablement, work management, and issue resolution as framed in our operations baseline. It is tempting for operations supervisors to get distracted by enablement initiatives because they impact the work their resources perform, which runs counter to our Comparative Advantage Ecosystem mindset. Operations supervisors often come from an operations execution background and don't have enablement skills and experience.

If our operations supervisory layer does not internalize its core responsibilities of overseeing operations and gets distracted by enablement initiatives, we will struggle to maintain discipline. It is even more challenging if operations supervisors do not support enablement resources and embrace improvements delivered into the operations baseline through strategic enablement initiatives.

I partnered with a sales team that struggled to follow the operations baseline. The lack of adherence to processes caused 90 percent of sales reps to achieve less than 60 percent of their achievable sales quota for multiple execution cycles. The sales executive struggled to coach the importance of a systemic approach to selling. The sales supervisors embraced the freedom mindset and advised the sales reps to be creative with sentiments like: "We want our reps to go after a prospect on Monday that they might have seen in an advertisement on TV on Sunday evening. . . ." But what if two sales reps saw that same advertisement? This company's execution and outcomes didn't improve until the supervisor roles were optimally staffed.

Consider these design questions to assess the level of discipline among operations resources:

Do senior executives embrace the company's operations baseline as the foundation for disciplined operations execution?

Are operations supervisors staffed effectively, and do they focus on their primary skill of coaching and overseeing day-to-day adherence to the operations baseline?

Are operations roles staffed with resources with role-specific skills and interest in disciplined execution of the operations baseline?

Once we establish a disciplined mindset across all levels of operations resources, we can manage with transparency.

Principle 3: Transparent operations execution starts with operations work planning.

What does adhering to our operations baseline look like each day? How do supervisors know how well each operations resource adheres to our baseline? How do supervisors know when to coach their resources on processes or role-specific skills? How do senior executives understand how effectively each team and individual is operating? How do we know each operations resource is adopting improvements injected by enablement initiatives?

Presenteeism was never a good way to manage work. When value creators with desk jobs went virtual during COVID-19, the limitations of presenteeism-based work management became much more exposed. During COVID-19, I took charge of a large team to transform operations execution because their historical approach of counting time spent at the office or email volumes proved ineffective.

Work planning is a necessary and straightforward concept that we introduced for enablement execution management. It also applies to operations execution. Although the aim and basic structure of work planning remain the same, **Operations Work Plans** are very different from enablement work plans. All five success factors – milestones, deliverables, action steps, single point of accountability, and hand-offs – still apply. But the way we create and use them is very different.

Operations work plans mirror The Company Way Processes.

Building operations execution work plans is easy, especially compared to enablement initiatives. Unlike enablement work plans, we do not have to create or design anything new. Operations work plans simply transform our process definitions into actionable, shareable, and monitorable formats. Figure F6 shows how the six process elements connect to the five work plan success factors labeled with the alphabet letters A through E.

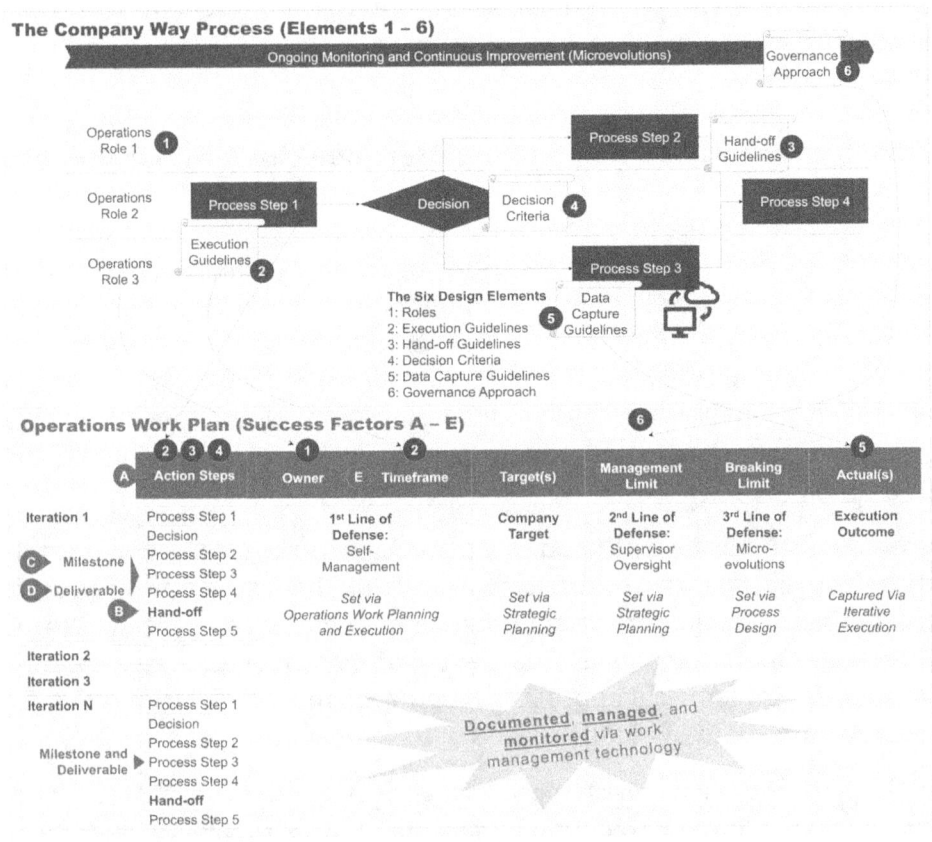

Figure F6. Transparent and defensible operations execution relies on the adoption of mature processes.

The process steps, the detailed execution guidelines, and the decision criteria from our process design must become a work plan's **action steps** because that's what resources are expected to do. The transitions between process steps and roles in our process design become the **hand-off** success factor in our operations work plan. The hand-off guidelines in our process design inform us to build additional action steps necessary to transition work between roles. The work plan's **milestones** come from a logical grouping of process steps that lead to meaningful interim outcomes. Our process design's execution and hand-off guidelines also articulate the appropriate **deliverables** for these milestones.

This firm connectivity of our mature process design to operations work plans is our path to maintaining discipline and creating transparency. Although we are lifting details for work plans from our process design, this relationship is paramount, and here is why.

Operations execution is iterative. Each operations resource executes processes several times each day, week, or month. Each time we execute a process, we require a **single point of accountability**, which is our final success factor for work plans. Our six process design elements include the articulation of roles and critical timeframes. We must translate them into a single name and an accountability timeframe for each action step and milestone in every iteration we perform. One or more operations resources in a role will execute the same process many times over. So, work plans are necessary to create accountability for every resource and each iteration.

Things To Remember: Operations Work Plans

Operations work plans convert a mature process design into an execution guide and tracker that operations resources can use to perform and record each process iteration. Each record of an operations work plan reflects a single iteration of the associated process.

Operations work plans are necessary to measure operations execution.

Recall Process-Data Symbiosis from Part C. Data reflects our process and its execution and how well we capture it. Process-Data Symbiosis comes to life when we capture each iteration of operations execution using work plans. Every iteration of a process will involve capturing action steps and recording information based on the data capture guidelines of that process. This is our company's data. The aggregation of data from many iterations forms the measurements of our leading indicators.

Operations work plans enable each operations resource to follow data capture guidelines during each iteration's execution. They allow supervisors to move past managing via presenteeism and manage based on the work being performed. Almost every company uses operations work plans for two or three of the most iterated processes, such as sales, customer service, or manufacturing. However, a mature operations execution environment expands this to the entire operations baseline.

A typical example of an operations work plan is tracking customer issue tickets. A well-run company relies on a strong process to resolve customer complaints. Solving customer issues requires operations resources to have ownership and timeline accountabilities. Each customer complaint ticket is an iterative log of a work plan mirroring the company's issue resolution process.

The intention to manage such common processes using work planning is a good start. But it is unlikely to move the needle unless work planning, managing those plans, and monitoring them is systemic. One-off efforts to manage common processes without organization-wide adoption of operations work plans indicate a weak system that considers operations work plans "paperwork."

Usually, one-off efforts fall off the wagon because no operations resource wants to be held more accountable than all other operations resources in the company. Senior executives will find it hard to hold one or two roles accountable via work plans and eventually increase their leniency. Even processes like sales execution and customer service tickets will become check-the-box exercises where the individual iterations will become decoupled from The Company Way Processes.

Our entire operations baseline has intertwined leading indicators for which we set targets through planning. So, we must track the when, what, how, and how much of every execution iteration of our operations baseline so that we can measure the maturity and execution effectiveness of operations across the company. In our balanced system mindset, our operations baseline breaks if only some processes are effectively executed and managed. So, we must build and manage work plans for all processes in our operations baseline.

Leverage technology enablers to manage work plans.

We could have done all of the above on paper and used to do so decades ago. Having said that, enabling the iterative execution of our operations baseline using software is a no-brainer in this digital age. Many out-of-the-box options exist for the core few company processes, like sales execution or customer service request handling.

All software that supports operations execution does the same thing. It interconnects information tables, and easy-to-navigate pages allow users to interact with them. Off-the-shelf options give these tables precise names and come with predefined columns, but their precision can be mistaken for universal applicability.

Remember, operations technology always follows a process. We must develop processes that fit our needs and then choose software to accommodate our process. Often, companies live in an inefficient or low-value-creating operations execution environment by relying too much on out-of-the-box software without maturing their operations baseline or ignoring well-defined processes. Recall our principles in Chapter C.2.

Most software allows us to mold tables and their columns to our needs and easily systematize our process. For example, I instituted a robust hiring process to mature the management approach at a company. During the first wave of improving the hiring process, we managed the process via emails and spreadsheets. But as we hired more, mistakes started creeping in. There was even an instance where I mixed up two candidates, one we wanted to hire and one we wanted to pass on.

The vital process needed to be operationally robust. So, I built the process into the work management software that the company already used. Codifying the hiring process into the software only took me two hours, allowing everyone involved in hiring to go through the same process with every candidate in every role. We logged all aspects of the hiring process, including interviewing, negotiating, and presentations given by candidates, in the work plan. It transformed the company's hiring process into a transparent and disciplined one.

Operations software options will only become better and easier to use. Leveraging them ensures our process-linked work plan and each iteration are documented and measured. However, using software for an operations work plan must follow an effective process design.

Embracing our operations baseline as the rule of law for day-to-day execution will help us find discipline. In addition, translating the operations baseline into work plans to manage every iteration of execution creates the transparency necessary to manage operations.

Empowered by this transparency, three lines of defense enable a system to execute in a predictive, preventative, and proactive manner and avoid mistakes caused by natural human tendencies.

Principle 4: Leading indicators to predict execution shortfalls and self-manage is the first line of operations defense.

The most fundamental aspect our company can control is ensuring value creators execute operations as designed. Our first line of defense makes sure we have empowered them to do so.

Remember, Newton's third law of motion states that actions have equal and opposite reactions. Each execution iteration against our operations baseline is an action. The expected reaction is the direct and causal impact of each action on the outcomes we desire. We designed our Chain of Controllability to create this causal relationship between these actions and reactions.

With transparent operations work plans, we don't have to wait for the reactions to become observable days or weeks later. Instead, we can predict those reactions by observing the leading indicators associated with the actions. Measurements of how well we perform action steps in the operations work plans predict the probability of achieving targets set in our aggregate operations plan.

Take sales execution as a sample process. If we effectively track and measure the quality of actions and decisions through each iteration of the sales process execution, we can predict the reaction we would receive from customers. Each iteration of our operations work plan tracks each sales execution, and one of those steps may be to make a phone call. Suppose we want reps to spend an average of thirty minutes on a phone call with prospective customers. We could predict that customers are far more likely to react positively to our sales inquiry days or weeks later than they would if the call were only three minutes long.

The good news is that predicting the future is possible. The bad news is that companies rarely achieve such predictability.

The fault is not with the idea. Instead, operations baseline immaturity or ineffective execution management are to blame. What if every sales rep has their own interpretation of what qualifies as an iteration to track? A rep may only log iterations if they spent significant time talking to a customer, and we would have no information on all the zero-minute calls, inflating the average call time. That's bad data. What if the process isn't well-articulated or trained on? Reps may log many calls with end users, while our process design intended that reps only log calls with buyers or approvers because only those calls lead to sales.

I once partnered with a company to improve value delivery. Their capability had both software and service dimensions. However, the productization was immature, and the operations resources needed to perform significant ad hoc manual error corrections before customers could see the value. Customers were regularly unhappy because this manual error correction was so mind-numbing that the responsible operations resources were not motivated to do it. Something had to change because not delivering value to customers is untenable.

I translated the error-checking portion of the process into a daily recurring action step in a work plan. It required every resource to address errors for two hours daily. If the resources addressed errors for two hours each day, then all of us could predict that we would meet the customers' needs by the end of the month. The converse was also true. The resources could self-manage their days and make up for days they fall behind. Monitoring the leading indicator for the error-checking step informed me which resources were executing well and self-directing. I could also predict which customers would send me an angry email based on which resources were not tracking well on this simple action.

Each operations resource must be systemically enabled to use leading indicator measurements associated with their everyday execution to self-manage and improve. In essence, this is each operations value creator performing their best according to the unit performance-based operations plan we set during strategic planning. Operations resources can explore learning sources to self-teach and use formal one-on-ones to receive coaching or escalate to get help on impediments to executing well. Self-empowerment of operations resources is our first line of defense.

Principle 5: Operations supervisors using management limits to prevent performance shortfalls is the second line of operations defense.

We can't manage solely by the progress of work plans, though. Operations resources executing as guided by our operations baseline are table stakes. An operations supervisor's responsibility is to empower operations resources using preset corrective actions when leading indicators reveal that individual value creators need help.

Management limits trigger supervisor and executive involvement.

The execution guidelines and governance approach from process design include targets, management limits, and breaking limits for the leading indicators across various building blocks of our operations baseline. Our deep analysis during the most recent strategic planning effort to create the unit performance operations plan ensures that our leading indicator targets and limits are current.

As we learned in Chapter C.3, management limits are thresholds defined to help supervisors perform their roles. These yellow flags trigger our second line of defense against operations execution challenges. Breaching management limits demands supervisor involvement to bring the execution quality within the acceptable range of management limits. This second line of defense is an opportunity to address breakdowns at an individual or role level, preventing negative lagging outcomes.

Recall that effective reporting does not require attention, barring breaches of limits. There is no reason to stare at a report beyond a quick comparison of measurements tracked through work plans against the associated management and breaking limits. Perpetually looking at reports without management limits does not help the supervisor make sound decisions. Is watching a stock price go up and down without any decision aids help us know when to buy or sell?

Using management limits to monitor processes is easy if we have a mature process design. It is a powerful execution management tool. It allows supervisors to sit back and focus on skills coaching and decision enablement instead of micromanagement. It will enable operations resources to have the breathing room to focus on using their skills instead of answering "Are we there yet?" questions. It optimizes our operations investment efficiency because everyone gets to focus on value-creating activities rather than status checks.

A supervisor will likely monitor several leading indicators associated with the processes executed by their operations resources. Crossing the management limits on any of them indicates that one or several execution iterations by one or more operations resources are showing significant enough aberration that we must worry it will lead to poor outcomes. It's time to act!

Going back to my delivery team from the last principle, what if there are too many errors to resolve in two hours? What if a resource just checked the box on two hours of error reviews without doing the work? Action-based work tracking is a good start, but more is needed.

Another leading indicator I monitored was how long an error stayed open before someone addressed it. I set a management limit of two days. Breaching this limit implied they had too many errors to handle in two hours, needed coaching to address the errors faster, or any other reason I could explore and remediate. However, the breach was still a leading indicator that allowed me to take corrective action before customers saw problems.

Use preset paths to limit impact of operations breakdowns.

Management limit triggers notify supervisors and executives to step in and perform their primary operations execution management role, which is to empower the individuals reporting to them. It is also important that the cavalry operates within our operations baseline and uses our company system. Support through this second line of defense must adhere to two factors.

The **first** factor is that supervisors and senior executives take constructive actions instead of just using the yellow flag as a stick. Asking an operations resource to fix the situation without offering support shifts blame and demonstrates incompetence. It looks good in TV shows but does not create value in real life. Unfortunately, this stick behavior is more common than one might think. Immature use of management approach levers place supervisors in critical roles without the necessary expertise, training, or natural instincts to manage.

Constructive corrective actions imply that the supervisor enters a diagnosis mode and gets their hands dirty. The diagnosis path will depend significantly on the company, market, process, metrics, and value creator being supported. This is a practical application moment for our Systems First philosophy. Breakdowns rarely happen only because of an individual.

However, it is also crucial that supervisors are comfortable holding their operations resources accountable if the underlying reason for the flag is recurring poor execution. Confronting direct reports and holding them accountable is difficult, but supervisory roles must be filled with resources with the skill and experience to do so professionally when necessary.

The **second** factor is the effective use of preset corrective actions baked into our processes and reporting design. In most situations where a yellow flag occurs, the root causes are predictable, and follow-throughs can be predefined in mature process designs. A good process design implies that a quick diagnosis would reveal the root cause and articulate a corresponding follow-on path. If supervisors have to figure out how to handle every aberration as though it's the first time it has occurred, then our process design lacks maturity.

Supervisors must demonstrate the discipline and humility to take the optimal follow-through paths to address the situation. Conversely, the supervisor must not place the situation, themselves, or the operations resources involved at the center of the universe and merely address symptoms. The relationship between the supervisor and a value creator must stay within the confines of the operations baseline.

These factors guide supervisory action and push us to embrace the discipline we need to play within our company's operations design. This helps us operate proactively instead of reactively after poor outcomes have already happened.

For example, a typical sales execution leading indicator is the length of time we have been trying to close a sale with a specific customer, and it's called aging. Aging indicates stagnation of each sales execution iteration.

In a simple real-life scenario, I set a management limit of sixty days to complete the first three milestones of a sales execution process. Any sales efforts stalled before the third milestone for over sixty days will require supervisory intervention.

The preset corrective action is for a sales supervisor to sit with each sales rep monthly to review every effort over sixty days. Specific remediations, like the supervisor engaging the prospect or closing the effort based on details of sales efforts thus far, were also set in place. This second line of defense moved stagnant good prospects to a sale, saved operations resources' time on prospects that were never likely to close, and provided the entire sales team with a clearer picture of the sales efforts that were likely to pan out.

The second line of defense trigger is not intended to highlight "bad" situations. It simply highlights areas where we can take and give help. Addressing operations shortfalls identified through management limit breaches and taking corrective actions helps us stay close to achieving the intended leading and lagging outcomes set during strategic planning.

Formal one-on-ones allow supervisors to engage in issue resolution via coaching and decision-making. In addition to employees raising risks and using the opportunities to drive decisions, one-on-ones are structured opportunities for supervisors to course-correct the actions of operations resources if the root cause remains within the purview of this supervisor–operations resource relationship.

But what if the root cause of a management limit breach overflows the supervisor–individual relationship or if we cross the breaking limits?

Principle 6: Microevolutions triggered by breaking limits are the third line of operations defense.

A root cause of a management limit breach that our operations baseline does not anticipate or address in time eventually results in breaching our breaking limit. So, an unanticipated root cause that triggers management limit multiple times is precisely the same as crossing the breaking limits. The latter could become apparent first if our attention to operations details is low. The third line of defense addresses repetitive breaches of the management limit that we don't know how to address or a more explicit red flag of breaching the breaking limit.

Problem-solving that bubbles over the supervisor–value creator relationship constitutes the third line of defense. If the root cause of a gap requires new solutions or the engagement of other functions, or if the supervisor cannot handle it, the third line kicks in.

Similarly, if breaking limits are triggered, the supervisor–individual construct needs help. The breaking limits are triggered when the first and second lines have consistently failed, whether we recognize it or not. The Congruence Architect and analytical enablement resources must monitor for repetitive management limits and breaking limit breaches across all metrics and are on the hook for effective problem-solving across all functions.

The third line of defense is to micro-evolve using our decision system to escalate unique root causes of operational flags. The decision ladder we covered in Chapter F.1 is the optimal pathway to address the unplanned or cross-functional operations gaps. The executive decision meetings offer a structured escalation path to discuss and decide on the path forward.

If your mind is running to an instance where a customer is extremely unhappy and demanding immediate action, and a supervisor feels the right course of action is to have an urgent meeting with another team to remedy the situation, hold that thought. That is firefighting 101. A screaming customer indicates a failure of operations execution management and both the first and second lines of defense. It is a raging red flag. Firefighting such a scenario is akin to pushing the situation under the carpet without understanding the root causes.

Doing nothing with intention is a powerful and disciplined corrective action.

If the root cause of operations shortfalls that rise to the third line is ineffective execution of our operations baseline, senior executives and the CEO must reinforce supervisors and operations resources to stay true to our operations baseline without succumbing to on-the-fly decisions. The maturity of our management approach addresses performance gaps at the supervisor or individual levels if we objectively believe our value engine is optimized to achieve the measurements we planned. We are staying within our operations baseline here.

Beyond execution ineffectiveness, we must understand the underlying reasons if our outcomes have breached our breaking limits positively. Think about this as unexpected **"good news."** Is our value engine more powerful than we gave it credit for during strategic planning? Did we consciously understate our targets in our strategic plans? Were our strategic planning assumptions on scaling our operations baseline too conservative?

The appropriate course of action is to stick with the execution of the operations baseline and consider these possibilities during the next macroevolution cycle, which is only months away. Do not overreact!

For instance, we anticipated that we'd get ten new customers, and fifteen wanted us to serve them. We must stay within our aggregate operations plan and politely nudge those five customers to stay patient until we are ready to serve them.

Alternatively, we realized we could produce fifteen widgets instead of the ten we thought were realistic for our manufacturing line. Again, we must stick to our plan. The extra five may not have customers, may spoil, and come at the additional cost of the raw materials.

Conversely, if we breach the breaking limits on the negative side, which is unexpected **"bad news,"** effective root cause analysis must methodically lead us forward.

One path that we cannot pursue is carelessly deviating from our operations baseline or our strategic plan. It's worth reiterating this on every page because it tends to be a widespread reaction. It never works! If we deviate from our operations baseline, we are left with nothing but chaos. So, what do we do?

Root cause analyses often suggest a need for strategic initiatives to improve our operations baseline because our company will always have incongruences. If we learn that we have a malignant tumor, would we start cutting ourselves up immediately or wait for a qualified surgeon to do so on a scheduled date with care and in a safe environment?

If our strategy development and planning efforts are mature, the root cause is likely already being addressed through a currently prioritized strategic enablement initiative or an initiative we deprioritized during strategic planning. Maybe the root cause is a new insight that didn't emerge during our recent macroevolution cycle. In any of these situations, inclinations to add strategic initiatives must wait for the next macroevolution cycle.

We live in a world of constraints, and we cannot do everything right now. Our enablement resources are already busy with their defined initiatives. One execution cycle flies by. Enablement initiatives take time to drive maturity improvements. Then, operations execution takes months to show progress in outcomes. Discipline and a cool head are paramount in execution management. Do not disrupt enablement execution.

However, if new information available through operations execution can improve an existing enablement effort, the initiative owner and change committee would welcome such contribution.

Additionally, a breaking limit breach could happen because maturity improvements from planned or in-flight enablement initiative execution could be running late. Recall that our targets are set with the expectation that operations improvements from strategic initiatives will help us perform at higher levels. If one or more enablement initiatives we commissioned are behind schedule, we must adjust the aggregate operations plan accordingly. If we are behind, we are behind. Getting excited about it doesn't change that. We can only mature how well we deploy the execution management principles in Chapter F.3.

For example, the introduction of a new capability could be delayed. One or more leading indicators around the activities or process outcomes of lead generation resources responsible for creating leads for this new capability could cross the breaking limit. In a mature operations ecosystem, we should see operations work plan measurements and management limits breached first before the third line is triggered. Regardless, our only path forward is to improve the practicality of our targets, management limits, and breaking limits in our aggregate operations plan to align with the new reality of the delayed enablement initiative execution.

Life doesn't always go according to plan. But if we don't maintain a plan, our performance will suffer. Even publicly traded companies refresh their targets when conditions change significantly enough.

One of the biggest lessons I learned throughout my career and life is that doing nothing is a very viable choice, assuming we understand the situation comprehensively. Often it is the correct yet hard choice.

Microevolutions improve operations without disrupting congruence.

Exploring breaking limit breaches also presents an opportunity for tactical improvement of a small part of our operations baseline with no new investment. This pathway is our microevolutions.

Microevolutions achieve hairline improvements without injecting incongruence into our operations baseline. They use our management approach and value engine principles for improvement opportunities. However, they must not cause a domino effect in our operations baseline. They must allow our company to operate within the constraints of our enablement, operations, and investment plans.

Microevolutions must embrace the Comparative Advantage Ecosystem mindset to allow experts to do their work. Let a process designer and analytical enablement resources improve narrow components of our operations baseline. We must use our decision and change management principles from Chapters F.1 and F.2 to ensure that microevolutions go through objective and well-communicated decisions and are effectively adopted.

Recall the error processing example. A discovery that two hours is too little time to address all the errors can trigger a microevolution. A microevolution could be to better prioritize which errors we address. Illustratively, we could say errors that happen before noon hurt customers far more than the ones that happen in the afternoon and that we will address only the former. This microevolution is self-contained and will not impact any other aspects of our operations baseline, which is absolutely critical.

A poor microevolution attempt would change the processing time from two to four hours daily. This may look innocuous. However, it directly impacts the operations resources' other responsibilities. It could create a domino that hurts customers in worse ways that we will never know without a deep analysis across the operations baseline that spans other functions and building blocks. This bleeds into the realm of a strategic initiative without connectivity to strategic planning.

The third line of defense must stay confined to these three actions. First, double down on the first and second lines of defense. Second, ensure the operations plans and their aggregate are feasible, and adjust the strategic plan to ensure we operate within reality. Third, self-contained hairline microevolutions could be made to specific building blocks to improve leading and lagging measurements without disrupting other portions of the operations baseline.

Formula 1 teams are some of the highest-functioning sports teams. They design and build a car for each new season. They make tactical improvements to squeeze the last millisecond of speed out of their design during the season. But they commit all strategic redesigns of their cars for the following season. We must embrace a similar macroevolution and micro-evolution mindset.

Leveraging the three lines of defense allows us to predictably manage operations and ensure we can course-correct before the final outcomes are revealed when it's too late to change our fate. It also enables supervisors and senior executives to nudge all operations resources to adhere to the intent of the operations baseline.

Principle 7: Countering the Hawthorne effect is an operations necessity.

Recall that I mentioned the Hawthorne effect early in the book. Every employee, supervisor, and senior executive in an operations baseline execution environment must internalize the concept of suboptimal reactions to management and monitoring.

Things To Remember: Hawthorne Effect

The Hawthorne effect is a simple idea that living things behave differently when observed.

In any situation where we set goals, human beings tend to cut corners to meet them. This applies to all of us. This tendency to cut corners becomes more prevalent when the gap between the goal and our ability to achieve the goal is high, or the pressure to achieve the goal is high.

Why does our form suffer when we significantly increase weight when we exercise? Our bodies cheat to meet the higher-weight goals we set.

Observation is a measurement of our operations. When a specific portion of operations is actively observed with the performers' knowledge, they will likely change their behavior to fit the observation.

Isn't this what we want? No! We want the performer to adhere to the intent of the behavior, not just the observable portion of the behavior.

All leading indicators are only proxies for behaviors. No single metric will ever measure 100 percent of a behavior's intent. Even two or three strong metrics that observe different elements of the same behavior will not be conclusive. We can only get close. This means we always leave room for the performer to intentionally or unintentionally cut corners to meet our measurement.

Wells Fargo Bank's account scandal in 2016 is an example of this facet. The company designed a great lagging indicator to report performance – the number of accounts per customer. Objectively, this is a good measure, and cross-selling different types of accounts to customers is good. However, this same metric was used for years to assess value creator performance. Eventually, Wells Fargo employees felt compelled to continue to improve this metric upwards. They figured out shortcuts, including creating unnecessary accounts for unsuspecting customers because they were being measured intently on this one measure.

We can find this facet playing out in any measurement. The most significant risk of the Hawthorne effect comes from highly intense reporting on particular metrics for extended periods. These three factors – high intensity, a few high-visibility metrics, and a long timeframe –give performers' subconscious brains good reasons and time to plot for measurable success, whether the real outcomes match the measurement or not.

A few years ago, I was revamping a sales analytics function where lead generation and conversion to sales were a struggle. Lead generation resources had a target number to produce each month. The CEO demanded that a daily report be sent to everyone highlighting the progress in lead generation. The numbers were bad in January, and the CEO sent a strongly worded email demanding corrective action. Amazingly, the February numbers were a complete reversal, and almost every operations resource created the allotted number of leads. Powerful email, right?

No single lead from this group turned into a sale in six months. The lead generation resources realized that they just had to schedule a meeting between a sales rep and anyone who might potentially take a meeting, no matter their relevance to the buying process. They set many meetings with executive assistants, people in unrelated departments, or contractors at prospects who didn't have any influence. That email was a stick without support and must not have gone out.

Supervisors and senior executives must never use measurements as a stick; measurements must be used as identifiers. The Hawthorne effect is a simple but powerful reality that we must predict through design efforts, proactively diagnose, and watch for during operations execution.

In our sales effort aging example, what if supervisors use the sixty-day management limit as a stick? The sales reps may only log their efforts if they are sure to win quickly to avoid triggering the sixty-day management limit. However, the company will have no information about what the sales reps are working on, and supervisors can't help them with leads that aren't easy wins.

Undesired behavior is likely when only one or two tactical and disjointed metrics are used, and they become overused. The impact of the Hawthorne effect is often hidden unless intentionally diagnosed. An experienced process designer and Congruence Architect must own the design of leading indicators used to monitor operations baseline execution.

Principle 8: Effective operations execution is the bridge to our future.

Our operations execution mantra is to embrace evolutionary enablement improvements, trust our operations baseline, and execute flawlessly using work plans and our three lines of defense. If our performance lags behind our leading indicators, the remediations sit in one of the topics we already discussed. When breaking limits are breached, we might find microevolution opportunities that improve our performance without injecting incongruences. The answer is never to go rogue and revert to Hail Mary tactics.

Focus on understanding how and why we win or lose without sacrificing discipline.

Our outcomes are only repeatable if we know why we win. We can only avoid repeating poor outcomes if we know why we lost. We will not know why we win or lose if we cannot connect our actions to outcomes.

If we have an outsized quarter of solid sales but achieved that without following our operations baseline, can we answer why we did so well? We cannot! We could find a correlation between our short-term success and some activity in our company. But how do we know which activity if our execution didn't match our operations baseline? Correlation does not imply causality. We are more likely to confirm an incorrect bias or two through a correlation analysis. Incrementally, our data is too poor to analyze if we don't execute based on our operations baseline.

Our Chain of Controllability designed our relationship between our execution and outcomes to be causal. Success decoupled from the execution of operations baseline often leads companies astray. Short-term success found by two or three individuals might leave us thinking that their approach is meaningful for others to follow. We might fall for recency bias that winning two or three similar customers in quick succession unexpectedly is a more meaningful trend than it truly is, which might lead us to sell to similar customers who may end up costing us more to serve than the revenue we get from them.

A series of events at a company I partnered with exemplifies the challenges of such decoupling. One sales rep leveraging a personal contact landed a large customer outside the company's sweet spot. This customer directly managed hundreds of residential homes in the US through their rental portal. Coincidentally, this was a good customer because they had access to data from these homes, and that data access is necessary for our company to create value. But was this one deal meaningful data? No, because we decided to pursue an easily winnable customer outside our sweet spot due to a personal relationship.

The sales rep then used this opportunity to pursue several other residential rental companies and convinced them that they could capture the same value as the first company. Again, it worked – from a sales perspective!

But here was the catch – the first customer was unique; they managed real estate directly and had the data that our company needed. It was sheer luck. Although the remaining customers considered themselves peers, their business models were not the same; they only invested in the residential properties but didn't directly manage them and thus didn't have the necessary data. As a result, creating post-sales value for these other customers was impossible for the account management team. The remaining customers were unhappy throughout and eventually canceled their contracts, for which the account management team was penalized. The relationship between execution and outcomes broke when the rep went after that first one-off prospect and ignored the sweet spot. The mistake was to think there was meaning in that lucky decoupled success.

A similar conundrum will plague us if we experience poor outcomes. We can only know what parts of the operations baseline failed us if we execute them to their intent. Otherwise, we will end up arbitrarily blaming our offerings, processes, or people involved rather than objectively solving the underlying root cause.

Execution discipline enables framing future purpose, corporate strategy, and strategic plan.

A mature operations baseline reflects our purpose-led strategy and associated strategic plan and initiatives. An execution cycle is a company-level reality test of whether our design works. Learning from our operations execution cycle is a necessity because, apart from a market analysis that anyone can do, all the unique company-specific information needed to frame our future comes from the performance of our operations baseline.

We can only build a future based on present reality if we know why we win and lose and what parts of our current company's design work or don't work.

Our actions, decisions, and customers' reactions are the only true sources of objective information that we can use to develop our next strategy and plan. Remember, data always follows a process. During planning, we modeled our entire company's operations as a giant process. Therefore, our company's data is only meaningful if we follow our operations baseline.

Conversely, if we cannot learn from our present operations baseline, our company will remain a perpetual startup in its maturity. Incongruences within and between the company's building blocks and system will continue to increase as we acquire more customers and add more value creators. Eventually, we will stall and regress.

Can we say that a specific capability is valued or not by customers if we aren't selling it as we framed in our operations baseline? Do we know the value created by a capability if we aren't teaching customers how to take advantage of it as we framed it in our operations baseline? Can we say that our selling process or compensation design is working well if we do not live by our core values or follow our processes?

No!

Consider these reflection questions as ones we must be able to answer based on our lessons from operations execution:

Are we staying true to our company's purpose and aligning the incentives of all our stakeholders?

Can we continue to do so? Must we reframe our company's purpose, including value exchange across stakeholders, expectations of profitability, and realistic lifecycle-specific risks?

What parts of our strategic decision proved to be correct? What didn't?

What strategic trade-offs and choices must we change in the next macroevolution cycle?

How effective was our strategic planning? Did we inject our strategy effectively into our operations baseline? Was our operations plan too optimistic, realistic, or too pessimistic?

How would customers characterize our value creation?

Did we invest efficiently?

Which building blocks of our operations baseline performed well? Which didn't?

How robust is our system?

These questions are not comprehensive. They must span every fundamental lever and underlying principle we discussed throughout the book. If we don't execute our operations baseline, we will not have objective information about our company, and we will not be able to answer these questions to continue to build towards the best version of our company. We will likely indulge in the same debates we did in previous years, and we won't have good answers on what is working and what isn't.

Every operations execution cycle leads us to an opportunity to reevaluate our company purpose and the next macroevolution, where we must ask ourselves the question: ***How aligned are our purpose, strategy, and operations?***

We must be disciplined and focus on delivering on our promises through our purpose, strategy, and operations to all our stakeholders – customers, employees, investors, partners, and even representatives of society.

Does all this feel exhausting? Building a holistic company that balances the incentives of all stakeholders in equilibrium requires us to maintain congruence at all levels of our company and across lifecycle stages. It's not meant to be easy. It's meant to be fulfilling and leave a positive legacy for all stakeholders who are part of our holistic company's lifecycle.

The Companies We Need.

PEOPLE are complicated. Everyone has different underlying motivations, and we all work with different sets of information. At the same time, we often interchangeably wear the hats of investors, employees, customers, partners, and society throughout our lives.

None of us would want to be in a personal relationship with an individual who takes and takes but brings little back to the table. So, we must not accept this mindset in the context of humanity's greatest invention: the value exchange relationship known as a company!

We need companies that balance the incentives of stakeholder groups. Such a One Company mindset is the only path to sustainable value creation and the effective and efficient use of investment, which, after all, is the premise of capitalism.

Our buying choices, which span volume, price, and company selection, are a vote and a capital contribution that impact all stakeholders, including other customers. Our choice to take a freebie or a discount may support an unsustainable, capital-engineered business model and hurt a sustainable one. Either we will pay for the free lunch later, or someone else will pay on our behalf.

Whether we have a humble retirement investment account or assets worth billions, we must internalize that capitalism is intended to create value from investment, not artificially boost the market price by telling stories.

As a value creator, leading large groups of people, making big decisions, and performing actions that impact others, all while being well-paid, is a luxury that many people in many parts of the world do not have. Attention to detail, so we understand the immediate and long-term ripple effects of our incentives, decisions, and actions, is a duty that comes with that luxury.

I no longer look at the extrinsic price or published results to understand the prosperity of companies. They often paint a manicured picture. Instead, I use the three philosophies, six parts, the levers within, and the underlying principles of the *Congruence™* method to assess a company's intrinsic nature through its everyday incentives, decisions, and behaviors.

It's up to all of us to ensure that we sidestep a societal bias for capital engineering that epitomizes short-termism and individualism. My hope is that you will use *Congruence™* to assess the companies you buy from, invest in, work at, or partner with. Committing our skills and energy to holistic companies that focus on value creation, capital efficiency, and sustainable profitability while balancing the incentives of all stakeholders is a necessity. It is a human evolutionary need to trust our most important institutions – companies – since they dictate the quality of our first breath as a newborn, our play, education, work, family, and health, and our final physical, mental, and economic state.

Definitions